T0342033

Embedded Linux Systems with the Yocto Project™

Embedded Linux Systems with the Yocto Project™

Rudolf J. Streif

PRENTICE
HALL

Boston • Columbus • Indianapolis • New York • San Francisco • Amsterdam • Cape Town
Dubai • London • Madrid • Milan • Munich • Paris • Montreal • Toronto • Delhi • Mexico City
São Paulo • Sydney • Hong Kong • Seoul • Singapore • Taipei • Tokyo

Library of Congress Cataloging-in-Publication Data
Names: Streif, Rudolf J., author.
Title: Embedded Linux systems with the Yocto project / Rudolf J. Streif.
Description: Boston : Prentice Hall, [2016] | Includes index.
Identifiers: LCCN 2016008130| ISBN 9780133443240 (hardcover : alk. paper) |
    ISBN 0133443248 (hardcover : alk. paper)
Subjects: LCSH: Software architecture. | Open source software. | Embedded
    computer systemsProgramming. | Linux.
Classification: LCC QA76.76.062 S77 2016 | DDC 006.2/2dc23
LC record available at https://lccn.loc.gov/2016008130

ISBN-13: 978-0-13-344324-0
ISBN-10: 0-13-344324-8

15 2023

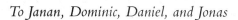

To Janan, Dominic, Daniel, and Jonas

Contents

Foreword

The embedded Linux landscape is a little bit like the Old West: different outposts of technology scattered here and there, with barren and often dangerous landscape in between. If you're going to travel there, you need to be well stocked, be familiar with the territory, and have a reliable guide.

Just as people moved West during the Gold Rush in the mid-1800s, developers are moving into the embedded Linux world with the rush to the Internet of Things. As increased population brought law, order, and civilization to the Old West, important new open source software projects are bringing order to embedded Linux.

The Yocto Project is a significant order-bringer. Its tools let you focus on designing your project (what you want to build) and devote only the necessary minimum of your time and effort to putting it all together (how you build what you want to build).

This book is your reliable guide. In logically ordered chapters with clear and complete instructions, it will help you get your work done and your IoT project to market. And with some luck, you'll have fun along the way!

Enjoy your adventure!

Arnold Robbins
Series Editor

Preface

Smart home. Smart car. Smart phone. Smart TV. Smart thermostat. Smart lights. Smart watch. Smart washer. Smart dryer. Smart fridge. Smart basketball. Welcome to the brave new world of smart everything!

The proliferation of embedded computers in almost everything we touch and interact with in our daily lives has moved embedded systems engineering and embedded software development into the spotlight. Hidden from the direct sight of their users, embedded systems lack the attractiveness of web applications with their flashy user interfaces or the coolness of computer games with their animations and immersive graphics. It comes as no surprise that computer science students and software developers hardly ever think of embedded software engineering as their first career choice. However, the "smart-everything revolution" and the Internet of Things (IoT) are driving the demand for specialists who can bridge hardware and software worlds. Experts who speak the language of electric schematics as well as programming languages are sought after by employers.

Linux has become the first choice for an explosively growing number of embedded applications. There are good reasons for this choice, upon which we will elaborate in the coming chapters. Through my journey as an embedded software developer for various industries, I have learned Linux for embedded systems the hard way. There is no shortage of excellent development tools for virtually any programming language. The vast majority of libraries and applications for Linux can easily be built natively because of their tooling. Even building the Linux kernel from scratch is almost a breeze with the kernel's own build system. However, when it comes to putting it all together into a bootable system, the choices are scarce.

The Yocto Project closes that gap by providing a comprehensive set of integrated tools with the OpenEmbedded build system at its center. From source code to bootable system in a matter of a few hours—I wish I had that luxury when I started out with embedded Linux!

What This Book Is and What It Is Not

A build system that integrates many different steps necessary to create a fully functional Linux OS stack from scratch is rather complex. This book is dedicated to the build system itself and how you can effectively use it to build your own custom Linux distributions. This book is not a tutorial on embedded Linux. Although Chapter 6 explains the basics of the Linux system architecture (as this foundation is necessary to understanding how the build system assembles the many different components into an operational system), I do not go into the details of embedded Linux as such. If you are a beginning embedded Linux developer, I strongly recommend Christopher Hallinan's excellent *Embedded Linux Primer*, published in this same book series.

In this book, you will learn how the OpenEmbedded build system works, how you can write recipes to build your own software components, how to use and create Yocto Project board support packages to support different hardware platforms, and how to debug build failures. You will learn how to build software development kits for application development and integrate them with the popular Eclipse integrated development environment (IDE) for seamless round-trip development.

Who Should Read This Book

This book is intended for software developers and programmers who have a working knowledge of Linux. I assume that you know your way around the Linux command line, that you can build programs on a Linux system using the typical tools, such as Make and a C/C++ compiler, and that you can read and understand basic shell scripts.

The build system is written entirely in Python. While you do not need to be a Python expert to use it and to understand how it works, having some core knowledge about Python is certainly advantageous.

How This Book Is Organized

Chapter 1, "Linux for Embedded Systems," provides a brief look at the adoption of Linux for embedded systems. An overview of the embedded Linux landscape and the challenges of creating custom embedded Linux distributions set the stage.

Chapter 2, "The Yocto Project," introduces the Yocto Project by jumpstarting an initial build of a Linux OS stack using the build system. It also gives an overview of the Yocto Project family of projects and its history.

Chapter 3, "OpenEmbedded Build System," explains the fundamentals of the build system, its workflow, and its architecture.

Chapter 4, "BitBake Build Engine," gives insight into BitBake, the build engine at the core of the OpenEmbedded build system. It explains the metadata concept of recipes, classes, and configuration files and their syntax. A Hello World project in BitBake style illustrates the build workflow. Through the information provided, you gain the necessary knowledge for understanding provided recipes and for writing your own.

Chapter 5, "Troubleshooting," introduces tools and mechanisms available to troubleshoot build problems and provides practical advice on how to use the tools effectively.

Chapter 6, "Linux System Architecture," provides the basics of a Linux operating system stack and explains how the different components are layered. It discusses the concepts of kernel space and user space and how application programs interact with the Linux kernel through system calls provided by the standard C library.

Chapter 7, "Building a Custom Linux Distribution," details how to use the Yocto Project to create your own customized Linux distribution. It starts with an overview of the Linux distribution blueprints available with the build system and how to customize them. It then demonstrates how to create a Linux distribution entirely from scratch using the build system tools. After completing this chapter, you will know how to build your own operating system images.

Chapter 8, "Software Package Recipes," explains BitBake recipes and how to write them to build your own software packages with the build system. The chapter provides various real-world recipe examples that you can try.

Chapter 9, "Kernel Recipes," examines the details of building the Linux kernel with the OpenEmbedded build system. It explains how the build system tooling interacts with the kernel's own build environment to set kernel configuration and apply patches. A discussion of how the build system handles out-of-tree kernel modules and incorporates building device trees with the build process closes this chapter.

Chapter 10, "Board Support Packages," introduces how the build system supports building for different hardware—that is, CPU architectures and systems. After an explanation of the Yocto Project board support package concepts, the chapter details how you can build a project using a board support package. We then look into the internals of Yocto Project board support packages and explain how to create your own with a practical example that you can put to use with actual hardware. The chapter concludes with creating bootable media images for different hardware configurations.

Chapter 11, "Application Development," describes Yocto Project support for developing applications for Linux OS stacks created with the build system. It provides hands-on instructions on how to build application development toolkits (ADT) that include all the necessary tools for round-trip application development. Examples illustrate how to use an ADT for application development using the command-line tools as well as with the Eclipse IDE. Step-by-step instructions teach how to remotely run and debug applications on an actual hardware target.

Chapter 12, "Licensing and Compliance," discusses requirements for compliance with open source licenses and the tools the Yocto Project provides to facilitate meeting them.

Chapter 13, "Advanced Topics," introduces several tools that help you scale the Yocto Project to teams. *Toaster* is a web-based graphical user interface that can be used to create build systems that can be controlled remotely from a web browser. *Build history* is a tool that provides tracking and audit capabilities. With *source mirrors*, you can share source packages to avoid repeated downloads and to control source versions for product delivery. Last but not least, *Autobuilder* provides an out-of-the-box continuous build and integration framework for automating builds, quality assurance, and release processes. Equipped with the knowledge from this chapter, you can effectively set up team environments for the Yocto Project.

The appendices cover popular open source licenses and alphabetical references of build system metadata layers and machines.

Hands-on Experience

The book is written to provide you with hands-on experience using the Yocto Project. You will benefit the most if you follow along and try out the examples. The majority of them you can work through simply with an x86-based workstation running a recent Linux distribution (detailed requirements are provided in Chapter 2). For an even better experience, grab one of the popular development boards, such as the BeagleBone, the MinnowBoard Max, or the Wandboard. The BeagleBone makes an excellent low-cost experimental platform. The other two boards offer more performance and let you gain experience with multicore systems.

Analyze the code and try to understand the examples produced in the book. Follow the steps and then veer off on your own by changing settings, applying your own configuration, and more. It is the best way to learn, and I can tell you, it is a lot of fun too. It is a great feeling to get your first own Linux distribution to work on a piece of hardware of your choice.

Register your copy of *Embedded Linux Systems with the Yocto Project*™ at informit.com for convenient access to downloads, updates, and corrections as they become available. To start the registration process, go to informit.com/register and log in or create an account. Enter the product ISBN (9780133443240) and click Submit. Once the process is complete, you will find any available bonus content under "Registered Products."

Acknowledgments

What you are holding in your hands is my first attempt at writing a technical book. Well, any book, for that matter. I humbly have to admit that I greatly underestimated the effort that goes into a project like this, the hours spent experimenting with things, finding the best way to make them work, and documenting everything in a concise and understandable fashion. During the process, I have come to truly appreciate the work of the many authors and technical writers whose books and manuals I have read and continue reading.

Foremost, I want to express my gratitude to my family, my loving wife, Janan, and my three wonderful boys, Dominic, Daniel, and Jonas. Without their support and their understanding, it would not have been possible for me to spend the many hours writing this text.

Special thanks go to the Yocto Project team. When I approached Dave Stewart, Project Manager for the Yocto Project at the time, and Jeffrey Osier-Mixon, the Yocto Project's Community Manager, they immediately welcomed the idea for the book and offered their support. Several individuals from the team were especially helpful with advice and answers to my questions: Beth Flanagan for Autobuilder, Belen Barros Pena and Ed Bartosh for Toaster, and Paul Eggleton and Khem Raj who jumped on many of the questions I posted to the Yocto Project mailing list.

Special thanks to Christopher Hallinan whose *Embedded Linux Primer: A Practical Real-World Approach* (Prentice Hall, 2006) inspired me to write this book on the Yocto Project.

I especially want to thank Debra Williams Cauley, Executive Acquisitions Editor, for her guidance and particularly her patience while this book was in the works. It took much longer than expected, and I am the only one to blame for the missed deadlines.

I cannot thank and praise enough my dedicated review team, Chris Zahn, Jeffrey Osier-Mixon, Robert Berger, and Bryan Smith, for their valuable contributions to the quality of the book in the form of corrections and suggestions for improvements.

I also want to thank the production team at Prentice Hall, Julie Nahil and Anna Popick, for their coordination and guidance through the process, and in particular Carol Lallier for her diligence in copyediting the manuscript.

Thanks also to the Linux Foundation and Jerry Cooperstein, who gave me the opportunity to develop the Linux Foundation's training course on the Yocto Project. Nothing teaches as well as teaching somebody else. Thank you to the students of the classes that I taught. Through your critical questions and feedback, I gained a lot of understanding for the many different problems you are facing when developing products with embedded Linux. One of your most asked questions was, "Is there a book on the Yocto Project?" Finally, I can say, "Yes."

About the Author

Rudolf Streif has more than twenty years of experience in software engineering as a developer as well as a manager leading cross-functional engineering teams with more than one hundred members. Currently, he is an independent consultant for software technology and system architecture specializing in open source.

He previously served as the Linux Foundation's Director of Embedded Solutions, coordinating the Foundation's efforts for Linux in embedded systems. Rudolf developed the Linux Foundation's training course on the Yocto Project, which he delivered multiple times to companies and in a crash-course variant during Linux Foundation events.

Rudolf has been working with Linux and open source since the early 1990s and developing commercial products since 2000. The projects he has been involved with include high-speed industrial image processing systems, IPTV head-end system and customer premises equipment, and connected car and in-vehicle infotainment.

In 2014, Rudolf was listed by *PC World* among the 50 most interesting people in the world of technology (http://tinyurl.com/z3tbtns).

Rudolf lives with his wife and three children in San Diego, California.

1

Linux for Embedded Systems

The *Internet of Things* is inspiring the imagination of visionaries and likewise the creativity of engineers. As a universal computing network of myriad connected devices collecting, analyzing, and delivering data in real-time, it carries the promise of a new era of information technology.

Devices comprising the Internet of Things need to meet an entirely new set of requirements and provide functionality previously not found in embedded systems. Connectivity, including through cellular data networks, is an obvious one, but there is also remote management, software configuration and updates, power efficiency, longevity, and, of course, security, to just name a few.

This changing landscape of embedded systems requires a different approach to building the software stacks that operate this new breed of connected hardware.

1.1 Why Linux for Embedded Systems?

Linux debuted as a *general-purpose operating system* (GPOS) for PC hardware with Intel x86 architecture. In his now famous post on news:comp.os.minix, Linux creator Linus Torvalds explicitly stated, "I'm doing a (free) operating system. . . . It is NOT portable (uses 386 task switching etc), and it probably never will support anything other than AT-harddisks . . .."

Driven by the rise of the Internet, Linux quickly evolved into a server operating system providing infrastructure for web servers and networking services for many well-founded reasons.

Nevertheless, Linux remained true to its GPOS origins in three major aspects that do not make it the premier choice of engineers for an embedded operating system at first:

- **Filesystem**: Linux is a file-based operating system requiring a filesystem on a block-oriented mass storage device with read and write access. Block-oriented mass storage typically meant hard drives with spinning platters, which are not practical for most embedded use cases.

- **Memory Management Unit (MMU)**: Linux is a multitasking operating system. Effective task switching mandates that individual processes have their private memory address space that can easily be mapped into physical memory when the process is running on the CPU. Microcontrollers that have been widely used for typical embedded applications do not provide an MMU.

- **Real Time**: Embedded systems running critical applications may require predictive responses with guaranteed timing within a certain margin of error, commonly referred to as *determinism*. The amount of error in the timing over subsequent iterations of a program or section thereof is called *jitter*. An operating system that can absolutely guarantee a maximum time for the operations it performs is referred to as a *hard real-time system*. An operating system that typically performs its operations within a certain time is referred to as *soft real-time*. Although several solutions providing real-time capabilities for Linux, most notably *PREEMPT-RT*, had been developed as early as 1996, they are still not part of the mainline Linux kernel.

During the last couple of years, advances in semiconductor technology have helped to overcome these hurdles for the adoption of Linux in embedded systems. Ubiquitously available, inexpensive, and long-term reliable flash memory devices used in many consumer products, such as digital cameras, are providing the necessary mass storage for the filesystem. Powerful system-on-chips (SoC) designs combining one or multiple general-purpose CPU cores with MMU and peripheral devices on a single chip have become the embedded systems engineer's choice of processor and are increasingly replacing the microcontroller in embedded applications.

Today we are seeing an explosive growth in the adoption of Linux for embedded devices. Virtually every industry is now touched by this trend. In Carrier-Grade Linux (CGL), the operating system has been adopted for products in public switched telephone networks and global data networks. Chances are that you carry a cellphone, watch television with a set-top box and high-definition television, surf the Internet with broadband modems and networking switches, find your way with a personal navigation device, and daily use many other devices that are powered by Linux.

There are many reasons for the rapid growth of embedded Linux. To name a few:

- **Royalties**: Unlike traditional proprietary operating systems, Linux can be deployed without any royalties.

- **Hardware Support**: Linux supports a vast variety of hardware devices including all major and commonly used CPU architectures: ARM, Intel x86, MIPS, and PowerPC in their respective 32-bit and 64-bit variants.

- **Networking**: Linux supports a large variety of networking protocols. Besides the ubiquitous TCP/IP, virtually any other protocol on any physical medium is implemented.
- **Modularity**: A Linux OS stack is composed of many different software packages. Engineers can customize the stack to make it exactly fit their application.
- **Scalability**: Linux scales from systems with only one CPU and limited resources to systems featuring multiple CPUs with many cores, large memory footprints, several networking interfaces, and much more.
- **Source Code**: The source code for the Linux kernel, as well as for all software packages comprising a Linux OS stack, is openly available.
- **Developer Support**: Because of its openness, Linux has attracted a huge number of active developers, and those developers have quickly built support for new hardware.
- **Commercial Support**: An increasing number of hardware and software vendors, including all semiconductor manufacturers as well as many independent software vendors (ISV), are now offering support for Linux through products and services.
- **Tooling**: Linux provides myriad tools for software development ranging from compilers for virtually any programming language to a steadily growing number of profiling and performance measurement tools important for embedded systems development.

These and many other reasons now make Linux the premier choice of embedded systems engineers, fueling its accelerated adoption for consumer and professional products.

1.2 Embedded Linux Landscape

Embedded systems are diverse. With the huge variety of hardware inevitably comes the burden of software adaptation, most notably the operating system, which provides abstraction from the hardware through its libraries and application programming interfaces (API). There is no one-size-fits-all, and you, as the systems engineer, will have to start somewhere with your embedded Linux project.

In the following paragraphs, we provide an overview of the most commonly used open source projects for embedded devices. Beyond those there are, of course, a couple of commercial embedded Linux offerings from operating system vendors (OSVs).

1.2.1 Embedded Linux Distributions

Similar to desktop and server Linux distributions, an ever-evolving variety of embedded Linux distributions is developed by community projects and commercial operating system vendors. Some of them are targeted for a specific class of embedded systems and devices, while others are more general in nature with the idea to provide a foundation rather than a complete system.

Android

Despite its primary target being mobile phones and tablet computers, Android (www.android.com, http://developer.android.com, http://source.android.com) is enjoying growing popularity as an operating system for all kinds of embedded devices. That does not come as any surprise, as its source code is freely available and includes a build system with configuration tools that lets developers adapt the system to different hardware devices.

In particular, if the target device is utilizing an ARM-based SoC and has a touch screen, then Android is a popular choice among systems engineers as the necessary support for the hardware is a core part of the system. Ports to Intel x86 architecture do exist, but there is much less hardware available, and development is typically also more expensive.

However, Android does not fill every need of embedded devices. While it utilizes the Linux kernel and other software packages generally found in a Linux OS stack, its fundamental architecture is different from a typical Linux OS stack. Android uses its own flavor of a C library with a reduced set of APIs, as well as its own filesystem layout and other specific extensions. These modifications make it less than straightforward to port standard Linux software packages to Android.

While Android is an open source project in the sense that the source code for the entire system is freely available and can be used, modified, and extended for any purpose with very few restrictions, developers cannot contribute their changes back to Android. Google alone controls the roadmap of the system. The CyanogenMod (www.cyanogenmod.org) community distribution based on Google's Android releases is trying to fill this void.

Nevertheless, the Linux kernel does owe Android one important extension: power management. While frowned upon by some Linux kernel developers because of their simplistic architecture, the Android Wake Locks have become the de facto standard of Linux power management.

Ångström Distribution

The Ångström Distribution, with its homepage at www.angstrom-distribution.org, is increasingly becoming an important resource for projects because of its growing list of supported *development boards*. Ångström is a community distribution that was started by a group of developers who worked on the *OpenEmbedded*, *OpenZaurus*, and *OpenSimpad* projects. Ångström has been using the OpenEmbedded tools from its beginning but is now adapting the architecture and structure of the Yocto Project.

OpenWrt

OpenWrt (www.openwrt.org) debuted as an open source operating system target-ing embedded devices that route network traffic such as broadband modems, routers, residential gateways, and other consumer premises equipment (CPE). OpenWrt's core components are the Linux kernel, uClibc, and BusyBox.

The first versions of OpenWrt were built on the Linksys GPL sources for their WRT54G residential gateway and wireless router and a root filesystem created with Buildroot—hence the name OpenWrt.

OpenWrt supports a wide variety of hardware devices and evaluation boards. OpenWrt's core strength is the exhaustive list of possibilities to configure network-ing technologies and protocols, including routing, mesh networking, firewall, address translation, port forwarding, load balancing, and much more.

While OpenWrt is intended to operate devices that typically run without regular human interaction, it provides a sophisticated web interface to comfortably access the many configuration options.

Its focus on connectivity and remote management make OpenWrt a favorite among systems engineers developing connected devices. A writable filesystem with package management makes it straightforward to add functionality even after the system has been deployed.

Embedded Versions of Full Linux Distributions

For many of the fully fledged Linux distributions for desktop, server, and cloud, vari-ants targeting embedded systems are now also available:

- Debian (www.emdebian.org)
- Fedora (https://fedoraproject.org/wiki/Embedded)
- Gentoo (https://wiki.gentoo.org/wiki/Project:Embedded)
- SUSE (https://tr.opensuse.org/MicroSUSE)
- Ubuntu (https://wiki.ubuntu.com/EmbeddedUbuntu)

For system builders and developers familiar with a desktop or server version of a particular Linux distribution, using its embedded variant provides the advantage of familiar tools, filesystem layout, and more.

1.2.2 Embedded Linux Development Tools

Besides utilizing an embedded Linux distribution, you can also build your own custom Linux OS stack with embedded Linux development tools. This gives you the most control and flexibility but in most cases requires more effort.

Baserock

Baserock is an open source project that provides a build system for Linux distributions, a development environment, and a development workflow in one package. Baserock's major characteristics are

- Git as the core to manage essentially everything from build instructions to build artifacts as a means to provide traceability
- Native compilation to avoid the complexity of cross-build environments
- Distributed builds across multiple systems using virtual machines

Currently, Baserock supports building for x86, x86_64, and ARMv7 architectures. The project's homepage is at http://wiki.baserock.org.

Buildroot

Buildroot is a build system for complete embedded Linux systems using GNU Make and a set of makefiles to create a cross-compilation toolchain, a root filesystem, a kernel image, and a bootloader image. The project's homepage is at http://buildroot.uclibc.org.

Buildroot mainly targets small footprint embedded systems and supports various CPU architectures. To jump start development it limits the choice of configuration options and defaults to probably the most commonly used ones for embedded systems:

- *uClibc* is the target library to build the cross-compilation toolchain. In comparison to the GNU C Library (glibc), uClibc is much more compact and optimized for small footprint embedded systems. uClibc supports virtually all CPU architectures as well as shared libraries and threading.
- *BusyBox* is the default set of command line utility applications.

These default settings enable building a basic embedded Linux system with Buildroot typically within 15 to 30 minutes, depending on the build host. However, these settings are not absolute, and the simple and flexible structure of Buildroot makes it easy to understand and extend. The internal cross-toolchain can be replaced by an external one such as *crosstool-ng*, and uClibc can be replaced with other C libraries.

Buildroot already supports many standard Linux packages, such as the X.org stack, GStreamer, DirectFB, and Simple DirectMedia Layer (SDL). The cross-toolchain can be used to build additional packages and have them included with the root filesystem.

Buildroot is very compact and straightforward to set up. A single-file (tarball) download and the installation of a few additional packages on the build host are all that are required to get started. After unpacking the tarball, the command `make menuconfig` launches a text-based user interface enabling configuration of a wide range of supported targets and setting of other options. In addition to *menuconfig*, Buildroot offers *gconfig* and *xconfig*, which are alternative graphical user interfaces.

Buildroot creates everything from source by downloading the source code files directly from the *upstream* projects. A nice feature is that offline builds can be done by downloading all the sources first using `make source`. Buildroot pre-fetches all necessary files and can then configure and run a build without further connectivity to the Internet.

OpenEmbedded

OpenEmbedded (www.openembedded.org) is a build framework composed of *tools*, *configuration data*, and *recipes* to create Linux distributions targeted for embedded devices. At the core of OpenEmbedded is the *BitBake* task executor that manages the build process.

Historically, OpenEmbedded was created by merging the work of the OpenZaurus project with contributions from other projects such as Familiar Linux and OpenSIMpad.

OpenEmbedded has been used to develop a variety of open source embedded projects, most notably the OpenMoko (http://wiki.openmoko.org) project dedicated to delivering a complete open source software stack for mobile phones.

OpenEmbedded, the Yocto Project, and the Ångström Distribution all have the same roots and build on and complement each other in various ways. We will explain the commonalities and differences in the next chapter when we dive into the details of the Yocto Project.

The Yocto Project

The Yocto Project is, of course, the subject of this book. It is listed here to complete this overview of the embedded Linux landscape. You can find its webpage at https://www.yoctoproject.org.

The Yocto Project is not a single open source project but represents an entire family of projects that are developed and maintained under its umbrella. This book describes many of the projects associated with the Yocto Project, in particular, Poky, the Yocto Project's reference distribution, which includes the OpenEmbedded build system and a comprehensive set of metadata.

The embedded Linux landscape is diverse. This list is not all-comprehensive, and there are many more open source projects providing solutions for developing embedded devices with Linux. The projects mentioned here are, in my opinion, the most active and most commonly used ones. Before reading on, you may want to take some time and visit the web pages of these projects. They will give you a good understanding of what the goals of these projects are and how they compare to each other.

There are also a number of commercial offerings complementing the embedded Linux landscape. Commonly, these offerings include cross-development toolchains, distribution builders, application development IDEs, and more. An increasing number of operating system vendors for embedded systems are using the Yocto Project as an upstream. They use the Yocto Project tools to create their product lines. Many of them are members of the Yocto Project and support it with engineering and financial resources.

1.3 A Custom Linux Distribution—Why Is It Hard?

Let's face it—building and maintaining an operating system is not a trivial task. Many different aspects of the operating system have to be taken into consideration to create a fully functional computer system:

- **Bootloader**: The bootloader is the first piece of software responsible for initializing the hardware, loading the operating system kernel into RAM, and then starting the kernel. The bootloader is commonly multistaged with its first stage resident in nonvolatile memory. The first stage then loads a second stage from attached storage such as flash memory, hard drives, and so on.

- **Kernel**: The kernel, as its name implies, is the core of an operating system. It manages the hardware resources of the system and provides hardware abstraction through its APIs to other software. The kernel's main functions are *memory management*, *device management*, and responding to *system calls* from application software. How these functions are implemented depends on the processor architecture as well as on peripheral devices and other hardware configuration.

- **Device Drivers**: Device drivers are part of the kernel. They provide application software with access to hardware devices in a structured form through kernel system calls. Through the device drivers, application software can configure, read data from, and write data to hardware devices.

- **Life Cycle Management**: From power on to shutdown, a computer system assumes multiple states during which it provides different sets of services to application software. Life cycle management determines what services are running in what states and in what order they need to be started to maintain a consistent operating environment. An important piece of life cycle management is also power management, putting a system into energy saving modes when full functionality is not required, and resuming fully operational mode when requested.

- **Application Software Management**: Application software and libraries make up the majority of software installed on a typical system, providing the end-user functionality. Frequently, many hundreds to multiple thousands of software packages are necessary for a fully operational system.

Linux and the plethora of open source software packages are like the building blocks of a construction kit. Unfortunately, it is more like a puzzle than like Legos. It can be a daunting task to figure out dependencies, incompatibilities, and conflicts between the different packages. Some packages even provide the same or similar functionality. Which one to choose? Eventually, you will have to draw your own blueprint to build the Linux distribution for your embedded project. In principal, you have two ways to go:

- **Top-down**: In this approach, you start with one of the many available Linux distributions and customize it according to your requirements by adding and/or removing software packages. The author took this approach many years ago with a high-speed image processing system running on x86 server hardware. It is a viable approach and has its appeal because using a tested and maintained distribution alleviates some of the more tedious tasks of building and maintaining your own distribution. And you may be able to get support for it. However, it may limit you in your choice of hardware, since most off-the-shelf Linux distributions are built for x86 hardware. And, of course, picking the right distribution to start off with and rightsizing it for your target device is not that simple either.

- **Bottom-up**: The bottom-up approach entails building your own custom Linux distribution from source code starting with a bootloader and the kernel and then adding software packages to support the applications for your target device. This approach gives you the most control (and you will learn a lot about Linux and operating systems in general), but it is also a challenging task. You will have to make many choices along the way, from selecting the right toolchain and setting kernel configuration options to choosing the right software packages. Some of these choices are interdependent, such as the choice of toolchain and target library, and taking the wrong turn can quickly send you down a dead end. After you have successfully built and deployed your own distribution, you are left with the burden of maintaining it—finding patches and security updates for the kernel and all the other packages you have integrated with your distribution.

This is where the strengths of the Yocto Project lie. It combines the best of both worlds by providing you with a complete tool set and blueprints to create your own Linux distribution from scratch starting with source code downloads from the upstream projects. The blueprints for various systems that ship with the Yocto Project tools let you build complete operating system stacks within a few hours. You can choose from blueprints that build a target system image for a basic system with command-line login, a system with a graphical user interface for a mobile device, a system that is Linux Standard Base compliant, and many more.

You can use these blueprints as a starting point for your own distribution and modify them by adding and/or removing software packages. The remaining chapters of this book walk you through the entire process of building and customizing your Linux distribution and creating your own blueprints using the Yocto Project tools, which will give you repeatable results every time you build your system.

1.4 A Word about Open Source Licensing

When building a system based on, or that includes, open source software, you will inevitably have to pay attention to open source licensing. Originating authors of software are of course free to choose whatever license they prefer for their works, which has led to a long and growing list of open source licenses. There is no single license, and whether you like it or not, you will have to deal with many of them. Some open source projects even use more than one software license. One of them is BusyBox.

One of the most common, if not *the* most common, open source licenses is the GNU General Public License (GPL).[1] Now in its third version, the GPL is widely considered the mother of open source licenses. Although some sources name the Berkeley Software Distribution (BSD) License, created in 1990, as the first open source license, the GPL predates it by a year, having been written by Richard Stallman and introduced in 1989.

One popular myth attributed to open source licenses is that open source software is free. However, the second paragraph of the GPL clarifies the common misunderstanding: "When we speak of free software, we are referring to freedom, not price." Professional engineering managers probably wholeheartedly agree—while you can download open source software for free, developing and deploying products based on it commonly carries significant engineering cost. In that sense, open source software is no different from commercial software offerings.

In comparison to commercial or closed source software licenses, open source licenses are *permissive*, meaning they grant you the freedom to use and run the software, the right to study and modify it, and the permission to distribute the original code and its modifications. This broad freedom makes it tempting to treat open source licenses rather casually. In one word: *Don't!* Open source licenses are binding and enforceable, as any commercial license is.

Most open source licenses explicitly stipulate a few major conditions you must comply with when shipping products based on open source:

- **Attribution**: Authors must be attributed as the creators of the work. You must not remove any copyright notices of any of the authors of the source code.
- **Conveyance**: Conveyance typically refers to conveying verbatim copies of the software's source code, conveying modified versions of the source code, and conveying non-source forms, such as binary files or firmware embedded in products. In the latter case, many open source licenses, including the GPL, require you to convey the corresponding source code with the product or auxiliary documentation.
- **Derivative Works**: This term commonly refers to a creation that includes all or major portions of a previously created work. What this exactly means for open source software is still unclear, since there are no legal test cases for it yet. Most typically, it refers to modification of the source code and/or additions to it but, for some licenses, also to linking, even dynamically at runtime, to libraries. Under the terms of the license, the author of a derivative work is required to distribute the work under exactly the same licensing term as the original work. This makes the license *self-perpetuating*.

This book was not written with the intention of providing legal advice concerning open source licensing. However, we strongly urge you to pay close attention to the licenses used by software packages you include with your product before actually

---

1. For a complete text of the GPL license, refer to Appendix A or see www.gnu.org/licenses/gpl.html.

shipping the product. While the legal field of open source licensing is still quite new, a growing number of legal experts are now specializing in this field. If in doubt, seek professional advice from the experts.

1.5 Organizations, Relevant Bodies, and Standards

As Linux and open source continue to grow their market share in computing, telecommunications, consumer electronics, industrial automation, and many other fields, organizations and standards are emerging to influence acceptance and adoption of Linux and open source technologies themselves as well as the principles of open collaboration and innovation they stand for.

This section introduces some of the organizations, bodies, and standards with which you may want to become familiar.

1.5.1 The Linux Foundation

The Linux Foundation (www.linuxfoundation.org) is a "non-profit consortium dedicated to fostering the growth of Linux. Founded in 2000, the Linux Foundation sponsors the work of Linux creator Linus Torvalds and is supported by leading technology companies and developers from around the world."

The Linux Foundation marshals the resources and contributions of its members and the open source community by

- Promoting Linux and providing a neutral environment for collaboration and education
- Protecting and supporting Linux development
- Improving Linux as a technical platform

The Linux Foundation directly sponsors the work of Linus Torvalds and other key Linux developers so that they remain independent and can focus on improving Linux. The Linux Foundation also sponsors several workgroups and collaborative projects to define standards and to advance Linux in certain areas and industries. Some of these projects are outlined in the following sections.

1.5.2 The Apache Software Foundation

More than 140 open source software projects are hosted by the Apache Software Foundation (ASF). For these projects, the ASF provides a collaboration framework including financial backing, intellectual property management, and legal support. The ASF website can be found at www.apache.org.

You are probably familiar with some of the most well-known ASF projects, such as the Apache HTTP Server, Ant build tool for Java, Cassandra cloud database, CloudStack cloud computing infrastructure, Hadoop distributed computing platform, and Tomcat web server for Java Servlet and JavaServer Pages.

All ASF projects and all software produced under the umbrella of the ASF are licensed under the terms of the *Apache Licenses*. One important property of the Apache Licenses is that contributors retain full rights to use their original contributions for any purpose outside the Apache projects while granting the ASF and the projects the rights to distribute and build upon their work.

1.5.3 Eclipse Foundation

The Eclipse Project (www.eclipse.org) was created in 2001 by IBM to build a support community of developers and software vendors around the Eclipse Platform. The Eclipse Platform started as a flexible IDE framework for software development tools. In 2004, the Eclipse Foundation was founded as a legal entity to marshal the resources of the project. The Eclipse Foundation provides IT infrastructure and IP management to the projects operating under its umbrella and supports their operations with development and engineering processes to ensure project transparency and product quality.

Besides the Eclipse IDE, the list of projects hosted under the auspices of the Eclipse Foundation includes development tools for virtually any programming language, software and data modeling tools, web development tools, and many more.

Embedded software development frameworks frequently build on top of the Eclipse IDE to offer convenient round-trip development including target debugging and profiling within the same IDE. The Yocto Project provides an Eclipse plug-in enabling the use of a Yocto Project–created toolchain directly from within the IDE.

1.5.4 Linux Standard Base

As outlined in previous sections, there are many ways to build a Linux OS stack. While flexibility is good, it comes with the burden of fragmentation. The goal of the *Linux Standard Base* (LSB) is to establish a set of common standards for Linux distributions. Common standards provide application developers assurance that the code that they develop on one Linux distribution will also run on other Linux distributions without additional adaptations.

In addition, LSB gives developers peace of mind when it comes to the continuity of a particular Linux distribution. As long as future versions of a distribution remain compliant with a particular LSB version, the application will continue to run on the future versions of the distribution too.

The LSB project provides a comprehensive set of specifications, documentation, and tools to test the compliance of a distribution with a particular LSB version.

While API and application binary interface (ABI) compliance may not necessarily be at the top of the list for embedded systems engineers, familiarizing yourself with the concepts and specifications may help with your embedded project in the long run. Even if you do not intend for third-party developers to contribute applications to your embedded platform, compliance considerations similar to those of the LSB project undoubtedly support the platform strategy of your products.

LSB is a Linux Foundation workgroup. You can find its website at www.linuxfoundation .org/collaborate/workgroups/lsb.

1.5.5 Consumer Electronics Workgroup

The Consumer Electronics (CE) Workgroup is a workgroup operating under the umbrella of the Linux Foundation. Its mission is to promote the use of Linux in embedded systems used in consumer electronics products as well as promote enhancement of Linux itself. The CE Workgroup started its work in 2003 as the Consumer Electronics Linux Forum (CELF) and merged with the Linux Foundation in 2010 for better alignment with the Linux community. You can find the CE Workgroup's website at www.linuxfoundation.org/collaborate/workgroups/celf.

One of the major activities of the CE Workgroup is the *Long-Term Support Initiative* (LTSI). LTSI's goal is to create and maintain a stable Linux kernel tree that is supported with relevant patches for about 2 to 3 years, which is the typical life of consumer electronic products such as smartphones, game consoles, and TV sets. LTSI details are published on http://ltsi.linuxfoundation.org.

1.6 Summary

Embedded Linux is already powering many devices and services you use on a daily basis. Generally unnoticed, it directs data traffic through Internet routers, puts high-definition pictures on TV screens, guides travelers inside navigation devices, measures energy consumption in smart meters, collects traffic information in roadside sensors, and much more. Linux and open source are powering the Internet of Things from connected devices to networking infrastructure and data processing centers. This chapter set the stage for the material to come, covering the following topics:

- Definition of embedded systems from the engineer's perspective and the broad set of responsibilities associated with taking an embedded product from design to production
- Technology developments contributing to the rapid adoption of Linux for embedded devices
- Overview of the embedded Linux landscape
- Challenges associated with building and maintaining an operating system stack
- Importance of open source licensing for embedded projects
- Several organizations and standards relevant to embedded Linux

1.7 References

Apache License, www.apache.org/licenses

The Apache Software Foundation, www.apache.org

Eclipse Foundation, www.eclipse.org

GNU GPL License, www.gnu.org/licenses/gpl.html

The Linux Foundation, www.linuxfoundation.org

Linux Standard Base, www.linuxfoundation.org/collaborate/workgroups/lsb

2

The Yocto Project

Yocto is the prefix of the smallest fraction for units of measurements specified by the International System of Units (abbreviated *SI* from French *Le Système International d'Unités*). It gives the name to the Yocto Project, a comprehensive suite of tools, templates, and resources to build custom Linux distributions for embedded devices. To say that the name is an understatement is an understatement in itself.

In this chapter we start *in medias res* with setting up the OpenEmbedded build system, provided by the Yocto Project in the Poky reference distribution, and building our first Linux OS stack relying entirely on the blueprint that Poky provides by default. The tasks we perform in this chapter set the stage for the coming chapters in which we analyze the various aspects of the Yocto Project from the Poky workflow to the OpenEmbedded build system, including the build engine BitBake, to customizing operating system stacks to board support packages and the application development toolkit, and much more.

We conclude with the relationship of the Yocto Project with OpenEmbedded and a glossary of Yocto Project terms.

2.1 Jumpstarting Your First Yocto Project Build

Getting your hands dirty—or learning by doing—is undoubtedly the best way to acquire new skills. Consequently, we start by building our first Linux OS stack for use with the QEMU (short for Quick Emulator, a generic open source machine emulator for different CPU architectures).

You learn how to prepare your computer to become a Yocto Project development host, obtain and install the build system, set up and configure a build environment, launch and monitor the build process, and finally verify the build result by booting your newly built Linux OS stack in the QEMU emulator.

The following section outlines the hardware and software prerequisites for a Yocto Project build host. If you do not wish to set up a build host right away, the Yocto Project provides a Build Appliance, a preconfigured system in a virtual machine, that lets you try out the Yocto Project tools without installing any software. Just jump ahead to Section 2.1.7, which outlines how to experiment with the Yocto Project Build Appliance.

2.1.1 Prerequisites

You probably have guessed it: to build a Linux system with the Yocto Project tools, you need a build host running Linux.

Hardware Requirements

Despite their capability to build Linux OS stacks, the Yocto Project tools require a build host with an x86 architecture CPU. Both 32-bit and 64-bit CPUs are supported. A system with a 64-bit CPU is preferred for throughput reasons. The Yocto Project's build system makes use of parallel processing whenever possible. Therefore, a build host with multiple CPUs or a multicore CPU significantly reduces build time. Of course, CPU clock speed also has an impact on how quickly packages can be built.

Memory is also an important factor. BitBake, the Yocto Project build engine, parses thousands of recipes and creates a cache with build dependencies. Furthermore, the compilers require memory for data structures and more. The tools do not run on a system with less than 1 GB of RAM; 4 GB or more is recommended.

Disk space is another consideration. A full build process, which creates an image with a graphical user interface (GUI) based on X11 currently consumes about 50 GB of disk space. If, in the future, you would like to build for more architectures and/or add more packages to your builds, you will require additional space. It is recommended that the hard disk of your system has at least 100 GB of free space. Since regular hard disks with large capacity have become quite affordable, we recommend that you get one with 500 GB or more to host all your Yocto Project build environments.

Since build systems read a lot of data from the disk and write large amounts of build output data to it, disks with higher I/O throughput rates can also significantly accelerate the build process. Using a solid-state disk can further improve your build experience, but these devices, in particular with larger capacity, are substantially higher in cost than regular disks with spinning platters. Whether you are using conventional hard drives or solid-state disks, additional performance gains can be realized with a redundant array of independent disks (RAID) setup, such as RAID 0.

Internet Connection

The OpenEmbedded build system that you obtain from the project's website contains only the build system itself—BitBake and the metadata that guide it. It does not contain any source packages for the software it is going to build. These are automatically downloaded as needed while a build is running. Therefore, you need a live connection to the Internet, preferably a high-speed connection.

Of course, the downloaded source packages are stored on your system and reused for future builds. You are also able to download all source packages upfront and build them later offline without a connection to the Internet.

Software Requirements

First of all, you will need a recent Linux distribution. The Yocto Project team is continually qualifying more and more distributions with each release. Using the previous to current release of one of the following distributions typically works without any issues:

- CentOS
- Fedora
- openSUSE
- Ubuntu

In general, both the 32-bit and the 64-bit variants have been verified; however, it is recommended that you use the 64-bit version if your hardware supports it. You can find a detailed list of all supported distributions in the *Yocto Project Reference Manual* located at www.yoctoproject.org/docs/current/ref-manual/ref-manual.html.

In addition to the Linux distribution, you need to install a series of software packages for the build system to run. We cover the installation in Section 2.1.3.

2.1.2 Obtaining the Yocto Project Tools

There are several ways for you to obtain the Yocto Project tools, or more precisely, the Yocto Project reference distribution, Poky:

- Download the current release from the Yocto Project website.
- Download the current release or previously released versions from the release repository.
- Download a recent nightly build from the Autobuilder repository.
- Clone the current development branch or other branches from the Poky Git repository hosted by the Yocto Project Git repository server.

The Yocto Project team releases a new major version of the build system every 6 months, in the April–May and October–November timeframes. All released versions of the Yocto Project tools have undergone multiple rounds of quality assurance and testing. They are stable and are accompanied with release notes and an updated documentation set describing the features. For Yocto Project novices, we recommend using the recent stable release.

Minor version releases that resolve issues but do not add any new features are provided as necessary between the 6-month release cycles. Since there are no new features, the documentation typically does not change with the minor releases.

Previous major and minor releases are archived and still available for download from the download repository. Sometimes new major releases introduce a new layer structure, new configuration files, and/or new settings in configuration files. Hence, migrating an existing build environment to the newer release may require migration effort. Staying with a previous release allows you to postpone or entirely put off migration.

Nightly builds track the current development status of the codebase in the Yocto Project Git repository. These builds have undergone basic quality assurance and Autobuilder testing. They are not tested as rigorously as the regular major and minor releases, but you get at least some confidence that the core functionality is operational.

Cloning the current development branch (*master* branch) from the Poky Git repository gives you direct access to the current state of the development effort. Modifications to this branch have not undergone any testing other than the tests the developers performed before signing off on their submissions. While the quality is generally high and any serious breakage of core functionality typically gets detected within a short period of time after a developer checked in a change, there is a good chance that the system may not work as expected. Unless you are directly involved in Yocto Project development, there is no immediate need to directly work with the master branch.

Besides the master branch, the Poky Git repository also contains milestone branches, development branches for the various versions, and a long list of tags referencing particular revisions of the various branches.

In the chapters to come, we outline how to download the Yocto Project releases from the various locations. We also explore the Yocto Project Git repositories for Poky, board support packages, the Linux kernel, and more in detail.

Downloading the Current Poky Release

Navigate to https://www.yoctoproject.org/downloads and click on the latest release of Poky. This URL directs you to a detailed download site with links to various download servers and mirrors. The site also contains the release information and an errata.

Downloading the release places a compressed archive of the Poky reference distribution named poky-<codename>-<release>.tar.bz2 on your system.

2.1.3 Setting Up the Build Host

Setting up your build host requires the installation of additional software packages. All of the four mainstream Linux distributions have those packages readily available in their package repositories. However, they differ in what packages are preinstalled as part of the distribution's default configuration.

After installing the additional packages, you need to unpack the Poky tarball, which includes all the necessary configuration data, recipes, convenience scripts, and BitBake.

BitBake requires Python with a major version of 2.6 or 2.7. BitBake currently does not support the new Python 3, which introduced changes to the language syntax and new libraries breaking backwards compatibility.

Installing Additional Software Packages

What command to use and what additional packages to install depends on the Linux distribution you installed on your build host.

To install the necessary packages on a CentOS build host, use the command in Listing 2-1.

Listing 2-1 **CentOS**

```
user@centos:~$ sudo yum install gawk make wget tar bzip2 gzip \
python unzip perl patch diffutils diffstat git cpp gcc gcc-c++ \
glibc-devel texinfo chrpath socat perl-Data-Dumper \
perl-Text-ParseWords perl-Thread-Queue SDL-devel xterm
```

For setup on a Fedora build host, execute the command in Listing 2-2.

Listing 2-2 **Fedora**

```
user@fedora:~$ sudo dnf install gawk make wget tar bzip2 gzip python \
unzip perl patch diffutils diffstat git cpp gcc gcc-c++ glibc-devel \
texinfo chrpath ccache perl-Data-Dumper perl-Text-ParseWords \
perl-Thread-Queue socat findutils which SDL-devel xterm
```

Listing 2-3 shows the installation command for an openSUSE build host.

Listing 2-3 **openSUSE**

```
user@opensuse:~$ sudo zypper install python gcc gcc-c++ git chrpath \
make wget python-xml diffstat makeinfo python-curses patch socat \
libSDL-devel xterm
```

On an Ubuntu build, run the command in Listing 2-4.

Listing 2-4 **Ubuntu**

```
user@ubuntu:~$ sudo apt-get install gawk wget git-core diffstat \
unzip texinfo gcc-multilib build-essential chrpath socat \
libsdl1.2-dev xterm
```

After a successful installation, you may want to verify that the correct version of Python has been installed: python --version. The output should show a major version number of 2.6 or 2.7.

Installing Poky

Installing Poky merely requires unpacking the compressed tarball you downloaded from the Yocto Project website earlier. We recommend that you create a subdirectory in your home directory for all things related to your Yocto Project builds. Listing 2-5 shows the necessary steps.

Listing 2-5   **Installing Poky**

```
user@buildhost:~$ mkdir ~/yocto
user@buildhost:~$ cd ~/yocto
user@buildhost:~$ tar xvfj <downloadpath>/poky-<codename>-release.tar.bz2
```

Now your build system is ready for setting up a build environment and creating your first Linux OS stack.

2.1.4 Configuring a Build Environment

Poky provides the script oe-init-build-env to create a new build environment. The script sets up the build environment's directory structure and initializes the core set of configuration files. It also sets a series of *shell variables* needed by the build system. You do not directly execute the oe-init-build-env script but use the source command to export the shell variable settings to the current shell:

```
$ source <pokypath>/oe-init-build-env <builddir>
```

Executing the command creates a new build environment in the current directory with the name provided by the parameter <builddir>. You may omit that parameter, and then the script uses the default build. After setting up the build environment, the script changes directory to the build directory.

Use the script in the form of Listing 2-6 to create a new build environment as well as to initialize an existing build environment previously created. When creating a new build environment the script provides you with some instructions.

Listing 2-6   **New Build Environment Setup**

```
You had no conf/local.conf file. This configuration file has therefore been
created for you with some default values. You may wish to edit it to use a
different MACHINE (target hardware) or enable parallel build options to take
advantage of multiple cores, for example. See the file for more information, as
common configuration options are commented.

The Yocto Project has extensive documentation about OE including a reference
manual which can be found at:
    http://yoctoproject.org/documentation

For more information about OpenEmbedded see their website:
    http://www.openembedded.org/

You had no conf/bblayers.conf file. The configuration file has been created
for you with some default values. To add additional metadata layers into your
configuration, please add entries to this file.
```

```
The Yocto Project has extensive documentation about OE including a reference
manual which can be found at:
    http://yoctoproject.org/documentation

For more information about OpenEmbedded see their website:
    http://www.openembedded.org/

### Shell environment set up for builds. ###

You can now run 'bitbake <target>'

Common targets are:
    core-image-minimal
    core-image-sato
    meta-toolchain
    meta-toolchain-sdk
    adt-installer
    meta-ide-support

You can also run generated qemu images with a command like 'runqemu qemux86'
```

Inside the newly created build environment, the script added the directory conf and placed the two configuration files in it: bblayers.conf and local.conf. We explain bblayers.conf in detail in Chapter 3, "OpenEmbedded Build System." For now we look only at local.conf, which is the master configuration file of our build environment.

In local.conf, various variables are set that influence how BitBake builds your custom Linux OS stack. You can modify the settings and also add new settings to the file to override settings that are made in other configuration files. We explain this inheritance and how to use it with various examples throughout this book. For our first build, we focus on a few settings and accept the defaults for the remaining ones. If you open the local.conf file in a text editor, you find the variable settings shown in Listing 2-7 (among many others, which along with comment lines we have removed from this listing).

Listing 2-7   **conf/local.conf**

```
BB_NUMBER_THREADS ?= "${@bb.utils.cpu_count()}"
PARALLEL_MAKE ?= "-j ${@bb.utils.cpu_count()}"
MACHINE ??= "qemux86"
DL_DIR ?= "${TOPDIR}/downloads"
SSTATE_DIR ?= "${TOPDIR}/sstate-cache"
TMP_DIR = "${TOPDIR}/tmp"
```

Lines starting with the hash mark (#) are comments. If a hash mark precedes a line with a variable setting, you need to remove the hash mark for the settings to become active. The values shown are the default values. BitBake uses those values even if you do not enable them explicitly. The variable settings shown in Listing 2-7 are the ones that you typically want to change after creating a new build environment. They are described in Table 2-1.

Table 2-1 **Configuration Variables**

Variable	Default Value	Description
BB_NUMBER_THREADS	${@bb.utils.cpu_count()}	Number of parallel BitBake tasks
PARALLEL_MAKE	-j ${@bb.utils.cpu_count()}	Number of parallel Make processes
MACHINE	qemux86	Target machine
DL_DIR	${TOPDIR}/downloads	Directory where source downloads are placed
SSTATE_DIR	${TOPDIR}/sstate_cache	Directory for shared state cache files
TMP_DIR	${TOPDIR}/tmp	Directory for build output

The default value for the two *parallelism options* BB_NUMBER_THREADS and PARALLEL_MAKE is automatically computed on the basis of the number of CPU cores in the system using all the available cores. You can set the values to less than the cores in your system to limit the load. Using a larger number than the number of physical cores is possible but does not speed up the build process. BitBake and Make spawn more threads accordingly, but they run only if there are CPU cores available. Never forget the quotes around the variable settings. Also note that for PARALLEL_MAKE, you have to include the -j, such as "-j 4" because this value is passed to the make command verbatim.

Setting the MACHINE variable selects the target machine type for which BitBake builds your Linux OS stack. Poky provides a series of standard machines for QEMU and a few actual hardware board target machines. Board support packages (BSPs) can provide additional target machines. For our first build, we choose qemux86, an emulated target machine with an x86 CPU.

The variable DL_DIR tells BitBake where to place the source downloads. The default setting places the files in the directory downloads beneath the top directory of your build environment. The variable TOPDIR contains the full (absolute) path to the build environment. Source downloads can be shared among multiple build environments. If BitBake detects that a source download is already available in the download directory, it does not download it again. Therefore, we recommend that you set the DL_DIR variable to point to a directory path outside of the build environment. When you no longer need a particular build environment, you can easily delete it without deleting all the source file downloads.

The same holds true for the SSTATE_DIR variable, which contains the path to the *shared state cache*. The OpenEmbedded build system produces a lot of intermediate output when processing the many tasks entailed in building the packages comprising the Linux OS stack. Similar to the source downloads, the intermediate output can be reused for future builds and shared between multiple build environments to speed up the build process. By default, the configuration places the shared state cache directory beneath the build environment's top directory. We suggest that you change the setting to a path outside the build environment.

The variable TMP_DIR contains the path to the directory where BitBake performs all the build work and stores the build output. Since the output stored in this directory is very specific to your build environment, it makes sense to leave it as a subdirectory to the build environment. The amount of data stored in this directory can eventually consume many gigabytes of hard disk space because it contains extracted source downloads, cross-compilation toolchains, compilation output, and images for kernel and root file systems for your target machines and more.

To conserve disk space during a build, you can add

```
INHERIT += rm_work
```

which instructs BitBake to delete the work directory for building packages after the package has been built.

2.1.5 Launching the Build

To launch a build, invoke BitBake from the top-level directory of your build environment specifying a build target:

```
$ bitbake <build-target>
```

We go into detail about what build targets are and how to use them to control you build output in the following chapters. For our first build we use a build target that creates an entire Linux OS stack with a GUI. From the top-level directory of the build environment you created and configured during the previous sections, execute the following:

```
$ bitbake core-image-sato
```

The core-image-sato target creates a root file system image with a user interface for mobile devices. Depending on your build hardware and the speed of your Internet connection for downloading the source files, the build can take anywhere from one to several hours.

You may also instruct BitBake to first download all the sources without building. You can do this with

```
$ bitbake -c fetchall core-image-sato
```

After the download completes, you can disconnect your build system from the Internet and run the build offline at a later point in time.

BitBake typically immediately aborts a build process if it encounters an error condition from which it cannot recover. However, you can instruct BitBake to continue building even if it encounters an error condition as long as there are tasks left that are not impeded by the error:

```
$ bitbake -k core-image-sato
```

The -k option tells BitBake to continue building until tasks that are not dependent on the error condition are addressed.

Figure 2-1   QEMU with `core-image-sato` target

2.1.6 Verifying the Build Results

Since our target machine is an emulated system, we can verify our build result by launching the QEMU emulator. For that purpose, Poky provides a convenient script that prepares the QEMU execution environment and launches the emulator with the proper kernel and root file system images:

```
$ runqemu qemux86
```

In its simplest form, the `runqemu` script is invoked with the machine target name. It then automatically finds the proper kernel and root file system images for the target in the build output. You have to enter your system administrator (or *sudo*) password for the script to set up the virtual network interface. Figure 2-1 shows the running system.

You can terminate your QEMU virtual machine by clicking on the *Shutdown* button on the *Utilities* screen. This properly shuts down the system by running through the shutdown sequence. Alternatively, you can simply type *Ctl-C* in the terminal where you launched QEMU.

2.1.7 Yocto Project Build Appliance

If you simply would like to try out the Yocto Project and Poky without setting up a Linux build host, you can use the *Yocto Project Build Appliance*. The Build Appliance is a complete Yocto Project build host, including a Linux OS with the software packages required by the OpenEmbedded build system and Poky installed, bundled as a virtual machine image. It even already includes all the source package downloads, speeding up your first build and allowing you to build offline without a network connection.

The Build Appliance download is located on the Yocto Project website at https://www.yoctoproject.org/download/build-appliance-0. The Build Appliance is provided as a compressed ZIP archive that you need to unpack on your system after downloading it.

To utilize the Build Appliance, you need either VMWare Player or VMWare Workstation installed on your computer. You can obtain either one of them matching the operating system on your computer from the download section of VMWare's website at www.vmware.com. Follow the installation instructions provided by VMWare.

Once you have installed VMWare Player or VMWare Workstation, the Build Appliance manual at https://www.yoctoproject.org/documentation/build-appliance-manual provides detailed instructions on how to configure the virtual machine and boot the Build Appliance.

Booting the Build Appliance directly launches the Hob GUI for BitBake, as shown in Figure 2-2.

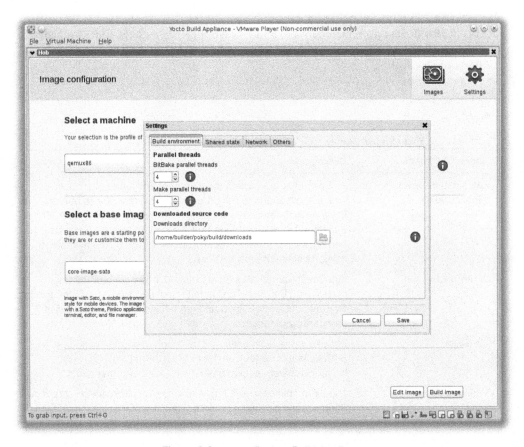

Figure 2-2   Yocto Project Build Appliance

Select *qemux86* from the drop-down box for the machine and *core-image-sato* for the base image. Then start the build. Depending on your host system and the virtual machine configuration, it may take multiple hours to build the image. You can observe the build process from the *Log* screen of Hob. The *Log* screen shows the packages to be built in a run-queue split up into the individual tasks. Currently running tasks are highlighted.

After the build completes, you can launch your image with the QEMU emulator directly from Hob.

2.2 The Yocto Project Family

The Yocto Project is not just a single open source project but combines multiple projects under one umbrella. You have already encountered the most prominent members of this family of projects: the OpenEmbedded build system, which includes BitBake and OpenEmbedded Core, and Poky, the Yocto Project reference distribution.

Essentially, all the members of the family support the OpenEmbedded build system. The Yocto Project team maintains the build system together with the OpenEmbedded Project, a separate organization. New functionality is added to the subprojects as the build system evolves.

Table 2-2 provides an overview of the subprojects maintained as part of the Yocto Project.

Table 2-2   **Yocto Project Family**

Internal Project	Description
Application Development Toolkit (ADT)	ADT provides a complete development environment for user space applications to run on operating system stacks built by Poky. An ADT comprises cross-development toolchains, the QEMU emulator, Linux kernel, and root file system images. Poky creates and packages an ADT directly from within the build environment using its configuration settings.
AutoBuilder	AutoBuilder automates builds through integration of the build system with Buildbot. The Yocto Project QA team uses AutoBuilder for continuous integration and regression testing with a set of standard build targets.
BitBake	BitBake is the build engine of the OpenEmbedded build system. BitBake is a build tool similar to Make or Ant with focus on building software packages and operating system stacks.
Build Appliance	The Build Appliance is a fully self-contained Poky build system on Ubuntu Linux packaged as a VMWare virtual machine image. It is a convenient way to try out Poky without installing a Linux build host and setting up Poky on it.

Table 2-2   **Yocto Project Family (*Continued*)**

Internal Project	Description
Cross-Prelink	Memory address locations of shared libraries are typically computed during runtime when the library is loaded into memory for the first time. Every time a program relying on a shared library is run, the loader has to locate the library in memory. Because libraries can move around in memory, this task causes a performance penalty that increases with the number of shared libraries that need to be resolved. Prelinking reduces this overhead by performing the dynamic linking of an executable in advance by precalculating the addresses. Cross-prelinking performs this process as part of the cross-development toolchain by emulating a runtime linker.
Eclipse IDE Plugin	The Yocto Project plugin for the Eclipse IDE integrates ADT into Eclipse, providing a cross-development workflow for user space applications. The plugin provides integration for cross-toolchains as well as for root file systems to be utilized with emulated and/ or hardware targets.
EGLIBC	EGLIBC is the embedded version of the GNU C Library (GLIBC). It offers the same APIs as GLIBC and tries to be source and binary compatible with it but is optimized for embedded systems. Optimization includes reduced footprint, improved support for cross-build and cross-testing, and configurable components. Although EGLIBC has been merged into GLIBC and reached end-of-life, we mention it here to provide context and history.
Hob	Hob is a GUI for BitBake. Hob allows configuration of a build environment, package selection, and image configuration from a convenient GUI rather than editing text files. Build processes can be directly launched and monitored from Hob. Hob is a layer contained in OpenEmbedded Core. Eventually, the Yocto Project team will discontinue Hob in favor of Toaster.
Matchbox	Matchbox is an open source window manager based on the X Window System targeted for embedded devices. It distinguishes itself from traditional desktop window managers in that it shows only one window at a time filling the entire screen. That feature makes it suitable for devices with smaller form factors.
OpenEmbedded Core	OpenEmbedded Core (OE Core) is the core collection of metadata in the OpenEmbedded build system. It consists of a collection of BitBake layers and classes and integration and utility scripts that are shared among OpenEmbedded-derived systems. OE Core is co-maintained by the OpenEmbedded Project and the Yocto Project.

Continues

Table 2-2   **Yocto Project Family (*Continued*)**

Internal Project	Description
Poky	Poky is the reference distribution of the Yocto Project. It provides a set of blueprints for preconfigured embedded Linux OS stacks as working examples. These blueprints can be used to bootstrap actual system development.
Pseudo	Building software packages frequently requires operations such as installing files into a system's root file system, changing file ownership or access permissions, and creating device nodes to be carried out as the system administrator. Pseudo is an application that provides a virtualized environment allowing such operations to succeed as though the user had system administrator privileges even if she is an ordinary user.
Swabber	The majority of software packages are configured to be built on a native system. Building them in cross-development environments frequently requires configuration changes and bears the inherent risk that a build uses components from the build host rather than from the cross-build environment. For instance, a path in a make file points to a file on the host system rather than the cross-build environment. Such *host pollution* of a cross-build can lead to hard-to-detect system failures not only during build time but also during runtime. Swabber provides a mechanism for detecting cross-build access beyond the boundaries of the build sandbox.
Toaster	Toaster is the new GUI for BitBake and the build system. It is web based and can be deployed as a distributed build service with remote access.

Although there is tight integration of the subprojects within the Yocto Project, the developers ensure that there are no cross dependencies and that the subprojects are interoperable and can also be used independently without the build system.

2.3 A Little Bit of History

Both OpenEmbedded and the Yocto Project have their roots in the OpenZaurus project, an open source project striving to improve the code of the first Linux-based personal digital assistant, the Sharp Zaurus SL-5000D. The SL-5000D, which first shipped in 2001, was a device targeted to developers, and Sharp provided the necessary tools to modify and update the ROM code of the device. At first, the project focused on repackaging the existing ROM code to make it more developer-friendly. Over time, the project evolved, and the original Sharp code was entirely replaced by a Debian-based Linux distribution built from source. It quickly outgrew its build system, making it necessary for the project to create a new device and distribution-independent build system. The OpenEmbedded project was born.

2.3.1 OpenEmbedded

The OpenEmbedded project debuted in 2003 by combining the efforts of the OpenZaurus project with contributions from other embedded Linux projects with similar goals, such as the Familiar Linux and OpenSIMpad projects.

The OpenEmbedded Project maintained the build system and the metadata that described how to build the software packages and assemble the operating system images as a common codebase. The number of packages added to the metadata inventory quickly grew to more than 2,100 recipes building over 5,000 packages.

In 2005, the project team decided to split the project into the BitBake build system and the OpenEmbedded metadata.

OpenEmbedded got support from various Linux distributions using it as their build system. Among them are the Ångström Distribution, Openmoko, WebOS, and others. Commercial entities adopted the system for their product offerings, among them MontaVista Software and OpenedHand, the startup that developed the Poky Linux distribution.

2.3.2 BitBake

BitBake, the build engine at the core of OpenEmbedded and the Yocto Project's Poky reference distribution, is derived from Portage, the build and package management system of Gentoo Linux. Portage comprises two components:

- **ebuild** is the actual build system that takes care of building software packages from source code and installing them.
- **emerge** is an interface to ebuild and a tool to manage ebuild package repositories, resolving dependencies and more.

All Portage tools are written in Python. BitBake evolved from Portage by extending it for building software packages with native and cross-development toolchains, supporting multiple package management systems and other functionality necessary for cross-building.

BitBake uses the same metadata syntax as the Portage build scripts but introduced new features such as an inheritance mechanism supported by classes, appending recipes, and global configuration files, among others.

2.3.3 Poky Linux

OpenEmbedded significantly simplified building Linux OS stacks for, but not limited to, embedded devices. However, it remained a challenge with quite a steep learning curve to modify and adapt the system to create different distributions and port the system to new hardware.

The software startup company OpenedHand originally developed Poky Linux, a versatile development platform as well as a Linux distribution for mobile devices, for internal use. Poky Linux provided the test platform for the company's Matchbox window manager for embedded devices. Matchbox is most notably used by the Nokia 770 and N800 tablet devices, Openmoko's Neo1973, and the One Laptop Per Child (OLPC) project's XO laptop computer.

Built with OpenEmbedded, the Poky Linux distribution provided a more intuitive way to configure operating system images for target devices. It also offered several blueprints for target device images that were easy to adapt and modify. Since Poky Linux was open source, it was quickly adopted by others to build embedded devices.

Intel Corporation acquired OpenedHand in 2008 with the goal to further develop Poky Linux as a universal distribution for embedded devices.

2.3.4 The Yocto Project

To build out Poky Linux to support many different architectures and hardware platforms, Intel was looking for other commercial entities—particularly other semiconductor manufacturers and embedded Linux companies—to support the project and contribute to it. As Intel is a dominant player in the chip market and has substantial resources, it proved difficult for Intel to get its competition and other companies to support it in its efforts to improve Poky Linux.

In 2010, Intel approached the Linux Foundation with the idea to create a collaborative project under the auspices of the Foundation with neutral stewardship. That effort would also include the open source community, particularly the OpenEmbedded project.

The Linux Foundation publicly announced the launch of the Yocto Project on October 26, 2010. On March 1, 2011, the Linux Foundation announced the alignment of the Yocto Project technology with OpenEmbedded and the support of multiple corporate collaborators to the project. This announcement was followed by another press release on April 6, 2011, communicating the formation of the Yocto Project Steering Group and the first Yocto Project software release.

2.3.5 The OpenEmbedded and Yocto Project Relationship

The technology alignment between OpenEmbedded and the Yocto Project brought several major improvements to both projects:

- **Aligned Development**: A common problem among open source projects is *fragmentation*: two projects with the same roots and similar goals fork and grow apart. Resources are divided and ultimately efforts are duplicated to provide similar functionality in both branches. Eventually, users and supporters are forced to make a decision between the two efforts. The tight alignment of OpenEmbedded and the Yocto Project ensures that users can get the benefits of both projects.

- **BitBake Metadata Layers**: Metadata layers enable logical grouping of recipes and configuration files into structures that can easily be included in and migrated to different build environments. Metadata layers also simplify dependency management, which is a complex task when building operating system stacks.
- **OpenEmbedded Core Metadata Layer**: The OpenEmbedded and Yocto Project development teams agreed to create a common metadata layer shared between the two projects and containing all the base recipes and configuration settings. Each project then adds additional metadata layers according to its goals.

Despite the close collaboration between OpenEmbedded and the Yocto Project, the two projects are separate entities. Both are open source projects, and both are supported by a community of open source developers as well as commercial entities.

OpenEmbedded focuses on cutting-edge technology, recipes, and a large set of board support packages for different hardware platforms. The Yocto Project focuses on the build system itself and tooling for cross-development. The goal of the Yocto Project is to provide powerful yet easy-to-use and well-tested tools together with a core set of metadata to jumpstart embedded system development. Additional board support packages and other components are offered through OpenEmbedded and the Yocto Project ecosystem.

The OpenEmbedded Project also maintains a layer index, which is a searchable database of layers, recipes, and machines. Looking for a recipe to build a particular open source package? Enter the name into the layer index, and chances are that somebody has already created a recipe for it.

2.4 Yocto Project Terms

Table 2-3 defines a set of terms commonly used in conjunction with and throughout the Yocto Project. Throughout this book, we use these terms consistently with their definitions provided here.

Table 2-3 **Yocto Project Terms**

Term	Description
Append file	An append file extends an existing recipe. BitBake verbatim appends the contents of an append file to the corresponding recipe, creating a single file before parsing it. Variables in an append file can override the same variables defined in the corresponding recipe. Append files use the `bbappend` extension.
BitBake	The build engine in the OpenEmbedded build system, BitBake is a task executor and scheduler. Its inputs are metadata files such as configuration files and recipes through which BitBake processing is controlled.

Continues

Table 2-3   **Yocto Project Terms (*Continued*)**

Term	Description
Board support package (BSP)	Documentation, binaries, code, and other implementation-specific support data in the BSP enable a given operating system to run on a particular target hardware platform. Sometimes a BSP also contains complete root file systems and a cross-development environment to create application programs running on the target hardware platform.
Class	In BitBake terminology, a class is a metadata file providing logic encapsulation and a basic inheritance mechanism allowing commonly used patterns to be defined once and used with many recipes. BitBake class files use the `bbclass` extension.
Configuration file	Configuration files are BitBake metadata files providing global definition and settings for variables that affect the build process.
Cross-development toolchain	A cross-development toolchain is a collection of software development tools allowing software development for target systems employing a different architecture than the development host. Architecture in this context refers to different CPU instruction sets (for instance, ARM, MIPS, PowerPC, x86) as well as different bit sizes (for instance, 8, 16, 32, and 64 bit). Typically, a cross-development toolchain includes one or more language compilers, an assembler, a linker, and often debuggers, emulators, and other tools that are specific to the target architecture.
Image	A binary file, often compressed, an image contains a bootloader, an operating system kernel, and a root file system to be copied to a storage medium from which the target system can boot and run. The term *image* is also used to mean just an operating system kernel (kernel image) or the root file system (root file system image).
Layer	In BitBake terminology, a layer is a collection of metadata (configuration files, recipes, etc.) organized into a file and directory structure. BitBake can include layers to extend its functionality. Yocto Project BSPs are provided as layers.
Metadata	In BitBake terminology, metadata includes all files that instruct BitBake how to execute build processes. BitBake metadata includes classes, recipes (with append files), and configuration files.
OpenEmbedded Core (OE Core)	A core set of metadata in the OpenEmbedded build system that is shared between OpenEmbedded and the Yocto Project, OE Core is a BitBake layer co-maintained by the OpenEmbedded Project and the Yocto Project.
Package	A package is a software bundle containing executable binaries, libraries, documentation, configuration information, and other files following a specific format that an operating system's package management system can install or uninstall. Packages commonly also include information on dependencies on and incompatibilities with other software packages that the package management system can use to automatically resolve and/or inform the user about.
	The Yocto Project also uses the term *package* to mean the recipes and other metadata used to build the respective software bundle. Dependent on the context, the term then refers either to the actual software bundle or to the metadata that builds the software bundle.

Table 2-3   **Yocto Project Terms (*Continued*)**

Term	Description
Package management system	A package management system is a collection of software tools automating the process of installing, upgrading, configuring, and removing software packages for a computer's operating system. It typically maintains a database of the installed software on the computer, including version information, dependencies, incompatibilities, and more, to prevent system faults through software mismatches and missing prerequisites.
Poky	Poky is the Yocto Project's reference distribution as well as the name of the default Linux distribution created by the build system. The Poky download package includes the OpenEmbedded build system as well as additional metadata for creating a sample embedded distribution called Poky.
Recipe	A recipe is a metadata file containing directives for BitBake on how to build a particular software package. Through its directives, a recipe describes from where to obtain the source code, what patches to apply and how to apply them, how to build the binaries and associated files, how to install the build results on a target system, how to create the packaged software bundle, and much more. Recipes also describe dependencies during build and runtime on other software packages, hence creating a logical hierarchy of the pieces required for the build process. Recipes use the bb file extension.
Task	BitBake recipes may contain executable metadata, or code, that BitBake executes during the build process. Execution steps can be grouped into metadata functions. A metadata function can be declared as a task by inserting it into the BitBake task list.
Upstream	In software development, particularly in open source, *upstream* references the direction to the originators, that is, the original authors or maintainers, of the software. Commonly, the term is used as a qualifier, such as *upstream repository* and *upstream patch*.

2.5 Summary

The Yocto Project is a family of projects related to embedded Linux software development. At its core is the OpenEmbedded build system and the Poky reference distribution. Originally developed by OpenedHand as Poky Linux, Poky evolved into the Yocto Project, a collaborative project under the auspices of the Linux Foundation. Supported by corporations and independent software developers, it aligned its technology with OpenEmbedded to form a broad community delivering state-of-the-art tools for developing embedded Linux systems.

Getting started with the Yocto Project is as simple as downloading the Build Appliance and booting it from the VMWare virtual machine manager. While the Build Appliance is not recommended for serious development, it offers a good introduction to the OpenEmbedded build system without the need to set up a Linux build host.

Installing a Linux build host for use with Poky requires a few more steps but avoids the overhead and performance impact of the virtual machine.

2.6 References

The Linux Foundation, *Linux Foundation and Consumer Electronics Linux Forum to Merge*, www.linuxfoundation.org/news-media/announcements/2010/10/linux-foundation-and-consumer-electronics-linux-forum-merge

The Linux Foundation, *Yocto Project Aligns Technology with OpenEmbedded and Gains Corporate Collaborators*, www.linuxfoundation.org/news-media/announcements/2011/03/yocto-project-aligns-technology-openembedded-and-gains-corporate-co

3

OpenEmbedded Build System

Poky is the Yocto Project's reference distribution. It includes the OpenEmbedded build system. It provides all the necessary tools, recipes, and configuration data required to build a Linux OS stack. As we saw in the previous chapter, Poky is a mostly self-contained system bundled as a simple archive. Only a few additional components need to be installed on the build host to use Poky.

This chapter starts by analyzing the typical workflow for open source software packages. It then explains how the OpenEmbedded work flow integrates building of individual software packages with the processes for creating a complete Linux OS stack and bootable filesystem images. Armed with this knowledge, we then have a detailed look at the Poky architecture and its components.

3.1 Building Open Source Software Packages

If you have built open source software packages for a Linux host system before, you may have noticed that the workflow follows a specific pattern. Some of the steps of this workflow you execute yourself, whereas others are typically carried out through some sort of automation such as Make or other source-to-binary build systems.

1. **Fetch**: Obtain the source code.

2. **Extract**: Unpack the source code.

3. **Patch**: Apply patches for bug fixes and added functionality.

4. **Configure**: Prepare the build process according to the environment.

5. **Build**: Compile and link.

6. **Install**: Copy binaries and auxiliary files to their target directories.

7. **Package**: Bundle binaries and auxiliary files for installation on other systems.

If you are building the software package only for use on the host system you use for building, then you would normally stop after installing the binaries on your system. However, if you are looking to distribute the binaries for installation and use on other systems, you would also include the *package* step, which creates an archive that can be used by the package management system for installation.

Let's have a look at the individual steps.

3.1.1 Fetch

It all starts with obtaining the source code for a software package. Typically, open source projects have a download area from where the source code together with instructions, documentation, and other information can be downloaded in the form of an archive, which commonly is also compressed. What theoretically sounds like a straightforward task in fact requires a lot of attention to detail. There are no generally adhered-to conventions when it comes to downloading source code packages.

Of course, each open source project has its own URL to access its website, file servers, and download areas. In addition, downloads may be accessible through one or more protocols, such as HTTP, HTTPS, FTP, SFTP, and others. Some projects may also provide access to released versions and development branches of their source code from a source control management (SCM) system such as Git, Subversion, Concurrent Versions System (CVS; also known as Concurrent Revisioning System), and more.

Commonly, sources obtained from remote locations such as download sites or repositories may be supplemented with patches and auxiliary files that are stored on a local filesystem.

For an automated build system such as the OpenEmbedded build system, this variety of ways to obtain the source code means it needs to be flexible and capable of handling this variety mostly transparently for the developer.

3.1.2 Extract

After the source code is downloaded, it must be unpacked and copied from its download location to an area where you are going to build it. Typically, open source packages are wrapped into archives, most commonly into compressed tar archives, but CPIO and other formats that serialize multiple files into a single archive are also in use. The most frequently used compression formats are GZIP and BZIP, but some projects utilize other compression schemes. Once again, a build system must be able to automatically detect the format of the source archive and use the correct tools to extract it.

If the sources are obtained from an SCM, extracting archives generally means *checking them out* from the SCM into the area where BitBake builds them.

3.1.3 Patch

Patching is the process of incrementally modifying the source code by adding, deleting, and changing the source files. There are various reasons why source code could require patching before building: applying bug and security fixes, adding functionality, providing configuration information, making adjustments for cross-compiling, and so forth. For instance, the Linux kernel requires a file that provides many hundreds of configuration settings to the kernel build system, such as target architecture, hardware information, device drivers, and many more.

Applying a patch can be as simple as copying a file into the directory structure of the source code. In this case, the build system of course needs to know where to copy the file to. Commonly, patches are applied using the patch utility, which takes a patch file as input that has been created with the diff utility. Diff compares an original file with a modified file and creates a differential file that includes not only the changes but also metadata such as the name and path of the file and the exact location of the modifications and a context. The format of the file is standardized and referred to as the *unified format*. A patch file using the unified format can contain information to patch multiple files at a time, and it can add or remove entire files. Because all information about the files being modified, added, or removed is contained within the patch file, the build system does not need to know anything about the directory structure of the source code to be patched.

The order in which patches are applied is of significance because patches may be dependent on each other. Applying a large number of patches in the correct order can be a difficult task. The Quilt patch management system greatly simplifies that task by creating a patch stack to maintain the order. Among many other functions, Quilt also allows for backing out patches that have been applied together with all dependent patches. Quilt is a series of shell scripts that was originally developed for the Linux kernel but is now also commonly used by many other open source projects.

3.1.4 Configure

Providing a software package in source code form serves, among others, the purpose that users can build the software themselves for a wide range of target systems. With variety comes diversity requiring the build environment for the software package to be configured appropriately for the target system. Accurate configuration is particularly important for *cross-build environments* where the CPU architecture of the build host is different from the CPU architecture of the target system.

Many software packages now use the GNU build system, also known as *Autotools*, for configuration. Autotools is a suite of tools aimed at making source code software packages portable to many UNIX-like systems. Autotools is a rather complex system reflecting the variety and diversity of target systems and dependencies. In a nutshell, Autotools creates a configure script from a series of input files that characterize a particular source code body. Through a series of processing steps, configure creates a makefile specifically for the target system. Autotools is frequently criticized for being hard to use. The difficulty, of course, depends on the perspective. From the user perspective, running a single script to configure the build environment of a source code package for a target system is certainly a huge benefit. Developers who want to provide that convenience to the users of their software need to understand the workings of Autotools and how to create the necessary input files correctly. Nevertheless, it is worth the effort and greatly simplifies building software packages with automated build systems such as the OpenEmbedded build system for many different target systems.

Some software packages use their own configuration system. In such cases, an automated build system needs to provide the flexibility to adjust the configuration step accordingly.

3.1.5 Build

The vast majority of software packages utilize Make to build binaries such as executable program files and libraries as well as auxiliary files from source code. Some software packages may use other utilities, such as CMake or qmake, for software packages using the Qt graphical libraries.

3.1.6 Install

The install step copies binaries, libraries, documentation, configuration, and other files to the correct locations in the target's filesystem. Program files are typically installed in /usr/bin, for user programs, and /usr/sbin, for system administration programs. Libraries are copied to /usr/lib and application-specific subdirectories inside /usr/lib. Configuration files are commonly installed to /etc. Although there are commonly used conventions on where to install certain files, software developers sometimes choose different directories to install files belonging to their software packages. The Filesystem Hierarchy Standard (FHS)[1] is a specification for the layout of filesystems for UNIX operating systems.

Most software packages provide an install target as part of their makefile, which performs the installation steps. Correctly written installation targets use the install utility to copy the files from the build environment to their respective target directories. The install utility can also set file ownership and permissions while copying the files.

3.1.7 Package

Packaging is the process of bundling the software, binaries, and auxiliary files into a single archive file for distribution and direct installation on a target system. Packaging can be as simple as a compressed tar archive that the user then extracts on the target system.

---

1. https://wiki.linuxfoundation.org/en/FHS

For convenience and usability, most software packages bundle their files for use with an installer or package management system. Some systems include the installation software with the software archive and create an executable file for self-contained installation. Others rely on a package manager that is already installed on the target system and only bundle the actual software together with metadata information for the package manager. All systems have in common that they not only copy the files from the software package to the target system but also verify dependencies and system configuration to avoid mismatching that eventually could render the system inoperable.

Linux systems commonly rely on a package management system that is part of the distribution rather than using self-contained installation packages. The advantages are that the package manager, as the only instance, maintains the software database on the system and that the software packages are smaller in size because they do not need to contain the installation software. However, the maintainers for each Linux distribution decide on its package management system, which requires software packages to be packaged multiple times for different target systems.

The most commonly used package management systems for Linux distributions are RPM Package Manager (RPM; originally Red Hat Package Manager) and dpkg, Debian's package management program. For embedded devices, the Itsy Package Management System (ipkg) has gained popularity. Ipkg is a lightweight system that resembles dpkg. Development of ipkg is discontinued, and many embedded projects that have been using ipkg are now using opkg, which was forked from ipkg by the Openmoko project. Opkg is written in C—it is actively maintained by the Yocto Project and used by OpenEmbedded and many other projects.

Install and package are not necessarily sequential steps. And they are also optional. If you are building a software package for local use only and not for redistribution, there is no need to package the software. If you are a package maintainer and create packages for redistribution, you may not need to perform the step to install the software package on your build system.

The steps outlined here are essentially the same whether you are building a software package natively or are performing a cross-build. However, you must consider many intricacies when setting up and configuring the build environment and building the package for a cross-build. We address the complexities of cross-building software throughout this book.

3.2 OpenEmbedded Workflow

Figure 3-1 illustrates the OpenEmbedded workflow. The workflow is not intrinsic to BitBake. BitBake does not establish a workflow at all. The workflow and its configuration are determined by the metadata, which is organized into different categories of files.

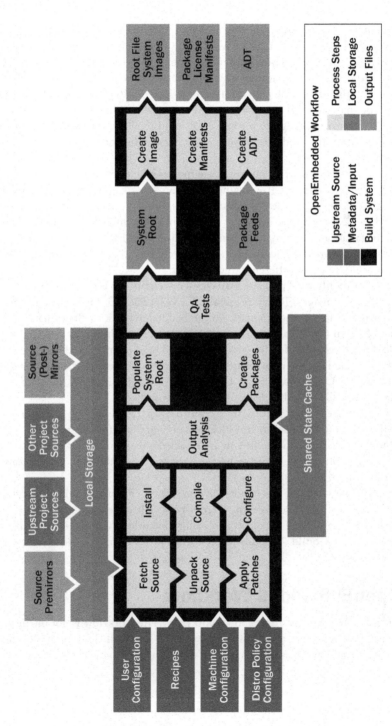

Figure 3-1   OpenEmbedded workflow

3.2.1 Metadata Files

Metadata files are subdivided into the categories *configuration files* and *recipes*.

Configuration Files

Configuration files contain global build system settings in the form of simple variable assignments. BitBake maintains the variable settings in a global data dictionary, and they can be accessed within any metadata file. A variable can be set in one configuration file and overwritten in another. Recipes can also set and overwrite variables, but the assignments made in recipes remain local to the recipe. BitBake employs a particular syntax for assigning metadata variables. Priorities for assigning and overwriting metadata variables are determined by various factors, such as layer structure, layer priorities, file parsing order, and assignment syntax. We explain the details of the BitBake metadata syntax and priorities in Chapter 4, "BitBake Build Engine."

BitBake distinguishes several different types of configuration files, but all have the common file extension .conf.

BitBake Master Configuration File (`bitbake.conf`)

BitBake's master or main configuration file is named `bitbake.conf`. BitBake expects this file to be present in all of the directories listed in its metadata search path. This file contains all the default configuration settings. Other configuration files and recipes commonly override some of the variable settings in this file according to their specific requirements.

The `bitbake.conf` file is part of the OpenEmbedded Core (OE Core) metadata layer and can be found in the configuration file subdirectory `conf` of that layer.

Layer Configuration (`layer.conf`)

The OpenEmbedded build system uses layers to organize metadata. A layer is essentially a hierarchy of directories and files. Every layer has its own configuration file named `layer.conf`. This file contains path settings and file patterns for the recipe files of the layer. The `layer.conf` file can be found in the `conf` subdirectory of the layer.

Build Environment Layer Configuration (`bblayers.conf`)

A build environment needs to tell BitBake what layers it requires for its build process. The file `bblayers.conf` provides BitBake with information on what layers to include with the build process and the filesystem paths where they are found. Each build environment has its own `bblayers.conf` file, which can be found in the `conf` subdirectory of the build environment.

Build Environment Configuration (`local.conf`)

Local configuration of a build environment is provided through a configuration file named `local.conf`. The `local.conf` file contains settings that apply to the particular build environment, such as paths to download locations, build outputs, and other files; configuration settings for the target system such as the target machine, package management system, and distribution policy; and many other settings. The `local.conf` file can be found in the `conf` subdirectory of the build environment.

Distribution Configuration (`<distribution-name>.conf`)

Distribution configuration files contain variable settings reflecting policies that apply for a particular distribution built by the OpenEmbedded build system. For the Poky reference distribution, the default image name is also *Poky*, and its configuration settings are contained in a file named `poky.conf`. Distribution policy settings typically include toolchain, C library, distribution name, and more. A distribution is selected by setting the variable `DISTRO` in the build environment's `local.conf` file. Of course, you are not limited to the distribution policies provided by Poky as a reference. You can create your own distribution policy file and use it with your build environment.

Distribution configuration files are typically found in the `conf/distro` subdirectory of a layer defining a distribution such as the `meta-yocto` layer.

Machine Configuration (`<machine-name>.conf`)

One of the most powerful features of the OpenEmbedded workflow is its capability to strictly separate parts of the build process that are dependent on the particular hardware system, the machine, and its architecture from the parts that do not depend on it. This capability greatly simplifies the creation of board support packages (BSP), allowing them to provide only the necessary parts that are dependent on the hardware and thus complementing the machine-independent pieces of the build system. Consequently, building the same Linux distribution for another machine is as straightforward as replacing one BSP with another.

A major part of this architecture consists of the machine configuration files that contain variable settings for machine dependencies referenced by the recipes that build software packages requiring machine-specific adaptions. Machine configuration files are named after the machine and can be found in the `conf/machine` subdirectory of a BSP layer.

Recipes

BitBake recipes form the core of the build system as they define the build workflow for each software package. The recipes contain the instructions for BitBake on how to build a particular software package by implementing the process steps outlined in Section 3.1. BitBake recipes are identified by their .bb file extension.

Recipes contain simple variable assignments as well as build instructions in the form of *executable metadata*, which are essentially functions that execute the process steps. We explain the details of executable metadata and BitBake tasks in the next chapter when discussing the internals of BitBake.

In contrast to configuration files, all variable assignments made within recipes are local to the recipe only. While recipes commonly reference variable settings made in configuration files and sometimes overwrite them for their purposes, all settings remain local to the recipe.

Many software packages are built in very similar ways using virtually identical build instructions following the same process steps. Repeatedly duplicating the same recipes while adjusting only a few parts that are specific to the software package would result in a lot of redundant effort. Hence, BitBake provides the concept of *classes*, a simple inheritance mechanism that allows recipes to easily share common workflows. Classes can be defined by any BitBake layer and are identified by their .bbclass file extension.

Another BitBake mechanism for recipes that fosters reuse is *append files*, which are identified by their .bbappend file extension. Append files are commonly used by layers building on top of other layers to tweak recipes contained in those layers for their special requirements. In most cases, they overwrite variable settings or modify them. Append files bear the same base filename as the core recipe from another layer that they are appending.

3.2.2 Workflow Process Steps

The workflow established by the OE Core metadata layer and executed by BitBake essentially follows the steps outlined in Section 3.1.

Source Fetching

The recipes call out the location of the sources such as source file packages, patches, and auxiliary files. BitBake can retrieve sources locally from the build host or remotely via network from external source repositories. Source files can be presented in a wide variety of formats such as plain and compressed tarballs. They can be retrieved via file transfer protocols as well as obtained from source control management (SCM) systems such as Git, SVN, and many more.[2]

Recipes specify the locations of the source files by including their URIs in the SRC_URI variable. The URIs in SRC_URI usually point to the upstream source repositories of the software package, such as the file download servers or the SCM of the upstream projects.

Before attempting to download a source software package from upstream repositories specified by the recipe's SRC_URI variable, BitBake first checks the local download directory to see whether the correct version of the source files has already been retrieved. If it cannot find the sources in the local download area, BitBake then attempts to retrieve the source files from a list of mirror file servers called *premirrors* if they are configured. If none of the premirrors contains the necessary files, BitBake next tries the actual upstream repositories, as specified in SRC_URI. If it cannot find the files there or if the upstream repositories are inaccessible, BitBake attempts to download the files from a second list of mirror servers. In the context of this book, we call these servers *postmirrors*, although in OpenEmbedded terminology, they are simply referred to as *mirrors*.

---

2. The complete list of protocols and SCM includes HTTP, FTP, HTTPS, Git, Subversion (SVN), Perforce (P4), Mercurial SCM (Hg), Bazar (BZR), CVS, Open Build Service (OSC), REPO, SSH, and SVK.

The Yocto Project maintains high-availability file servers on which the team places all upstream software packages. The Poky distribution configuration instructs BitBake to use the Yocto Project mirrors before attempting to download files directly from upstream repositories. Using the Yocto Project mirrors makes builds less dependent on the availability of the upstream file servers.

You may also set up mirrors as part of your own build infrastructure to maintain direct control of the sources included with your builds.

Source Unpacking and Patching

Once the sources are downloaded into the local download directory, they are extracted into the local build environment. If any patches were specified as part of the source download, then they are applied using Quilt. Commonly, source packages are not suitable for cross-building, and hence the majority of the patches are integration patches modifying the source for proper building with BitBake.

Configure, Compile, and Install

Through its classes, OpenEmbedded provides various schemes to build standard software packages, such as Make-based packages, GNU Autotools–based packages, and CMake-based packages. These schemes offer standardized ways to specify custom environment settings. We explore the details of building packages with BitBake using the standard schemes and customizing them in Chapter 8, "Software Package Recipes."

Although configuring, compiling, and installing are distinct steps in the build process, they are typically addressed within the same class because all of them involve invoking parts of the package's own build system.

The install step is executed using the pseudo[3] command, allowing the creation of special files and permissions for owner, group, and others to be set correctly. All files are installed into a private system root directory residing within the build environment for the particular package.

Output Analysis and Packaging

During output analysis, the software generated and installed by the previous step is categorized according to its functionality: runtime files, debug files, development files, documentation, locales. This allows the files to be split up into multiple physical packages for the package management system.

Following the analysis, the packages are created using one or more of the common packaging formats RPM, dpkg, and ipkg.

BitBake creates packages for the package management system classes contained in the variable PACKAGE_CLASSES in the build environment's configuration file local.conf. Although BitBake can create packages for one or more of the classes, it uses only the first one listed to create the final root filesystem for the distribution.

---

3. https://www.yoctoproject.org/tools-resources/projects/pseudo

Image Creation

The various images for the root filesystem of the distribution are created using the package feeds from the packaging step. The packages are installed from the package feeds into a root filesystem staging area using the package management system.

Which packages are installed into an image is decided on by image recipes that assemble a functional set for a working system based on the defined set of requirements. For example, a minimal image may contain just enough packages to boot the system for console operation with a minimal set of basic applications, whereas an image with a graphical user interface may include an X server and many other application packages.

Image creation is handled by the `core-image` class, which, among many other tasks, evaluates the variable `IMAGE_INSTALL` for a list of packages to be included with the image.

Images can be created in a variety of formats, including `tar.bz2` for extraction in a formatted filesystem and other formats, such as `ext2`, `ext3`, `ext4`, and `jffs`, that can be directly bit-copied to a suitable storage device.

SDK Generation

As an additional step, which is not part of the standard build process, with the goal of creating a bootable operating system stack, a software development kit (SDK) can be created.

An SDK contains native applications for the development host, such as cross-tool-chain, QEMU emulator, and installation scripts. It may also contain root filesystem images for use with the emulator that are based on the contents of the image creation step. The SDK can then be used by application developers to create and test applications using the very same environment that has been used to build the target system without actually using the OpenEmbedded build system.

The SDK with its tools may be used on the development host directly from the command line as well as through the integration with the Eclipse IDE. For the latter, the Yocto Project provides a plug-in for Eclipse that can directly be installed from the Eclipse workbench.

3.3 OpenEmbedded Build System Architecture

Three base components make up the OpenEmbedded build system architecture:

- Build system
- Build environment
- Metadata layers

Figure 3-2 depicts the components and their relationship to each other.

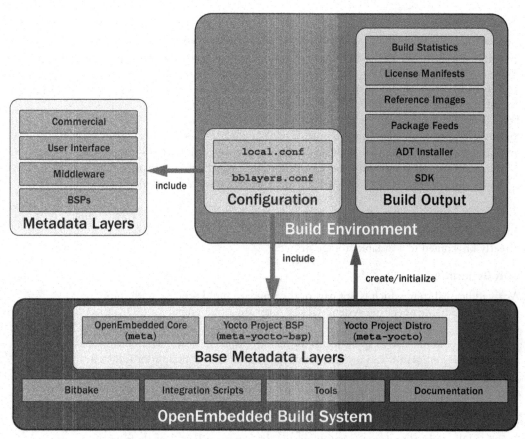

Figure 3-2   Poky architecture

The OpenEmbedded build system provides all of the necessary components, other than a few additional software packages that come with any Linux distribution, for building embedded Linux OS stacks. Included are the BitBake build engine; a set of integration scripts that provide additional functionality for convenience; various tools; OE Core, the core set of metadata required by BitBake to build images; and the entire documentation set in DocBook format. The Poky reference distribution also includes a minimum set of base metadata layers: Yocto Project BSP (meta-yocto-bsp) and Yocto Project Distribution (meta-yocto).

As we saw in Chapter 2, "The Yocto Project," the script oe-init-build-env creates and initializes the build environment. This script is one of the scripts contained within the build system. A build system and build environments form a 1:*n* relationship: a build system can be associated with any number of build environments, but a build environment can be associated with only one build system. This is an important limitation you need to be aware of when you are using more than one Yocto Project release at a time. You can use a build environment only with the version of the build system it was originally created with. Using a build system to initialize a build environment that is different from the one originally used to create the build environment leads to build failures.

A build system always has to include metadata layers, which provide recipes and configuration files. When you create a build environment with the `oe-init-build-env` script of the build system, the script automatically sets up a `conf/bblayers.conf` file that includes the three base layers: `meta`, `meta-yocto-bsp`, and `meta-yocto`. These base layers are sufficient to build the standard Poky reference distribution. However, as an embedded Linux developer, you eventually want to create your own distribution, add your own software packages, and potentially provide your own BSP for your target hardware. This goal is accomplished by including other metadata layers with the build system.

In the following section, we explore the structures of the build system, the build environment, and the metadata layers in more detail.

3.3.1 Build System Structure

Whether you download the Poky distribution in the form of a tarball and extract it or you directly clone it from the Yocto Project Git repository, it installs as a simple structure consisting of directories and files in a single directory similar to Listing 3-1 (the directory names are italicized to distinguish them from the filenames).

Listing 3-1   **OpenEmbedded Build System Structure**

```
yocto@yocto-dev:~/yocto$ tree -L 1 poky
poky
├── bitbake
├── documentation
├── LICENSE
├── meta
├── meta-hob
├── meta-selftest
├── meta-skeleton
├── meta-yocto
├── meta-yocto-bsp
├── oe-init-build-env
├── oe-init-build-env-memres
├── README
├── README.hardware
└── scripts

9 directories, 5 files
```

Because the OpenEmbedded build system is mostly self-contained and does not install any of its components into the system directories of your build host, it is rather easy to use multiple versions of the build system with different build environments on the same build host. This is a very convenient feature because you eventually develop and maintain a product generation with one version of the build system while developing the next generation with a newer version to take advantage of new functionality and features.

BitBake, the build engine, is an integral part of the OpenEmbedded build system. It evolves with the build system, and the Yocto Project developers add new functionality to BitBake to support new features required by the build system. Consequently, BitBake is included with the build system, and you can find it in the `bitbake` subdirectory. Be aware that some Linux distributions include a BitBake package that you can install using the distributions package management system. If you have BitBake installed on your development host as part of the distribution, we recommend uninstalling it because it may interfere with the version contained in the build system. The build system and BitBake are matched to each other. Inadvertently using a BitBake version that does not match the build system may result on build failures.

The `bitbake` directory contains a `doc` subdirectory that contains the BitBake documentation and man pages. The documentation is written in DocBook format, and you can build PDF and HTML versions of the manual by invoking the `make` command. We have a closer look at BitBake in the next chapter.

The `documentation` directory contains the documentation for the Poky build system. The following are the various manuals you can also find on the Yocto Project's website:

- Application Development Toolkit User's Guide (adt-manual)
- BSP Developer's Guide (bsp-guide)
- Development Manual (dev-manual)
- Linux Kernel Development Manual (kernel-dev)
- Profiling and Tracing Manual (profile-manual)
- Reference Manual (ref-manual)
- Yocto Project Quick Start (yocto-project-qs)
- Toaster Manual (toaster-manual)

The respective manuals are provided as sources in DocBook format in separate directories. To create a manual in PDF and HTML formats, use the command

```
$ make DOC=<manual>
```

replacing <manual> with the name of the directory. For example,

```
$ make DOC=mega-manual
```

creates a "mega-manual" that contains all the manuals in one file.

The LICENSE file contains the licensing information for the Poky build system. A mix of MIT and GPLv2 licenses are used. BitBake is licensed under the GPLv2 license, and all metadata is licensed under the MIT license. If there is any source code included in the tree for individual recipes, such as patches, it is licensed under the license stated in the respective recipe.

License information for any other files is either explicitly stated in the respective file or, in the absence thereof, defaults to GPLv2.

It is important to note that there can be, and commonly is, a difference in licensing of the source code of a package and the metadata (recipe) that builds that package. Be sure not to confuse the two because it can have implications for the product you are developing.

The directories starting with `meta` are all metadata layers:

- **meta**: OE Core metadata layer
- **meta-hob**: Metadata layer used by the Hob graphical user interface for BitBake
- **meta-selftest**: Layer for testing BitBake that is used by the `oe-selftest` script
- **meta-skeleton**: Template layer you can use to create your own layers
- **meta-yocto**: Yocto Project distribution layer
- **meta-yocto-bsp**: Yocto Project BSP layer

We explain the structure of metadata layers in Section 3.3.3.

The script `oe-init-build-env` creates and initializes build environments. It is used in two ways: to create an empty build environment with default settings and to initialize a build environment that has previously been created. We used the former in Chapter 2 to create our first build environment. The script's command line is

```
$ oe-init-build-env <buildenv>
```

with `<buildenv>` being substituted for the name of the build environment. If no build environment name is provided, then the script uses the default name `build`. The script creates a subdirectory in the current directory using the provided build environment name. Inside that directory, it creates a subdirectory named `conf` in which it creates the two configuration files `bblayers.conf` and `local.conf` that are required for every build environment. After that, the script initializes all necessary shell environment variables and changes directory to the build environment.

If the build environment directory already exists and is an OpenEmbedded build environment, then `oe-init-build-env` only initializes the shell environment variables and changes directory.

The second script, `oe-init-build-env-memres`, also creates and initializes build environments like `oe-init-build-env` but also launches a memory-resident BitBake server, which is listening on a TCP port for commands. This easily allows for running BitBake on remote build servers and controlling it from a local system over the network. The script's command line is

```
$ oe-init-build-env <buildenv> <port>
```

Either the `<port>` argument or both arguments, `<buildenv>` and `<port>`, can be omitted, in which cases the defaults `build` and `12345` are used.

Finally, there is the subdirectory `scripts`, which contains a collection of integration and support scripts for working with Yocto Project builds. The most commonly used scripts are as follows:

- **bitbake-whatchanged**: Lists all components that need to be rebuilt as a consequence of changes made to metadata between two builds

- **cleanup-workdir**: Removes build directories of obsolete packages from a build environment

- **create-recipe**: Creates a recipe that works with BitBake

- **hob**: Launches Hob, the graphical user interface for BitBake

- **runqemu**: Launches the QEMU emulator

- **yocto-bsp**: Creates a Yocto Project BSP layer

- **yocto-kernel**: Configures Yocto Project kernel recipes inside a Yocto Project BSP layer

- **yocto-layer**: Creates a metadata layer that works with BitBake

Throughout this book, we use these and other scripts form the `scripts` subdirectory. We explain their use and functions when we first introduce them.

3.3.2 Build Environment Structure

The OpenEmbedded build system carries out all its work inside a build environment. The build environment, too, has a specific layout and structure. The layout with all directories and files in it is created automatically by the build system. The build environment structure of directories and files is deeply nested. Listing 3-2 shows the first two levels of the structure after a build has been run.

Listing 3-2   **Build Environment Structure**

```
yocto@yocto-dev:~/yocto$ tree -L 2 build
x86/
├── bitbake.lock
├── cache
│   ├── bb_codeparser.dat
│   ├── bb_persist_data.sqlite3
│   └── local_file_checksum_cache.dat
├── conf
│   ├── bblayers.conf
│   ├── local.conf
│   └── sanity_info
└── tmp
    ├── abi_version
    ├── buildstats
    ├── cache
    ├── deploy
    │   ├── images
    │   ├── licenses
```

```
|   ├── deb
|   ├── ipk
|   └── rpm
├── log
├── qa.log
├── saved_tmpdir
├── sstate-control
├── stamps
├── sysroots
├── work
|   ├── all-poky-linux
|   ├── i586-poky-linux
|   ├── qemux86-poky-linux
|   └── x86_64-linux
└── work-shared
```

A newly created build environment contains only the subdirectory conf with the two files bblayers.conf and local.conf. We encountered the latter in Chapter 2 when we set up and configured our first build environment. This file contains all the configuration settings for the build environment. You can also add variable settings to it that locally override settings from included layers.

The bblayers.conf file contains the layer setup for the build environment. Listing 3-3 shows a typical bblayers.conf file.

Listing 3-3 **bblayers.conf**

```
# LCONF_VERSION: version number for bblayers.conf
# It is increased each time build/conf/bblayers.conf
# changes incompatibly
LCONF_VERSION = "6"

BBPATH = "${TOPDIR}"
BBFILES ?= ""

BBLAYERS ?= " \
  /absolute/path/to/poky/meta \
  /absolute/path/to/poky/meta-yocto \
  /absolute/path/to//poky/meta-yocto-bsp \
  "
BBLAYERS_NON_REMOVABLE ?= " \
  /absolute/path/to/poky/meta \
  /absolute/path/to/poky/meta-yocto \
  "
```

The most important variable in this file is BBLAYERS, which is a space-delimited list of paths to all the layers included by this build environment. This is the place where you would add additional layers to be included with your build environment. The file also sets BBPATH to the top-level directory of the build environment and initializes the recipe file list BBFILES with an empty string.

Other directories and files are created during the build process. All build output is placed into the `tmp` subdirectory. You can configure this directory by setting the `TMPDIR` variable in the `conf/local.conf` file of the environment. Build output inside the `tmp` directory is organized into a variety of subdirectories:

- **buildstats**: This subdirectory stores build statistics organized by build target and date/time stamp when the target was built.
- **cache**: When BitBake initially parses metadata, it resolves dependencies and expressions. The results of the parsing process are written into a cache. As long as the metadata has not changed, BitBake retrieves metadata information from this cache on subsequent runs.
- **deploy**: The build output for deployment, such as target filesystem images, package feeds, and licensing information, is contained in the `deploy` subdirectory.
- **log**: Here is where you can find the BitBake logging information created by the *cooker* process.
- **sstate-control**: This subdirectory contains the manifest files for the shared state cache organized by architecture/target and task.
- **stamps**: BitBake places completion tags and signature data for every task organized by architecture/target and package name into this subdirectory.
- **sysroots**: This subdirectory contains root filesystems organized by architecture/target. Contents includes a root filesystem for the build host containing cross-toolchain, QEMU, and many tools used during the build process.
- **work**: Inside this directory, BitBake creates subdirectories organized by architecture/target where it builds the actual software packages.
- **work-shared**: This subdirectory is similar to `work` but is for shared software packages.

There are also two files inside the `tmp` directory that are worth explaining: `abi_version` and `saved_tmpdir`. The former contains the version number for the layout of the `tmp` directory. This number is incremented when the layout changes and allows verification if the build environment is compatible with the build system. The latter contains the absolute filesystem path of the `tmp` directory. Many files residing inside the `tmp` directory contain absolute filesystem paths. That arrangement, unfortunately, makes the directory not relocatable. Although this restriction may be inconvenient, the `saved_tmpdir` file allows you to easily check whether the directory has been moved from its original location.

While build environments, and in particular the `tmp` directory typically located within them, cannot be easily relocated, BitBake can essentially re-create all contents of the `tmp` directory from the shared state cache. The shared state cache stores the intermediate output of the tasks identified by a signature that is created from its input metadata, such as task code, variables, and more. As long as the input does not change, the signature does not change, causing BitBake to use the output from the shared state cache rather than running the task. That shortens build time considerably, particularly for tasks that can take a long time to run, such as configuring or compiling.

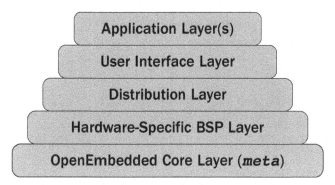

Figure 3-3 Layer architecture

3.3.3 Metadata Layer Structure

Metadata layers are containers to group and organize recipes, classes, configuration files, and other metadata into logical entities. Layers commonly build on and extend each other. The OE Core layer forms a foundation for the layer architecture of the Poky build system. It provides recipes for a core set of software packages that are needed by most Linux OS stacks, including, of course, the Linux kernel but also bootloaders, graphics, networking, and many other packages. OE Core also provides the base classes to build software packages, package the software with package management systems, create filesystem images, and extend the BitBake functionality.

The OE Core layer by itself, complemented by BitBake and the convenience and integration scripts, is sufficient for building a Linux OS stack for an emulated device. OE Core includes basic image targets as well as machine definitions for the QEMU emulator for ARM, MIPS, PowerPC, x86, and x86_64 architectures.

A build environment for a device operating system stack would typically include other layers, such as a BSP layer for actual hardware; a distribution layer specifying the OS configuration for user accounts, system startup, and more; and a user interface layer and application layers for the user space applications providing the device functionality. Figure 3-3 depicts the architecture.

Layer Layout

All layers, no matter what purpose they serve, have the same basic structure shown in Listing 3-4 (directory names are italicized to distinguish them from the filenames).

Listing 3-4 **Layer Layout**

```
meta-<layername>
├── conf
│   ├── layer.conf
│   ├── machine
│   │   ├── <machine 1>.conf
│   │   ├── <machine 2>.conf
│   │   ├── ...
│   │   └── <machine m>.conf
```

```
|    ├── distro
|    |    ├── <distro 1>.conf
|    |    ├── <distro 2>.conf
|    |    ├── ...
|    |    └── <distro r>.conf
├── classes
|    ├── class<1>.bbclass
|    ├── class<2>.bbclass
|    ├── ...
|    └── class<1>.bbclass
├── recipes-<category 1>
|    ├── <package a>
|    |    ├── <package a>_<version 1>.bb
|    |    └── <package a>_<version 2>.bb
|    ├── <package b>
|    |    ├── <package b>_<version 1>.bb
|    |    └── <package b>_<version 2>.bb
|    ├── ...
|    └── <package z>
├── recipes-<category 2>
|    └── ...
└── recipes-<category n>
     └── ...
```

A metadata layer is essentially a structure comprising directories and files. The name of the top-level directory of the layer does not strictly matter; however, by convention, all layer directory names start with the term meta followed by a hyphen and the name of the layer.

Every layer must include a conf subdirectory that must contain the layer configuration file layer.conf. BitBake requires this file to set up paths and search patterns for metadata files. Listing 3-5 shows the boilerplate layer.conf file.

Listing 3-5 **layer.conf**

```
# Add the layer's directory to BBPATH
BBPATH =. "${LAYERDIR}:"

# Add the layer's recipe files to BBFILES
BBFILES += "${LAYERDIR}/recipes-*/*/*.bb \
            ${LAYERDIR}/recipes-*/*/*.bbappend"

# Add the name of the layer to the layer collections
BBFILE_COLLECTIONS += "layername"

# Set the recipe file search pattern
BBFILE_PATTERN_layername = "^${LAYERDIR}/"

# Set the priority of this layer
BBFILE_PRIORITY_layername = "5"

# Set version of this layer
# (should only be incremented if changes break compatibility)
LAYERVERSION_layername = "2"
```

```
# Specify other layers this layer depends on. This is a white space-
# delimited list of layer names. If this layer depends on a particular
# version of another layer, it can be specified by adding the version
# with a colon to the layer name: e.g., anotherlayer:3.
LAYERDEPENDS_layername = "core"
```

The first assignment adds the layer's directory to the BBPATH variable. The variable LAYERDIR is expanded by BitBake to the canonical path name of the layer. Then the layer's recipes are added to the BBFILES variable. You can see that the wildcard expressions match the layout of the recipes' directories in the layer. Wildcards for both recipes and recipe append files need to be added to BBFILES.

BBFILE_COLLECTIONS is a list of layer names delimited by spaces. Each layer adds its name to the list. BBFILE_PATTERN contains a regular expression to match the recipes of this layer within the BBFILES variable. This variable is conditional on the layer, and hence the variable name needs to be suffixed with the name of the layer.[4]

Since layers depend on and extend each other, the order of processing is important. Therefore, each layer is assigned a priority by setting the variable BBFILE_PRIORITY. Layer priorities range from 1 to 10 with 1 being the lowest and 10 being the highest priority. If two layers use the same priority, then their order in the BBLAYERS variable of the file bblayers.conf file determines the priority.

Optionally, a layer can also define a version number by setting the variable LAYERVERSION. The layer version can be used together with the LAYERDEPENDS variable to prevent including incompatible versions of a layer. If a layer depends on other layers, these dependencies can be set by adding the layers to the LAYERDEPENDS variable, which contains a list of space-delimited layer names. If the dependency is on a particular version of the layer, the version number can be specified by adding a colon and the version number.

The conf subdirectory may contain other files and directories, in particular, the distro and machine subdirectories. These are optional. Typically, only a distribution layer would contain a distro subdirectory, and only BSP layers normally contain the machine subdirectory. If present, each of these two subdirectories contain files for distribution and machine configuration.[5]

If a layer defines its own classes, they are located in the classes subdirectory.

The layer's recipes are grouped by category and package. A category is a collection of packages that logically belong together. For example, the category recipes-connectivity of the OE Core metadata layer contains recipes that build packages for networking, telephony, and other connectivity software. Within each category subdirectory, there are subdirectories for the different software packages. These package subdirectories contain recipes, patches, and other files required to build the software package. Commonly, a package subdirectory contains recipes to build different versions of the particular package.

---

4. We discuss conditional variable settings in Chapter 4.

5. We explain distribution layers and BSP layers in the following chapters.

Creating Layers

Using layers for BSPs, application software, distribution policy, and so forth, makes a lot of good sense for your own projects. Most projects start out small, but then more and more functionality is added. Even if you have only one or two recipes to begin with, it is good practice to place your recipes into your own layer rather than add them to the OE Core layer or any of the Yocto Project layers.

Your own layers separate your recipes from the common recipes, making it easy for you to migrate from one version of the OpenEmbedded build system to the next. You only need to create a new build environment with the newer build system and include your layers into this build environment.

By using `bbappend` files in your layers, you can adjust recipes from common layers rather than duplicate or rewrite them. Consider the recipes in `meta/recipes-kernel/linux` for building the Linux kernel. For the most part, they already provide everything necessary for building the kernel. For your own BSP layer, you normally need to tweak only a couple of settings to fully support your target hardware. Rather than duplicating the kernel recipe, you can use `bbappend` files or include files to customize the base recipe to your requirements.

Creating layers is simple and straightforward with the `yocto-layer` script. After sourcing a build environment, this script is readily available in your command search path. Simply invoke the script as

```
$ yocto-layer create <layername>
```

The script prompts you for the priority of your new layer if you would like to create an example recipe and/or an example `bbappend` file and then creates the layer including the `conf/layer.conf` file and example files in the current directory. All you need to do is add the layer to the `BBLAYERS` variable in the `conf/bblayers.conf` file of your build environment to include it with the build process. Of course, you also have to modify the example recipes and/or new recipes, configuration files, and classes as your project requires.

3.4 Summary

This chapter presented an overview of the build system, its workflow, and its components.

- Open source software packages are most commonly built following a standard workflow.
- The OpenEmbedded build system automates the workflow steps for the many hundreds of packages that are built from source code to create a fully functional Linux OS stack.
- BitBake not only builds the software packages but also packages executables, libraries, documentation, and more into packages that can be utilized by the common package management systems dpkg, RPM, and ipgk.

- The build system creates root filesystem images that can be installed on target systems.
- Optionally, BitBake can build an SDK that includes cross-development tools for developers to build applications for the target systems.
- The three core components that make up the architecture are the OpenEmbedded build system, build environment, and metadata layers.
- The Poky reference distribution includes the OpenEmbedded build system as well as the three metadata layers OE Core (`meta`), Yocto Distribution (`meta-yocto`), and Yocto BSP (`meta-yocto-bsp`), which are automatically added to a build environment when it is created.
- Layers group metadata into logical entities such as BSPs, distribution layer, application layers, and more.

3.5 References

Yocto Project Documentation, https://www.yoctoproject.org/documentation/current

4

BitBake Build Engine

BitBake is a build tool comparable to Make and Apache Ant. However, because of its flexible and extensible architecture, BitBake's capabilities go far beyond what typical software build engines provide. BitBake's metadata syntax not only enables variables and execution of simple commands but also can embed entire shell scripts and Python functions.

BitBake is derived from Portage, the build and package management system used by the Gentoo Linux distribution. BitBake is written entirely in Python, making it mostly platform independent as long as the platform provides a Python runtime environment.

Like any software build tool, BitBake on its own does not provide the functionality to build a software package. It must be complemented by build instructions that are included in metadata files. BitBake metadata files are comparable to Make's makefiles and to Ant's build.xml files. OpenEmbedded and the Yocto Project provide the necessary metadata to build thousands of software packages and integrate them into filesystem images containing fully functional Linux OS stacks.

4.1 Obtaining and Installing BitBake

BitBake is a core component of the OpenEmbedded build system, described in the previous chapter. BitBake is a Yocto Project subproject jointly maintained by OpenEmbedded and the Yocto Project. BitBake source repositories were originally hosted on http://developer.berlios.de/projects/bitbake, but the active development branches were moved to the OpenEmbedded Git repository at http://git.openembedded.org/bitbake after the creation of the Yocto Project.

The build system that you download from the Yocto Project website or clone from the Yocto Project Git repository always includes the version of BitBake matching Poky's metadata. Therefore, when using Poky, you do not have to worry about downloading and installing BitBake.[1] However, if you are interested in using BitBake for other projects, such as to track the current BitBake development status, or are looking to contribute to BitBake, you can download it from the OpenEmbedded repository and install it on your system.

We illustrate the download and installation of BitBake so you can see how BitBake works. It is a useful setup to experiment with BitBake and learn about its inner workings without the integration that comes with the OpenEmbedded build system.

4.1.1 Using a Release Snapshot

Compressed tar archives of released BitBake versions can be downloaded via web browser from the OpenEmbedded Git repository or using the wget command:

```
wget https://git.openembedded.org/bitbake/snapshot/bitbake-1.17.0.tar.bz2
```

Executing

```
tar xvjf bitbake-1.17.0.tar.bz2 -C ~
```

extracts the archive into your home directory, creating a subdirectory named bitbake-1.17.0 containing the BitBake sources.

4.1.2 Cloning the BitBake Development Repository

The command

```
git clone git://git.openembedded.org/bitbake.git ~/bitbake
```

clones the BitBake Git repository into the directory bitbake in your home directory and check out the master branch. As usual with Git repositories, the master branch is the actual development branch.

4.1.3 Building and Installing BitBake

The BitBake source tree contains a setup.py script that allows you to precompile the BitBake Python source modules, create the documentation, and eventually install BitBake on your system.

---

1. Using a version of BitBake other than the one included with the build system is discouraged. BitBake is tightly integrated with the build system that provides it.

From the directory where you have extracted or cloned the BitBake source, execute

```
./setup.py build
```

to compile BitBake and to create the documentation in HTML and PDF formats from the DocBook sources. Compiling BitBake requires the Python Lex-Yacc (PLY) package to be installed on your system. Virtually all Linux distributions provide this package. Executing

```
./setup.py install
```

installs BitBake and its libraries into the default Python installation directory on your development system, which on most Linux distributions is /usr/lib/python<version>/site-packages. Installing BitBake is of course optional, as you can use BitBake directly from its source directory.

4.2 Running BitBake

If you have worked with Make before, you know that you can execute it without any parameters, and Make looks for a file called GNUmakefile, makefile, or Makefile in the current directory and builds the default target it finds in the file. Ant is quite similar, as it searches for a file named build.xml in the current directory. Both tools also allow you to explicitly specify a file containing the build instructions as a command-line parameter.

BitBake essentially works in the same way. However, BitBake always must be called with the base name of a recipe or target as a parameter:

```
$ bitbake core-image-minimal
```

In this example, core-image-minimal corresponds to the recipe core-image-minimal.bb. However, unlike Make and Ant, BitBake does not automatically look for the recipe in the current directory. BitBake requires that you set up an execution environment before it can locate and execute build instructions.

4.2.1 BitBake Execution Environment

When launched, BitBake first searches for the conf/bblayers.conf configuration file in the current working directory (see Listing 4-1).

Listing 4-1 **conf/bblayers.conf**

```
BBPATH = "${TOPDIR}"
BBFILES ?= ""

BBLAYERS ?= " \
  /path/to/directory/for/layer1 \
  /path/to/directory/for/layer2 \
  /path/to/directory/for/layer3 \
  "
```

Although this file is optional, it is present in any BitBake build environment using the layer architecture, which includes all build environments created by the Yocto Project tools. BitBake expects this file to contain a variable called BBLAYERS, which contains a list of paths to directories where the layers included in the build environment can be found. Each of these layer directories is expected to contain a file named conf/layer.conf (see Listing 4-2).

Listing 4-2 **conf/layer.conf**

```
# We have a conf and classes directory, add to BBPATH
BBPATH .= ":${LAYERDIR}"

# We have recipes-* directories, add to BBFILES
BBFILES += "${LAYERDIR}/recipes-*/*/*.bb \
        ${LAYERDIR}/recipes-*/*/*.bbappend"

BBFILE_COLLECTIONS += "layer1"
BBFILE_PATTERN_layer1 = "^${LAYERDIR}/"
BBFILE_PRIORITY_layer1 = "6"
```

The purpose of the layer configuration file conf/layer.conf is to set up the variables BBPATH and BBFILES correctly so that BitBake can find the recipes, classes, and configuration files contained in the layer:

- **BBPATH**: BitBake uses this variable to locate classes (.bbclass files) in a subdirectory named classes and configuration files (.conf files) in a subdirectory called conf and subdirectories thereof. The variable contains a list of colon-delimited directory paths.

- **BBFILES**: This variable contains a list of paths with wildcards, for the recipe files.

A layer typically adds the path to its own top-level directory to the list of paths contained in BBPATH. BitBake automatically sets the variable LAYERDIR to the path to the top-level directory of a layer when it begins parsing the files in that layer.

The layer also adds the paths to the recipe files it provides to a list of file paths contained in the BBFILES variable. The file paths represent the directory structure that contains the recipes of the layer, which is, by convention, a layout with two levels of subdirectories, as explained in Chapter 3, "OpenEmbedded Build System."

The three variables BBFILE_COLLECTIONS, BBFILE_PATTERN, and BBFILE_PRIORITY provide BitBake with information on how to locate and treat the recipes of this layer in regard to other layers:

- **BBFILE_COLLECTIONS**: Contains a list of the names of configured layers. This list is used by BitBake to find other BBFILE_* variables in its data directory. Each layer typically adds its own name to the list.

- **BBFILE_PATTERN**: A regular expression telling BitBake how to locate recipe files from this layer within BBFILES. The value that a layer sets this variable to corresponds to the paths it adds to the BBFILES variable. Since all paths in BBFILES typically begin with the top-level directory of the layer, the regular expression reflects that convention. The name of the variable must be appended with an underscore and the name of the layer.

- **BBFILE_PRIORITY**: Assigns a priority to the recipes contained in this layer. The name of the variable must be appended with the name of the layer.

A larger priority value corresponds to a higher priority. Priorities are especially important if a recipe with the same name appears in more than one layer. In that case, BitBake picks the recipe from the layer with the higher priority even if the recipe contained in the layer with lower priority has a later version than the recipe of the layer with the higher priority.

The priority also determines in what order BitBake appends append files to the recipes. An append file from a layer with higher priority is added after an append file from a layer with lower priority.

In most cases, you execute BitBake directly from the top-level directory of the execution or build environment. If, for some reason, execution from the top-level directory is not desirable, you can set the BBPATH variable before launching BitBake:

```
$ BBPATH="/absolute/path/to/build_env" bitbake <target>
```

Note that BitBake expects the BBPATH variable to contain an absolute path; otherwise, it does not find the configuration file conf/bblayers.conf.

After parsing conf/bblayers.conf, BitBake looks for the configuration file conf/bitbake.conf, which provides the build system setup. If layers are not used and therefore no conf/bblayers.conf file is present, then the BBPATH variable needs to be set up as shown previously, and the file conf/bitbake.conf must contain variable assignments for BBFILES.

After locating and parsing conf/bitbake.conf and other configuration files, BitBake locates and parses all classes. At least one class, base contained in the file base.bbclass, must be present for BitBake to operate correctly. This class provides the basic functions and tasks, including the default build task.

4.2.2 BitBake Command Line

Running BitBake with the --help option provides an overview of the tool's command-line options (see Listing 4-3).

Listing 4-3 **BitBake Command-Line Options**

```
$ bitbake --help
Usage: bitbake [options] [recipename/target ...]

    Executes the specified task (default is 'build') for a given set of
    target recipes (.bb files). It is assumed there is a conf/bblayers.conf
    available in cwd or in BBPATH which will provide the layer, BBFILES and
    other configuration information.
```

```
Options:
  --version              show program's version number and exit
  -h, --help             show this help message and exit
  -b BUILDFILE, --buildfile=BUILDFILE
                         Execute tasks from a specific .bb recipe directly.
                         WARNING: Does not handle any dependencies from
                         other recipes.
  -k, --continue         Continue as much as possible after an error. While
                         the target that failed and anything depending on it
                         cannot be built, as much as possible will be built
                         before stopping.
  -a, --tryaltconfigs    Continue with builds by trying to use alternative
                         providers where possible.
  -f, --force            Force the specified targets/task to run
                         (invalidating any existing stamp file).
  -c CMD, --cmd=CMD      Specify the task to execute. The exact options
                         available depend on the metadata. Some examples
                         might be 'compile' or 'populate_sysroot' or
                         'listtasks' may give a list of the tasks available.
  -C INVALIDATE_STAMP, --clear-stamp=INVALIDATE_STAMP
                         Invalidate the stamp for the specified task such as
                         'compile' and then run the default task for the
                         specified target(s).
  -r PREFILE, --read=PREFILE
                         Read the specified file before bitbake.conf.
  -R POSTFILE, --postread=POSTFILE
                         Read the specified file after bitbake.conf.
  -v, --verbose          Output more log message data to the terminal.
  -D, --debug            Increase the debug level. You can specify this more
                         than once.
  -n, --dry-run          Don't execute, just go through the motions.
  -S, --dump-signatures
                         Don't execute, just dump out the signature
                         construction information.
  -p, --parse-only       Quit after parsing the BB recipes.
  -s, --show-versions    Show current and preferred versions of all recipes.
  -e, --environment      Show the global or per-package environment complete
                         with information about where variables were
                         set/changed.
  -g, --graphviz         Save dependency tree information for the specified
                         targets in the dot syntax.
  -I EXTRA_ASSUME_PROVIDED, --ignore-deps=EXTRA_ASSUME_PROVIDED
                         Assume these dependencies don't exist and are
                         already provided (equivalent to ASSUME_PROVIDED).
                         Useful to make dependency graphs more appealing.
  -l DEBUG_DOMAINS, --log-domains=DEBUG_DOMAINS
                         Show debug logging for the specified logging
                         domains.
  -P, --profile          Profile the command and save reports.
  -u UI, --ui=UI         The user interface to use (e.g. knotty, hob,
                         depexp).
  -t SERVERTYPE, --servertype=SERVERTYPE
                         Choose which server to use, process or xmlrpc.
  --revisions-changed    Set the exit code depending on whether upstream
                         floating revisions have changed or not.
  --server-only          Run bitbake without a UI, only starting a server
                         (cooker) process.
  -B BIND, --bind=BIND   The name/address for the bitbake server to bind to.
```

```
--no-setscene          Do not run any setscene tasks. sstate will be
                       ignored and everything needed, built.
--remote-server=REMOTE_SERVER
                       Connect to the specified server.
-m, --kill-server      Terminate the remote server.
--observe-only         Connect to a server as an observing-only client.
```

At first look, the number of command-line options seems overwhelming, but they can easily be broken down into a few functionality blocks.

Displaying Program Version and Help

The command-line options --version and --help or -h print the program version number and the help information in Listing 4-3, respectively, to the console.

Executing Builds with Dependency Handling

Calling BitBake with a target, the base name of the recipe file without the .bb extension, runs the default task as defined by the variable BB_DEFAULT_TASK, typically build:

```
$ bitbake core-image-minimal
```

BitBake evaluates all the dependencies of the target and the task and executes all dependent tasks in correct order imposed by the dependency chain before actually building the target. An unfulfilled dependency causes an error.

Any error condition causes BitBake to stop execution even if other tasks are ready to be executed. Using the -k option,

```
$ bitbake -k core-image-minimal
```

instructs BitBake to continue building even if one or more tasks have failed. BitBake builds as much as possible until the failed task or tasks become gating for the target and anything dependent on it.

Using a target without version and revision always builds the latest version of a software package or the version specified by the variable PREFERRED_VERSION. Version and revision numbers can be added to the target name to build a specific version regardless whether it is the latest version and regardless of the value of PREFERRED_VERSION. The commands

```
$ bitbake editor-1.0
$ bitbake editor-2.0-r3
```

build version 1.0 and version 2.0/revision r3 of the editor software package respectively.

Executing Builds without Dependency Handling

Using the -b or --buildfile option with the name of the recipe file, including the .bb extension, executes the default task of the recipe but without building dependencies:

```
$ bitbake -b core-image-minimal.bb
$ bitbake --buildfile=core-image-minimal.bb
```

If any of the dependencies of core-image-minimal are not fulfilled, BitBake exits with an error message without attempting to build the dependencies.

Executing Specific Tasks

Specific tasks of a target can be executed using the -c or --cmd options:

```
$ bitbake editor -c compile
$ bitbake editor --cmd=compile
```

As they are with executing the default task, all dependencies are honored and built if they are not yet fulfilled. Using

```
$ bitbake -b editor.bb -c compile
$ bitbake -b editor.bb --cmd=compile
```

attempts to run the compile task without building any dependencies.

Forcing Execution

BitBake creates a timestamp for each successfully completed task. If, on subsequent runs of a task, the task's time stamp is current or later then the time stamps of all the tasks that task depends on BitBake does not run the task. The options -C or --clear-stamp instruct BitBake to run a task regardless of the time stamp:

```
$ bitbake zlib -C compile
$ bitbake zlib --clear-stamp=compile
```

These options can also be combined with the -b or --buildfile options.

The -C or --clear-stamp also automatically run all dependent tasks. If you only need to force execution for a specific task without running all dependent tasks, use the -f or --force options:

```
$ bitbake zlib -c compile -f
$ bitbake zlib -c compile --force
```

An important function of any build system is the capability to determine what parts of the build process must be executed again if any of the input changes. For that purpose, BitBake implements the shared state cache. The shared state cache operates on the task level and determines for each task for every recipe what its input is and stores what output a task adds to the build process. If a task's input has not changed, then its output does not change on a subsequent build. If that is the case, then BitBake obtains and restores the task's output from the shared state cache rather than running the actual task. The operation of obtaining and restoring task output from the shared state cache is referred to as *set-scene*. If set-scene is not desired, then it can be turned off using the --no-setscene option:

```
$ bitbake zlib -c compile --no-setscene
```

The --no-setscene option can also be combined with the -b or --buildfile options.

The shared state cache is powerful functionality that can tremendously speed up build processes by reusing already processed task output from the cache.

Displaying Metadata

For debugging purposes, it can be very useful to list all the metadata. The option -e or -environment shows all metadata, variables, and functions immediately after BitBake has completed the parsing process:

```
$ bitbake -e
$ bitbake --environment
```

When used with a target or recipe name, the command displays the environment settings that BitBake applies to building that package:

```
$ bitbake -e zlib
$ bitbake -environment zlib
```

These options can also be combined with the -b or --buildfile options.

Because displaying all metadata including the functions produces a lot of output scrolling by on the screen, it is advisable to use a utility such as grep to filter for the desired information.

Another useful option is -s or --show-versions, which displays a list of all recipes and the version numbers:

```
$ bitbake -s
$ bitbake --show-versions
```

These options always list the entire roster of recipes, and using a filter utility may help to shorten the list to the items you are looking for.

Creating Dependency Graphs

BitBake can create graphs describing package dependencies in the DOT language. DOT is a plain text graph description language that can describe undirected and directed graphs and annotate them as well as the nodes and edges with attributes. Software applications from the Graphviz package (www.graphviz.org) can read DOT files and render them in graphical form. The command

```
$ bitbake -g zlib
```

creates, in the current working directory, three files describing the dependencies of the zlib package using the DOT language:

- **package-depends.dot**: Dependency graph on the actual package level detailing the subpackages, such as zlib-dev and zlib-dgb
- **task-depends.dot**: Dependency graph on the task level
- **pn-depends.dot**: Dependency graph on the package name level not detailing the subpackages

Alternatively to the -g option, the --graphviz option can be used.

If the Graphviz package is installed on your development system, you can create graphical renditions of the dependency graphs from these files. The command

```
$ dot -Tpng -o pn-depends.png pn-depends.dot
```

creates an image file in png format containing the dependency graph. The dependency graphs tend to get rather large because all dependencies, including common ones such as the compiler and C library, are represented. You can omit common packages using the -I or --ignore-deps options:

```
$ bitbake -g zlib -I expat
$ bitbake -g zlib --ignore-deps="expat"
```

These commands remove the expat package from the dependency graph. Unfortunately, you have to specify each package individually to be removed from the dependency graph, as there is no way to remove common dependencies altogether with a single option.

The dependency graphs generated by BitBake also include transitive dependencies, making the graphs larger than necessary. You can remove the transitive dependencies using the `tred` command from the Graphviz package:

```
$ tred pn-depends.dot > pn-depends-notrans.dot
```

BitBake also includes a built-in visualization for dependency graphs, the dependency explorer. Using

```
$ bitbake -g -u depexp zlib
```

launches the dependency explorer, shown in Figure 4-1.

The dependency explorer lists runtime, build-time, and reverse dependencies per package. Runtime dependencies are all dependencies a software package requires during execution. The build-time dependencies must be fulfilled when the software package is built. And the reverse dependencies list shows all packages that depend on this package.

Providing and Overriding Configuration Data

The options -r or --read and -R or --postread offer a convenient way to provide additional configuration data or to override existing settings without modifying any configuration files of the build environment, such as bitbake.conf or local.conf.

As an alternative to directly setting variables through the shell at the command line, as we saw earlier, -r or --read can be used to provide configuration data to BitBake before the tool reads any other files:

```
$ bitbake -r prefile.conf <target>
$ bitbake --read prefile.conf <target>
```

This technique can be used for automatic build systems in lieu of a bblayers.conf file to set up the BBPATH and BBLAYERS variables to dynamically set up build environments.

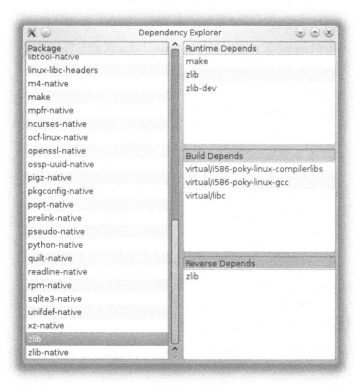

Figure 4-1   Dependency explorer

Using

```
$ bitbake -R postfile.conf <target>
$ bitbake --postread postfile.conf <target>
```

easily allows overriding variable settings made by any other configuration file of the build environment, as BitBake processes `postfile.conf` after it completes parsing all other configuration files. For example, machine or distribution settings can be dynamically overridden, or variables can be set for debugging purposes.

Running BitBake Server

BitBake is a client–server application. Every time you run BitBake, it starts a server or backend process called *cooker* in the background and a client or frontend process for the user interface. The cooker backend process does all the metadata file processing as well as the actual building, eventually spawning multiple threads. When launched together in this all-in-one mode, backend and frontend processes use pipe–based interprocess communication (IPC) to exchange information.

Backend and frontend processes can also be launched independently and on different systems, allowing you to remotely start and monitor build processes. To launch a BitBake server process from a build environment, use:

```
$ bitbake --server-only --servertype=xmlrpc --bind=<ip>:<port>
```

This command starts a BitBake server as a background process listening on the IP address <ip> and port <port>. You can bind the server to any IP address, such as localhost or the IP address of any network interface of your build system. You may also use any port number as long as it is not privileged or currently in use. You must specify --servertype=xmlrpc when launching a BitBake server. While this seems redundant, since process and xmlrpc are currently the only two IPC methods supported and process cannot be used with server mode, BitBake may support additional IPC methods for server mode in the future.

To connect to a running BitBake server using the default text-terminal-type user interface and execute commands, use

```
bitbake --servertype=xmlrpc --remote-server=<ip>:<port> <target>
```

which starts the build process for <target> on the remote server.

4.3 BitBake Metadata

BitBake uses metadata to control the build process. In general, metadata describes the software packages, how they are built, and how they relate to and depend on each other. BitBake distinguishes two types of metadata:

- **Variables**: Variables are assigned values and expressions that evaluate to values. Variables can be globally valid for the entire build system or locally valid for the current context, such as for a particular recipe. Many BitBake metadata variables contain not only a single value but a space-delimited list of values.

- **Executable Metadata**: Executable metadata are functions and tasks embedded in recipes and classes that are executed by BitBake within the context of a recipe.

Metadata is organized in five categories of files:

- **Configuration Files (.conf)**: Metadata placed in configuration files is global and affects all recipes referencing them. Configuration files may contain only variables with no executable metadata. If the same variable is assigned in multiple configuration files, then the order established by the layer priority determines which setting prevails. The configuration file bitbake.conf has the lowest priority, and the local configuration file of the build environment local.conf has the highest.

- **Recipe Files (.bb)**: Recipes contain the metadata that describes a particular software package and how that software package is built. A recipe typically provides executable metadata in the form of tasks with instructions for downloading, unpacking, patching, compiling, packaging, and installing the software package.

- **Class Files (.bbclass)**: Class files provide a simple inheritance mechanism for recipes to share the same build instructions. BitBake searches for class files inside of the classes subdirectory of a layer. Recipes can include class files by simply referencing them by their name using the inherit directive. Classes are global, meaning that recipes located in a layer can inherit classes from any other layer the build environment includes.

- **Append Files (.bbappend)**: Append files are extensions to recipe files. Typically, a layer uses append files to extend a recipe contained in another layer. The append file must have the same base name as the recipe it extends but with the .bbappend extension instead of the .bb extension. An append file must also have the same path relative to the layer's root directory as the recipe it is appending. Append files either add additional metadata or modify metadata defined in the recipe. The content of an append file is literally appended to the original recipe. If append files from different layers append the same recipe, the layer priority determines in which order BitBake appends the files to the recipe.

- **Include Files (.inc)**: Any metadata file can include other files using the include and require directives. Include files commonly provide metadata that is shared among multiple metadata files. The content of the include file is inserted into the including metadata file at the position of the respective directive. Include files themselves may also include other files. This of course bears the risk of circular inclusion, which BitBake detects and warns about. File inclusion is not limited to the same layer, but a recipe in one layer can include a file from another. The .inc file extension is purely conventional. A metadata file can include any other metadata file; however, files containing executable metadata may be included only by recipes, append files, and classes.

BitBake parses the metadata files immediately after starting and creates a metadata cache. This cache is essentially a persistent form of BitBake's metadata dictionary. As long as there are no changes to the metadata, BitBake reads it from the cache, significantly reducing start time.

4.4 Metadata Syntax

BitBake metadata files employ a specific syntax that is rather straightforward. To some extent, it is similar to what you may be familiar with from Makefiles and shell scripts.

4.4.1 Comments

Comments in metadata files are prefixed with a hash symbol: #. Comments must start on the first column unless they are placed inside of shell or Python functions (see Listing 4-4).

Listing 4-4   **Comments**

```
# This is a comment.

    # This is an invalid comment, which causes a parse error.

SUMMARY = "Sample file with comments" # this comment is also invalid

helloworld () {
    # comments in shell functions can start on any column
    # and can also be added after statements
    echo "Hello World!" # this is okay in a shell function
}

python printdate () {
    # comments in Python functions can start on any column
    # and can also be added after statements
    import time
    print time.strftime("%Y%m%d", time.gettime()) # ok too
}
```

As it is with any programming language, the frequent use of meaningful comments makes your code easier to read and understand for others and is always encouraged.

4.4.2 Variables

BitBake variables are typeless. BitBake treats all values assigned to variables as strings.

Variable Names

BitBake variable names may contain uppercase and lowercase letters, numbers, and the special characters underscore (_), hyphen (-), period (.), plus (+), and tilde (~). They can also begin with any of these characters.

While any of the preceding characters are allowed in variable names, only uppercase letters and the underscore are used by convention, and all variable names start with an uppercase letter.

Variable Scope

Variables defined in configuration files—that is, files that end in .conf—are global and visible in all recipes. Variables defined in recipes are local to the recipe only. Recipes have their own namespace, and global variables assigned a new value in a recipe retain that value only when BitBake processes that recipe.

Variable Assignment

All BitBake variable assignments are *string literals* with balanced delimiters that enclose the value. The delimiters are either double (") or single (') quotes. Double quotes are preferred by convention.

Direct Value Assignment (=)

A variable can be assigned a value using the = sign. Using

```
VAR = "value"
```

assigns value to the variable VAR. Quotation inside a variable assignment can be achieved by using the backlash (\) as escape character or single quotes:

```
VAR1 = "This is a \"quotation\" inside a variable assignment"
VAR2 = "This is a second 'quotation' inside a variable assignment"
```

The second method is preferred for readability.

Default Value Assignment (?=)

Variables can be assigned default values using the ?= assignment operator:

```
A ?= "value1"
B ?= "value2"
B ?= "value3"
C ?= "value4"
C = "value5"
```

If a variable has not previously been set, it is assigned the default value. If it has been set prior to the default value assignment, it retains its value. In the preceding assignment sequence, A contains value1 if it has not been previously set. B contains value2 because the first use of the ?= operator sets the variable.

The = operator overrides any previous default value assignment; hence C contains value5.

Weak Default Value Assignment (??=)

When using the weak or lazy default assignment operator ??=, value assignment does not occur until the end of the parsing process, so that the last rather than the first ??= assignment to a variable is used:

```
A ??= "value1"
B ??= "value2"
B ??= "value3"
C ?= "value4"
C ??= "value5"
D = "value6"
D ??= "value7"
```

In this example, A contains value1 if it has not been previously set. B contains value3 if it has not been previously set because the assignment does not occur until the end of the parsing process. C contains value4 and D contains value6 because the ?= and = operators override the ??= operator.

Variable Expansion

BitBake variables can reference the content of other BitBake variables:

```
VAR1 = "jumps over"
VAR2 = "The quick brown fox ${VAR1} the lazy dog."
```

The content of a variable is referenced using the `${}` reference operator with the variable name. In the example, VAR2 contains `The quick brown fox jumps over the lazy dog`.

Immediate Variable Expansion

Variable expansion does not occur until the variable is actually used. Simply assigning an expression containing variable expansion does not expand the referenced variable. The assignment operator `:=`, however, causes an immediate expansion on assignment:

```
VAR1 = "jumps over"
VAR2 = "${VAR1} the lazy dog. "
VAR1 = "falls on"
VAR3 = "The rain in Spain ${VAR1} the plain."
VAR4 := "The quick brown fox ${VAR2}"
```

The variable VAR4 contains `The quick brown fox falls on the lazy dog`. because VAR1 contained in the assignment of VAR2 is not expanded until the content of VAR2 is referenced during the assignment to VAR4 using the `:=` operator. By then, however, the value of VAR1 has been set to `falls on`.

Python Variable Expansion

BitBake can evaluate Python expressions in variable assignments:

```
DATE = "${@time.strftime('%A %B %d, %Y', time.gmtime())}"
TODAY := "Today is: ${DATE}."
```

The `@` operator tells BitBake to treat the expression following it as Python code. The code must evaluate to a value. In the example, TODAY would contain a value similar to `Today is: Friday April 1, 2016`.

Variable Appending and Prepending

Variable content can be concatenated with other string literals and content from other variables using the append and prepend operators.

Appending (+=) and Prepending (=+) with Space

The `+=` and `=+` operators append and prepend variables respectively while adding a single space between the values:

```
VAR1 = "12"
VAR1 += "34"
VAR2 = "89"
VAR2 =+ "67"
VAR3 = "5"
VAR3 =+ "${VAR1}"
VAR3 += "${VAR2}"
```

This example results in variable VAR1 containing 12 34, variable VAR2 containing 67 89, and variable VAR3 containing 12 34 5 67 89.

Appending (.=) and Prepending (=.) without Space

The .= and =. operators append and prepend variables respectively without placing an additional space between the values:

```
VAR1 = "12"
VAR1 .= "34"
VAR2 = "89"
VAR2 =. "67"
VAR3 = "5"
VAR3 =. "${VAR1}"
VAR3 .= "${VAR2}"
```

This example results in variable VAR1 containing 1234, variable VAR2 containing 6789, and variable VAR3 containing 123456789.

Appending and Prepending Using the _append and _prepend Operators

Variable values can also be appended and prepended using the special _append and _prepend operators that are added to the variable names:

```
VAR1 = "12"
VAR1_append = "34"
VAR2 = "89"
VAR2_prepend = "67"
VAR3 = "5"
VAR3_prepend = "${VAR1}"
VAR3_append = "${VAR2}"
```

This example results in variable VAR1 containing 1234, variable VAR2 containing 6789, and variable VAR3 containing 123456789.

The _append and _prepend operators do not insert any spaces. If spaces are required, you have to include them with the string literal.

Removing (_remove)

Single values in variables containing space-delimited value lists can be removed using the _remove operator:

```
VAR1 = "123 456 789 123456789 789 456 123 123 456"
VAR1_remove = "123"
VAR1_remove = "456"
```

This example results in the variable VAR1 containing the string 789 123456789 789.

Conditional Variable Assignment

The variable OVERRIDES contains a list of values separated by colons. Each one of the values represents a condition that needs to be fulfilled:

```
OVERRIDES = "conda:condb:condc"
```

BitBake processes the conditions from right to left, meaning that the ones to the right take precedence over the ones to the left.

Conditional Variable Setting

A variable is set conditionally by appending the condition to the variable name with an underscore (_):

```
OVERRIDES = "sun:rain:snow"
PROTECTION = "unknown"
PROTECTION_sun = "lotion"
```

In this example, the variable PROTECTION contains lotion because the condition sun is contained in the OVERRIDES list. Consider the following example where both conditions are contained in the OVERRIDES list:

```
OVERRIDES = "sun:rain:snow"
PROTECTION_rain = "umbrella"
PROTECTION_snow = "sweater"
```

In this example, the variable PROTECTION contains sweater because the condition snow has higher priority than the condition rain.

In the following example, the variable PROTECTION contains umbrella because the condition hail is not contained in the OVERRIDES list:

```
OVERRIDES = "sun:rain:snow"
PROTECTION_rain = "umbrella"
PROTECTION_hail = "duck"
```

Like any other metadata, the variable OVERRIDES can also reference the contents of other variables:

```
OVERRIDES = "sun:rain:snow:${OTHER}"
OTHER = "hail"
```

Conditional variable setting allows the assignment of a default value overriding it with a specific value if the particular condition is met. This method is frequently used by the build system when, for instance, specific parameters need to be passed to the compiler for compiler machine–dependent code.

Conditional Appending and Prepending

Conditions can also be used for appending and prepending variables:

```
OVERRIDES = "sun:rain:snow"
PROTECTION = "sweater"
PROTECTION_append_rain = " umbrella"
```

This example results in PROTECTION being set to sweater umbrella.

Appends and prepends with higher priority (more to the right of the OVERRIDES list) take precedence as is the case with conditional variable assignment. For the example to work correctly you have to modify the OVERRIDES variable in the configuration file bitbake.conf as it is defined there already.

4.4.3 Inclusion

Metadata files can include other metadata files to allow for shared settings. A common use case is recipes that build the different versions of the same software package. The include file provides the shared settings, such as build instructions, installation directories, and more, which are complemented by the actual recipe with settings specific for the version to be built, such as the download location and the name of the source file.

BitBake offers two inclusion directives for *optional* and *required* inclusion:

```
include optional.inc   # optional inclusion
require mandatory.inc  # required inclusion
```

When using option inclusion with the `include` directive, BitBake attempts to locate the include file but silently continue operation even if it cannot find the file. Conversely, `required` inclusion with the required directive causes BitBake to exit with an error message.

For the majority of use cases, including a file with the `required` directive is preferred because it warns you if BitBake cannot locate the include file, protecting against mistakes such as typos in pathnames and filenames. However, it is sometimes desirable to provide a customization method that does not require changing a metadata file directly. For such cases, placing an `include` directive into the metadata file provides a mechanism for optional customization. If customization is desired, the include file can be provided, but if it is not necessary and the include file does not exist, BitBake simply ignores the inclusion.

The `include` and `required` directives can be used with relative and absolute paths:

```
include file1.inc
include meta-test/recipes-core/images/file2.inc
required /home/build/yocto/file3.inc
```

When relative paths are used, BitBake tries to locate the file using the list of file paths specified by the `BBPATH` variable. BitBake uses the first file it finds that has the correct path segment and filename.

After BitBake locates the include file, it parses its contents and inserts the contents into the including file at the very position it encountered the inclusion directive. Hence, include files can override settings previously made by the including file, and vice versa, making it important that the inclusion directives are placed at the proper position in the including file.

Of course, an include file must adhere to the BitBake metadata syntax of the including file. Recipes and classes can include files that contain configuration settings as well as executable metadata. Configuration files, however, can only include files that contain configuration settings but no executable metadata, since the latter is not supported in configuration files.

Included files can themselves include other files. That practice bears the risk of circular inclusion, particularly for files included with relative paths because of the search order of `BBPATH`. BitBake, however, detects circular inclusion and terminates with an error message.

4.4.4 Inheritance

Through classes, BitBake provides a simple inheritance mechanism. Classes can be inherited by recipes, append files, and other classes using the `inherit` directive:

```
inherit myclass
```

Classes are metadata files with the filename extension .bbclass that are placed inside the classes subdirectory of metadata layers. The inherit directive only uses the class name, which is the base name of class filename without the extension. It can be used only in recipes, append files, and other class files.

At first glance, inheritance seems to be very similar and eventually redundant to inclusion. The difference, however, lays in how BitBake processes and parses classes:

- BitBake identifies classes by their class name and not by their filename and path, which means class names must be unique across all metadata layers included by a build environment.

- BitBake parses classes once after it has completed parsing the configuration files and before it parses the recipes. Include files are parsed when BitBake encounters an inclusion directive. If the same include file is included by multiple other files, BitBake parses the same file multiple times within the context of the including file. That makes classes a more efficient mechanism for build instructions that are shared by many different recipes. However, using include files for recipes building different versions of the same software package is a good choice. since typically only one version at a time of a particular software package is built.

- BitBake's DataSmart copy-on-write (COW) data store maintains only one copy of the class, even if the class file is used by hundreds of recipes, whereas using include files may lead to duplication of data.

The use of common classes simplifies many recipes. For example, the autotools class for building software packages utilizing the GNU Autotools configuration mechanisms can reduce a recipe to a few lines of code (see Listing 4-5).

Listing 4-5   **Using the autotools Class**

```
SUMMARY = "GNU nano - an enhanced clone of the Pico text editor"

LICENSE = "GPLv3"
LIC_FILES_CHKSUM = "file://COPYING;md5=f27defe1e96c2e1ecd4e0c9be8967949"

DEPENDS = "ncurses"
PR = "r0"

PV_MAJOR = "${@bb.data.getVar('PV',d,1).split('.')[0]}\
.${@bb.data.getVar('PV',d,1).split('.')[1]}"

SRC_URI = "http://www.nano-editor.org/dist/v${PV_MAJOR}/nano-${PV}.tar.gz\
           file://ncursesw.patch"

SRC_URI[md5sum] = "af09f8828744b0ea0808d6c19a2b4bfd"

inherit autotools gettext
RDEPENDS_${PN} = "ncurses"
```

The preceding recipe builds the GNU nano editor, which is an autotooled software package. The recipe itself only specifies SRC_URI and package name, while all the complexities of building autotooled software packages are hidden within the autotools class.

4.4.5 Executable Metadata

Recipes, append files, and classes can include definitions of executable metadata. Executable metadata are shell or Python functions that BitBake can execute.

BitBake treats executable metadata exactly the same as variables: the function name is stored in the data dictionary together with the function code that represents the assigned value. Consequently, functions can be appended and prepended like regular variables and may also have metadata attributes.

The scope of metadata functions defined in recipes and append files is local to the particular file, whereas functions defined in classes are global.

Shell Functions

Shell functions are defined in a metadata file exactly as you would define them in a regular shell script (see Listing 4-6).

Listing 4-6   **Executable Metadata Shell Function**

```
helloworld () {
    echo "Hello, World!"
}
```

The code inside the function's body follows regular shell syntax. In fact, BitBake calls the shell interpreter /bin/sh when executing shell functions. Ideally, all shell functions should be written agnostic to the particular shell interpreter the system defaults to. On all Linux distributions officially supported by the Yocto Project, the default shell interpreter is the Bourne Again Shell (bash). To make your own code portable, it is advisable do avoid shell-specific extensions and stay with the common denominator for bash derivatives, such as .sh, .bash, .ksh, and .zsh.

Python Functions

Executable metadata can also be defined as Python functions (see Listing 4-7).

Listing 4-7   **Executable Metadata Python Function**

```
python printdate () {
    import time
    print time strftime('%Y%m%d', time.gettime())
}
```

They keyword python tells BitBake that the code following it is to be interpreted as Python code.

Using Python for executable metadata allows you to import any Python module and take advantage of the many functions available. Inside the function body, you must pay attention to Python's indentation scheme for code blocks. It is advisable to use spaces instead of tabs for indentation.

Global Python Functions

Functions can be defined globally using the def keyword regardless of the file they are defined in, as shown in Listing 4-8.

Listing 4-8   **Global Python Function**

```
def machine_paths(d):
    """List any existing machine specific filespath directories"""
    machine = d.getVar("MACHINE", True)
    filespathpkg = d.getVar("FILESPATHPKG", True).split(":")
    for basepath in d.getVar("FILESPATHBASE", True).split(":"):
        for pkgpath in filespathpkg:
            machinepath = os.path.join(basepath, pkgpath, machine)
            if os.path.isdir(machinepath):
                yield machinepath
```

The syntax is exactly the same as for defining any standard Python function.

Since the function is global, it can be called from any other Python metadata function.

Anonymous Python Functions

Recipes, append files, and classes may define anonymous Python functions using the __anonymous keyword as the function's name or by omitting the function name altogether (see Listing 4-9).

Listing 4-9   **Anonymous Python Function**

```
python __anonymous () {
    # Anonymous function using the __anonymous keyword
    ...
}
python () {
    # Anonymous function omitting the function name
    ...
}
```

BitBake executes anonymous functions at the end of the parsing process of a particular unit. For example, an anonymous function defined inside a recipe is executed after the recipe has been parsed.

Tasks

The previous sections described how to define shell and Python functions as executable metadata. The question is, how can BitBake execute functions from metadata files? We have already seen how BitBake executes anonymous functions after completing parsing of a recipe or class.

BitBake recognizes special functions called *tasks*. Tasks are defined in recipes and classes and can be

- Directly invoked from the BitBake command line for a particular recipe.
- Automatically executed by BitBake as part of the build process.

Listing 4-10 provides examples.

Listing 4-10   **Defining Tasks**

```
python do_clean () {
    # task to clean remove build output
    ...
}
addtask clean
do_build () {
    # task to build the software package
    ...
}
addtask build
do_download () {
    # task to download sources
    ...
}
addtask download before do_build
do_unpack () {
    # task to unpack sources
    ...
}
addtask unpack before do_build after do_download
do_compile () {
    # task to compile software package
    ...
}
addtask compile before do_build after do_unpack
do_install () {
    # task to install binaries, libraries, and documentation
    ...
}
addtask install after do_build
```

To define a shell or Python function as a task, its name must be prefixed with do_. Other than that, a task is exactly like any other executable metadata. The directive addtask is used to add a task to the BitBake task list and to define a task execution chain.

The code in Listing 4-10 defines the task `clean` and adds it to the task list with `addtask`. This technique allows for the task to be invoked from the BitBake command line. Let's assume the code of Listing 4-10 is placed inside a recipe called `myrecipe.bb`. Using

```
bitbake myrecipe -c clean
```

invokes the `clean` task of the recipe. The recipe adds the tasks `build`, `download`, `unpack`, `compile`, and `install`, using `before` and `after` together with the `addtask` directive, creating an execution chain. Running

```
bitbake myrecipe -c build
```

runs first the `download` task, then the `unpack` task, then the `compile` task, then the `build` task, and finally the `install` task.

When BitBake is invoked with the recipe as parameter but without specifying a task to be run, then it runs the default task. The default task is defined by the variable `BB_DEFAULT_TASK`. This variable is set by the base class to

```
BB_DEFAULT_TASK ?= "build"
```

making `build` the default task similar to the `all` target for makefiles. Recipes and classes can of course override `BB_DEFAULT_TASK` setting it to a different task.

Accessing BitBake Variables from Functions

BitBake variables can be accessed from both shell and Python functions.

Accessing Variables from Shell Functions

From within shell functions, BitBake variables can be directly accessed using the variable expansion notation (see Listing 4-11).

Listing 4-11   **Accessing Variables from Shell Functions**

```
BPN = "myapp-v1"
MAKE = "make"
EXTRA_OEMAKE = "CFLAGS='-W -Wall -Werror -Wundef -Wshadow ${CFLAGS}'"

do_compile () {
        bbnote ${MAKE} ${EXTRA_OEMAKE} "$@"
        ${MAKE} ${EXTRA_OEMAKE} "$@" || die "oe_runmake failed"
}

do_install () {
        BPN = "myapp"
        docdir = "docs"
        install -d ${D}${docdir}/${BPN}
}
```

Variables can be read as well as written from shell functions. However, writing a variable only changes its value locally within the scope of the shell script. In the Listing 4-11,

BPN is a BitBake variable that is overridden in the do_install function. The overridden value is valid only for the do_install function. That convention is easily understood considering that BitBake creates a shell script for the do_install function with all variable settings and expansions and then executes that script.

Accessing Variables from Python Functions

Accessing BitBake variables from Python functions is slightly more complicated than from shell functions, since BitBake variables cannot be read or written directly but must be retrieved from and manipulated through the BitBake data dictionary using special functions (see Listing 4-12).

Listing 4-12   **Accessing Variables from Python Functions**

```
HELLO = "Hello, World!"
DATE = ""

python printhello () {
        hello = d.getVar('HELLO', True)
        print hello
}

python setdate () {
        import time
        date = time.strftime('%A %B %d, %Y', time.gettime())
        d.setVar('DATE', date)
}
```

The functions getVar and setVar provide access to variables through BitBake's data dictionary, which is referenced by the global Python variable d. BitBake's data dictionary is implemented as a Python class. The functions getVar and setVar are methods of that class. The first parameter for both functions is the name of the variable to be accessed. The second parameter for getVar is a Boolean value telling the function whether to expand the variable's expression. The second parameter for setVar is the new value of the variable.

Creating a Local Data Dictionary Copy

Using setVar with the global data dictionary modifies that variable globally and changes its value for all following operations. If that is not desired, a copy of the data dictionary can be made:

```
localdata = d.createCopy()
```

The createCopy method creates a new reference for the data dictionary. Since Bit-Bake's data dictionary uses COW, an actual copy of a variable is not created until it is accessed by a write operation.

Accessing Variables Containing Value Lists

Many BitBake variables contain value lists whose values are separated by a delimiter. Commonly, these list variables are converted into Python arrays after they are retrieved from the data dictionary (see Listing 4-13).

Listing 4-13   **Accessing Variable Lists**

```
python do_download () {
        uris = (d.getVar('SRC_URI', True) or "").split(" ")
        for uri in uris:
            # process the source URIs
            ...
}
```

The sample code of Listing 4-13 retrieves the variable SRC_URI from the data dictionary, which is a string of space-delimited URIs. It then splits the string into an array of strings using the split operator. The term or "" returns an empty string if the variable SRC_URI is not found in the data dictionary to make the code failsafe.

You find variants of this sample code frequently used in recipes and classes to retrieve and process variable lists.

Appending and Prepending Functions

Like variables, functions can be appended and prepended using the _append and _prepend operators (see Listing 4-14).

Listing 4-14   **Appending and Prepending Functions**

```
python printdate () {
    import time
    print time.strftime('%A %B %d, %Y', time.gettime())
}

python printdate_prepend () {
    print ('Today is: ')
}

python printdate_append () {
    print('MOTD: A good day for the Yocto Project.')
}
```

The code in Listing 4-14 would result in a combined printdate function (see Listing 4-15).

Listing 4-15   **Combined Function**

```
python printdate () {
    print ('Today is: ')
```

```
    import time
    print time strftime('%A %B %d, %Y', time.gettime())
    print('MOTD: A good day for the Yocto Project.')
}
```

Of course, you would normally not append or prepend functions in the same file.
Typical use cases for appending or prepending are recipes that inherit a class and add to
a function defined by that class or an append file that extends a function defined by the
recipe it appends.

Appending and prepending works for both shell and Python functions.

4.4.6 Metadata Attributes

All BitBake metadata—that is, variables as well as functions—can have *attributes*,
also referred to as *flags*. Attributes provide a way of tagging extra information to the
metadata.

BitBake metadata syntax provides for setting attributes by adding the name of the
attribute in brackets to the variable or function name:

```
VAR[flag] = "flagvalue"
```

Attributes can be appended and prepended using the +=, =+, .=, and =. operators.
Expressions to assign value to attributes may use variable expansion. However, it is not
possible to read an attribute's value via BitBake metadata syntax.

The value of an attribute can be read and written from Python functions using the
BitBake data dictionary methods getVarFlag and setVarFlag (see Listing 4-16).

Listing 4-16   **Metadata Attributes (Flags)**

```
func[run] = "1"

python func () {
    run = d.getVarFlag('func', 'run')
    if run == 1:
        # do some work
        ...
        d.setVarFlag('func', 'run', 0)
    else:
        # do not run at this time
}
```

The first argument to the method getVarFlag is the name of the variable, and the
second is the name of the flag. The method setVarFlag uses three parameters: variable
name, flag name, and flag value.

4.4.7 Metadata Name (Key) Expansion

Expansion can also be applied to metadata names. The actual expansion happens at the very end of the data parsing process immediately before conditional assignment, appending, and prepending.

```
A${B} = "foo"
B = "2"
A2 = "bar"
```

The variable A2 contains foo, since the entire evaluation of the expression A${B} = "foo" is not evaluated until the end of the parsing process after the expression A2 = "bar".

4.5 Source Download

In the beginning there is the source, and the source can be anywhere and presented in any format. Consequently, a build system capable of building a Linux OS stack consisting of many hundreds of software packages must be able to retrieve them from a vast variety of sources, often referred to as *upstream repositories*. Upstream repositories can be local or remote file servers or software configuration or revision control systems such as Git, Subversion, and many others. Source code may be packaged in the form of archives, such as tar, that are commonly compressed using various formats. When using source control management (SCM), source code is typically checked out file by file in the form of source trees.

Besides providing the necessary functionality for retrieving source code packages from many different sources, it is imperative that the build system offers a consistent and transparent way of accessing repositories from the build recipes without requiring the end user to know about the specifics of the repository and protocol implementations.

BitBake provides the necessary framework through its *fetcher* architecture. In BitBake terminology, fetching is the process of obtaining source files. The Python Fetch class from the BitBake fetch2 library (bitbake/lib/bb/fetch2) presents a uniform interface for source code fetching through source URIs following the format

```
<scheme>://[<user>[:<pwd>]@]<host>[:<port>]/<path>[;<key>=<value>;..]
```

For the most part, the BitBake fetcher URIs are compliant with the IETF standard of RFC3986 except for the handling of paths. RFC3986 provides for *absolute* and *relative* paths. The standard defines valid absolute path references as

```
file://hostname/absolute/path/to/file
file:///absolute/path/to/file
```

BitBake supports the second form for absolute paths but does not recognize the first form. Valid relative paths can be specified according to the standard as

```
file:relative/path/to/file
```

BitBake does support relative paths using that format and additionally recognizes the format

```
file://relative/path/to/file
```

which is not compliant with RFC3986. This format is supported for backwards compatibility with earlier implementations of the fetcher library to avoid rewriting older recipes.

BitBake URIs also have no notion of *queries* and *fragments* provided by the IETF standard.

The Fetch base class defers actual processing of a URI and accessing the resource to a specific implementation identified by the *scheme* of the URI. The optional parameter list is dependent on the particular implementation of the fetcher. Certain schemes may access resources that require authentication with a user name and a password. Those can be included with the URI using the standard notation.

An important detail of the Fetch base class is that the source URI parameter passed to it during instantiation may contain not just a single URI but a list of URIs in the preceding format that may even use different schemes.

4.5.1 Using the Fetch Class

Although BitBake provides the fetcher architecture and the fetcher implementations, it does not provide a default task for fetching source files. To use the fetchers, you have to implement a task in your recipes or, preferably, inside a BitBake class. Listing 4-17 shows the implementation of a sample do_fetch task.

Listing 4-17   **Sample do_fetch Task**

```
1  python do_fetch() {
2
3    bb.note("Downloading sources from ${SRC_URI} ...")
4
5    src_uri = (d.getVar('SRC_URI', True) or "").split()
6    if len(src_uri) == 0:
7       bb.fatal("Empty URI")
8
9    try:
10      fetcher = bb.fetch2.Fetch(src_uri, d)
11      fetcher.download()
12   except bb.fetch2.BBFetchException:
13      bb.fatal("Could not fetch source tarball.")
14
15   bb.note("Download successful.")
16 }
17
18 addtask fetch before do_build
```

Line 5 of the sample task first obtains the SRC_URI variable from the BitBake data dictionary. This variable is assumed to contain a space-delimited list of URIs to the source repositories. The list is converted into a Python list variable (or array). Line 10 then creates a `fetcher` object from the `Fetch` base class. Line 11 attempts to download the sources from the repositories. The other code of the sample task provides logging information for debugging and handles exceptions raised by the fetcher.

A recipe using this `do_fetch` task would simply have to specify the `SRC_URI` variable. All the actual work of downloading the sources is handled by the task and the fetcher implementation. As a matter of fact, the `base.bbclass` provided by the OpenEmbedded Core (OE Core) metadata layer implements a `do_fetch` task very similar to the sample.

That leaves one question that the code of the sample task does not directly answer: Where do the fetchers download the sources to? If you analyze the code of the BitBake fetcher library, you notice that the fetchers expect the variable `DL_DIR` to contain the path of the directory to which they download the source file.

4.5.2 Fetcher Implementations

BitBake provides implementations of fetchers for virtually all common types of upstream repositories used for open source projects. The following sections discuss the most commonly used fetchers and their parameters individually.

Local File Fetcher

The local file fetcher retrieves files from filesystems that can be accessed using the `file://` URI scheme. That does not necessarily mean that these files reside on the local host. They could very well be located on filesystems that are mounted from remote file servers.

Paths contained in the URI can be absolute or relative:

```
SRC_URI = "file:///absolute/path/to/file"
SRC_URI = "file://relative/path/to/file"
```

In the case of a relative path, the fetcher uses the variables `FILESPATH` and `FILESDIR` to locate the file:

- `FILESPATH` contains a list of paths separated by colons (:). The fetcher searches for the file starting with the first path in the list. Each directory is searched until there is a first match. If there are multiple directories containing a file with that name, the fetcher downloads the first file it finds.

- If none of the directories are contained in `FILESPATH`, the fetcher checks whether the variable `FILESDIR` is set. If it is set and contains a single valid path, the fetcher uses that path to locate the file.

The fetcher raises an error if the file does not exist in the case of an absolute path or if neither `FILESPATH` nor `FILESDIR` includes a path that contains the file in the case of a relative path.

The local file fetcher does not actually "download"—that is, copy the file from the location specified by the URI to `DL_DIR`. Instead, its download method only verifies that the file exists. Local files are accessed directly from their original location.

Commonly, SRC_URI specifies a single file. However, the fetcher can also access multiple files either by using wildcards anywhere in the path name or SRC_URI or by pointing SRC_URI to a directory:

```
SRC_URI = "file://*/*.patch"
SRC_URI = "file://path/to/dir"
```

Both forms work equally with absolute and relative paths.

The implementation of the local file fetcher can be found in the file bitbake/lib/bb/fetch2/local.py.

HTTP/HTTPS/FTP Fetcher

Frequently, sources are downloaded from upstream file servers using HTTP, HTTPS, or FTP protocol. BitBake provides a fetcher implementation for these protocols using the GNU Wget utility by default. However, the command, including any command-line options, can be specified by setting the FETCHCMD_wget variable.

Following are the parameters supported by this fetcher:

- **md5sum**: MD5 checksum for download verification. If provided, the fetcher computes the MD5 checksum for the downloaded file and compares it to the value provided with this parameter. If they differ, the fetcher raises an error.
- **sha256sum**: SHA256 checksum for download verification. If provided, the fetcher computes the SHA256 checksum for the downloaded file and compares it to the value provided with this parameter. If they differ, the fetcher raises an error.
- **downloadfilename**: If provided, the fetcher renames the downloaded file to this filename.
- **name**: Symbolic reference for the URI.

Providing a checksum for download verification is mandatory for the fetcher. Either of the parameters md5sum or sha256sum must be provided. If both are provided, they must match both.

Following are examples for SRC_URI:

```
SRC_URI = "http://host.site.org/downloads/srcpkg.tar.gz;md5sum=12345"
SRC_URI = "https://host.site.org/downloads/srcpkg.tar.gz;sha256sum=6789"
SRC_URI = "ftp://user:pwd@host.site.org/repo/srcpkg.tar.gz;md5sum=12345"
SRC_URI = \
"ftp://host.site.org/srcpkg.tar.tgz;md5sum=12345;downloadfilename=file.tgz"
```

The large MD5 and SHA256 checksums can make the SRC_URIs hard to read and to maintain. Therefore, they can be specified outside the SRC_URI using this syntax:

```
SRC_URI = "http://host.site.org/downloads/srcpkg.tar.gz"
SRC_URI[md5sum] = "12345"
SRC_URI[sha256sum] = "6789"
```

When specifying more than one URI in SRC_URI, symbolic references need to be used in order to provide the checksums for all downloads outside the SRC_URI variable:

```
SRC_URI = "http://host.site.org/downloads/srcpkg1.tar.gz;name=pkg1
           ftp://host.anothersite.org/downloads/srcpkg2.tgz;name=pkg2"
SRC_URI[pkg1.md5sum] = "12345"
SRC_URI[pkg2.sha256sum] = "6789"
```

The implementation of the HTTP/HTTPS/FTP fetcher can be found in the file bitbake/lib/bb/fetch2/wget.py.

SFTP Fetcher

The SFTP fetcher allows downloading files from secure FTP sites with or without authentication:

```
SRC_URI = "sftp://host.site.org/downloads/srcpkg.tgz;md5sum=12345"
SRC_URI = "sftp://user@host.site.org/downloads/srcpkg.tgz;md5sum=12345"
```

Using a password in the URI for authentication is not supported. You have to use SSH keys for authentication.

The fetcher expects the sftp command to be available on your development host. There is no BitBake variable for this fetcher to override the command and command-line options.

The SFTP fetcher supports the same parameters as the HTTP/HTTPS/FTP fetcher: md5sum, sha256sum, downloadfilename, and name.

The implementation of the SFTP fetcher can be found in the file bitbake/lib/bb/fetch2/sftp.py.

Git Fetcher

Git has become the SCM of choice for many open source projects, and of course the Linux kernel community is using it to manage the kernel development. The fetcher clones repositories and is capable of checking out multiple branches at the same time.

The parameters supported by this fetcher are as follows:

- **protocol**: Transfer protocol to use for accessing the repository. The supported protocols are git, file, ssh, http, https, and rsync. If the parameter is omitted, the fetcher defaults to git.

- **branch**: Branch to check out. If the parameter is omitted, the fetcher defaults to master. Multiple branches can be specified by separating them with commas.

- **name**: Symbolic names for the branches. If multiple branches are checked out, then the number of names provided by this parameter must match the number of branches.

- **tag**: Git tag to retrieve from the branch. If the parameter is not provided, the fetcher defaults to HEAD.

- **rebaseable**: Tells the fetcher that the upstream repository may rebase in the future, causing the tags and their SHA1 hashes to change. The parameter instructs the fetcher to preserve the local cache so that future merges can be carried out. Set the parameter to `rebaseable=1` for a rebaseable Git repository. The default is `rebaseable=0` if the parameter is not provided.
- **nocheckout**: Instructs the fetcher to not check out source code from the branches when unpacking. That instruction is useful for recipes that use their own code for checking out the source code. The default value if the parameter is not provided is `nocheckout=0`. Set it to `nocheckout=1` if the recipe uses its own code for source handling.
- **bareclone**: Tells the fetcher to create a bare clone of the repository and not to check out source code from the branches. Use this option for recipes that provide their own routines to check out source code from branches and track branch requirements. The default value if the parameter is not provided is `bareclone=0`. Set it to `bareclone=1` if the recipe uses its own routines.

Following are examples for the Git fetcher's `SRC_URI`:

```
SRC_URI = "git://git.site.org/git/repo.git;branch=develop"
SRC_URI = "git://git.site/org/git/repo.git;tag=0C12ABD"
SRC_URI = "git://git.site.org/git/repo.git;protocol=http"
```

A common mistake is to set the scheme at the beginning of the URI to `http` (or another protocol) when trying to access a Git repository using a different protocol rather than specifying the `protocol` parameter. That, of course, does not work because the scheme tells the BitBake fetcher infrastructure what fetcher to use. The scheme implies the protocol but can be overridden with the `protocol` parameter.

The implementation of the Git fetcher can be found in the file `bitbake/lib/bb/fetch2/git.py`.

Git Submodules Fetcher

The Git submodules fetcher is an extension of the Git fetcher handling repositories whose tree embeds foreign Git trees. The fetcher detects whether a Git repository contains submodules and updates them after cloning the main repository.

The scheme of the fetcher is `gitsm`. URI format and parameters are the same as for the Git fetcher.

```
SRC_URI = "gitsm://git.site.org/git/repo.git;branch=develop"
```

The implementation of the Git submodules fetcher can be found in the file `bitbake/lib/bb/fetch2/gitsm.py`.

Subversion (SVN) Fetcher

For checking out source code modules from Subversion repositories, BitBake provides the SVN fetcher.

The parameters supported by this fetcher are as follows:

- **protocol**: Transfer protocol to use for accessing the repository. The supported protocols are svn, svn+ssh, http, and https. If the parameter is omitted, the fetcher defaults to svn.

- **module**: The repository module to check out. This parameter is required.

- **rev**: The revision of the module to check out. If the parameter is omitted, HEAD is used.

The SVN fetcher can be used without or with authentication:

```
SRC_URI = "svn://svn.site.org/trunk;module=library;rev=12345;protocol=http"
SRC_URI = "svn://user:passwd@svn.anothersite.org/svn;module=trunk"
```

The implementation of the Subversion fetcher can be found in the file bitbake/lib/bb/fetch2/svn.py.

Concurrent Versions System (CVS) Fetcher

Repositories using Concurrent Versions System (CVS) can be accessed using the CVS fetcher. The parameters supported by this fetcher are presented in Table 4-1.

Table 4-1   Parameters Supported by the CVS Fetcher

method	Method to use for accessing the repository. The supported methods are pserver, dir, and ext. The methods pserver and ext are used for accessing repositories on remote servers, and dir accesses a repository on a local filesystem. If method=ext, the fetcher reads the environment variable CVS_RSH to determine the access method, which is typically CVS_RSH="ssh". If the parameter is omitted, the fetcher defaults to pserver.
port	TCP/IP port for accessing a repository on a remote server.
rsh	Provide the external access method rather than using CVS_RSH.
module	The repository module to check out. This parameter is required.
tag	The revision of the module to check out. If the parameter is omitted, the head of the repository is checked out.
date	The source date to check out, which is provided by the parameter in the form YYYYMMDDHHMM.
norecurse	Run CVS only in the current working directory rather than recursively updating all subdirectories. When this parameter is provided, the fetcher adds the -l option to the command line of the cvs command.
localdir	The name of the local directory to which the fetcher checks out the module. If the parameter is omitted, then the directory has the name of the module.

Table 4-1   **Parameters Supported by the CVS Fetcher (*Continued*)**

`fullpath`	After checking out a module, the fetcher creates a tar archive of it. If `fullpath` is not set, then the tar archive's path names include only the name of the top-level directory, which is typically the module name. If `fullpath` is set, the archive's path names include the full path.

Following are examples for URIs supported by this fetcher:

```
SRC_URI = "cvs://user@cvs.site.org/cvs;module=src;tag=V0-23-1"
SRC_URI = "cvs://user:pwd@cvs.site.org/cvs;module=src;localdir=sitesrc"
```

The implementation of the CVS fetcher can be found in the file `bitbake/lib/bb/fetch2/cvs.py`.

Other Fetchers

In addition to the fetchers described in detail in the previous sections, BitBake supports these less commonly used repositories and revision control systems:

- **Bazaar**: Fetcher for the GNU Project revision control system Bazaar. The scheme is `bzr://`. The fetcher implementation can be found in the file `bitbake/lib/bb/fetch2/bzr.py`.
- **Mercurial**: Fetcher for the cross-platform, distributed revision control system Mercurial. The scheme is `hg://`. The fetcher implementation can be found in the file `bitbake/lib/bb/fetch2/hg.py`.
- **Open Build Service**: Fetcher to access sources managed by the Open Build Service (OBS) used by the SUSE Linux distribution. The scheme is `osc://`. The fetcher implementation can be found in the file `bitbake/lib/bb/fetch2/osc.py`.
- **Perforce**: Fetcher to access sources managed by the proprietary commercial revision control system Perforce. The scheme is `p4://`. The fetcher implementation can be found in the file `bitbake/lib/bb/fetch2/perforce.py`.
- **Repo**: Fetcher to access Git repositories that use the Android `repo` tool for repository management. The scheme is `repo://`. The fetcher implementation can be found in the file `bitbake/lib/bb/fetch2/repo.py`.
- **SVK**: Fetcher to access sources from SVK repositories. The scheme is `svk://`. The fetcher implementation can be found in the file `bitbake/lib/bb/fetch2/svk.py`.

URI syntax and usage of these fetchers follow the same rules as for the more mainstream fetchers. The fetchers may use additional or different parameters to accommodate the their particular functionality.

4.5.3 Mirrors

Recipes set the SRC_URI variable to the upstream location of the source code. In addition to SRCI_URI, BitBake supports mirror download sites from which it can alternatively obtain source code packages.

BitBake uses a defined sequence to access locations and sites for files:

1. BitBake first checks the local download directory specified by DL_DIR that the files provided in SRC_URI have already been downloaded. If that is the case, it skips accessing any upstream and mirror sites and uses the files in DL_DIR. If some of the files are present and others are not, BitBake incrementally downloads the files. If SRC_URI is an SCM repository, it verifies the correct branches and tag in DL_DIR and eventually updates them as required.

2. If files provided in SRC_URI are not available locally, BitBake attempts to download them from mirror sites specified by the PREMIRRORS variable.

3. If the premirror sites do not provide the package, BitBake uses SRC_URI to download the files directly from the upstream project site.

4. If downloading from the upstream project site is unsuccessful, BitBake uses the mirror sites provided by the MIRRORS variable.

5. If none of the download sites provide the required files, BitBake posts an error message.

Using mirrors and the preceding sequence is BitBake's default behavior. If you do not want to use mirrors, you need to set either the PREMIRRORS or MIRRORS variables or both to an empty string.

The PREMIRRORS and MIRRORS variables specify lists of tuples consisting of a regular expression for the key to match the SRC_URI and URI pointing to the respective mirror:

```
MIRRORS = "\
ftp://.*/.*     http://downloads.mirrorsite.org/mirror/sources/ \n \
http://.*/.*    http://downloads.mirrorsite.org/mirror/sources/ \n \
https://.*/.*   http://downloads.mirrorsite.org/mirror/sources/ \n \
git://.*/.*     http://downloads.mirrorsite.org/mirror/sources/ \n \
svn://.*/.*     http://downloads.mirrorsite.org/mirror/sources/ \n"
```

Key and URI of a tuple are separated by one or more space characters, and the tuples are separated from each other with newline characters. Typically, mirrors use HTTP protocol for file download but other file download protocols, such as FTP, HTTPS, and SFTP, are valid too as long as BitBake has a fetcher for it.

Operation for file downloads is straightforward. For instance, if BitBake encounters an SRC_URI using the FTP scheme, it looks for a matching key in the MIRROR variable and then substitutes the scheme and path of SRC_URI for the mirror's URI. Using the above mirror list

```
SRC_URI - "ftp://ftp.sitc.org/downloads/file.tgz"
```

effectively turns into

```
SRC_URI = "http://downloads.mirrorsite.org/mirror/sources/file.tgz"
```

However, how do mirrors work for SCM repositories such as Git if the URI of the mirror points to a file download site? In that case, BitBake expects the repository to be packaged into a tarball. It downloads the tarball from the mirror and locally extracts the repository it contains.

The Yocto Project provides a source mirror on high-availability infrastructure at http://downloads.yoctoproject.org/mirror/sources. This mirror is enabled by default by the Poky reference distribution policy for all Yocto Project build environments.

Creating Mirrors

Creating your own mirror site has advantages, such as minimizing network access for teams and controlling the sources from which your product's Linux distribution is built. You can create your own mirror site by downloading all source packages from the Yocto Project mirror and placing them into a directory of an intranet server. You can also create a mirror from the download directory of a Yocto Project build environment you have been using for building a Linux distribution for your project. Your local download directory already contains all the necessary sources, but not yet in a format that is suitable for a mirror site. By default, and to save build time, BitBake does not create source tarballs for SCM repositories. You can instruct BitBake to create the tarballs in your local download directory by adding

```
BB_GENERATE_MIRROR_TARBALLS = "1"
```

to your conf/local.conf file. After your build has finished successfully, simply copy all the files in your download directory to your mirror server. You have to copy the files. You cannot use symbolic links to the files because the fetchers do not follow symbolic links.

After your mirror server is set up, you can use its URI for the MIRRORS and PREMIRRORS variables.

4.6 HelloWorld—BitBake Style

The preceding sections explained the BitBake essentials and set the stage for employing BitBake as a build system. Now it is time to put it to work with a simple example—the BitBake HelloWorld. This may not be the most primitive example you can do with BitBake, but it demonstrates how to use it for building an open source software package for the build host as a target.

The example builds the nano text editor (http://nano-editor.org) from source. Nano uses GNU Autotools for configuration. For this example to work on your build host, you need to have the GNU development package including Autotools installed. You of course also need BitBake.

First we need to set up a build environment for our BitBake HelloWorld project. Listing 4-18 shows its layout.

Listing 4-18   **BitBake HelloWorld Build Environment Layout**

```
yocto@yocto-dev:~/bitbake$ tree -L 3 bbhello
bbhello/
├── classes
│   └── base.bbclass
├── conf
│   ├── bblayers.conf
│   └── bitbake.conf
└── meta-hello
    ├── conf
    │   └── layer.conf
    └── recipes-editor
        └── nano
```

We simply copied BitBake's default files base.bbclass and bitbake.conf into the build environment from the BitBake installation directory. For the purpose of this example, they contain all the required settings.

The file bblayers.conf sets up the build environment and also includes our meta-hello layer, which eventually contains the recipe to build the nano editor (see Listing 4-19).

Listing 4-19   **bblayers.conf**

```
# Initialize BBPATH with the top-level directory of the
# build environment.
BBPATH := "${TOPDIR}"
# Initialize BBFILES to an empty string as it is set up
# by the layer.conf files of the layers.
BBFILES ?= ""

# Add our layer to BBLAYERS.
BBLAYERS = " \
  ${TOPDIR}/meta-hello \
  "
```

The file first sets the BBPATH variable to the build environment's top-level directory and initializes BBFILES to an empty string. Then it adds the meta-hello layer to BBLAYERS. For simplicity, this example is all self-contained and includes the meta-hello within the build environment.

As outlined earlier, all BitBake layers must contain a layer.conf configuration file, which is shown in Listing 4-20.

Listing 4-20   **layer.conf**

```
# Add the path of this layer to BBPATH
BBPATH .- ":${LAYERDIR}"
```

```
# Add recipes and append files to BBFILES
BBFILES += "${LAYERDIR}/recipes-*/*/*.bb \
            ${LAYERDIR}/recipes-*/*/*.bbappend"

# Set layer search pattern and priority
BBFILE_COLLECTIONS += "hello"
BBFILE_PATTERN_hello := "^${LAYERDIR}/"
BBFILE_PRIORITY_hello = "5"
```

The file is essentially a copy of the boilerplate template. The only adjustments necessary are to the search pattern and the priority settings.

Last, we need a recipe to build the nano editor. We place this recipe into the subdirectory recipes-editor of the layer's top-level directory meta-hello. The full path to the recipes in our layer matches the expression in BBFILES of layer.conf. Listing 4-21 shows the recipe.

Listing 4-21   **nano.bb**

```
SUMMARY = "Recipe to build the 'nano' editor"

PN = "nano"
PV = "2.2.6"

SITE = "http://www.nano-editor.org/dist"
PV_MAJOR = "${@bb.data.getVar('PV',d,1).split('.')[0]}"
PV_MINOR = "${@bb.data.getVar('PV',d,1).split('.')[1]}"

SRC_URI = "${SITE}/v${PV_MAJOR}.${PV_MINOR}/${PN}-${PV}.tar.gz"
SRC_URI[md5sum] = "03233ae480689a008eb98feb1b599807"
SRC_URI[sha256sum] = \
"be68e133b5e81df41873d32c517b3e5950770c00fc5f4dd23810cd635abce67a"

python do_fetch() {
    bb.plain("Downloading source tarball from ${SRC_URI} ...")
    src_uri = (d.getVar('SRC_URI', True) or "").split()
    if len(src_uri) == 0:
        bb.fatal("Empty URI")
    try:
        fetcher = bb.fetch2.Fetch(src_uri, d)
        fetcher.download()
    except bb.fetch2.BBFetchException:
        bb.fatal("Could not fetch source tarball.")
    bb.plain("Download successful.")
}

addtask fetch before do_build

python do_unpack() {
    bb.plain("Unpacking source tarball ...")
    os.system("tar x -C ${WORKDIR} -f ${DL_DIR}/${P}.tar.gz")
    bb.plain("Unpacked source tarball.")
}

addtask unpack before do_build after do_fetch
```

```
python do_configure() {
    bb.plain("Configuring source package ...")
    os.system("cd ${WORKDIR}/${P} && ./configure")
    bb.plain("Configured source package.")
}

addtask configure before do_build after do_unpack

python do_compile() {
    bb.plain("Compiling package...")
    os.system("cd ${WORKDIR}/${P} && make")
    bb.plain("Compiled package.")
}

addtask compile before do_build after do_configure

do_clean[nostamp] = "1"
do_clean() {
    rm -rf ${WORKDIR}/${P}
    rm -f ${TMPDIR}/stamps/*
}

addtask clean
```

This recipe utilizes many of the major concepts of BitBake metadata syntax: variable setting, variable expansion, Python variable expansion, variable attributes, accessing BitBake variables from Python code, Python tasks, shell tasks, and more.

To build the nano text editor, simply execute

```
$ bitbake nano
```

from the top-level directory of the build environment. If everything works, you should see output similar to Listing 4-22.

Listing 4-22   **Building the Nano Text Editor**

```
$ bitbake nano
NOTE: Not using a cache. Set CACHE = <directory> to enable.
Parsing recipes: 100% |##################################| Time: 00:00:00
Parsing of 1 .bb files complete (0 cached, 1 parsed). 1 targets,
   0 skipped, 0 masked, 0 errors.
NOTE: Resolving any missing task queue dependencies
NOTE: Preparing runqueue
NOTE: Executing RunQueue Tasks
Downloading source tarball from
   http://www.nano-editor.org/dist/v2.2/nano-2.2.6.tar.gz ...
Download successful.
Unpacking source tarball ...
Unpacked source tarball.
Configuring source package ...
Configured source package.
Compiling package...
Compiled package.
NOTE: Tasks Summary: Attempted 5 tasks of which 0 didn't need to be rerun and all
succeeded.
```

The nano executable is located in `tmp/work/nano-2.2.6-r0/nano-2.2.6/src` from where you can run it.

You can clean your build environment with

```
$ bitbake nano -c clean
```

Of course, this is a very simple example. A build system, such as the OpenEmbedded build system, that builds an entire Linux OS stack must provide much more functionality and includes hundreds of recipes and many classes. Additionally, the OpenEmbedded build system is capable of building for different architectures and many different machine types for which it also builds the necessary cross-toolchains.

4.7 Dependency Handling

Rarely does a build system build just a single software package. If multiple software packages are built, dependencies commonly exist between some of those packages, meaning that the build system must be able to handle such dependencies. The build system must be able to detect all changes made to a package, re-execute any tasks that were invalidated by the changes, and then also re-execute any tasks from software packages that depend on the output of one or more tasks of the changed package.

Build systems typically distinguish between two types of dependencies:

- **Build Dependencies**: Components that are required for a software package to be successfully built. These can be header files, static libraries, or other components.
- **Runtime Dependencies**: Components that are required for a software package to correctly operate. These can be libraries, configuration files, or other components.

To express dependencies, the build system must implement a way for software packages to announce their name or functionality as well as a way for other software packages to reference that name or functionality as a dependency.

4.7.1 Provisioning

BitBake recipes for software packages use the PROVIDES variable to announce their name and functionality that other recipes then can use to express their dependency on that package. BitBake offers three different variants of provisioning, which in this book are referred to as *implicit provisioning*, *explicit provisioning*, and *symbolic provisioning*.

Implicit Provisioning

BitBake derives the values for package name, package version, and package revision from the filename of a recipe. It uses these values for provisioning unless they are explicitly overridden by the recipe's content, as explained in the next section.

BitBake recipe filenames follow the convention

```
<package name>_<package version>_<package revision>.bb
```

The convention concatenates package name, package version, and package revision with underscores; for example,

```
nano_2.2.6_r0.bb
```

BitBake parses the filename and assigns the variables PN, PV, and PR accordingly:

```
PN = "nano"
PV = "2.2.6"
PR = "r0"
```

If a recipe name does not provide the package revision, PR defaults to r0, and if it does not provide the package version, PV defaults to 1.0. You cannot, however, specify the package revision without specifying the package version when using implicit provisioning through the recipe name. If you want to provide the package revision without specifying the package version, you have to use explicit provisioning. However, it typically does not make much sense to do so, since the package revision is meaningful only in the context of the package version.

Through the assignment

```
PROVIDES_prepend = "${PN} "
```

a package always announces its package name.

Explicit Provisioning

The three variables PN, PV, and PR can explicitly set by the recipe itself by assigning values to them. Such explicit provisioning overrides any settings derived from the filename. BitBake sets the PROVIDES variable accordingly.

Symbolic Provisioning

Recipes can also override or add to the PROVIDES variable that can be used to specify a symbolic name for that package. Dependent packages can then reference the symbolic name. This is useful if multiple packages or multiple versions of the same package provide the same functionality:

```
PROVIDES =+ "virtual/editor"
```

This statement used in the recipe for the nano text editor would add the symbolic name virtual/editor to the list of names. It is always recommended to add a symbolic name to PROVIDES rather than overriding the variable altogether. What the symbolic name actually is does not matter, but to avoid inadvertent collision of a symbolic name with the name of an actual other recipe, developers have adopted the convention to use the prefix virtual/ for symbolic names.[2]

---

2. Because of the forward slash in the symbolic name, it is obvious that on Linux build hosts, a symbolic name can never collide with the name of an actual recipe because on UNIX systems, the forward slash is used to delimit path segments.

Clearly, if multiple packages are using the same symbolic name, the build system must have a way to determine which recipe to use. We address this issue in Section 4.7.3.

4.7.2 Declaring Dependencies

Recipes declare build dependencies and runtime dependencies by adding the names of packages they depend on to the DEPENDS and RDEPENDS variables, respectively:

```
DEPENDS = "libxml2-native gettext-native virtual/libiconv ncurses"
RDEPENDS = "base-files run-postinsts"
```

Both variables contain a space-delimited list of actual or symbolic names of the packages on which they depend. Of course, those packages must provide their names through the PROVIDES variable, as outlined in the previous section.

Although dependencies are declared on the *recipe level*, it would be rather inefficient to enforce them on the recipe level. For example, enforcing build dependencies on the recipe level would mean that all tasks of a recipe building a package must have completed successfully before the first task of a recipe that depends on that package can start. That would be less than optimal for a parallel build process because tasks such as fetching the source code, unpacking it, patching it, and so forth, are not dependent on another package having completed its build successfully. However, tasks that configure and compile a package are dependent on the successful completion of the build process of a package. Therefore, BitBake enforces dependencies on the task level. Enforcement is achieved using the metadata attributes deptask and rdeptask. Each task has a deptask attribute that contains a space-delimited list of tasks that must have completed from each of the packages listed in DEPENDS:

```
do_configure[deptask] = "do_populate_staging"
```

For the code example, the do_populate_staging task of each recipe contained in DEPENDS must have completed before this recipe's do_configure_task can run.

The rdeptask attribute fulfills the same function for runtime dependencies:

```
do_package_write[rdeptask] = "do_package"
```

In this example, the do_package_write task of a recipe cannot run before all of the packages it depends on during runtime have completed their packaging step.

4.7.3 Multiple Providers

Through symbolic provisioning, multiple packages potentially can fulfill another package's build and/or runtime dependencies. For example, there could be two packages providing text editor functionality for an e-mail program. The e-mail program itself does not care which one of the two text editor packages provides the functionality as long as one of them is available:

```
editor1.bb:    PROVIDES = "virtual/editor"
editor2.bb:    PROVIDES = "virtual/editor"
mailer.bb:     RDEPENDS = "virtual/editor"
```

Both editor packages provide the `virtual/editor` functionality that the mailer package requires. How does BitBake choose which one of the two editor packages to build? Through the `PREFERRED_PROVIDER` variable, you can select which of the packages that provide `virtual/editor` BitBake builds:

```
PREFERRED_PROVIDER_virtual/editor = "editor2"
```

Most commonly, this variable is placed into a configuration file such as your distribution policy configuration file.

4.8 Version Selection

Many metadata layers include multiple recipes to build different versions of the same software package. For example, the OE Core metadata layer provides multiple recipes to build different versions of the Linux kernel.

By default, BitBake always chooses the recipe that builds the latest version of a package, as indicated by the `PV` variable. However, you can override the default behavior by specifying the `PREFERRED_VERSION` variable:

```
PREFERRED_VERSION_editor = "1.1"
```

You must set this variable conditional on the actual package name. Sometimes the version number is appended with additional information, such as the Git tag or a minor version number. In this case, you tell BitBake by adding a percent sign (%) to the version string that the additional information is irrelevant:

```
PREFERRED_VERSION_linux-yocto = "3.10%"
```

Recipes may set the `DEFAULT_PREFERENCE` variable to indicate a lower or higher priority than its version number:

```
editor_1.1.bb: DEFAULT_PREFERENCE = "6"
editor_1.2.bb: DEFAULT_PREFERENCE = "0"
```

By default, BitBake would choose the `editor-1.2.bb` recipe over the `editor-1.1 bb` recipe because it is the later version. However, by using `DEFAULT_PREFERENCE`, the priority of the recipe building the older version is elevated. The default value for `DEFAULT_PREFERENCE` is 5.

It is recommended that you use `DEFAULT_PREFERENCE` only for experimental recipes that build newer versions to lower their priority:

```
editor_2.0.bb: DEFAULT_PREFERENCE = "-1"
```

Using `DEFAULT_PREFERENCE` other than for lowering the priority for experimental recipes can easily lead to undesirable results and confusion if you are not aware that a recipe is using it.

4.9 Variants

Recipes commonly build one variant of a software package that is intended for the target system. However, for some packages, variants are needed for different applications. A typical example is a compiler that is needed in a target variant and in a native or host variant. To enable building multiple variants of a package from the same recipe, BitBake provides the BBCLASSEXTEND variable:

```
BBCLASSEXTEND += "native"
```

If this directive is used in a recipe, it instructs BitBake to build a native variant of the software package for the build host in addition to the target variant. The mechanism behind this functionality is that BitBake executes the recipe a second time inheriting the native class. For this mechanism to work correctly, you must define the native class in a file called native.bbclass.

BBCLASSEXTEND contains a list of classes that is space-delimited, allowing you to execute the recipe as many times as you need it with different classes.

Variables or tasks contained in a recipe may need to contain different values or perform different processing steps based on what variant is currently built. That can be achieved by conditionally overriding variables or tasks. Using

```
VARIABLE_class-target = "target value"
VARIABLE_class-native = "native value"
```

assigns VARIABLE different values dependent on what variant BitBake is building. All variables and tasks that do not use the variant overrides are shared by all variants.

The variant target is implicit. There is also no class target defined. All other classes used in BBCLASSEXTEND must be defined by their respective .bbclass files.

4.10 Default Metadata

BitBake defines, uses, and relies on several default metadata objects. You find them referenced in many recipes and classes. In the following sections, we discuss this core list of variables and tasks.

Of course, OpenEmbedded, Poky, and other metadata layers add more metadata as they extend BitBake's functionality. We discuss many of those extensions and their metadata when we introduce them in the context of building a custom Linux distribution in Chapter 7, developing recipes for software packages in Chapter 8, configuring and compiling the Linux kernel in Chapter 9, and developing board support packages in Chapter 10.

4.10.1 Variables

BitBake references and uses several variables. It expects those variables to be set, or it raises an error and terminates execution. BitBake derives some of these variables internally from its current context and sets them accordingly. Others are set to default values by the bitbake.conf file. For a third category, you have to provide the settings explicitly for your project.

Internally Derived Variables

BitBake derives the values for the following variables from its current contexts and sets them accordingly:

- **FILE**: Full path to the file that BitBake is currently processing. The file can be a configuration file, a recipe, a class, and so on.
- **LAYERDIR**: BitBake sets this variable to the full path to the directory of the current layer when it processes the files of that layer.
- **TOPDIR**: BitBake sets this variable to the full path to the directory from where you have executed BitBake. BitBake expects you to either run it from the top-level directory of your build environment or explicitly set this variable to the top-level directory of your build environment, as shown earlier.

Project-Specific Variables

These variables are specific to your BitBake project. You need to set them explicitly for your project.

- **BBFILES**: Space-delimited list of paths for recipe files. The layer.conf configuration file for a layer extends this variable to add its own recipes.
- **BBLAYERS**: BitBake sets this variable to the full path to the directory of the current layer when it processes the files of that layer.
- **BBPATH**: BitBake uses this variable to locate classes (.bbclass files) in a subdirectory named classes and configuration files (.conf files) in a subdirectory called conf and subdirectories thereof. The variable contains a list of colon-delimited directory paths. Layers typically add their top-level directory to this variable: BBPATH .= ":${LAYERDIR}".

Standard Runtime Variables

The standard runtime variables are referenced by many of the BitBake modules. Hence, they must contain valid values for BitBake to operate correctly. These variables are typically initialized by the conf/bitbake.conf file. The BitBake source package provides a conf/bitbake.conf file containing default settings. If you start a BitBake project from scratch, as we did for the HelloWorld example, you can use this file as a starting point.

The OE Core metadata layer, which forms the foundation of the Poky build system, includes a conf/bitbake.conf file that initializes a much larger list of variables to meet the requirements of the many classes included with that layer. As we explore more of Poky's functionality in the coming chapters, we introduce these variables within their appropriate context.

- **B**: Full path of the directory in which BitBake builds a source package. This is typically the same directory BitBake extracts the package's source to: B = ${S}. For out-of-tree builds, B can be set to point to a different build directory.

- **BUILD_ARCH**: CPU architecture of the build host. In most cases, the value is automatically derived using BUILD-ARCH = ${@os.uname()[4])}, which returns the system's architecture on Linux systems.

- **CACHE**: Full path of the directory for the metadata cache, which typically resides inside the build environment: CACHE = ${TOPDIR}/cache. When BitBake is first run in a build environment, it parses all metadata files and recipes and creates a cache from which it reads during subsequent runs. This improves execution speed. A metadata change invalidates the cache and causes BitBake to re-create it.

- **CVSDIR**: Full path to the directory to which BitBake checks out CVS repositories. The default is for this directory to be a subdirectory of the download directory: CVSDIR = ${DL_DIR}/cvs.

- **D**: Full path to the directory to which a task such as an installation task or an image creation task places its output. For example, an installation task using make install references this variable for the installation path.

- **DEPENDS**: The variable describes package dependencies as a space-delimited list of package names.

- **DEPLOY_DIR**: Full path to the base directory where BitBake places all the files for deployment, such as target images, package feeds, and license manifests. By default, this directory resides inside the build environment: DEPLOY_DIR = ${TMPDIR}/deploy.

- **DEPLOY_DIR_IMAGE**: Full path to the directory to which BitBake copies target binary images. It typically points to a subdirectory of DEPLOY_DIR: DEPLOY_DIR_IMAGE = ${DEPLOY_DIR}/images.

- **DL_DIR**: Full path to the download directory. The default setting places this directory inside the build environment: DL_DIR = ${TMPDIR}/downloads. To avoid downloading the same source files multiple times and taking up time and disk space when working with more than one build environment, it is recommended to set the variable to a path outside a build environment.

- **FILE_DIRNAME**: Full path to the directory that contains the file that BitBake is currently processing. The value is automatically derived using FILE_DIRNAME = ${@os.path.dirname(bb.data.getVar('FILE'))}.

- **FILESDIR**: Full path to a directory where BitBake looks for local files. BitBake uses this variable only if it cannot find the file in any of the directories listed in FILESPATH. The most common use case for this variable is in append files.

- **FILESPATH**: This variable contains a colon-separated list of full directory paths that are searched by BitBake's local file fetcher for matching local files. The default setting is FILESPATH = "${FILE_DIRNAME}/${PF}:${FILE_DIRNAME}/${P}:${FILE_DIRNAME}/${PN}:${FILE_DIRNAME}/files:${FILE_DIRNAME}".

- **GITDIR**: Full path to the directory to which BitBake checks out Git repositories. The default is for this directory to be a subdirectory of the download directory: GITDIR = ${DL_DIR}/git.

- **MKTEMPCMD**: Command that BitBake uses to create temporary files: MKTMPCOMMAND = "mktemp -q ${TMPBASE}".

- **MKTEMPDIRCMD**: Command that BitBake uses to create temporary directories: MKTMPCOMMAND = "mktemp -d -q ${TMPBASE}".

- **OVERRIDES**: Colon-delimited priority list of conditional overrides. BitBake processes the list from right to left, so that the ones listed later take precedence.

- **P**: Package name and version concatenated with a dash: P = "${PN}-${PV}".

- **PERSISTENT_DIR**: Full path to the directory where BitBake stores files persistently. The default setting is PERSISTENT_DIR = "${TOPDIR}/cache". The CACHE and the PERSISTENT_DIR variables are used interchangeably. Either one of them must be set. If PERSISTENT_DIR is not set, BitBake falls back to CACHE.

- **PF**: Package name, version, and revision concatenated with dashes: PF = "${PN}-${PV}-${PR}".

- **PN**: Package name derived from the recipe filename.

- **PR**: Package revision derived from the recipe name or explicitly set.

- **PROVIDES**: Space-delimited list of names declaring what a package provides. Other recipes can use these names to declare their dependencies on this package.

- **PV**: Package version derived from the recipe filename or explicitly set.

- **S**: Full path to the directory where BitBake places the unpacked sources. By default, this is a subdirectory of the working directory for the package: S = "${WORKDIR}/${P}".

- **SRC_URI**: Download URI for source packages.

- **SRCREV**: Source revision for use with downloads from SCM.

- **SVNDIR**: Full path to the directory to which BitBake checks out Subversion repositories. The default is for this directory to be a subdirectory of the download directory: GITDIR = ${DL_DIR}/svn.

- **T**: Full path to a directory where BitBake stores temporary files, such as task code and task logs, when processing a package recipe. By default, this directory resides inside the package's work directory: T = "${WORKDIR}/tmp".

- **TARGET_ARCH**: CPU architecture for which BitBake is building.

- **TMPBASE**: Full path of a directory that BitBake uses to create temporary files and directories with the MKTMPCMD and MKTEMPDIRCMD commands. BitBake modules, classes, and tasks set this variable according to their requirements.

- **TMPDIR**: Full path to the top-level directory where BitBake places all the build output, such as package builds, root filesystem stages, image, and package feeds. It typically resides inside the build environment: TMPDIR = "${TOPDIR}/tmp". The choice of name for this variable and its default setting is a little unfortunate. While the files and directories created within TMPDIR are temporary in a sense that BitBake can always re-create them, the directory actually contains all the build output and artifacts. That makes the directory actually more important than its name suggests.

- **WORKDIR**: Full path to the directory where BitBake builds a package and also stores all log information related to the package's build progress. The default setting is WORKDIR = "${TMPDIR}/work/${PF}".

As you can see, many of the variables reference other variables, particularly the paths for files and directories. This creates a very flexible architecture that lets you easily customize your build environments by simply changing a few variables in a single configuration file.

4.10.2 Tasks

The BitBake code also includes a default implementation of the base class provided by the base.bbclass. You can use this class as a starting point for your own BitBake-based build system. The OE Core metadata layer, of course, provides an extended base class. BitBake's default base.bbclass provides the following tasks:

- **build**: This is the default task that BitBake uses when executing a recipe unless another task is set by the variable BB_DEFAULT_CLASS. The default base class does not actually implement anything useful to execute. You need to either override it in your recipes or use it as an anchor for other tasks, as we did in our HelloWorld example.

- **listtasks**: Executing this task with any target shows all the tasks that are applicable to the target. That includes the tasks that the target's recipe defines as well as any tasks the recipe inherits from classes. Note that the tasks must be listed in the order of their task hashes and not alphabetically or in the order of their execution.

4.11 Summary

This chapter presented an overview of BitBake, the build engine behind OpenEmbedded and Poky.

- BitBake is jointly developed by OpenEmbedded and the Yocto Project as a core component of the OpenEmbedded build system, shared by both projects. Yocto Project releases of the Poky reference distribution include a version of BitBake that matches Poky's metadata for the particular release.

- BitBake requires an execution or build environment with certain metadata variables to be set correctly. Poky includes shell scripts to correctly set up and initialize build environments.

- BitBake metadata distinguishes between variables and executable metadata or functions. Metadata functions can be implemented as shell or Python code. Tasks are specially declared metadata functions that are executed by BitBake as part of the build process of a target or that can be explicitly invoked from the BitBake command line.

- Metadata is organized into configuration files, recipes, classes, append files, and include files.
- BitBake's metadata syntax provides a variety of expressions to manipulate variable contents. Variables may contain single values or lists of values separated by a delimiter.
- Conditional variable assignment and variable appending and prepending allow overriding variables based on the context. The OVERRIDES variable contains the priority list of conditions.
- Metadata functions implemented as shell code can access metadata variables directly, whereas Python functions need to access them via the BitBake data dictionary.
- Return values from Python metadata functions can directly be assigned to metadata variables.
- BitBake's dependency handling allows the declaration of dependencies on the package level. To optimize parallel execution, BitBake enforces the dependencies on the task level.
- Symbolic names for packages allow packages to declare dependencies based on the provided functionality rather than the name of the implementing package. The PREFERRED_PROVIDER variable allows the selection of the implementing package.
- Packages may provide multiple recipes to build different versions of the package. BitBake always builds the latest package with the highest version number unless a different version is specified by the PREFERRED_VERSION variable.
- Variants or class extensions provide a mechanism for building the same package multiple times for different applications, such target or build host, without rewriting the entire recipe.

4.12 References

BitBake's source package includes documentation in DocBook format that can be formatted for HTML or PDF output. Online documentation is available at www.yoctoproject.org/docs/2.0/bitbake-user-manual/bitbake-user-manual.html. The ultimate BitBake documentation is, of course, its source code.

5

Troubleshooting

As a software developer, you are well aware that it is never a question of *if* but *when* there is an issue with building software. Troubleshooting failures of a complex build system can be a daunting task. Failures can be rooted in many different areas of the build system: the code in recipes and classes, configuration file settings, cross-development, the software package to be built, packaging, and more. It always comes down to

- Locating and identifying the cause of the failure, and
- Finding and applying a solution

Having the right tools at hand and knowing how to use them effectively saves a lot of time and effort for correctly locating and identifying the root cause of a problem. The OpenEmbedded build system provides a set of tools that assist you in finding the problem that causes your build failure. Finding a solution for the problem, however, can be even more challenging. Due to the potentially large variety of the problems and their origins, there is no single and simple answer to how to solve a build problem. Problem solving is a lot about experience in recognizing patterns in issues and modifying and applying solutions found for similar issues. We don't discourage you from problem solving, but we encourage you to set realistic expectations. Depending on your experience in software development, you find solutions to some problems rather easily, while others present a greater challenge. Nevertheless, chances are that you are not the only one experiencing a particular problem. The Internet and its search engines make it much easier for software developers to find solutions for almost anything.

The following sections explain the various debugging tools provided by the Open-Embedded build system and how to use them.

5.1 Logging

BitBake logs all events occurring during the build process. The events logged by BitBake are

- Debug statements inserted into executable metadata
- Output from any command executed by tasks and other code
- Error messages emitted by any command executed by tasks and other code

All log messages are routed to various log files from which they can be retrieved. BitBake creates log files for every task that it executes as well as for its own main build process. All output sent to stdout or stderr by any command executed by BitBake tasks and other code is redirected to the log files. During normal operation BitBake does not show any logging output while running unless there is a warning or error condition.

5.1.1 Log Files

BitBake maintains separate log files for all of its processes. That includes its cooker process, which is the main build process, as well as for every task of every recipe. The cooker process spawns a separate process for each task it runs.

General Log Files

BitBake stores all general log files, such as the cooker's look file, in the directory pointed to by the LOG_DIR variable. By default, this directory is a subdirectory called log inside the directory for the temporary build files:

```
LOG_DIR = "${TMPDIR}/log"
```

Inside that directory, you find a subdirectory for each BitBake process, such as cooker. The log files are further subdivided by the target machine. For example, if you are building for the qemux86 machine, the cooker subdirectory contains a qemux86 subdirectory that contains the actual log files. Although this setup requires some effort navigating through a tree of directories, it more easily allows you to find the relevant log file.

BitBake names the log files using the timestamp at the time the process was started, effectively maintaining a history of log files. Having a history of log files and comparing files from subsequent builds to each other can help you track down build failures effectively. Rather than using local time, BitBake always uses Coordinated Universal Time (UTC) for its timestamps, making them easily comparable when utilizing remote build servers in different time zones.

The cooker log file contains all the logging output that BitBake also writes to the console when running. Listing 5-1 shows a short cooker log file for just an image from prebuilt packages.

Listing 5-1 **Cooker Log File**

```
NOTE: Resolving any missing task queue dependencies

Build Configuration:
BB_VERSION        = "1.21.1"
BUILD_SYS         = "x86_64-linux"
NATIVELSBSTRING   = "Fedora-18"
TARGET_SYS        = "i586-poky-linux"
MACHINE           = "qemux86"
DISTRO            = "poky"
DISTRO_VERSION    = "1.5+snapshot-20140210"
TUNE_FEATURES     = "m32 i586"
TARGET_FPU        = ""
meta
meta-yocto
meta-yocto-bsp    = "master:095bb006c3dbbfbdfa05f13d8d7b50e2a5ab2af0"


NOTE: Preparing runqueue
NOTE: Executing SetScene Tasks
NOTE: Executing RunQueue Tasks
NOTE: Running noexec task 2051 of 2914 (ID: 4, /develop/yocto/yocto-git/poky/meta/
recipes-core/images/core-image-minimal.bb, do_fetch)
NOTE: Running noexec task 2052 of 2914 (ID: 0, /develop/yocto/yocto-git/poky/meta/
recipes-core/images/core-image-minimal.bb, do_unpack)
NOTE: Running noexec task 2053 of 2914 (ID: 1, /develop/yocto/yocto-git/poky/meta/
recipes-core/images/core-image-minimal.bb, do_patch)
NOTE: Running noexec task 2910 of 2914 (ID: 9, /develop/yocto/yocto-git/poky/meta/
recipes-core/images/core-image-minimal.bb, do_package_write)
NOTE: Running task 2911 of 2914 (ID: 8, develop/yocto/yocto-git/poky/meta/recipes-
core/images/core-image-minimal.bb, do_populate_lic)
NOTE: Running task 2912 of 2914 (ID: 7, develop/yocto/yocto-git/poky/meta/recipes-
core/images/core-image-minimal.bb, do_rootfs)
NOTE: recipe core-image-minimal-1.0-r0: task do_populate_lic: Started
NOTE: recipe core-image-minimal-1.0-r0: task do_populate_lic: Succeeded
NOTE: recipe core-image-minimal-1.0-r0: task do_rootfs: Started
NOTE: recipe core-image-minimal-1.0-r0: task do_rootfs: Succeeded
NOTE: Running noexec task 2914 of 2914 (ID: 12, /develop/yocto/yocto-git/poky/
meta/recipes-core/images/core-image-minimal.bb, do_build)
NOTE: Tasks Summary: Attempted 2914 tasks of which 2907 didn't need to be rerun
and all succeeded.
```

One of the important pieces of information contained in the cooker log file is the build configuration, which tells you what settings this build used. That information is very valuable when debugging issues of the "it worked yesterday, why does it not work today?" kind. Frequently, a change in configuration can cause a build to fail, and comparing cooker log files from a successful build to the one of the failed build may help track down the issue. The following variables make up the build configuration listed at the beginning of a cooker log file:

- **BB_VERSION**: The BitBake version number. BitBake evolves together with the metadata layers. Using newer versions of metadata layers, such as OpenEmbedded

Core with an older version of BitBake, may cause issues. That is one of the reasons Poky packages the core metadata layers with BitBake. BitBake is, however, backwards compatible, allowing you to use a newer version with older metadata layers.

- **BUILD_SYS**: Type of the build system. The variable is defined in `bitbake.conf` as `BUILD_SYS = "${BUILD_ARCH}${BUILD_VENDOR}-${BUILD_OS}"`. `BUILD_ARCH` contains the output of `uname -m`, `BUILD_OS` contains the output of `uname -s`, and `BUILD_VENDOR` is a custom string that is commonly empty.

- **NATIVELSBSTRING**: Distributor ID and release number concatenated with a dash as obtained by the `lsb_release` command.

- **TARGET_SYS**: Type of the target system. This variable is defined in `bitbake.conf` as `TARGET_SYS = "${TARGET_ARCH}${TARGET_VENDOR}${@['-' + d.getVar('TARGET_OS', True), ''][d.getVar('TARGET_OS', True) == ('' or 'custom')]}"`.

- **MACHINE**: The target machine BitBake is building for.

- **DISTRO**: The name of the target distribution.

- **DISTRO_VERSION**: The version of the target distribution.

- **TUNE_FEATURES**: Tuning parameters for the target CPU architecture.

- **TARGET_FPU**: Identification for the floating-point unit of the target architecture.

- **meta[-xxxx]**: Branch and commit ID for the metadata layers if they were checked out from a Git repository.

For the example of Listing 5-1, the author has used Poky checked out from the Yocto Project's Git repository on a Fedora 18 build host using 64-bit architecture on x86. The target system is a 32-bit Linux system built for QEMU using the Poky distribution policy.

Task Log Files

BitBake creates a log file for every task it runs for every recipe. By default, BitBake stores task log files in the directory pointed to by the `T` variable. By default, this directory is a subdirectory of the work directory of the recipe:

```
T = "${WORKDIR}/temp"
```

That is the case for all tasks but the *clean* tasks that clean a working directory. Since running clean tasks eventually also deletes the work directory and its subdirectories, the `T` variable is conditionally set to

```
T_task-clean = "${LOGDIR}/cleanlogs/${PN}"
```

for clean tasks. The log files are sorted into subdirectories named according to the package name of the recipe they are executed for.

Log files for tasks are named `log.do_<taskname>.<pid>`, where `pid` is the process ID of the task when it was run by BitBake. The process ID is used to distinguish task logs of multiple executions of the same task. That makes it straightforward to compare before and after scenarios and compare successful task execution to failed execution. Larger process numbers typically mean more current runs. A symbolic link named log .do_<taskname> points to the log file containing the log output of the most current run.

Unless there is incorrect syntax in a metadata file, virtually all build failures are related to the execution of a task of a recipe. BitBake offers a great deal of help when locating the log file for the failed task by printing its full path to the console together with the error message. Listing 5-2 shows a failing task for a recipe that builds the nano text editor.

Listing 5-2 **Task Failure**

```
NOTE: Resolving any missing task queue dependencies

Build Configuration:
BB_VERSION        = "1.21.1"
BUILD_SYS         = "x86_64-linux"
NATIVELSBSTRING   = "Fedora-18"
TARGET_SYS        = "i586-poky-linux"
MACHINE           = "qemux86"
DISTRO            = "poky"
DISTRO_VERSION    = "1.5+snapshot-20140211"
TUNE_FEATURES     = "m32 i586"
TARGET_FPU        = ""
meta-mylayer      = "<unknown>:<unknown>"
meta
meta-yocto
meta-yocto-bsp    = "master:095bb006c3dbbfbdfa05f13d8d7b50e2a5ab2af0"

NOTE: Preparing runqueue
NOTE: Executing SetScene Tasks
NOTE: Executing RunQueue Tasks
ERROR: This autoconf log indicates errors, it looked at host include and/or
library paths while determining system capabilities.
Rerun configure task after fixing this. The path was
'/develop/yocto/yocto-git/x86/tmp/work/i586-poky-linux/nano/2.3.1-r0/nano-2.3.1'
ERROR: Function failed: do_qa_configure
ERROR: Logfile of failure stored in:
.../tmp/work/i586-poky-linux/nano/2.3.1-r0/temp/log.do_configure.17865
ERROR: Task 5 (.../meta-mylayer/recipes-apps/nano/nano_2.3.1.bb,
do_configure) failed with exit code '1'
NOTE: Tasks Summary: Attempted 550 tasks of which 545 didn't need to be rerun and
1 failed.
No currently running tasks (550 of 558)

Summary: 1 task failed:
  .../meta-mylayer/recipes-apps/nano/nano_2.3.1.bb, do_configure
Summary: There were 3 ERROR messages shown, returning a non-zero exit code.
```

Lines starting with ERROR contain the relevant information on the build failure, such as a hint to the root cause of the problem, the task that failed, and the complete path to the log file. You can simply use the path to the log file to view it in your preferred editor for additional information on why the task failed. Even if you clear the console or close its window, you can always retrieve this output later from the cooker log file.

5.1.2 Using Logging Statements

One of the more commonly used, if not the most commonly used, methods for debugging in programming is inserting debug messages into the code that allow following the execution path and examining data by printing variable content.

BitBake provides several levels to indicate the severity of messages:

- **Plain**: Logs the message exactly as passed without any additional information.
- **Debug**: Logs the message prefixed with DEBUG:. The logging function also expects a numeric parameter between 1 and 3 indicating the debug level. However, only for Python functions is the debug level actually evaluated. For shell functions, all messages are logged regardless of the debug level.
- **Note**: Logs the message prefixed with NOTE:. It is used to inform the user about a condition or information to be aware of.
- **Warn**: Logs the message prefixed with WARNING:. Warnings indicate problems that eventually should be taken care of by the user; however, they do not cause a build failure.
- **Error**: Logs the message prefixed with ERROR:. Errors indicate problems that need to be resolved to successfully complete the build. However, the build can continue until there are no tasks left to build.
- **Fatal**: Logs the message prefixed with FATAL:. Fatal conditions cause BitBake to halt the build process right after the message has been logged.

All messages are written into the respective log file dependent on the context. Note, warn, error, and fatal messages are also outputted to the console. Debug messages are written to the console only if BitBake's debug level is equal to or higher than the level of the message. BitBake debug levels are set by adding the -D parameter to the BitBake command line.

```
bitbake -D <target>
bitbake -DD <target>
bitbake -DDD <target>
```

select debug level 1, 2, or 3, respectively. Plain messages are never written to the console.

Log messages can be inserted into any function defined in files that support executable metadata: that is, recipes, append files, and classes. For both Python and shell executable metadata, logging functions that match the log levels are provided (see Table 5-1).

The Python functions are implemented as part of the BitBake library. You can find the implementation in the file bitbake/lib/bb/__init__.py. BitBake's Python logging utilizes and extends the Python logging classes. The file bitbake/lib/bb/msg.py provides formatting and filtering classes for the log messages. In particular, the class

Table 5-1 **Log Functions**

Log Level	Python Function	Shell Function
PLAIN	bb.plain(message)	bbplain message
DEBUG	bb.debug(level, message)	bbdebug level message
NOTE	bb.note(message)	bbnote message
WARN	bb.warn(message)	bbwarn message
ERROR	bb.error(message)	bberror message
FATAL	bb.fatal(message)	bbfatal message

BBLogFormatter provides colorizing for the different message levels. If colorizing is enabled, warning messages appear in yellow, and error and fatal messages are printed in red.

The shell functions are implemented by the logging.bbclass, which is provided by the OE Core metadata layer.

The pseudocode in Listings 5-3 and 5-4 illustrate the use of the logging functions for Python and shell executable metadata.

Listing 5-3 **Python Logging Example**

```
python do_something() {
    bb.debug(2, "Starting to do something...")
    if special_condition:
        bb.note("Met special condition.")
    bb.debug(2, "Processing input")
    if warning_condition:
        bb.warn("Upper limit out of bounds, adjusting to maximum.")
    if error_condition:
        bb.error("Recoverable error, proceeding, but needs to be fixed.")
    if fatal_condition:
        bb.fatal("Division by 0, unable to proceed, exiting.")
    bb.plain("The result of doing something is 'mostly nothing'.")
    bb.debug(2, "Done with doing something.")
```

Listing 5-4 **Shell Logging Example**

```
do_something() {
    bbdebug 2 "Starting to do something..."
    if [ special_condition ]; then
        bbnote "Met special condition."
    fi
    bbdebug 2 "Processing input"
    if [ warning_condition ]; then
        bbwarn "Upper limit out of bounds, adjusting to maximum."
    fi
    if [ error_condition ]; then
        bberror "Recoverable error, proceeding, but needs to be fixed."
    fi
```

```
if [ fatal_condition ]; then
    bbfatal "Division by 0, unable to proceed, exiting."
fi
bbplain "The result of doing something is 'mostly nothing'."
bb.debug 2 "Done with doing something."
```

It is desirable and encouraged that you use logging messages in your own classes and recipes where useful. Messages that indicate the processing progress should use the debug level. Messages that indicate warnings and errors should use the appropriate levels. Typically, you should not use the fatal level but instead use the error level, which gives BitBake the chance to complete the processing of other tasks running in parallel, clean up, and leave the build environment in a consistent state. Using fatal causes BitBake to cease execution immediately, which potentially could leave a build environment in a state from which BitBake may not be able to recover automatically on subsequent execution.

5.2 Task Execution

For any given recipe, BitBake executes a series of tasks in a particular sequence as defined by the dependencies. Using the command listtasks for a recipe gives you a list of all the tasks that are defined for that recipe (see Listing 5-5).

Listing 5-5   Listing Tasks for a Recipe

```
user@buildhost:~$ bitbake busybox -c listtasks

[... omitted for brevity ...]

NOTE: Preparing runqueue
NOTE: Executing RunQueue Tasks
do_build                      Default task for a recipe - depends on all
                              other normal tasks required to 'build' a
                              recipe
do_checkuri                   Validates the SRC_URI value
do_checkuriall                Validates the SRC_URI value for all recipes
                              required to build a target
do_clean                      Removes all output files for a target
do_cleanall                   Removes all output files, shared state
                              cache, and downloaded source files for a
                              target
do_cleansstate                Removes all output files and shared state
                              cache for a target
do_compile                    Compiles the source in the compilation
                              directory
do_compile_ptest_base         Compiles the runtime test suite included in
                              the software being built
do_configure                  Configures the source by enabling and
                              disabling any build-time and configuration
                              options for the software being built
do_configure_ptest_base       Configures the runtime test suite included
                              in the software being built
```

```
do_devshell                    Starts a shell with the environment set up
                               for development/debugging

[... omitted for brevity ...]
```

The output is a list of all tasks in alphabetical order with short descriptions of what each task does. However, it does not provide you with information about which tasks are run during a regular build process and in which order they are run.

As we saw in Chapter 3, "OpenEmbedded Build System," the build process for any software package pretty much follows these standard steps:

1. **Fetch**: Retrieve the package source code archives for download sites, or clone source repositories as well as all applicable patches and other local files.

2. **Unpack**: Extract source code, patches, and other files from their archives.

3. **Patch**: Apply the patches.

4. **Configure**: Prepare the sources for building within the target environment.

5. **Build**: Compile the sources, archive the objects into libraries, and/or link the objects into executable programs.

6. **Install**: Copy binaries and auxiliary files to their target directories of an emulated system environment.

7. **Package**: Create the installation packages, including any manifests, according to the chosen package management systems.

You can follow the build chain by analyzing the task dependencies created by the classes in the OE Core metadata layer by searching for the keyword addtask through the class files:

```
$ grep addtask *.bbclass
```

Using the output, you can determine the task dependencies (see Listing 5-6).

Listing 5-6 **Task Dependencies**

```
base.bbclass:          addtask fetch
base.bbclass:          addtask unpack after do_fetch
patch.bbclass:         addtask patch after do_unpack
base.bbclass:          addtask configure after do_patch
license.bbclass:       addtask populate_lic after do_patch before do_build
base.bbclass:          addtask compile after do_configure
base.bbclass:          addtask install after do_compile
staging.bbclass:       addtask populate_sysroot after do_install
package.bbclass:       addtask package before do_build after do_install
package_deb.bbclass:   addtask package_write_deb before do_package_write
                       after do_packagedata do_package
package_ipk.bbclass:   addtask package_write_ipk before do_package_write
                       after do_packagedata do_package
```

```
package_rpm.bbclass:     addtask package_write_rpm before do_package_write
                         after do_packagedata do_package
package.bbclass:         addtask package_write before do_build
                         after do_package
base.bbclass:            addtask build after do_populate_sysroot
```

For Listing 5-6, we used the tasks that apply to the typical user space software package. Special packages such as the kernel use a different process. We also ordered the list by the execution sequence and omitted tasks that are not relevant for the typical package build process.

5.2.1 Executing Specific Tasks

Executing tasks individually for a given recipe and making adjustments in between consecutive executions can be very helpful when debugging build failures.

Using

```
$ bitbake <target> -c <task>
```

executes `<task>` for the given `<target>` recipe. A common scenario is that you build a package for the first time, discover an error when compiling the package, make adjustments to the source code or modify settings, and then run the `compile` task again to verify whether your changes have resolved the problem:

```
$ bitbake busybox
[...]
[make some changes to the source code]
$ bitbake busybox -c compile
```

Rerunning tasks individually allows you to make changes at any stage of the build process and then execute only the task that is affected by the changes. Because BitBake creates log files for each execution of the task, distinguished by the process ID, you easily can analyze the effects of your modifications.

Once your changes have the desired outcome, you need to integrate them with the regular build process. Since modifications made inside the build directory of a package are not permanent and are wiped out when cleaning the build directory, you have to add them to the build process by modifying the recipe, creating an append file, including additional patches, and so forth.

5.2.2 Task Script Files

For each execution of a task, BitBake creates a script file that contains the commands it executes when running the task. The task script files are located in the same directory as the task log files:

```
T = "${WORKDIR}/temp"
```

Task script files are named

```
run.do_<taskname>.<pid>
```

The `<pid>` extension is used to distinguish script files for the same task from multiple executions. The file `run.do_<taskname>` without a process ID extension is a symbolic link that points to the script file that BitBake executed for the most recent run of the task.

Script files for Python tasks are executed from within the BitBake environment from which they inherit and access the BitBake data dictionary. Script files for shell tasks contain the entire environment and are executed by spawning a process. In many cases, they can be run directly from the command line.

The file `log.task_order` contains a list of the tasks and their corresponding script files together with the process IDs for the most recent execution.

5.3 Analyzing Metadata

The entire BitBake build process is driven by metadata. Executable metadata provide the process steps, which are configured through values of the different variables. Many of these variables are dependent on the execution context of the particular recipe. For example, variables such as `SRC_URI` are defined by every recipe. Many variables also reference other variables, which are expanded within the execution context. Conditional variable setting and appending are powerful concepts to dynamically adjust the execution context but also add complexity when debugging build failures.

From simple typos in variable names and settings to incorrect variable expansion and conditional assignments, there are many opportunities for the build process to fail or to produce incorrect output. Hence, it is important to be able to analyze variable settings the build system uses within different contexts. The command

```
$ bitbake -e
```

prints the entire data dictionary for the global BitBake environment to the console. This is useful to examine the default settings before they get potentially overridden by the particular recipe context. Using the command with a target shows the data dictionary entries for that particular target:

```
$ bitbake -e <target>
```

A drawback of this command is that it lists variables as well as functions, since functions are nothing else but executable metadata. BitBake stores variables and functions in the same data dictionary. Listing the code of every function makes the output rather cumbersome to analyze. Unfortunately, neither BitBake nor OE Core provides functionality to list only the variables. However, that can easily be added by including the code in Listing 5-7 into a class file.

Listing 5-7 showvars Task

```
addtask showvars
do_showvars[nostamp] = "1"
python do_showvars() {
        # emit only the metadata that are variables and not functions
        isfunc = lambda key: bool(d.getVarFlag(key, 'func'))
        vars = sorted((key for key in bb.data.keys(d) \
                if not key.startswith('__')))
        for var in vars:
                if not isfunc(var):
                        try:
                                val = d.getVar(var, True)
                        except Exception as exc:
                                bb.plain('Expansion of %s threw %s: %s' % \
                                        (var, exc.__class__.__name__, str(exc)))
                        bb.plain('%s="%s"' % (var, val))
}
```

When used with

```
$ bitbake <target> -c showvars
```

the task lists all the variables but not the functions of the target's execution environment in alphabetical order.

5.4 Development Shell

Build failures that originate from compiling and linking of sources to objects, libraries, and executables are challenging to debug when cross-building. You cannot just change to the source directory, type make, examine the error messages, and correct the issue. Build environments for software packages are typically configured for native builds on the host system. A cross-build environment requires a different and often rather complicated setup for tools, header files, libraries, and more to correctly operate.

The Poky reference distribution creates cross-build environments for its own BitBake build process. Through the command devshell, it can also provide cross-build environments in a shell to the developer. The command

```
$ bitbake <target> -c devshell
```

launches a terminal with a cross-build environment for target. The setup of the cross-build environment exactly matches the one that Poky is using for its own builds. Within that shell you can use the development tools as you would for a native build on your build host. The environment references the correct cross-compilers as well as any header files, libraries, and other files required to build the software package.

If any of the dependencies of the software package you are targeting with the devshell command have not been built, Poky builds them beforehand.

If you are using BitBake from a graphical user interface with window manager, it automatically tries to determine the terminal program to use and open it in a new window. The variable OE_TERMINAL controls what terminal program to use. It is typically set to auto. You can set it to one of the supported terminal programs in the conf/ local.conf file of your build environment. The terminal program must be installed on your development host. You can disable the use of the devshell altogether by setting OE_TERMINAL = "none".

5.5 Dependency Graphs

In Chapter 4, "BitBake Build Engine," we saw how packages can declare direct build-time and runtime dependencies on other packages using the DEPENDS and RDEPENDS variables in their recipes. You can easily realize how this practice can lead to long and complex chains of dependencies.

BitBake, of course, must be able to resolve these dependency chains to build the packages in the correct order. Using its dependency resolver, BitBake can also create dependency graphs for analysis and debugging.

BitBake creates dependency graphs using the DOT plain text graph description language. DOT provides a simple way of describing undirected and directed graphs with nodes and edges in a language that can be read by humans and computer programs alike. Programs from the Graphviz[1] package as well as many others can read DOT files and render them into graphical representations.

To create dependency graphs for a target, invoke BitBake with the -g or --graphviz options. Using

```
$ bitbake -g <target>
```

creates the following dependency files for target:

- **pn-buildlist**: This file is not a DOT file but contains the list of packages in reverse build order starting with the target.
- **pn-depends.dot**: Contains the package dependencies in a directed graph declaring the nodes first and then the edges.
- **package-depends.dot**: Essentially the same as pn-depends.dot but declares the edges for a node right after the node. This file may be easier to read by humans because it groups the edges ending on a node with the node.
- **task-depends.dot**: Declares the dependencies on the task level.

BitBake also provides a built-in user interface for package dependencies, the dependency explorer. You can launch the dependency explorer with

```
$ bitbake -g -u depexp <target>
```

The dependency explorer lets you analyze build-time and runtime dependencies as well as reverse dependencies (the packages that depend on that package) in a graphical user interface, as shown in Figure 5-1.

---

1. www.graphviz.org

Figure 5-1   Dependency explorer

If the Graphviz package is installed on your development system, you can use it to create visual renditions of the dependency graphs:

```
$ dot -Tpng pn-depends.dot -o pn-depends.png
```

creates a PNG image from the DOT file.

5.6 Debugging Layers

BitBake's layer architecture provides an elegant way of organizing recipes. However, it also introduces complexity, particularly when multiple layers provide the same recipe and/or modify the same recipe with append files.

The bitbake-layers tool provides several functions that help with analyzing and debugging layers used by a build environment. Invoking

```
$ bitbake-layers help
```

provides a list of commands that can be used with the tool:

- **help**: Without any argument or by specifying `help` as argument, the tool shows a list of the available commands. If you provide a command, it shows additional help for that command.

- **show-layers**: Displays a list of the layers used by the build environment together with their path and priority.

```
$ bitbake-layers show-layers
layer                    path                                    priority
==========================================================================
meta                     /path/to/poky/meta                          5
meta-yocto               /path/to/poky/meta-yocto                     5
meta-yocto-bsp           /path/to/poky/meta-yocto-bsp                 5
meta-mylayer             /path/to/meta-mylayer                        1
```

- **show-recipes**: Displays a list of recipes in alphabetical order including the layer providing it.

```
$ bitbake-layers show-recipes
Parsing recipes..done.
=== Available recipes: ===
acl:
  meta                   2.2.52
acpid:
  meta                   1.0.10
adt-installer:
  meta                   0.2.0
alsa-lib:
  meta                   1.0.27.2
alsa-state:
  meta                   0.2.0
alsa-tools:
  meta                   1.0.27
[...]
```

- **show-overlayed**: Displays a list of overlaid recipes. A recipe is overlaid if another recipe with the same name exists in a different layer.

```
$ bitbake-layers show-overlayed
Parsing recipes..done.
=== Overlayed recipes ===
mtd-utils:
  meta                   1.5.0
  meta-mylayer           1.4.9
```

When building an overlaid recipe, BitBake issues a warning and builds the recipe from the layer with the highest priority.

- **show-appends**: Displays a list of recipes with the files appending them. The appending files are shown in the order they are applied.

```
$ bitbake-layers show-appends
Parsing recipes..done.
=== Appended recipes ===
alsa-state.bb:
  /.../meta-yocto-bsp/recipes-bsp/alsa-state/alsa-state.bbappend
psplash_git.bb:
  /.../meta-yocto/recipes-core/psplash/psplash_git.bbappend
[...]
```

- **show-cross-depends**: Displays a list of all recipes that are dependent on metadata in other layers.

```
$ bitbake-layers show-cross-depends
Parsing recipes..done.
meta-yocto/recipes-core/tiny-init/tiny-init.bb RDEPENDS
          meta/recipes-core/busybox/busybox_1.22.1.bb
meta-yocto/recipes-core/tiny-init/tiny-init.bb inherits
          meta/classes/base.bbclass
meta-yocto/recipes-core/tiny-init/tiny-init.bb inherits
          meta/classes/patch.bbclass
meta-yocto/recipes-core/tiny-init/tiny-init.bb inherits
          meta/classes/terminal.bbclass
```

- **flatten <directory>**: Flattens the layer hierarchy by resolving recipe overlays and appends and writing the output into a single-layer directory provided by the parameter directory. Several rules apply:

  - If the layers contain overlaid recipes, the recipe from the layer with the highest priority is used. If the layers have the same priority, then the order of the layers in the BBLAYERS variable of the conf/bblayers.conf file of the build environment determine which recipe is used.

  - If multiple layers contain non-recipe files (such as images, patches, or similar) with the same name in the same subdirectory, they are overwritten by the one from the layer with the highest priority.

  - The conf/layer.conf file from the first layer listed in the BBLAYERS variable in conf/bblayers.conf of the build environment is used.

  - The contents of the append files are simply added to the respective recipe according to the layer priority or their order in the BBLAYERS variable if layers appending the same recipe have the same priority.

5.7 Summary

This chapter introduced a variety of tools provided by the OpenEmbedded build system to assist with troubleshooting build failures. Isolating the root cause of a problem is only the first step. The second step is finding a solution, which can be even more challenging. However, in many cases, other developers may have encountered the same or a similar problem, and searching the Internet frequently produces one or more discussions about the problem and potential solutions.

- Log files are a good starting point to identify the area of failure. Task log files contain the entire output of the commands a task executes.

- Inserting your own log messages into recipes and classes can help in pinpointing build failures.

- Executing specific tasks multiple times allows for comparing results. Task log files are not overwritten by consecutive runs.

- Printing metadata shows variables within their task contexts, including variable expansions and conditional assignments.
- The development shell allows execution of `make` targets within the same cross-build environment that BitBake uses.
- Dependency graphs support tracing build failures due to unresolved dependencies between software packages.
- The bitbake-layers utility provides a set of functions assisting with debugging build environments using multiple layers.

Linux System Architecture

In the previous chapters, we introduced the core concepts and components of the Yocto Project and the OpenEmbedded build system. Before we explore in detail how we can build our own custom Linux distributions with the Yocto Project, it is time to take a step back and look at what makes up a Linux system.

Understanding the architecture of a Linux system provides the context for the methods employed by OpenEmbedded Core (OE Core) to create the various system components, such as root filesystem images, kernel images, and bootloaders.

We start with a look at the anatomy of a Linux system and then break it down into its components.

6.1 Linux or GNU/Linux?

You may have noticed that in some contexts, a Linux OS is referred to as *Linux* and in others to as *GNU/Linux*. The reason behind this distinction is that the name Linux, strictly speaking, refers only to the Linux kernel as the foundation or core of an operating system.

For an operating system to be useful, many more applications and libraries are required—development tools, compilers, editors, shells, utilities, and more—that are not part of the kernel. A large variety of those applications are provided by the GNU Project started by Richard Stallman in 1984. Probably the best-known tools from the GNU Project are the GCC compiler, the GLIBC library and the EMACS editor. Less known about the GNU Project is that it also includes an operating system kernel called *Hurd*.[1]

---

1. https://www.gnu.org/software/hurd/hurd.html

Because virtually all Linux OSes used for desktop and server applications include many of the GNU Project software packages, many consider the name *GNU/Linux* a more appropriate name for the operating system, while *Linux* is appropriate when referring just to the kernel.

Embedded Linux OSes typically do not include a large variety of tools and applications, since they are dedicated to specific use cases. Commonly, in addition to the specific applications necessary for the embedded device, you find a limited set of standard tools such as a shell, an editor, and a few utilities. Frequently, that set of applications is provided in a single toolbox such as BusyBox.

6.2 Anatomy of a Linux System

Figure 6-1 depicts a high-altitude overview of the Linux system architecture. The *bootloader* is not strictly part of the Linux system, but it is necessary to start the system and therefore relevant in the context of building a fully functional system with the Yocto Project.

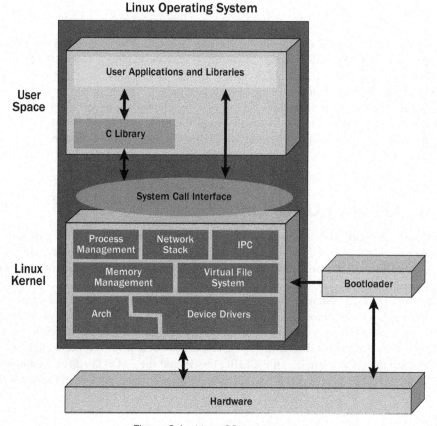

Figure 6-1   Linux OS architecture

A Linux OS can be divided into two levels, the *kernel space* and the *user* or *application space*. This distinction is not just conceptual but originates from the fact that code from the kernel space is executed in a different processor operating mode than code from the user space.

All kernel code is executed in *unrestricted* or *privileged* mode.[2] In this mode, any instruction of the instruction set of the architecture can be executed. Application code, by contrast, is executed in *restricted* or *user mode*. In this mode, instructions that directly access hardware—input/output (I/O) instructions—or otherwise can alter the state of the machine are not permitted. Access to certain memory regions is typically also restricted.

Changing from user mode to kernel mode requires the CPU to switch contexts, which is achieved by special instructions that are dependent on the architecture. For example, on legacy x86 CPUs, the `int 80h` software interrupt or trap fulfilled that purpose. Newer x86_64 CPUs provide the `syscall` instruction, which is used instead of the `int 80h` trap.

6.3 Bootloader

Although the bootloader plays only a very short role in the life cycle of a system during startup, it is a very important system component. To some extent, configuring a bootloader is a common task for any Linux system running on standard PC-style hardware. For embedded systems, setting up a bootloader becomes a very special task, since hardware for embedded systems not only differs significantly from the standard PC architecture but also comes in many different variants. That is true not only for the different CPU architectures but also for the actual CPU or system-on-chips (SoC) as well as for the many peripherals that, combined with the CPU or SoC, make up the hardware platform.

Frequently, bootloaders are divided into two categories: *loaders* and *monitors*. In the former case, the bootloader provides only the mere functionality to initialize the hardware and load the operating system. In the latter case, the bootloader also includes a command-line interface through which a user can interact with the bootloader, which can be used for configuration, reprogramming, initialization, and testing of hardware and other tasks. With these functions, monitors offer a great deal of flexibility to the engineer during system development but also pose some challenges when deploying the product. End users should not be able to inadvertently enter the monitor mode.

There is no shortage in bootloaders for Linux. Discussing even just the most commonly used bootloaders in detail can fill an entire book. In this section, we focus on the role of the bootloader and introduce the most prevalent ones, highlighting those that are supported by the Yocto Project.

---

2. As it is with almost anything, there are exceptions to the rule. The uClinux project (http://www.uclinux.org) builds a Linux system that targets microcontrollers without memory management systems.

6.3.1 Role of the Bootloader

After power is applied to a processor board, the majority of the hardware components need to be initialized before any software application can be executed. Each processor architecture has its own set of initialization steps that need to be performed before the hardware can be used. The bootloader typically just initializes the hardware necessary for the operating system kernel to boot. All other hardware and peripherals are initialized by the operating system itself at a later stage of the boot process. Once the operating system kernel takes control of the hardware, it may reinitialize hardware components originally set up by the bootloader.

Most processors have a default address from which they read the first instruction to be executed. Other processors read that address from a defined location. Hardware designers use that information to arrange the layout and address range of the bootrom accordingly. While commonly referred to as *bootrom*, this device often is electrically erasable programmable read-only memory (EEPROM) or, nowadays, flash memory.

The bootrom contains what is typically referred to as the *first-stage bootloader*. This bootloader can be just a couple of lines of code that load a secondary bootloader from a secure digital (SD) chip or a more complex system that provides functionality to initialize peripheral hardware and boot the system from other devices such as hard drives or network adapters. An example of the latter is the BIOS found in standard PCs.

The most important step during the early initialization of the hardware performed by the bootloader is the initialization of memory and memory controller. Commonly, CPUs start in real mode with a direct mapping between logical and physical addresses. In real mode, the CPU does not use a memory management unit (MMU), which provides abstraction and mapping between virtual and physical memory as well as memory protection and relocation. The operating system kernel typically initializes the MMU as one of its first hardware configuration steps. Depending on the platform, however, it might be necessary for the bootloader to enable and configure the MMU.

After the hardware is initialized, the bootloader locates the operating system, typically the kernel, loads it into memory, passes configuration parameters, and hands over control to the operating system. At this point, the bootloader has completed its responsibilities and terminates. The operating system later reclaims all memory space used by the bootloader.

6.3.2 Linux Bootloaders

As a Linux system developer you have many choices for a bootloader for your project. Bootloaders differ in functionality, processor, and operating system support. Many of them can boot not only Linux but also other operating systems. Another distinction is from what media they can boot the operating system. Besides floppy disk, hard drives, and USB storage devices, many of them can also boot from LAN via BOOTP and TFTP.

When choosing a bootloader, architecture and boot media support come first. During development, monitor functionality can significantly speed up round-trip engineering and optimizing boot parameters. However, when development has finished and the finalized product is deployed, monitor functionality may become a liability, as users may inadvertently (or purposely) enter the monitor mode. Some of the bootloaders offering monitor capabilities can be reconfigured to allow or disallow access to the monitor features or can protect the monitor mode with a password. The safest option, however, is to remove monitor capabilities at compile time.

Table 6-1 provides an overview of some of the bootloaders commonly used with Linux. Not all of the bootloaders presented in the table have Yocto Project or OpenEmbedded recipes. They are included for a more complete picture of Linux bootloaders. Not all embedded systems are created equal, and eventually you may find yourself writing a recipe for a bootloader that better fits your application than the ones that are supported by the Yocto Project by default.

Virtually all bootloaders allow the selection of different systems from a menu before the default is booted after a configurable timeout. This is common practice for laptop, desktop, and server computers, giving users the choice to boot a failsafe or limited system or a previously working configuration after the system has been modified. For

Table 6-1 **Linux Bootloaders**

Bootloader	Description	Yocto Project Recipe	Monitor	Architectures	License	Homepage
LILO (LInux LOader)	Default bootloader for many Linux distributions	No	No	x86	BSD	http://lilo.alioth .debian.org
ELILO (EFI LILO)	LILO for UEFI-based PC hardware	No	No	x86	GPLv2	http://elilo .sourceforge.net
GNU GRUB	GNU LILO successor	Yes	No	x86	GPLv3	www.gnu.org/ software/grub
SYSLINUX	Lightweight bootloader	Yes	No	x86	GPLv2+	www.syslinux.org
U-Boot	Universal bootloader popular for embedded systems	Yes	Yes	ARM, MIPS, PPC, SuperH, x86, m86k	GPLv2	www.denx.de/ wiki/U-Boot
BURG	Branch of GNU GRUB	No	No	x86	GPLv3	https://code .google.com/p/burg
systemd-boot	Minimal bootloader for UEFI-based PC hardware	Yes	No	x86	LGPL 2.1	https://wiki. archlinux.org/index .php/Systemd-boot
RedBoot	Red Hat Embedded Debug and Bootstrap firmware based on cCos real-time OS	No	Yes	ARM, MIPS, PPC, SuperH, x86, m68k	eCos	http://ecos .sourceware.org/ redboot

embedded systems, this functionality can be utilized to fall back to an earlier version if, for instance, a system upgrade has failed.

Before we discuss the bootloaders in more detail, a note about architecture: references to x86 almost always imply the PC platform. This platform is mostly standardized in terms of memory layout, buses, and peripherals. It also includes the BIOS, a first-stage bootloader that also provides configuration information to secondary bootloaders and the operating system. This makes it much different from other architectures, such as ARM and PPC, for which there are no standardized platforms. Although the different platforms use CPUs with the same architecture memory layout, buses and peripherals can greatly differ. Those platforms typically also do not have a BIOS or any other standardized means to obtain the system configuration. That requires the bootloader to be specifically adapted to the particular platform.

LILO

The LInux LOader (LILO) was once the standard bootloader for virtually all Linux distributions for x86 systems. Originally developed by Werner Almesberger from 1992 to 1998, John Coffman took over maintenance from 1999 to 2007, and Joachim Wiedorn has been maintaining the project since 2010. Although GNU GRUB has successively replaced LILO as the default bootloader for many Linux distributions since 2013, the project is still active. LILO's main advantage over many other bootloaders is that it is filesystem agnostic. The operating system can exist on any filesystem, including NTFS, EXT4, FAT32, and the relatively new BTRFS, and LILO can launch it regardless. LILO can directly boot Linux kernel images from floppy disks and hard drives. LILO is very well documented and remains a viable choice for many applications where a more complex bootloader such as GRUB is not required.

ELILO

The EFI-based LInux LOader (ELILO) is a branch of LILO made by Hewlett-Packard to support EFI-based hardware. In addition, it handles network booting via BOOTP, DHCP, and TFTP protocols.

GRUB

The GNU GRand Unified Bootloader (GRUB) was originally designed and implemented by Erich Stefan Boleyn. It started replacing LILO as the mainstream bootloader for Linux distributions from 2013 on.

GRUB was eventually replaced with GRUB 2 and is now known as *GRUB Legacy*. Today the term *GRUB* typically refers to GRUB 2.

The PUPA research project created the foundation for GRUB 2 and eventually evolved into it. GRUB 2 is a complete rewrite and is related to GRUB Legacy only by its name. GRUB 2 utilizes the network drivers from the Etherboot[3] open source software package for handling network booting via BOOTP, DHCP, and TFTP protocols.

---

3. http://etherboot.org/wiki/index.php

SYSLINUX

The Syslinux Project is an umbrella project covering multiple lightweight bootloaders for different purposes:

- **SYSLINUX**: Bootloader for FAT and NTFS filesystems that can handle hard drives, floppy disks, and USB drives.
- **ISOLINUX**: Bootloader for bootable El Torito CD-ROMs.
- **EXTLINUX**: Bootloader for Linux EXT2/EXT3/EXT4 and BTRFS filesystems.
- **PXELINUX**: Bootloader for network booting via BOOTP, DHCP, and TFTP using the Preboot Execution Environment (PXE) supported by the majority of the networking hardware.

While stable, Syslinux is an active project with the latest releases also supporting booting EFI-based hardware.

U-Boot

U-Boot, the Universal Bootloader, also known as *Das U-Boot*, can be considered the Swiss army knife among the embedded Linux bootloaders. Based on the PPCBoot and ARMBoot projects and originally developed by Wolfgang Denk of DENX Software Engineering, U-Boot is one of the most feature-rich, flexible, and actively developed bootloaders currently available.

Extensive support for hardware platforms is only one of the many features of U-Boot. At the time of this writing, U-Boot supports more than 1,000 platforms, of which more than 600 are PowerPC based and more than 300 are ARM based. If your project uses any of these architectures, chances are that your hardware platform is already supported by U-Boot. And even if it is not, you most likely will find a close match from which you can derive your own platform support code.

U-Boot also supports device trees for platform configuration. Device trees, also referred to as *open firmware* or *flattened device trees (FDTs)*, are data structures in byte code format containing platform-specific parameters, such as register locations and sizes, addresses, interrupts, and more, required by the Linux kernel to correctly access the hardware and boot. U-Boot copies the device tree data structures to a memory location. The idea behind device trees is to provide platform configuration parameters during runtime, allowing the Linux kernel to be compiled for multiple platforms without specific information about the particular platform.

U-Boot is very well documented. The main documentation is *The DENX U-Boot and Linux Guide (DULG)*.[4] Besides that guide, there is a very detailed README file included with the U-Boot sources.

U-Boot source repositories are located at http://git.denx.de.

---

4. www.denx.de/wiki/DULG/Manual

BURG

The Brand-new Universal loadeR from GRUB (BURG) is a recent bootloader derived from GRUB. The intention is to support a wider variety of operating systems and the ability to have different themes to customize the appearance of the bootloader during startup. BURG is not yet widely used, as it has not been adopted by the mainstream Linux distributions. Like GRUB, it supports only x86 systems but provides all the features of GRUB, including network booting via BOOTP, DHCP, and TFTP.

systemd-boot

systemd-boot is a simple bootloader targeting UEFI systems. It executes images that are located on an EFI System Partition (ESP). All configuration files for the bootloader as well as operating system images need to reside inside the ESP. Linux kernels need to be configured for EFI booting by setting the CONFIG_EFI_STUB parameter so that systemd-boot can directly execute them as EFI images.

RedBoot

The Red Hat Embedded Debug and Bootstrap Firmware (RedBoot) is a bootloader based on the eCos hardware abstraction layer. eCos is a free, open source, real-time operating system targeting embedded applications. eCos and RedBoot were originally developed and maintained by Red Hat, but the company has discontinued development and all sources have since been relicensed under the GPL. Active development and maintenance have been taken over by the company eCosCentric,[5] which has been formed by the core eCos developers from Red Hat.

Because of its eCos heritage, RedBoot supports many embedded hardware platforms for virtually all architectures, among them ARM, MIPS, PPC, and x86.

RedBoot's networking support includes BOOTP and DHCP. It can download images over Ethernet using TFTP as well as over serial connections using X- or Y-modem protocols.

Monitor functionality with an interactive command-line interface allows RedBoot configuration, image download and management, as well as boot scripting. Such features can be used for development as well as for systems deployed in the field for remote updating.

6.4 Kernel

The two primary functions of an operating system's kernel are to

- Manage the computer's resources
- Allow other programs to execute and access the resources

---

5. www.ecoscentric.com

The core resources of a computer are typically composed of

- **CPU**: The CPU is the execution unit for programs. The kernel is responsible for allocating programs to processors (*scheduling*) and setting up the execution environment (*dispatching*).

- **Memory**: Memory stores instructions as well as data for the programs. Multiple programs compete for the memory, and programs can demand more memory than physically available in the system (*virtual memory*). The kernel is responsible for allocating memory to the programs, protecting memory, and deciding what happens if a program requests more memory than available, which in most cases is less than the physical memory of the computer.

- **I/O Devices**: I/O devices represent sources and sinks for data such as keyboard, mouse, display, network interfaces, storage, and more. The kernel is responsible for servicing program requests to exchange data with devices through a uniform programming interface that abstracts from the specifics of the underlying hardware.

Operating system kernel architectures are typically categorized as *monolithic kernel* or *microkernel*. Monolithic kernels execute all kernel functions, including device drivers within the core kernel process and memory context. Microkernels execute only core functions, such as process and memory management within the core kernel context, and execute device drivers as separate user space processes. A microkernel allows for easier system configuration and maintenance because device drivers can be loaded and unloaded while the system is running. That convenience, however, comes at a performance cost, since microkernels use interprocess communication (IPC) to exchange data between kernel modules.

Although the Linux kernel provides loadable kernel modules for device drivers that can be loaded and unloaded during runtime, Linux is considered a monolithic kernel, since these modules are directly inserted into the kernel's execution context. Because they are running within the kernel's execution context, Linux kernel modules have access to all system resources, including memory. Hence, IPC is not necessary for exchanging data, and therefore there is no performance hit.

Proponents of the microkernel architecture claim that it is superior to the monolithic kernel architecture, since it is a cleaner design and faulty device drivers cannot compromise the entire system. According to them, this advantage outweighs the performance hit due to increased context switches and IPC. This issue has been a long-standing debate between Linus Torvalds and Andrew S. Tanenbaum, the creator of the Minix OS.[6]

---

6. Andrew S. Tanenbaum, "Linux Is Obsolete," January 29, 1992, https://groups.google.com/forum/#!msg/comp.os.minix/wlhw16QWltI/XdksCA1TR_QJ.

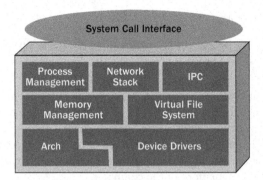

Figure 6-2   Linux kernel subsystems

6.4.1 Major Linux Kernel Subsystems

The Linux kernel is divided into a set of major subsystems that are shown in Figure 6-2.

Architecture-Dependent Code

Although the majority of the Linux kernel code is independent of the architecture it is executed on, there are portions that need to take the CPU architecture and the platform into consideration.

Inside the Linux kernel source tree, all architecture and platform-specific code is located in the linux/arch subdirectory. Within that subdirectory is another directory for each architecture supported by the Linux kernel. Every architecture directory contains a subdirectory kernel containing the architecture-specific kernel code. The assembly file head.S (or different head_*.S files for some architectures) provides the startup code for the CPU.

Device Drivers

Device drivers handle all the devices that the Linux kernel supports. In most cases, these are hardware devices, but some drivers implement software devices. One example is the software watchdog timer.

Device drivers make up the vast majority of the Linux kernel code. Inside the Linux source tree, device driver code is located in the linux/drivers directory, which is further divided into subdirectories for the various drivers supporting certain device categories, such as Bluetooth, FireWire, I2C SCSI, and many more.

Memory Management

Only the kernel has unrestricted access to the system's physical memory and is therefore responsible for safely allowing processes to access it. Most modern CPUs contain an MMU providing virtual addressing of a memory space that is typically much larger than the actual physical memory of the system. Virtual addressing allows each process to have its own private memory space that is protected (by the kernel) from other processes.

While a process runs, the kernel must ensure that the process's virtual memory space is mapped to physical memory. Memory is mapped from virtual addresses to physical addresses in pages, or segments, that on Linux are typically 4 k in size.[7] However, that does not mean that a process can allocate only 4 k of memory at a time. Linux provides what is called a *slab allocator*. While based on 4 k pages, slab allocation allows larger chunks of memory to be allocated, eliminates fragmentation caused by allocations and deallocations, and reuses previously allocated memory by tracking the usage states of slabs.

Virtual addressing allows allocation of more memory than is physically present in the system. When physical memory is exhausted, the kernel can move pages from the memory onto external storage such as a hard drive. This process is called *swapping* because memory pages are swapped from memory onto the disk. Most embedded systems do not have a hard disk, however. While swapping to flash devices is possible, it is rather inefficient and reduces the life span of the flash device.

You can find the memory management code in the linux/mm directory of the kernel source tree.

Virtual Filesystem

A *filesystem* is an organizational scheme for persistent data storage after an application terminates. It provides mechanisms to write, read, update, and erase data and manages the available space on the storage medium.

Unlike other operating systems, Linux gives users the choice of many different filesystems for a variety of applications and storage media. Besides the core Linux filesystems ext2, ext3, and ext4, Linux offers support for many others, including VFAT, NTFS, ZFS, and the new Btrfs.

With a broad variety comes the challenge of providing an abstraction between applications' requirements for persistent storage from the details of the filesystem. For basic operations such as creating, writing, and reading files and browsing directories, applications must not need to be aware of the type of file system their data is stored on.

For this purpose, the Linux kernel provides a common abstraction interface for file operations known as the virtual file system (VFS). The VFS is a switching fabric between the underlying filesystem implementations and file operations of the system call interface (SCI). The filesystem implementations are essentially data management plugins that reside between the VFS layer above and a unified data buffer below. The purpose of the data buffer is to optimize data access to the physical storage devices. The data buffer layer implements a common set of APIs and functions for data access from

---

7. The default page size of the Linux kernel has been 4 k for the longest time because it has been a good compromise between granularity and management overhead, as the Linux kernel maintains a 64-byte (dependent on architecture and debug options) management structure per page. For a system with 4 GB of RAM, this means 64 MB; for 16 GB, it is 256 MB. Server systems with a lot of memory typically use a larger page size to reduce the amount of memory needed for the page tables. The page size is defined in asm/page.h as #define PAGE_SIZE (1UL << PAGE_SHIFT) and can be changed by modifying PAGE_SHIFT.

the filesystem implementations and to the underlying device drivers that handle the specifics of the storage devices.

An interesting aspect of the VFS is that it is not limited to filesystems residing on physical storage devices but likewise provides the same uniform interface for network filesystems, such as Network File System (NFS) and Server Message Block (SMB), as well as for pseudo-filesystems such as the proc filesystem.

Sources for VFS and the filesystem reside in the linux/fs directory of the Linux kernel source tree.

Process Management

The kernel's process management is responsible for the execution of processes. The application programming domain typically distinguishes between processes and threads. In this context, *process* refers to the execution context of an application, and *thread* refers to independent execution paths inside a process. A process has at least one thread, its main thread, from which it can spawn additional threads. All threads of a process share the same execution context, memory space, and other resources. Therefore, threads are also commonly referred to as *lightweight processes*.

The Linux kernel does not separate the two concepts of processes and threads. Both of them are implemented as threads that represent a complete execution context comprising code, data, stack, and CPU registers.

Process management allocates the core resource of a computer system, the CPUs. As threads compete for the available CPUs, it is the task of the *scheduler* to select the threads eligible to run and assign them to the available CPUs (or CPU cores). The Linux kernel's default scheduling algorithm is the Completely Fair Scheduler (CFS). The goal of the CFS is to maximize overall CPU utilization while also maximizing interactive performance of the system. Like the earlier O(1) scheduler, which it replaced, CFS provides a scheduling time, which is independent of the number of processes waiting to be scheduled.

The Linux kernel also offers real-time scheduling policies with static priorities. The latest addition to the real-time scheduling policies is deadline scheduling, a policy that uses dynamic priorities based on the closest expiring deadline.

Network Stack

The Linux kernel's network stack is essentially modeled after the well-known ISO Open Systems Interconnection (OSI) layered architecture, as defined by ISO/IEC 7498-1.

On the network layer, Linux of course supports the IPv4 and IPv6 protocols but also AppleTalk, IPX, X.25, Frame Relay, and others. Transport layer protocols include TCP, UDP, SPX, and more.

The *socket layer* provides the abstraction between application programs and the networking protocol stacks in the kernel. A socket is a communication endpoint, which is defined by its *domain* and *type*. The domain indicates the protocol family such as IPv4 (AF_INET) or IPv6 (AF_INET6). Type indicates the communication semantics, such as connection-based two-way byte streams (SOCK_STREAM) or raw protocol access (SOCK_RAW).

The network stack implementations can be found in `linux/net` inside the Linux kernel source tree.

Interprocess Communication

IPC is a set of methods for data exchange between processes or threads. IPC methods are typically subdivided into message passing, shared memory, synchronization, and data streams.

Implementation of the Linux kernel IPC methods can be found in `linux/ipc`. These functions create the core for the higher-level abstractions of the System V and POSIX (Portable Operating System Interface) IPC mechanisms.

System Call Interface

The SCI is the connection between the Linux kernel and applications running in user space. Through the SCI, the kernel provides a common API of function calls for process management, file management, device management, interprocess communication, and system management.

The Linux kernel's SCI comprises over 300 functions. The exact number is dependent on the architecture. The majority of the functions are common, though their implementations may be architecture-dependent. Some functions may be architecture-specific and only supported by a particular architecture. The SCI implementation can be found in `linux/kernel` with the architecture-dependent portions in the subdirectories of `linux/arch`.

Each system call represents a defined entry point from user space into the kernel. A system call always constitutes a CPU context switch from user mode into kernel or privileged mode. On legacy x86 CPUs, this context switch was invoked by issuing the `int 80h` software interrupt or trap. Newer x86 CPUs provide the `sysenter` instruction, which is more efficient than a trap. Every system call has a unique number by which it is identified. This number is also referred to as the *system call slot*. The number is the key through which the SCI multiplexes and de-multiplexes the system calls through a single API. You can find the number belonging to a particular system call in the file `/usr/include/asm/unistd.h`. Depending on the architecture, this file may include other files containing the actual list of system calls.

If manual pages are installed on your system, you can use `man syscalls` or `info syscalls` for more information on the system calls.

With the strace tools, you can trace system calls and signals. For instance,

```
$ strace ls
```

shows the system calls in their sequential call order used by the `ls` command to list the entries of the current directory. The strace sources are also a great resource for the system calls for the different architectures. You can find the project's source on Source-Forge at http://sourceforge.net/projects/strace. In the code tree under the directory `linux`, there are subdirectories for the various architectures. Each of these subdirectories contains a file called `syscallent.h`, which lists all the system calls supported by that architecture in order of their slot.

For each architecture, the Linux kernel sources maintain system call tables. For x86 architecture, you can find them in `arch/x86/syscalls/syscall_32.tbl` for 32-bit and `arch/x86/syscalls/syscall_64.tbl` for 64-bit.

There is not a single location inside the Linux kernel source tree where all the system calls are implemented. However, you can easily find the implementation of a particular system call by its name from within the Linux source tree using the command shown in Listing 6-1.

Listing 6-1   **Implementation of the exit System Call**

```
yocto@yocto-dev:~/linux$ grep -rA3 'SYSCALL_DEFINE.\?(exit,' *
kernel/exit.c:SYSCALL_DEFINE1(exit, int, error_code)
kernel/exit.c-{
kernel/exit.c-   do_exit((error_code&0xff)<<8);
kernel/exit.c-}
```

The example uses the exit system call. Simply replace exit in the command line with a different system call name to find the implementation for that system call. The example also shows the definition of system call functions using the SYSCALL_DEFINE macro. Depending on the number of parameters the system call function expects, a different macro with the number of parameters in its name is used.

Invoking system call functions requires saving all the CPUs' registers, passing the system call number and its parameters in specific registers, and then issuing the trap. What exactly needs to be done, and how, is dependent on the architecture and is usually written in assembly code. Typically, user space applications do not invoke system calls directly, although they could, but through wrapper functions contained in the C Library.

6.4.2 Linux Kernel Startup

Now that we have discussed the major kernel subsystems, let's have a high-altitude look at the Linux kernel startup process. For the context of this discussion, it is sufficient to understand how control is passed from the bootloader to the kernel and then finally to the first user space application program, the init process. In reality, the Linux kernel runs through many stages of initialization for the various hardware components and subsystems. Many of these stages are dependent on the hardware platform.

After the bootloader has copied the Linux kernel image into memory, it passes control to the *bootstrap loader* that is a prepended part of the kernel image. To save space, the kernel image is typically compressed, and it is the bootstrap loader's responsibility to create the proper execution environment for the kernel, decompress the kernel, relocate the kernel in memory, and then pass control to it. The bootstrap loader directly passes control to the kernel entry point inside a module, which is called head.o for most architectures.

The module head.o contains architecture-specific but platform-independent initialization code for the particular CPU architecture. This module is derived from the assembly language file head.s, which is located inside the directory linux/arch/<ARCH>/kernel, where <ARCH> is replaced by the particular architecture.

At a high-level, the head.o module performs the following tasks:

- Verifies the correct architecture and CPU
- Detects CPU type and functionality, such as hardware floating-point capabilities
- Enables the CPU's MMU and creates the initial table of memory pages
- Establishes basic error reporting and handling
- Switches to non-architecture-specific kernel startup function start_kernel() in main.c

The file main.c in linux/init contains the bulk of the Linux kernel startup code, from architecture setup, kernel command-line processing, and initialization of the first kernel thread to mounting the root filesystem and executing the first user space application program.

After performing a basic set of kernel initialization, the start_kernel() function calls rest_init(), which spawns the first kernel thread. This thread is spawned by calling kernel_thread() with the function kernel_init() as the first parameter. This function becomes the init thread. At this point, there are now two threads running: start_kernel() and kernel_init(). The former kicks off the scheduler and then loops forever in the cpu_idle() function. The latter becomes the init() thread, the parent of all user space processes with the process ID (PID) of 1.

At the end, kernel_init() launches the first user space application. If an init command was passed as part of the kernel command line, kernel_init() first attempts to start that program. If no init command was passed, the function then tries a set of default programs that it loads from the root filesystem. It tries /sbin/init, /etc/init, /bin/init, and /bin/sh in this order until one succeeds. If none succeeds, the kernel exits with the well-known error message "No init found. Try passing init= option to the kernel. See Linux Documentation/init.txt for guidance."

Typically, the first user space process is part of an init or a startup system that then launches other user processes. The init systems typically used by Linux desktops and servers are System V Init, systemd, and Upstart. Embedded systems commonly use more lightweight startup systems such as BusyBox or directly launch their core application.

6.5 User Space

Now that the kernel has completed its initialization, launched the init process, and within it executed the first user space application, the system has entered *userland* or *user space*. User space is all the code that runs outside the operating system's kernel and includes all the libraries and application programs. User space provides all the functionality required for the system to serve its intended purpose.

Configuration of the user space and which libraries and application programs it includes differ from system to system. However, there is always one library that virtually all systems include: the C Standard Library (LIBC). Just as the init process is the parent of all processes, LIBC can be considered the parent of all libraries.

Even the canonical Hello World! application shown in Listing 6-2 requires a lot of logistics to put the two words on the screen.

Listing 6-2   **Hello World**

```
#include <stdio.h>
int main() {
    printf("Hello World!\n");
    return 0;
}
```

This program calls printf(), which is one of many functions provided by the LIBC APIs, alleviating the burden on application programmers to perform the more tedious tasks of implementing core functionality required by virtually any program. The LIBC APIs are specified by the ANSI C Standard. For UNIX systems, the ANSI C Standard is described as part of the POSIX library, which is a superset of it. POSIX is an IEEE standard. The current version is *POSIX.1-2008* or *IEEE Std 1003.2008*.

Many of the LIBC APIs directly map to the kernel's systems calls. In fact, frequently, the implementation of the function is merely a wrapper around the system call.

For Linux systems, multiple implementations of LIBC are available. They vary by footprint of the library itself, compatibility with the ANSI C Standard, performance, modularity, and configurability. Table 6-2 provides an overview of the common implementations.

Table 6-2   **C Standard Libraries for Linux**

Library	Description	Yocto Project Support	Configurable	License	Homepage
GLIBC	GNU implementation of LIBC	Yes	Partially	LGPL	https://www.gnu.org/software/libc
EGLIBC	Embedded version of GLIBC optimized for footprint and cross-compilation (now merged into GLIBC)	Yes	Yes	LGPL	www.eglibc.org/home
uClibc	Created to support Linux systems not requiring memory management	Yes	No	LGPL	www.uclibc.org
Bionic libc	LIBC for Android systems; optimized for footprint	No	No	3-clause BSD	https://android.googlesource.com/platform/bionic/

Table 6-2 **C Standard Libraries for Linux (*Continued*)**

Library	Description	Yocto Project Support	Configurable	License	Homepage
dietlibc	Small footprint library with cross-build support	No	Partially	LGPL, Commercial	www.fefe.de/dietlibc
musl	A lightweight LIBC, optimized for small footprint and performance	Yes	No	MIT	www.musl-libc.org
klibc	Subset of LIBC originally designed for Linux kernel initialization	No	No	GPL, BSD	ftp://ftp.kernel.org/pub/linux/libs/klibc
Newlib	Targeted for embedded systems for virtually any architecture; conglomeration of several library parts	No	Yes	Multiple free software licenses	www.sourceware.org/newlib

The goal of EGLIBC is to be a lightweight and configurable LIBC that supports cross-build and is binary-compatible with GLIBC. Binary compatibility allows application programs compiled for GLIBC to execute on systems with EGLIBC without requiring recompilation. Other LIBC implementations typically provide compatibility only of the APIs and require recompilation.

While originally intended for embedded systems, an increasing number of desktop and server Linux distributions have made EGLIBC their default. Therefore, efforts have been ongoing to phase out the different EGLIBC and GLIBC branches in favor of a common development effort under the umbrella of GLIBC. As of the writing of this book, EGLIBC has now officially been merged into GLIBC. We mention EGLIBC here for historic reasons.

6.6 Summary

A Linux OS stack is made up of many different components. In this chapter, we examined its architecture to create a foundation for the discussions on how the OpenEmbedded build system builds the components and assembles them into a working Linux system.

- Bootloaders play a short but important role during system startup. A bootloader's responsibility is to initialize the hardware, and load and boot the OS kernel.

- The Linux kernel is a large and complex project. It is divided into various subsystems that provide the kernel's functionality and abstract it from the underlying hardware.
- The kernel's SCI is the bridge between the kernel and user space applications.
- *User space* or *userland* refers to all the code that runs outside the kernel. The kernel starts the first user space process.
- LIBC provides a common set of APIs and functions for application programs. LIBC eliminates the need for application developers to deal with the intricacies of the system and makes application programs portable between different systems.

6.7 References

Kernel Documentation, https://www.kernel.org/doc/Documentation

7

Building a Custom Linux Distribution

In the preceding chapters, we laid the foundation for using the Yocto Project tools to build custom Linux distributions. Now it is time that we put that knowledge to work.

Chapter 2, "The Yocto Project," outlined the prerequisites for the build system and how to set up your build host, configure a build environment, and launch a build that creates a system ready to run in the QEMU emulator. In this chapter, we reuse that build environment. If you have not yet prepared your build system, we recommend that you go back to Chapter 2 and follow the steps. Performing a build using Poky's default settings validates your setup. It also downloads the majority of the source code packages and establishes a shared state cache, both of which speed up build time for the examples presented in this chapter.

In Chapter 3, "OpenEmbedded Build System," and Chapter 4, "BitBake Build Engine," we explained the OpenEmbedded build system and the BitBake syntax. This and following chapters show examples or snippets of BitBake recipes utilizing that syntax. While the syntax is mostly straightforward and resembles typical scripting languages, there are some constructs that are particular to BitBake. Referring to Chapter 4, you find syntax examples and explanations.

When experimenting with the Yocto Project, you eventually encounter build failures. They can occur for various reasons, and troubleshooting can be challenging. You may want to refer to Chapter 5, "Troubleshooting," for the debugging tools to help you track down build failures.

Chapter 6, "Linux System Architecture," outlined the building blocks of a Linux distribution. While bootloader and the Linux kernel are indispensable for a working

Linux OS stack, user space makes up its majority. In this chapter, we focus on customizing Linux OS stacks with user space libraries and applications from recipes provided by the Yocto Project and other compatible layers from the OpenEmbedded project.

7.1 Core Images—Linux Distribution Blueprints

The OpenEmbedded Core (OE Core) and other Yocto Project layers include several example images. These images offer root filesystem configurations for typical Linux OS stacks. They range from very basic images that just boot a device to a command-line prompt to images that include the X Window System (X11) server and a graphical user interface. These reference images are called the *core images* because the names of their respective recipes begin with core-image. You can easily locate the recipes for the core images with the find command from within the installation directory of your build system (see Listing 7-1).

Listing 7-1   **Core Image Recipes**

```
user@buildhost:~/yocto/poky$ find ./meta*/recipes*/images -name "*.bb" \
                           -print
./meta/recipes-core/images/core-image-minimal-initramfs.bb
./meta/recipes-core/images/core-image-minimal-mtdutils.bb
./meta/recipes-core/images/build-appliance-image_8.0.bb
./meta/recipes-core/images/core-image-minimal-dev.bb
./meta/recipes-core/images/core-image-minimal.bb
./meta/recipes-core/images/core-image-base.bb
./meta/recipes-extended/images/core-image-full-cmdline.bb
./meta/recipes-extended/images/core-image-testmaster-initramfs.bb
./meta/recipes-extended/images/core-image-lsb-sdk.bb
./meta/recipes-extended/images/core-image-lsb-dev.bb
./meta/recipes-extended/images/core-image-lsb.bb
./meta/recipes-extended/images/core-image-testmaster.bb
./meta/recipes-graphics/images/core-image-x11.bb
./meta/recipes-graphics/images/core-image-directfb.bb
./meta/recipes-graphics/images/core-image-weston.bb
./meta/recipes-graphics/images/core-image-clutter.bb
./meta/recipes-qt/images/qt4e-demo-image.bb
./meta/recipes-rt/images/core-image-rt-sdk.bb
./meta/recipes-rt/images/core-image-rt.bb
./meta/recipes-sato/images/core-image-sato-dev.bb
./meta/recipes-sato/images/core-image-sato-sdk.bb
./meta/recipes-sato/images/core-image-sato.bb
./meta-skeleton/recipes-multilib/images/core-image-multilib-example.bb
```

You can look at the core images as Linux distribution blueprints from which you can derive your own distribution by extending them. All core image recipes inherit the core-image class, which itself inherits from image class. All images set the IMAGE_INSTALL variable to specify what packages are to be installed into the root filesystem. IMAGE_INSTALL is a list of packages and package groups. Package groups are collections of packages. Defining package groups alleviates the need to potentially list hundreds of single packages in the `IMAGE_INSTALL` variable. We explain package groups in a coming section of this chapter. Image recipes either explicitly set `Image_INSTALL` or extend its default value provided by the `core-image` class, which installs the two package groups `packagegroup-core-boot` and `packagegroup-base-extended`. The default creates a working root filesystem that boots to the console.

Let's have a closer look at the various core images:

- **core-image-minimal**: This is the most basic image allowing a device to boot to a Linux command-line login. Login and command-line interpreter are provided by BusyBox.

- **core-image-minimal-initramfs**: This image is essentially the same as `core-image-minimal` but with a Linux kernel that includes a RAM-based initial root filesystem (initramfs).

- **core-image-minimal-mtdutils**: Based on `core-image-minimal`, this image also includes user space tools to interact with the memory technology device (MTD) subsystem in the Linux kernel to perform operations on flash memory devices.

- **core-image-minimal-dev**: Based on `core-image-minimal`, this image also includes all the development packages (header files, etc.) for all the packages installed in the root filesystem. If deployed on the target together with a native target toolchain, it allows software development on the target. Together with a cross-toolchain, it can be used for software development on the development host.

- **core-image-rt**: Based on `core-image-minimal`, this image target builds the Yocto Project real-time kernel and includes a test suite and tools for real-time applications.

- **core-image-rt-sdk**: In addition to `core-image-rt`, this image includes the system development kit (SDK) consisting of the development packages for all packages installed; development tools such as compilers, assemblers, and linkers; as well as performance test tools and Linux kernel development packages. This image allows for software development on the target.

- **core-image-base**: Essentially a `core-image-minimal`, this image also includes middleware and application packages to support a variety of hardware such as WiFi, Bluetooth, sound, and serial ports. The target device must include the necessary hardware components, and the Linux kernel must provide the device drivers for them.

- **core-image-full-cmdline**: This minimal image adds typical Linux command-line tools—bash, acl, attr, grep, sed, tar, and many more—to the root filesystem.

- **core-image-lsb**: This image contains packages required for conformance with the Linux Standard Base (LSB) specification.

- **core-image-lsb-dev**: This image is the same as the `core-image-lsb` but also includes the development packages for all packages installed in the root filesystem.

- **core-image-lsb-sdk**: In addition to `core-image-lsb-dev`, this image includes development tools such as compilers, assemblers, and linkers as well as performance test tools and Linux kernel development packages.

- **core-image-x11**: This basic graphical image includes the X11 server and an X11 terminal application.

- **core-image-sato**: This image provides X11 support that includes the OpenedHand Sato user experience for mobile devices. Besides the Sato screen manager, the image also provides several applications using the Sato theme, such as a terminal, editor, file manager, and several games.

- **core-image-sato-dev**: This image is the same as `core-image-sato` but also includes the development packages for all packages installed in the root filesystem.

- **core-image-sato-sdk**: In addition to `core-image-sato-dev`, this image includes development tools such as compilers, assemblers, and linkers as well as performance test tools and Linux kernel development packages.

- **core-image-directfb**: An image that uses DirectFB for graphics and input device management, DirectFB may include graphics acceleration and a windowing system. Because of its much smaller footprint compared to X11, DirectFB is the preferred choice for lower-end embedded systems that need graphics support but not the entire functionality of X11.

- **core-image-clutter**: This is an X11-based image that also includes the Clutter toolkit. Clutter is based on OpenGL and provides functionality for animated graphical user interfaces.

- **core-image-weston**: This image uses Weston instead of X11. Weston is a compositor that uses the Wayland protocol and implementation to exchange data with its clients. This image also includes a Wayland-capable terminal program.

- **qt4e-demo-image**: This image launches a demo application for the embedded Qt toolkit after completing the boot process. Qt for embedded Linux provides a development framework of graphical applications that directly write to the framebuffer instead of using the X11.

- **core-image-multilib-example**: This image is an example of the support of multiple libraries, typically 32-bit support on an otherwise 64-bit system. The image is based on a core image and adds the desired multilib packages to `IMAGE_INSTALL`.

The following three images are not reference images for embedded Linux systems. We include them in this discussion for completeness purposes.

- **core-image-testmaster, core-image-testmaster-initramfs**: These images are references for testing other images on actual hardware devices or in QEMU. They are deployed to a separate partition to boot into and then use scripts to deploy the image under test. This approach is useful for automated testing.

- **`build-appliance-image`**: This recipe creates the Yocto Project Build Appliance virtual machine images that include everything needed for the Yocto Project build system. The images can be launched using VMware Player or VMware Workstation.

Studying the reference image recipes is a good way to learn how these images are built and what packages comprise them. The core images are also a good starting point for your own Linux OS stack. You can easily extend them by adding packages and package groups to IMAGE_INSTALL. Images can only be extended, not shrunk. To build an image with less functionality, you have to start from a smaller core image and add only the packages you need. There is no simple way to remove packages. The majority of them are added through package groups, and you would need to split up the package group if you do not want to install a package included with it. Of course, if you are removing a package, you also have to remove any other packages that depend on it.

There are several ways you can add packages and package groups to be included with your root filesystem. The following sections explain them and also provide information on why you would want to use one method over another.

7.1.1 Extending a Core Image through Local Configuration

The simplest method for adding packages and package groups to images is to add IMAGE_INSTALL to the conf/local.conf file of your build environment:

```
IMAGE_INSTALL_append = " <package> <package group>"
```

As we have seen, image recipes set the IMAGE_INSTALL variable adding packages and package groups. To extend an image, you have to append your packages and packages group to the variable. You may wonder why we use the explicit _append operator instead of the += or .+ operators. Using the _append operator unconditionally appends the specified value to the IMAGE_INSTALL variable after all recipes and configuration files have been processed. Image recipes commonly explicitly set the IMAGE_INSTALL variable using the = or ?= operators, which may happen *after* BitBake processed the settings in conf/local.conf.

For example, adding

```
IMAGE_INSTALL_append = " strace sudo sqlite3"
```

installs the strace and sudo tools as well as SQLite in the root filesystem. When using the _append operator, you always have to remember to add a space in front of the first package or package group, as this operator does not automatically include a space.

Using IMAGE_INSTALL in the conf/local.conf of your build environment unconditionally affects all images you are going to build with this build environment. If you are looking to install additional packages only to a certain image, you can use conditional appending:

```
IMAGE_INSTALL_append_pn-<image> = " <package> <package group>"
```

This installs the specified packages and package groups only into the root filesystem of image. For example,

```
IMAGE_INSTALL_append_pn-core-image-minimal = " strace"
```

installs the strace tool only into the root filesystem of core-image-minimal. All other images are unaffected.

Using IMAGE_INSTALL also affects core images, that is, images that inherit from the core-image class, as well as images that inherit directly from the image class. For convenience purposes, the core-image class defines the variable CORE_IMAGE_EXTRA_INSTALL. All packages and package groups added to this variable are appended to IMAGE_INSTALL by the class. Using

```
CORE_IMAGE_EXTRA_INSTALL = "strace sudo sqlite3"
```

adds these packages to all images that inherit from core-image. Images that inherit directly from image are not affected. Using CORE_IMAGE_EXTRA_INSTALL is a safer and easier method for core images than appending directly to IMAGE_INSTALL.

7.1.2 Testing Your Image with QEMU

You can easily test your image with the QEMU emulator. Even though you eventually build a system for the target hardware of your product, using QEMU for testing makes good sense for the following reasons:

- The round-trip time for launching QEMU is much quicker than deploying an image to actual hardware.
- Frequently, hardware is not yet available when software development begins.
- Yocto Project board support packages (BSP) make it simple to switch from QEMU to hardware and back.

In Chapter 2, when performing our first build, we used QEMU to verify the build output. The Poky reference distribution provides the script runqemu that greatly simplifies the task of launching QEMU by providing the necessary parameters. In its simplest form, you launch the script with a single parameter

```
$ runqemu qemux86
```

which tells the script to locate the latest kernel and root filesystem image builds for the provided QEMU machine and otherwise launch QEMU with default parameters. The parameter values match the QEMU machine types in conf/local.conf.

When working with different root filesystem images, you probably want to select the particular image when running QEMU. For example, you have built core-image-minimal and core-image-base using the preceding command line, since runqemu launches whatever image you last built. Using the command as follows lets you choose the image:

```
$ runqemu qemux86 core-image-minimal
```

The script automatically selects the correct kernel and uses the latest `core-image-minimal` root filesystem. For even more control, you can directly specify the kernel image and root filesystem image file:

```
$ runqemu <path>/bzImage-qemux86.bin <path>/core-image-minimal-qemux86.ext3
```

QEMU and the `runqemu` script are handy tools for rapid round-trip application development, which we explore in Chapter 11, "Application Development."

7.1.3 Verifying and Comparing Images Using the Build History

When building a product, you find yourself frequently modifying your images, adding new packages, and removing extraneous packages to trim the footprint. A tool that enables you to easily verify and compare image builds with each other can simplify that otherwise tedious task.

To help maintain build output quality and enable comparison between different builds, BitBake provides build history, which is implemented by the `buildhistory` class. This class records information about the contents of all packages built and about the images created by the build system in a Git repository where you can examine them. Build history is disabled by default. To enable it, you need to add

```
INHERIT += "buildhistory"
BUILDHISTORY_COMMIT = "1"
```

to the `conf/local.conf` file of your build environment. Please note that `INHERIT` (uppercase) is a variable to which you have to add the `buildhistory` class. It is different from the `inherit` (lowercase) directive used by recipes and classes to inherit functionality from classes. Every time you do a build, `buildhistory` creates a commit to the Git repository with the changes.

The `buildhistory` Git repository is stored in a directory as defined by the `BUILDHISTORY_DIR` variable. The default value of this variable is set to

```
BUILDHISTORY_DIR ?= "${TOPDIR}/buildhistory"
```

After enabling `buildhistory` and running a build, you see a `buildhistory` directory added to the top-level directory of your build environment. The directory contains the two subdirectories `images` and `packages`. The former contains build information about the images you build, the latter information on the packages. We analyze the `buildhistory` Git repository in Chapter 13, "Advanced Topics." Here we just look at the `images` subdirectory. Inside the `images` subdirectory, the images are sorted into further subdirectories by target machine, target C library, and image name:

```
${TOPDIR}/buildhistory/images/<machine>/<clib>/<image>
```

For the build of our `core-image-minimal` for qemux86 using the default EGLIBC target library, you find the image history in

```
${TOPDIR}/buildhistory/images/qemux86/eglibc/core-image-mininal
```

The files in that directory give you detailed information on what makes up your image:

- **image-info.txt**: Overview information about the image in form of the most important variables, such as DISTRO, DISTRO_VERSION, and IMAGE_INSTALL
- **installed-packages.txt**: A list of the package files installed in the image, including version and target information
- **installed-package-names.txt**: Similar to the previous file but contains only the names of the packages without version and target information
- **files-in-image.txt**: A list of the root filesystem with directory names, file sizes, file permissions, and file owner

Simply searching the file installed-package-names.txt gives you information on whether or not a package has been installed.

7.1.4 Extending a Core Image with a Recipe

Adding packages and package groups to CORE_IMAGE_EXTRA_INSTALL and IMAGE_INSTALL and in conf/local.conf may be straightforward and quick, but doing so makes a project hard to maintain and complicates reuse. A better way is to extend a predefined image through a recipe. Listing 7-2 shows a simple recipe that extends core-image-base.

Listing 7-2   **Recipe Extending core-image-base**

```
DESCRIPTION = "A console image with hardware support for our IoT device"

require recipes-core/images/core-image-base.bb

IMAGE_INSTALL += "sqlite3 mtd-utils coreutils"
IMAGE_FEATURES = "dev-pkgs"
```

The example includes the recipe for core-image-base and adds packages to IMAGE_INSTALL and an image feature to IMAGE_FEATURES. We explain what image features are and how to utilize them to customize image in the next section.

A couple of things to consider when extending images with recipes:

- Unlike classes, you need to provide the path relative to the layer for BitBake to find the recipe file to include, and you need to add the .bb file extension.
- While you can use either include or require to include the recipe you are extending, we recommend the use of require, since it causes BitBake to exit with an explicit error message if it cannot locate the included recipe file.
- Remember to use the += operator to add to IMAGE_INSTALL. Do not use = or := because they overwrite the content of the variable defined by the included recipe.

For BitBake to actually be able to use this recipe as a build target, you have to add it to a layer that is included into your build environment via the `conf/bblayers.conf` file. It is not recommended that you add your recipes to the core Yocto Project layers, such as `meta`, `meta-yocto`, and others, because it makes it hard to maintain your build environment if you upgrade to a newer version of the Yocto Project. Instead, you should create a layer in which to put your recipes.

Creating a layer for one recipe may seem like a lot of overhead, but hardly any project ever stays small. What may start with one recipe eventually grows into a sophisticated project with recipes for images, packages, and package groups. In Chapter 3, we introduced the `yocto-layer`, which makes creating layers a breeze.

7.1.5 Image Features

Image features provide certain functionality that you can add to your target images. This can be additional packages to be installed, modification of configuration files, and more.

For example, the `dev-pkgs` image feature adds the development packages, which typically include headers and other files required for development, for all packages installed in the root filesystem. Using this image feature is a convenient way to enable a target image for development without having to explicitly specify the development packages in the `IMAGE_INSTALL` variable. For deployment, you can then simply remove the `dev-pkgs` image feature.

Installation of image features is controlled by the two variables `IMAGE_FEATURES` and `EXTRA_IMAGE_FEATURES`. The former is used in image recipes to define the required set of image features. The latter is typically used in the `conf/local.conf` file to define additional image features that, of course, then affect all images built with that build environment. The content of `EXTRA_IMAGE_FEATURES` is simply added to `IMAGE_FEATURES` by the `meta/conf/bitbake.conf` configuration file.

Image features are defined by different classes. The list of currently available image features contains the following:

- Defined by `image.bbclass`:
  - **debug-tweaks**: Prepares an image for development purposes. In particular, it sets empty root passwords for console and Secure Shell (SSH) login.
  - **package-management**: Installs the package management system according to the package management class defined by `PACKAGE_CLASSES` for the root filesystem.
  - **read-only-rootfs**: Creates a read-only root filesystem. This image feature works only if System V Init (SysVinit) system is used rather than `sytemd`.
  - **splash**: Enables showing a splash screen instead of the boot messages during boot. By default, the splash screen is provided by the `psplash` package, which can be customized. You can also define an alternative splash screen package by setting the `SPLASH` variable to a different package name.

- Defined by `populate_sdk_base.bbclass`:
  - **dbg-pkgs**: Installs the debug packages containing symbols for all packages installed in the root filesystem.
  - **dev-pgks**: Installs the development packages containing headers and other development files for all packages installed in the root filesystem.
  - **doc-pkgs**: Installs the documentation packages for all packages installed in the root filesystem.
  - **staticdev-pkgs**: Installs the static development packages such as static library files ending in *.a for all packages installed in the root filesystem.
  - **ptest-pkgs**: Installs the package test (ptest) packages for all packages installed in the root filesystem.
- Defined by `core-image.bbclass`:
  - **eclipse-debug**: Installs remote debugging tools for integration with the Eclipse IDE, namely the GDB debugging server, the Eclipse Target Communication Framework (TCF) agent, and the OpenSSH SFTP server.
  - **hwcodecs**: Installs the hardware decoders and encoders for audio, images, and video if the hardware platform provides them.
  - **nfs-server**: Installs Network File System (NFS) server, utilities, and client.
  - **qt4-pkgs**: Installs the Qt4 framework and demo applications.
  - **ssh-server-dropbear**: Installs the lightweight SSH server Dropbear, which is popular for embedded systems. This image feature is incompatible with ssh-server-openssh. Either one of the two, but not both, can be used.
  - **ssh-server-openssh**: Installs the OpenSSH server. This image feature is incompatible with ssh-server-dropbear. Either one of the two, but not both, can be used.
  - **tools-debug**: Installs debugging tools, namely the GDB debugger, the GDB remote debugging server, the system call tracing tool strace, and the memory tracing tool mtrace for the GLIBC library if it is the target library.
  - **tools-profile**: Installs common profiling tools such as oprofile, powertop, latencytop, lttng-ust, and valgrind.
  - **tools-sdk**: Installs software development tools such as the GCC compiler, Make, autoconf, automake, libtool, and many more.
  - **tools-testapps**: Installs test applications such as tests for X11 and middleware packages like the telephony manager oFono and the connection manager ConnMan.
  - **x11**: Installs the X11 server.
  - **x11-base**: Installs the X11 server with windowing system.
  - **x11-sato**: Installs the OpenedHand Sato user experience for mobile devices.

It matters what classes define the image features when creating your own image recipes and choosing the image class to inherit. The class `image` inherits `populate_sdk_base` and thus all image features defined by those two classes are available to images that inherit `image`. Image features defined by `core-image` are available only to images that inherit that class, which in turn inherits `image` and with it also `populate_sdk_base`.

7.1.6 Package Groups

We have touched on package groups a couple of times during this discussion of creating custom Linux distribution images. Package groups are bundles of packages that are referenced by a name. Using that name in the `IMAGE_INSTALL` variable installs all the packages defined by the package group into the root filesystem of your target image.

The Yocto Project and OE Core layers define a common set of package groups that you can readily use for your images. You can also create your own package groups containing packages from any layer, including your own. We first describe the package groups defined by the Yocto Project and OE Core layers and then look into the details on how package groups are defined.

Predefined Package Groups

Package groups are defined by recipes. Conventionally, the recipe files begin with `packagegroup-` and are placed inside `packagegroup` subdirectories of the respective recipe categories. For instance, you can find package group recipes related to the Qt development framework in the subdirectory `meta/recipes-qt/packagegroups`.

Using

```
find . -name "packagegroup-*" -print
```

from the installation directory of the Yocto Project build system gives you a list of all the package group recipes for the predefined package groups of the Yocto Project build system.

Following are the most common predefined package groups:

- **packagegroup-core-ssh-dropbear**: Provides packages for the Dropbear SSH server popular for embedded systems because of its smaller footprint compared to the OpenSSH server. This package group conflicts with `packagegroup-core-ssh-openssh`. You can include only one of the two in your image. The `ssh-server-dropbear` image feature installs this package group.

- **packagegroup-core-ssh-openssh**: Provides packages for the standard OpenSSH server. This package group conflicts with `packagegroup-core-ssh-dropbear`. You can include only one of the two in your image. The `ssh-server-openssh` image feature installs this package group.

- **packagegroup-core-buildessential**: Provides the essential development tools, namely the GNU Autotools utilities autoconf, automake, and libtool; the GNU binary tool set binutils which includes the linker ld, assembler as, and other tools;

the compiler collection cpp; gcc; g++; the GNU internationalization and localization tool gettext; make; libstc++ with development packages; and pkgconfig.

- **packagegroup-core-tools-debug**: Provides the essential debugging tools, namely the GDB debugger, the GDB remote debugging server, the system call tracing tool strace, and, for the GLIBC target library, the memory tracing tool mtrace.

- **packagegroup-core-sdk**: This package group combines the packagegroup-core-buildessential package group with additional tools for development such as GNU Core Utilities coreutils with shell, file, and text manipulation utilities; dynamic linker ldd; and others. Together with packagegroup-core-standalone-sdk-target, this package group forms the tools-sdk image feature.

- **packagegroup-core-standalone-sdk-target**: Provides the GCC and standard C++ libraries. Together with packagegroup-core-sdk, this package group forms the tools-sdk image feature.

- **packagegroup-core-eclipse-debug**: Provides the GDB debugging server, the Eclipse TCF agent, and the OpenSSH SFTP server for integration with the Eclipse IDE for remote deployment and debugging. The image feature eclipse-debug installs this package group.

- **packagegroup-core-tools-testapps**: Provides test applications such as tests for X11 and middleware packages like the telephony manager oFono and the connection manager ConnMan. The tools-testapps image feature installs this package group.

- **packagegroup-self-hosted**: Provides all necessary packages for a self-hosted build system. The build-appliance image target uses this package group.

- **packagegroup-core-boot**: Provides the minimum set of packages necessary to create a bootable image with console. All core-image targets install this package group. The core-image-minimal installs just this package group and the postinstallation scripts.

- **packagegroup-core-nfs**: Provides NFS server, utilities, and client. The nfs-server image feature installs this package group.

- **packagegroup-base**: This recipe provides multiple package groups that depend on each other as well as on machine and distribution configuration. The purpose of these package groups is to add hardware, networking protocol, USB, filesystem, and other support to the images dependent on the machine and distribution configuration. The two top-level package groups are packagegroup-base and packagegroup-base-extended. The former adds hardware support for Bluetooth, WiFi, 3G, and NFC only if both the machine configuration and the distribution configuration require them. The latter also adds configuration for those technologies if the distribution configuration requires them. However, the machine configuration does not support them directly but provides support for PCI, PCMCIA, or USB host. This package group allows you to create an image with support for devices that can physically be added to the target device; for example, via USB hotplug. Most commonly, images providing hardware support use `packagegroup-base-extended` rather than `packagegroup-base` for dynamic hardware support; for example, `core-image-base`.

- **packagegroup-cross-canadian**: Provides SDK packages for creating a toolchain using the Canadian Cross technique, which is building a toolchain on system A that executes on system B to create binaries for system C. A use case for this package group is to build a toolchain with the Yocto Project on your build host that runs on your image target but produces output for a third system with a different architecture than your image target.

- **packagegroup-core-tools-profile**: Provides common profiling tools such as oProfile, PowerTOP, LatencyTOP, LTTng-UST, and Valgrind. The `tools-profile` image feature uses this package group.

- **packagegroup-core-device-devel**: Provides distcc support for an image. Distcc allows distribution of compilation across several machines on a network. The distcc must be installed, configured, and running on your build host. On the target you must define the cross-compiler variable to use distcc instead of the local compiler (e.g., `export CC="distcc"`).

- **packagegroup-qt-toolchain-target**: Provides the package to build applications for the X11-based version of the Qt development toolkit on the target system.

- **packagegroup-qte-toolchain-target**: Provides the package to build applications for the embedded version of the Qt development toolkit on the target system.

- **packagegroup-core-qt**: Provides all necessary packages for a target system using the X11-based version of the Qt development toolkit.

- **packagegroup-core-qt4e**: Provides all necessary packages for a target system using the embedded Qt toolkit. The `qt4e-demo-image` installs this package group.

- **packagegroup-core-x11-xserver**: Provides the X.Org X11 server only.

- **packagegroup-core-x11**: Provides `packagegroup-core-x11-xserver` plus basic utilities such as xhost, xauth, xset, xrandr, and initialization on startup. The x11 image feature installs this package group.

- **packagegroup-core-x11-base**: Provides `packagegroup-core-x11` plus middleware and application clients for a working X11 environment that includes the Matchbox Window Manager, Matchbox Terminal, and a fonts package. The x11-base image feature installs this package group.

- **packagegroup-core-x11-sato**: Provides the OpenedHand Sato user experience for mobile devices, which includes the Matchbox Window Manager, Matchbox Desktop, and a variety of applications. The x11-sato image feature installs this package group. To utilize this package group for your target image, you also have to install `packagegroup-core-x11-base`.

- **packagegroup-core-clutter-core**: Provides packages for the Clutter graphical toolkit. To use the toolkit for your target image, you also have to install `packagegroup-core-x11-base`.

- **packagegroup-core-directfb**: Provides packages for the DirectFB support without X11. Among others, the package group includes the directfb package and the directfb-example package, and it adds touchscreen support if provided by the machine configuration.

- **packagegroup-core-lsb**: Provides all packages required for LSB support.

- **packagegroup-core-full-cmdline**: Provides packages for a more traditional Linux system by installing the full command-line utilities rather than the more compact BusyBox variant.

When explaining the different package groups, we used the terms *provide* and *install* somewhat liberally, since the package group recipes actually do not provide or install any packages. They only create dependencies that cause the build system to process the respective package recipes, as we see in the next section.

Several of the package groups are used by image features, which raises the question whether to use an image feature or to use the package group the image feature uses.

Package Group Recipes

Package groups are defined by recipes that inherit the packagegroup class. Package group recipes are different from typical package recipes, as they do not build anything or create any output. Package group recipes only create dependencies that trigger the build system to process the recipes of the packages the package groups reference.

Listing 7-3 shows a typical package group recipe.

Listing 7-3   **Package Group Recipe**

```
SUMMARY = "Custom package group for our IoT devices"
DESCRIPTION = "This package group adds standard functionality required by \
               our IoT devices."

LICENSE = "MIT"

inherit packagegroup
PACKAGES = "\
   packagegroup-databases \
   packagegroup-python \
   packagegroup-servers"

RDEPENDS_packagegroup-databases = "\
   db \
   sqlite3"

RDEPENDS_packagegroup-python = "\
   python \
   python-sqlite3"

RDEPENDS_packagegroup-servers = "\
   openssh \
   openssh-sftp-server"
```

```
RRECOMMENDS_packagegroup-python = "\
    ncurses \
    readline \
    zip"
```

Names of package group recipes, although not enforced or required by the build system, should adhere to the convention `packagegroup-<name>.bb`. You also would want to place them in the subdirectory `packagegroup` of the recipe category the package groups are integrating. If package groups span recipes and possibly package groups from multiple categories, it is good practice to place them into the `recipes-core` category.

The basic structure of package group recipes is rather simple. As should any recipe (and we go into the details of writing recipes in Chapter 8, "Software Package Recipes"), a package group recipe should provide a SUMMARY of what the recipe does. The DESCRIPTION, which can provide a longer, more detailed explanation, is optional, but it is good practice to add it. Any recipe also needs to provide a LICENSE for the recipe itself. All package group recipes must inherit the `packagegroup` class.

The names of the actual package groups are defined by the PACKAGES variable. This variable contains a space-delimited list of the package group names. In the case of Listing 7-3, these are `packagegroup-databases`, `packagegroup-python`, and `packagegroup-servers`. By convention, package group names begin with `packagegroup-`. Although the build system does not require it, it is good practice if you adhere to it for your own package group names.

For each package group, the recipe must define its dependencies in a conditional `RDEPENDS_<package-group-name>` variable. These variables list the required dependencies, which can be packages or package groups.

The `RRECOMMENDS_<package-group-name>` definitions are optional. As we saw in Chapter 3, recommendations are weak dependencies that cause a package to be included only if it already has been built.

You can reference package groups from other variables, such as IMAGE_INSTALL, which of course causes these package groups to be installed in a target image. You can also use them to create dependencies for other package groups for a hierarchy. You must avoid circular dependencies of package groups. That may sound simple and straightforward but can easily happen by mistake in rather complex environments. BitBake, however, aborts with an error message in the case of a circular package group dependency.

Package group recipes can also be directly used as BitBake build targets. For example, if the name of the package group recipe is `packagegroup-core-iot.bb`, you can build all the packages of the package groups defined by the recipe using

```
$ bitbake packagegroup-core-iot
```

Doing so allows testing the package groups before referencing them by image builds, which simplifies debugging.

7.2 Building Images from Scratch

Section 7.1 detailed the Yocto Project core images and how to extend them through setting `IMAGE_INSTALL`, `CORE_IMAGE_EXTRA_INSTALL`, `IMAGE_FEATURES`, and `EXTRA_IMAGE_FEATURES` in `conf/local.conf` and in recipes extending predefined image recipes. Eventually, you may want to create your custom Linux distribution image from scratch without relying on one of the reference images.

A custom image recipe must inherit either the `image` or the `core-image` class. The latter is essentially an extension of the former and defines additional image features, as described earlier in Section 7.1.5. Which one to choose for custom image recipes depends on your requirements. However, inheriting `core-image` generally is sound advice, since the image features are made available but only installed if explicitly requested.

Listing 7-4 shows the simplest image recipe that creates a bootable console image.

Listing 7-4　**Basic Image Recipe**

```
SUMMARY = "Custom image recipe that does not get any simpler"
DESCRIPTION = "Well yes, you could remove SUMMARY, DESCRIPTION, LICENSE."

LICENSE = "MIT"

inherit core-image
```

The recipe creates an image with the core packages to boot and hardware support for the target device because the `core-image` class adds the two package groups `packagegroup-core-boot` and `packagegroup-base-extended` to `IMAGE_INSTALL` by default. Also added to `IMAGE_INSTALL` by the class is the variable `CORE_IMAGE_EXTRA_INSTALL`, which allows for simple image modification through `conf/local.conf`, as described earlier.

The basic image with `package-group-core-boot` and `package-base-extended` provides a good starting point that easily can be extended by adding to `IMAGE_INSTALL` and `IMAGE_FEATURES`, as shown in Listing 7-5.

Listing 7-5　**Adding to the Basic Image**

```
SUMMARY = "Custom image recipe adding packages and features"
DESCRIPTION = "Append to IMAGE_INSTALL and IMAGE_FEATURES for \
               further customization. "

LICENSE = "MIT"

# We are using the append operator (+=) below to preserve the default
# values set by the core-image class we are inheriting.
IMAGE_INSTALL += "mtd-utils"
IMAGE_FEATURES += "splash"

inherit core-image
```

Within image recipes, you append directly to IMAGE_INSTALL and IMAGE_FEATURES using the += operator. Do not use EXTRA_IMAGE_FEATURES or CORE_IMAGE_EXTRA_INSTALL in your image recipe. These variables are reserved for use in conf/local.conf where they are directly assigned and overwrite any values assigned by the image recipe.

An image recipe that does not rely on the default values for IMAGE_INSTALL and IMAGE_FEATURES is equally simple, as Listing 7-6 shows.

Listing 7-6 **Core Image from Scratch**

```
SUMMARY = "Custom image recipe from scratch"
DESCRIPTION = "Directly assign IMAGE_INSTALL and IMAGE_FEATURES for \
               for direct control over image contents."

LICENSE = "MIT"

# We are using the assignment operator (=) below to purposely overwrite
# the default from the core-image class.
IMAGE_INSTALL = "packagegroup-core-boot packagegroup-base-extended \
                ${CORE_IMAGE_EXTRA_INSTALL} mtd-utils"
IMAGE_FEATURES = "${EXTRA_IMAGE_FEATURES} splash"

inherit core-image
```

At first glance, the image recipes of Listings 7-5 and 7-6 look rather similar. In fact, the two recipes produce exactly the same image. The differences are subtle but significant. Listing 7-5 uses the append operator += for IMAGE_INSTALL and IMAGE_FEATURES to take advantage of the default values provided by the core-image class. Listing 7-6 uses the assignment operator = to purposely overwrite the default values.

Overwriting the default values gives you the most control over the content of your image, but you also have to take care of the basics yourself. For any image, you would most likely always want to include packagegroup-core-boot to get a bootable image. Whether you want the hardware support that packagegroup-base-extended provides depends on your requirements. Also at your disposal is CORE_IMAGE_EXTRA_INSTALL: if you do not explicitly add it to IMAGE_FEATURES, you will not be able to use this variable in conf/local.conf for local customization of your target image, but it may make sense to do so for a controlled build environment for production.

The same holds true for IMAGE_FEATURES and EXTRA_IMAGE_FEATURES. If you use the assignment operator with IMAGE_FEATURES and purposely do not add EXTRA_IMAGE_FEATURES, it is not included, which means that the debug-tweaks image feature is not applied, and you need to provide passwords for shell and SSH logins. Again, this makes sense for production build environments where you do not want local configuration settings to override the settings of your production images.

7.3 Image Options

The following sections discuss a list of options that affect how the Yocto Project build system creates your root filesystem images.

7.3.1 Languages and Locales

Additional languages for different territories can easily be added to a root filesystem or your image by adding the IMAGE_LINGUAS variable to an image recipe. Using

```
IMAGE_LINGUAS = "en-gb pt-br"
```

adds the specific language packages for British English and Brazilian Portuguese to the image. However, not all software packages provide locales separated by language and territory. Some of them provide the locale files only by language. In this case, the build system defaults to installing the correct language local files regardless of the territory.

The minimum default for all packages is en-us and is always installed. In addition, the image class defines

```
IMAGE_LINGUAS ?= "de-de fr-fr en-gb"
```

Any additional locale packages, of course, occupy additional space in your root filesystem image. Therefore, if your device does not require any additional language support, it is good practice to set

```
IMAGE_LINGUAS = ""
```

in image recipes.

The build system ignores the languages for packages that do not provide them.

7.3.2 Package Management

The build system can package software packages using the four different packaging formats dpkg (Debian Package Management), opkg (Open Package Management), RPM (Red Hat Package Manager), and tar. Only the first three can be used to create root filesystems. Tar does not provide the necessary metadata package information and database to log what packages in what versions have been installed, which packages conflict with each other, and so on.

The variable PACKAGE_CLASSES in conf/local.conf of your build environment controls what package management systems are used for your builds:

```
PACKAGE_CLASSES = "package_rpm package_ipk package_tar"
```

You can declare more than one packaging class, but you have to provide at least one. The build system creates packages for all classes specified; however, only the first packaging class in the list is used to create the root filesystem of your distribution images. The first packaging class in the list must not be tar.

The build system stores the package feeds organized by the package management system in separate directories in tmp/deploy/<pms>, where <pms> is the name of the respective package management system. Inside those directories, the packages are further subdivided into common, architecture, and machine-dependent packages.

What package management system should you choose for your project? That depends on the requirements of your project. Here are some considerations you may want to take into account:

- Opkg creates and utilizes less package metadata than dpkg and RPM. That makes building faster, and the packages are smaller.
- Dpkg and RPM offer better dependency handling and version management than opkg because of the enhanced package metadata.
- The RPM package manager is written in Python and requires Python to be installed on the target to install packages during runtime of the system.

By default, the build system does not install the package manager on your target system. If you are looking to install packages during runtime of your embedded system, you have to add the package manager using its image feature:

```
IMAGE_FEATURES += "package_management"
```

The build system automatically installs the correct package manager depending on the first entry of PACKAGE_CLASSES.

The package management system for your root filesystem is ultimately controlled by the variable IMAGE_PKGTYPE. This variable is set automatically by the order of the packaging classes defined by PACKAGE_CLASSES. The first packaging class in the list sets the variable. We recommend that you do not set this variable directly.

7.3.3 Image Size

The final size of the root filesystem is dependent on multiple factors and is computed by the build system using the function _get_rootfs_size() in the Python module meta/lib/oe/image.py. The computation takes into account the actual space required by the root filesystem and the following variable settings. It also ensures that the final root filesystem image size is always sufficient to hold the entire image. Hence, even if you set IMAGE_ROOTFS_SIZE to a specific value, the final image may be larger than that value, but it is never smaller.

- **IMAGE_ROOTFS_SIZE**: Defines the size in kilobytes of the created root filesystem image. The build system uses this value as a request or recommendation. The final root filesystem image size may be larger depending on the actual space required. The default value is 65536.
- **IMAGE_ROOTFS_ALIGNMENT**: Defines the alignment of the root filesystem image in kilobytes. If the final size of the root filesystem image is not a multiple of this value, it is rounded up to the nearest multiple of it. The default value is 1.
- **IMAGE_ROOTFS_EXTRA_SPACE**: Adds extra free space to the root filesystem image. The variable specifies the value in kilobytes. For example, to add an additional 4 GB of space, set the variable to IMAGE_ROOTFS_EXTRA_SPACE = "4194304". The default value is 0.
- **IMAGE_OVERHEAD_FACTOR**: This variable specifies a multiplicator for the root filesystem image. The factor is applied after the actual space required by the root filesystem has been determined. The default value is 1.3.

After the build system has created the root filesystem in the staging area, a directory specified by the variable `IMAGE_ROOTFS`, it calculates its actual size in kilobytes using `du -ks ${IMAGE_ROOTFS}`. The function `_get_rootfs_size()` computes the final root filesystem image size, as shown by Listing 7-7 in pseudocode.

Listing 7-7   Root Filesystem Image Size Computation in Pseudocode

```
_get_rootfs_size():

  ROOTFS_SIZE =`du -ks ${IMAGE_ROOTFS}`
  BASE_SIZE = ROOTFS_SIZE * IMAGE_OVERHEAD_FACTOR

  if (BASE_SIZE < IMAGE_ROOTFS_SIZE):
     IMG_SIZE = IMAGE_ROOTFS_SIZE + IMAGE_ROOTFS_EXTRA_SPACE
  else:
     IMG_SIZE = BASE_SIZE + IMAGE_ROOTFS_EXTRA_SPACE

  IMG_SIZE = IMG_SIZE + IMAGE_ROOTFS_ALIGNMENT - 1
  IMG_SIZE = IMG_SIZE % IMAGE_ROOTFS_ALIGNMENT

  return IMG_SIZE
```

Most commonly, your image recipes set `IMAGE_ROOTFS_SIZE` and `IMAGE_ROOTFS_EXTRA_SPACE` to adjust the final root filesystem image size. If you are concerned with the footprint of your root filesystem, then you may also want to reduce `IMAGE_OVERHEAD_FACTOR` or set it to 1 to shrink your image.

7.3.4 Root Filesystem Types

Eventually, you use the root filesystem image to create a bootable medium for your target or to launch the QEMU emulator. For that purpose, the build system provides the `image_types` class that can create a root filesystem for various filesystem types.

Your image recipes do not use the `image_types` class directly but rather set the variable `IMAGE_FSTYPES` to one or more of the filesystem types provided by the class. Using

```
IMAGE_FSTYPES = "ext3 tar.bz2"
```

creates two root filesystem images, one using the ext3 filesystem and one that is a tar archive compressed using the bzip2 algorithm.

The `image_types` class defines the variable `IMAGE_TYPES`, which contains a list of all image types you can specify in `IMAGE_FSTYPES`. The list shows the filesystem types ordered by core type. Commonly, some of the core types are also used in compressed formats to preserve space. If a compression algorithm is used for the filesystem, the name of the core type is appended with the compression type: `<core name>.<compression type>`.

- **tar, tar.gz, tar.bz2, tar.xz, tar.lz3**: Create uncompressed and compressed root filesystem images in the form of tar archives.

- **ext2, ext2.gz, ext2.bz2, ext2.lzma**: Root filesystem images using the ext2 filesystem without or with compression.

- **ext3**, **ext3.gz**: Root filesystem images using the ext3 filesystem without or with compression.

- **btrfs**: Root filesystem image with B-tree filesystem.

- **jffs2**, **jffs2.sum**: Uncompressed or compressed root filesystems based on the second generation of the Journaling Flash File System (JFFS2). Since JFFS2 directly supports NAND flash devices, it is a popular choice for embedded systems. It also provides journaling and wear-leveling.

- **cramfs**: Root filesystem image using the compressed ROM filesystem (cramfs). The Linux kernel can mount this filesystem without prior decompression. The compression uses the zlib algorithm that compresses files one page at a time to allow random access. This filesystem is read-only to simplify its design, as random write access with compression is difficult to implement.

- **iso**: Root filesystem image type using the ISO 9660 standard for bootable CD-ROM. This filesystem type is not a standalone format. It uses ext3 as the underlying filesystem type.

- **hddimg**: Root filesystem image for bootable hard drives. It uses ext3 as the actual filesystem type.

- **squashfs**, **squashfs-xz**: Compressed read-only root filesystem type specifically for Linux, similar to cramfs but with better compression and support for larger files and filesystems. SquashFS also has a variable block size from 0.5 kB to 64 kB over the fixed 4 kB block size of cramfs, which allows for larger file and filesystem sizes. SquashFS uses gzip compression, while squashfs-xz uses Lempel–Ziv–Markov (LZMA) compression for even smaller images.

- **ubi**, **ubifs**: Root filesystem images using the unsorted block image (UBI) format for raw flash devices. UBI File System (UBIFS) is essentially a successor to JFFS2. The main differences between the two is that UBIFS supports write caching. Using ubifs in IMAGE_FSTYPES just creates the ubifs root filesystem image. Using ubi creates the ubifs root filesystem image and also runs the ubinize utility to create an image that can be written directly to a flash device.

- **cpio**, **cpio.gz**, **cpio.xz**, **cpio.lzma**: Root filesystem images using uncompressed or compressed copy in and out (CPIO) streams.

- **vmdk**: Root filesystem image using the VMware virtual machine disk format. It uses ext3 as the underlying filesystem format.

- **elf**: Bootable root filesystem image created with the mkelfImage utility from the Coreboot project (www.coreboot.org).

Once again, which image types to use depends entirely on the requirements of your project, particularly on your target hardware. Boot device, bootloader, memory constraints, and other factors determine what root filesystem types are appropriate for your project. Our recommendation is to specify the root filesystem types ext3 and tar, or better, one of the compressed formats such as tar.bz2, in the image recipe. The ext3 format allows you to easily boot your root filesystem with the QEMU emulator for testing. The tar filesystem can easily be extracted onto partitioned and formatted media. The machine configuration files for your target hardware can then add additional root filesystem types appropriate for it.

7.3.5 Users, Groups, and Passwords

The class extrausers provides a comfortable mechanism for adding users and groups to an image as well as setting passwords for user accounts (see Listing 7-8).

Listing 7-8   **Modifying Users, Groups, and Passwords**

```
SUMMARY = "Custom image recipe from scratch"
DESCRIPTION = "Directly assign IMAGE_INSTALL and IMAGE_FEATURES for \
               for direct control over image contents."

LICENSE = "MIT"

# We are using the assignment operator (=) below to purposely overwrite
# the default from the core-image class.
IMAGE_INSTALL = "packagegroup-core-boot packagegroup-base-extended \
                 ${CORE_IMAGE_EXTRA_INSTALL}"

inherit core-image
inherit extrausers

# set image root password
ROOT_PASSWORD = "secret"
DEV_PASSWORD = "hackme"

EXTRA_USERS_PARAMS = "\
  groupadd developers; \
  useradd -p `openssl passwd ${DEV_PASSWORD}` developer; \
  useradd -g developers developer; \
  usermod -p `openssl passwd ${ROOT_PASSWORD}` root; \
  "
```

The listing adds a group named developers and a user account named developer and adds the user account to the group. It also changes the password for the root account. Commands for adding and modifying groups, users, and passwords are added to the variable EXTRA_USERS_PARMS, which is interpreted by the class. The commands understood by the class are

- **useradd**: Add user account
- **usermod**: Modify user account
- **userdel**: Remove user account
- **groupadd**: Add user group

- **groupmod**: Modify user group
- **groupdel**: Remove user group

The class executes the respective Linux utilities with the corresponding names. Hence, the options are exactly the same and can easily be found in the Linux man pages. Note that the individual commands must be separated with a semicolon.

Using the option -p with the commands useradd and usermod sets the password of the user account. The password must be provided as the password hash. You can either calculate the password hash manually and add it to the recipe or, as shown in the example, have the recipe calculate it.

A word about the root user account: the build system sets up the root user for an image with an empty password if debug-tweaks is included with IMAGE_FEATURES. Removing debug-tweaks replaces the empty root password with *, which disables the account, so logging in as root from the console is no longer possible. For production use, we strongly recommend removing debug-tweaks from the build. If your embedded system requires console login capability, you can either set the root password as shown previously or add the sudo recipe and set up user accounts as *sudoers*.

For example, if you want to give the developer user account *sudoer* privileges, simply add sudo to IMAGE_INSTALL and usermod -a -G sudo developer to EXTRA_USERS_PARAMS.

7.3.6 Tweaking the Root Filesystem

For further customization of the root filesystem after it has been created by the build system and before the actual root filesystem images are created, ROOTFS_POSTPROCESS_COMMAND is available (see Listing 7-9). The variable holds a list of shell functions separated by semicolons.

Listing 7-9 **ROOTFS_POSTPROCESS_COMMAND**

```
SUMMARY = "Custom image recipe from scratch"
DESCRIPTION = "Directly assign IMAGE_INSTALL and IMAGE_FEATURES for \
               for direct control over image contents."

LICENSE = "MIT"

# We are using the assignment operator (=) below to purposely overwrite
# the default from the core-image class.
IMAGE_INSTALL = "packagegroup-core-boot packagegroup-base-extended \
                ${CORE_IMAGE_EXTRA_INSTALL}"

inherit core-image

# Additional root filesystem processing
modify_shells() {
    printf "# /etc/shells: valid login shells\n/bin/sh\n/bin/bash\n" \
          > ${IMAGE_ROOTFS}/etc/shells
}
ROOTFS_POSTPROCESS_COMMAND += "modify_shells;"
```

The example adds the bash shell to /etc/shells. Be sure to always use the += operator to add to ROOTFS_POSTPROCESS_COMMAND, as the build system adds its own postprocessing commands to it.

Sudo Configuration

If you followed the example on giving a user sudoer privileges in the previous paragraph, you probably noticed that it does not work unless you uncomment the line %sudo ALL=(ALL) ALL in /etc/sudoers. A simple shell function added to ROOTFS_POSTPROCESS_COMMAND takes care of that when the root filesystem image is created (see Listing 7-10).

Listing 7-10   **Sudo Configuration**

```
modify_sudoers() {
    sed 's/# %sudo/%sudo/' < ${IMAGE_ROOTFS}/etc/sudoers > \
        ${IMAGE_ROOTFS}/etc/sudoers.tmp
    mv ${IMAGE_ROOTFS}/etc/sudoers.tmp ${IMAGE_ROOTFS}/etc/sudoers
}
ROOTFS_POSTPROCESS_COMMAND += "modify_sudoers;"
```

The script simply uncomments the line using sed.

SSH Server Configuration

All core images automatically include an SSH server for remote shell access to the system. By default, the server is configured to allow login with user name and password. Using public key infrastructure (PKI) provides an additional level of security but requires configuration of the root server and installation of keys into the root filesystem. A ROOTFS_POSTPROCESS_COMMAND can also easily be used to accomplish that task (see Listing 7-11).

Listing 7-11   **SSH Server Configuration**

```
configure_sshd() {
    # disallow password authentication
    echo "PasswordAuthentication no" >> ${IMAGE_ROOTFS}/etc/ssh/sshd_config
    # create keys in tmp/deploy/keys
    mkdir -p ${DEPLOY_DIR}/keys
    if [ ! -f ${DEPLOY_DIR}/keys/${IMAGE_BASENAME}-sshroot ]; then
        ssh-keygen -t rsa -N '' \
            -f ${DEPLOY_DIR}/keys/${IMAGE_BASENAME}-sshroot
    fi
    # add public key to authorized_keys for root
    mkdir -p ${IMAGE_ROOTFS}/home/root/.ssh
    cat ${DEPLOY_DIR}/keys/${IMAGE_BASENAME}-sshroot.pub \
        >> ${IMAGE_ROOTFS}/home/root/.ssh/authorized_keys
}
ROOTFS_POSTPROCESS_COMMAND += "configure_sshd;"
```

The script first disables authentication with user name and password for SSH. It then creates a key pair in tmp/deploy/keys inside the build environment using the name of the root filesystem image, essentially the name of the image recipe. If a previous build has already created a set of keys, they are preserved. Finally, the script adds the public key to the `authorized_keys` file in `/home/root/.ssh`, which is typical for SSH configuration. Login keys for other users can be created in a similar way.

This method works well if you do not require different keys for each device that you build, as every copy of the root filesystem of course contains the same keys. If you need different keys or, in general, individual configuration for your devices, then you need to devise a provisioning system for your device production.

7.4 Distribution Configuration

The build system provides a mechanism for global configuration that applies to all images built. This mechanism is called *distribution configuration* or *distribution policy*. It is simply a configuration file that contains variable settings. The distribution configuration is included through the `DISTRO` variable setting in the build environment configuration file `conf/local.conf`:

```
DISTRO = "poky"
```

The variable setting corresponds to a distribution configuration file whose base name is the same as the variable's argument with the file extension `.conf`. For the preceding example, the build system searches for a distribution configuration file with the name `poky.conf` in the subdirectory `conf/distro` in all metadata layers included by the build environment.

7.4.1 Standard Distribution Policies

The Yocto Project provides several distribution configuration files for standard configuration policies:

- **poky**: Poky is the default policy for the Yocto Project's reference distribution Poky. It is a good choice for getting started with the Yocto Project and as a template for your own distribution configuration files.

- **poky-bleeding**: This distribution configuration is based on `poky` but sets the versions for all packages to the latest revision. It is commonly used by the Yocto Project developers for integration test purposes. You may, of course, use it, but be aware that there could be issues with packages with incompatible versions.

- **poky-lsb**: This distribution configuration is for a stack that complies with LSB. It is preferably used with the `core-image-lsb` image target and image targets derived from it. It inherits the base settings from `poky` and adds global configuration settings to enable security and includes default libraries required for LSB compliance.

- **poky-tiny**: This distribution configuration tailors the settings to yield a very compact Linux OS stack for embedded devices. It is based on `poky` but provides only the bare minimum functionality necessary to support the hardware and a BusyBox environment. It does not support any video but only a serial console. Because of its slim configuration, only the `core-image-minimal` image target and image targets based on it can be built with the `poky-tiny` distribution configuration.

The standard distribution policies, particularly `poky`, are good starting points for your own distribution configuration. Let's have a closer look at the `poky` distribution configuration to understand how distribution policies are set and how we can use them for our own projects.

7.4.2 Poky Distribution Policy

You can find the file `poky.conf` containing the Poky distribution policy in the `meta-yocto/conf/distro` directory of the build system. We replicated its contents here for convenience, reformatted the file to fit on the page, grouped the variable settings into logical blocks, and added some comments (see Listing 7-12).

Listing 7-12   **Poky Distribution Policy meta-yocto/conf/distro/poky.conf**

```
# Distribution Information

DISTRO = "poky"
DISTRO_NAME = "Poky (Yocto Project Reference Distro)"
DISTRO_VERSION = "1.6+snapshot-${DATE}"
DISTRO_CODENAME = "next"
MAINTAINER = "Poky <poky@yoctoproject.org>"
TARGET_VENDOR = "-poky"

# SDK Information
SDK_NAME = \
    "${DISTRO}-${TCLIBC}-${SDK_ARCH}-${IMAGE_BASENAME}-${TUNE_PKGARCH}"
SDK_VERSION := \
    "${@'${DISTRO_VERSION}'.replace('snapshot-${DATE}','snapshot')}"
SDK_VENDOR = "-pokysdk"
SDKPATH = "/opt/${DISTRO}/${SDK_VERSION}"

# Distribution Features
# Override these in poky based distros
POKY_DEFAULT_DISTRO_FEATURES = "largefile opengl ptest multiarch wayland"
POKY_DEFAULT_EXTRA_RDEPENDS = "packagegroup-core-boot"
POKY_DEFAULT_EXTRA_RRECOMMENDS = "kernel-module-af-packet"

DISTRO_FEATURES ?= "${DISTRO_FEATURES_DEFAULT} ${DISTRO_FEATURES_LIBC} \
                    ${POKY_DEFAULT_DISTRO_FEATURES}"

# Preferred Versions for Packages
PREFERRED_VERSION_linux-yocto ?= "3.14%"
PREFERRED_VERSION_linux-yocto_qemux86 ?= "3.14%"
PREFERRED_VERSION_linux-yocto_qemux86-64 ?= "3.14%"
PREFERRED_VERSION_linux-yocto_qemuarm ?= "3.14%"
PREFERRED_VERSION_linux-yocto_qemumips ?= "3.14%"
PREFERRED_VERSION_linux-yocto_qemumips64 ?= "3.14%"
PREFERRED_VERSION_linux-yocto_qemuppc ?= "3.14%"
```

```
# Dependencies
DISTRO_EXTRA_RDEPENDS += " ${POKY_DEFAULT_EXTRA_RDEPENDS}"
DISTRO_EXTRA_RRECOMMENDS += " ${POKY_DEFAULT_EXTRA_RRECOMMENDS}"

POKYQEMUDEPS = "${@bb.utils.contains( \
    "INCOMPATIBLE_LICENSE", "GPLv3", "", "qemu-config",d)}"
DISTRO_EXTRA_RDEPENDS_append_qemuarm = " ${POKYQEMUDEPS}"
DISTRO_EXTRA_RDEPENDS_append_qemumips = " ${POKYQEMUDEPS}"
DISTRO_EXTRA_RDEPENDS_append_qemuppc = " ${POKYQEMUDEPS}"
DISTRO_EXTRA_RDEPENDS_append_qemux86 = " ${POKYQEMUDEPS}"
DISTRO_EXTRA_RDEPENDS_append_qemux86-64 = " ${POKYQEMUDEPS}"

# Target C Library Configuration
TCLIBCAPPEND = ""

# Target Architectures for QEMU
# (see meta/recipes-devtools/qemu/qemu-targets.inc)
QEMU_TARGETS ?= "arm i386 mips mipsel ppc x86_64"
# Other QEMU_TARGETS "mips64 mips64el sh4"

# Package Manager Configuration
EXTRAOPKGCONFIG = "poky-feed-config-opkg"

# Source Mirrors
PREMIRRORS ??= "\
bzr://.*/.*   http://downloads.yoctoproject.org/mirror/sources/ \n \
cvs://.*/.*   http://downloads.yoctoproject.org/mirror/sources/ \n \
git://.*/.*   http://downloads.yoctoproject.org/mirror/sources/ \n \
gitsm://.*/.* http://downloads.yoctoproject.org/mirror/sources/ \n \
hg://.*/.*    http://downloads.yoctoproject.org/mirror/sources/ \n \
osc://.*/.*   http://downloads.yoctoproject.org/mirror/sources/ \n \
p4://.*/.*    http://downloads.yoctoproject.org/mirror/sources/ \n \
svk://.*/.*   http://downloads.yoctoproject.org/mirror/sources/ \n \
svn://.*/.*   http://downloads.yoctoproject.org/mirror/sources/ \n"

MIRRORS =+ "\
ftp://.*/.*     http://downloads.yoctoproject.org/mirror/sources/ \n \
http://.*/.*    http://downloads.yoctoproject.org/mirror/sources/ \n \
https://.*/.*   http://downloads.yoctoproject.org/mirror/sources/ \n"

# Build System Configuration

# Configuration File and Directory Layout Versions
LOCALCONF_VERSION = "1"
LAYER_CONF_VERSION ?= "6"
#
# OELAYOUT_ABI allows us to notify users when the format of TMPDIR changes
# in an incompatible way. Such changes should usually be detailed in the
# commit that breaks the format and have been previously discussed on the
# mailing list with general agreement from the core team.
#
OELAYOUT_ABI = "8"

# Default hash policy for distro
BB_SIGNATURE_HANDLER ?= 'OEBasicHash'

# Build System Checks
```

```
# add poky sanity bbclass
INHERIT += "poky-sanity"

# The CONNECTIVITY_CHECK_URIs are used to test whether we can successfully
# fetch from the network (and warn you if not). To disable the test, set
# the variable to be empty.
# Git example url: \
#      git://git.yoctoproject.org/yocto-firewall-test;protocol=git;rev=HEAD

CONNECTIVITY_CHECK_URIS ?= " \
              https://eula-downloads.yoctoproject.org/index.php \
              http://bugzilla.yoctoproject.org/report.cgi"

SANITY_TESTED_DISTROS ?= " \
              Poky-1.4 \n \
              Poky-1.5 \n \
              Poky-1.6 \n \
              Ubuntu-12.04 \n \
              Ubuntu-13.10 \n \
              Ubuntu-14.04 \n \
              Fedora-19 \n \
              Fedora-20 \n \
              CentOS-6.4 \n \
              CentOS-6.5 \n \
              Debian-7.0 \n \
              Debian-7.1 \n \
              Debian-7.2 \n \
              Debian-7.3 \n \
              Debian-7.4 \n \
              SUSE-LINUX-12.2 \n \
              openSUSE-project-12.3 \n \
              openSUSE-project-13.1 \n \
              "

# QA check settings - a little stricter than the OE-Core defaults
WARN_QA = "textrel files-invalid incompatible-license xorg-driver-abi \
           libdir unknown-configure-option"
ERROR_QA = "dev-so debug-deps dev-deps debug-files arch pkgconfig la \
            perms useless-rpaths rpaths staticdev ldflags pkgvarcheck \
            already-stripped compile-host-path dep-cmp \
            installed-vs-shipped  install-host-path packages-list \
            perm-config perm-line perm-link pkgv-undefined \
            pn-overrides split-strip var-undefined version-going-backwards"
```

The file shown in the listing is from the head of the Yocto Project Git repository at the writing of this book. Depending on what version of the Yocto Project tools you are using, this file may look slightly different. The file is an example of a distribution policy only. It provides the variable settings most commonly associated with the configuration of a distribution. You are not limited to using just the settings shown in the listing, and you can remove settings if you do not need them for your project.

Distribution Information

This section of the distribution policy file contains settings for general information about the distribution.

- **DISTRO**: Short name of the distribution. The value must match the base name of the distribution configuration file.

- **DISTRO_NAME**: The long name of the distribution. Various recipes reference this variable. Its contents are shown on the console boot prompt.

- **DISTRO_VERSION**: Distribution version string. It is referenced by various recipes and used in filenames' distribution artifacts. It is shown on the console boot prompt.

- **DISTRO_CODENAME**: A code name for the distribution. It is currently used only by the LSB recipes and copied into the lsb-release system configuration file.

- **MAINTAINER**: Name and e-mail address of the distribution maintainer.

- **TARGET_VENDOR**: Target vendor string that is concatenated with various variables, most notably target system (TARGET_SYS). TARGET_SYS is a concatenation of target architecture (TARGET_ARCH), target vendor (TARGET_VENDOR), and target operating system (TARGET_OS), such as i586-poky-linux. The three parts are delimited by hyphens. The TARGET_VENDOR string must be prefixed with the hyphen, and TARGET_OS must not. This is one of the many unfortunate inconsistencies of the OpenEmbedded build system. You may want to set this variable to your or your company's name.

SDK Information

The settings in this section provide the base configuration for the SDK.

- **SDK_NAME**: The base name that the build system uses for SDK output files. It is derived by concatenating the DISTRO, TCLIBC, SDK_ARCH, IMAGE_BASENAME, and TUNE_PKGARCH variables with hyphens. There is not much reason for you to change that string from its default setting, as it provides all the information needed to distinguish different SDKs.

- **SDK_VERSION**: SDK version string, which is commonly set to DISTRO_VERSION.

- **SDK_VENDOR**: SDK vendor string, which serves a similar purpose as TARGET_VENDOR. Like TARGET_VENDOR, the string must be prefixed with a hyphen.

- **SDKPATH**: Default installation path for the SDK. The SDK installer offers this path to the user during installation of an SDK. The user can accept it or enter an alternative path. The default value /opt/${DISTRO}/${SDK_VERSION} installs the SDK into the /opt system directory, which requires root privileges. A viable alternative would be to install the SDK into the user's home directory by setting SDKPATH = "${HOME}/${DISTRO}/${SDK_VERSION}".

Distribution Features

These feature settings provide specific functionality for the distribution.

- **DISTRO_FEATURES**: A list of distribution features that enable support for certain functionality within software packages. The assignment in the poky.conf distribution policy file includes DISTRO_FEATURES_DEFAULT and DISTRO_FEATURES_LIBC.

Both contain default distribution feature settings. We discuss distribution features and how they work and the default configuration in the next two sections.

Preferred Versions

Version settings prescribe particular versions for packages rather than the default versions.

- **PREFERRED_VERSION**: Using PREFERRED_VERSION allows setting particular versions for software packages if you do not want to use the latest version, as it is the default. Commonly, that is done for the Linux kernel but also for software packages on which your application software has strong version dependencies.

Dependencies

These settings are declarations for dependencies required for distribution runtime.

- **DISTRO_EXTRA_RDEPENDS**: Sets runtime dependencies for the distribution. Dependencies declared with this variable are required for the distribution. If these dependencies are not met, building the distributions fails.
- **DISTRO_EXTRA_RRECOMMENDS**: Packages that are recommended for the distribution to provide additional useful functionality. These dependencies are added if available but building the distribution does not fail if they are not met.

Toolchain Configuration

These settings configure the toolchain used for building the distribution.

- **TCMODE**: This variable selects the toolchain that the build system uses. The default value is default, which selects the internal toolchain built by the build system (gcc, binutils, etc.). The setting of the variable corresponds to a configuration file tcmode-${TCMODE}.inc, which the build system locates in the path conf/distro/include. This allows including an external toolchain with the build system by including a toolchain layer that provides the necessary tools as well as the configuration file. If you are using an external toolchain, you must ensure that it is compatible with the Poky build system.
- **TCLIBC**: Specifies the C library to be used. The build system currently supports EGLIBC, uClibc, and musl. The setting of the variable corresponds to a configuration file tclibc-${TCLIBC}.inc that the build system locates in the path conf/distro/include. These configuration files set preferred providers for libraries and more.
- **TCLIBCAPPEND**: The build system appends this string to other variables to distinguish build artifacts by C library. If you are experimenting with different C libraries, you may want to use the settings

```
TCLIBCAPPEND = "-${TCLIBC}"
TMPDIR .= "${TCLIBCAPPEND}"
```

in your distribution configuration, which creates a separate build output directory structure for each C library.

Mirror Configuration

The settings in this section configure the mirrors for downloading source packages.

- **PREMIRRORS** and **MIRRORS**: The Poky distribution adds these variables to set its mirror configuration to use the Yocto Project repositories as a source for downloads. If you want to use your own mirrors, you can add them to your distribution configuration file. However, since mirrors are not strictly distribution settings, you may want to add these variables to the local.conf file of your build environment. Another alternative would be to add them to the layer.conf file of a custom layer.

Build System Configuration

These settings define the requirements for the build system.

- **LOCALCONF_VERSION**: Sets the expected or required version for the build environment configuration file local.conf. The build system compares this value to the value of the variable CONF_VERSION in local.conf. If LOCALCONF_VERSION is a later version than CONF_VERSION, the build system may be able to automatically upgrade local.conf to the newer version. Otherwise, the build system exits with an error message.

- **LAYER_CONF_VERSION**: Sets the expected or required version for the bblayers.conf configuration file of a build environment. The build system compares this version to the value of LCONF_VERSION set by bblayers.conf. If LAYER_CONF_VERSION is a later version than LCONF_VERSION, the build system may be able to automatically upgrade bblayers.conf to the newer version. Otherwise, the build system exits with an error message.

- **OELAYOUT_ABI**: Sets the expected or required version for the layout of the output directory TMPDIR. The build system stores the actual layout version in the file abi_version inside of TMPDIR. If the two are incompatible, the build system exits with an error message. This typically happens only if you are using a newer version of the build system with a build environment that was created by a previous version and the layout changed incompatibly. Deleting TMPDIR resolves the issue by re-creating the directory.

- **BB_SIGNATURE_HANDLER**: The signature handler used for signing shared state cache entries and creating stamp files. The value references a signature handler function that, because of its complexity, is typically implemented in Python. The code in meta/lib/oe/sstatesig.py implements OEBasic and OEBasicHash based on the BitBake signature generators SignatureGeneratorBasic and SignatureGeneratorBasicHash defined by bitbake/lib/bb/siggen.py and illustrates how to insert your own signature handler function. The two signature handlers are principally the same, but OEBasicHash includes the task code in the signature, which causes any change to metadata to invalidate stamp files and shared state cache entries without explicitly changing package revision numbers. Using the default value of OEBasicHash is typically sufficient for most applications.

Build System Checks

These configuration variables control various validators to catch build system misconfigurations.

- **INHERIT += "poky-sanity"**: Inherits the class poky-sanity, which is required to perform the build system checks. It is recommended that you include this directive in your own distribution configuration files.
- **CONNECTIVITY_CHECK_URIS**: A list of URIs that the build system tries to verify network connectivity. In the case of Poky, these point to files on the Yocto Project's high-availability infrastructure. If you intend to use your own mirrors for downloading source packages, you could use URIs pointing to files on your mirror servers to verify proper connectivity.
- **SANITY_TESTED_DISTROS**: A list of Linux distributions the Poky build system has been tested on. The build system verifies the Linux distribution it is running on against this list. If that distribution is not in the list, Poky displays a warning message and starts the build process regardless. Poky runs on most current Linux distributions, and in most cases, building works just fine even if the distribution is not officially supported.

QA Checks

The QA checks are defined and implemented by meta/classes/insane.bbclass. This class also defines the QA tasks that are included with the build process. QA checks are performed after configuration, packaging, and other build tasks. The following two variables define which QA checks cause warning messages and which checks cause the build system to terminate the build with an error message:

- **WARN_QA**: A list of QA checks that create warning messages, but the build continues
- **ERROR_QA**: A list of QA checks that create error messages, and the build terminates

The preceding list represents the most common variable settings used by a distribution configuration. For your own distribution configuration, you may add and/or omit variables as needed.

7.4.3 Distribution Features

Distribution features enable support for certain functionality within software packages. Adding a distribution feature to the variable DISTRO_FEATURES adds the functionality of this feature to software packages that support it during build time. For instance, if a software package can be built for console as well as graphical user interfaces, then adding x11 to DISTRO_FEATURES configures that software package so that it is built with X11 support. Unlike the x11 image feature, this does not mean that the X11 packages are installed in your target root filesystem. The distribution feature only prepares a software package for X11 support so that it uses X11 on a system where the X11 base packages are installed.

Using DISTRO_FEATURES gives you granular control over how software packages are built. If you do not need a particular functionality, omitting the distribution feature enabling it typically results in a smaller footprint for a particular software package.

Using

```
$ grep -R DISTRO_FEATURES *
```

from the installation directory of your build system gives you a list of all the recipes and include files that use DISTRO_FEATURES to conditionally modify configuration settings or build processes dependent on what distribution features are enabled.

Recipes typically scan DISTRO_FEATURES using

```
bb.utils.contains('DISTRO_FEATURES', <feature>, <true_val>, <false_val>)
```

to determine if a particular distribution feature is enabled by DISTRO_FEATURES. The function returns true_val if DISTRO_FEATURES contains feature and false_val otherwise. That makes it convenient for the developer to assign values to BitBake variables or use the function in if-then-else statements. Typically, this is used by the do_configure task to modify the configuration based on DISTRO_FEATURES. For some packages, it may provide flags to makefiles.

A prime example is the recipe to build the EGLIBC library. EGLIBC allows enabling functionality by setting configuration options. The file meta/recipes-core/egligc/egilbc-options.inc, which is included by the recipe, sets the configuration options based on the distribution features provided by DISTRO_FEATURES.

The following list shows the most common distribution features that you can add to DISTRO_FEATURES to enable functionality in software packages globally across your distribution:

- **alsa**: Enable support for the Advanced Linux Sound Architecture (ALSA), including the installation of open source compatibility modules if available.

- **bluetooth**: Enable support for Bluetooth.

- **cramfs**: Enable support for the compressed filesystem CramFS.

- **directfb**: Enable support for DirectFB.

- **ext2**: Enable support and include tools for devices with internal mass storage devices such as hard disks instead of flash devices only.

- **ipsec**: Enable support for authentication and encryption using Internet Protocol Security (IPSec).

- **ipv6**: Enable support for Internet Protocol version 6 (IPv6).

- **irda**: Enable support for wireless infrared data communication as specified by the Infrared Data Association (IrDA).

- **keyboard**: Enable keyboard support, which includes loading of keymaps during boot of the system.

- **nfs**: Enable client NFS support for mounting NFS exports on the system.

- **opengl**: Include the Open Graphics Library (OpenGL), which is an application programming interface for rendering 2D and 3D graphics. OpenGL runs on different platforms and provides bindings for most common programming languages.

- **pci**: Enable support for the PCI bus.

- **pcmcia**: Enable PCMCIA and CompactFlash support.

- **ppp**: Enable Point-to-Point Protocol (PPP) support for dial-up networking.

- **smbfs**: Enable support and include clients for Microsoft's Server Message Block (SMB) for sharing remote filesystems, printers, and other devices over networks.

- **systemd**: Include support for the system management daemon (systemd) that replaces the SysVinit script-based system for starting up and shutting down a system.

- **sysvinit**: Include support for the SysVinit system manager.

- **usbgadget**: Enable support for the Linux-USB Gadget API Framework that allows a Linux device to act like a USB device (slave role) when connected to another system.

- **usbhost**: Enable USB host support allowing client devices such as keyboards, mice, cameras, and more to be connected to the system's USB ports and detected by it.

- **wayland**: Enable support for the Wayland compositor protocol and include the Weston compositor.

- **wifi**: Enable WiFi support.

- **x11**: Include the X11 server and libraries.

The list does not include the distribution features for the configuration of the C library. These distribution features all begin with `libc-`. They enable support for functionality provided by the C library if the C library is configurable like the Yocto Project's default C library glibc. If you are using glibc, then you do not have to worry about setting these distribution features, as they are inherited from the default distribution setup, which is covered in the next section.

If you have already been working with the Yocto Project, you may have noticed that there is also a variable called MACHINE_FEATURES and that the permissible list of machine features has a large intersection with the distribution feature list. For example, both MACHINE_FEATURES and DISTRO_FEATURES provide the feature bluetooth. Enabling Bluetooth in DISTRO_FEATURES causes the Bluetooth packages for hardware support to be installed and also enables Bluetooth support for various software packages. However, enabling Bluetooth in MACHINE_FEATURES only causes the Bluetooth packages for hardware support to be installed. This gives you control over functionality on the machine and the distribution level. We discuss machine features in detail when we are looking into Yocto Project board support packages.

7.4.4 System Manager

The build system supports SysVinit, the traditional script-based system manager, as well as the system management daemon (systemd), a replacement for SysVinit that offers better prioritization and dependency handling between services and the ability to start services in parallel to speed up the boot sequence.

SysVinit is the default system manager for Linux distributions built by Poky. You do not have to change the configuration if you want to use SysVinit.

To enable systemd, you need to add it to the distribution features and set it as the system manager. Add the following to your distribution configuration file:

```
DISTRO_FEATURES_append = " systemd"
VIRTUAL-RUNTIME_init_manager = "systemd"
```

The first line installs systemd in the root filesystem. The second line enables it as the system manager. Installing and enabling systemd does not remove SysVinit from your root filesystem if it is also included in DISTRO_FEATURES. If you are using one of the standard distribution configurations, such as poky, then you can remove it from DISTRO_FEATURES with

```
DISTRO_FEATURES_BACKFULL_CONSIDERED = "sysvinit"
```

which is easier than redefining DISTRO_FEATURES altogether. For your own distribution configuration, you can of course simply omit SysVinit from the DISTRO_FEATURES list.

The SysVinit initscripts to start the individual system services are typically part of the package that provides the service. To conserve space in the root filesystem, you may not want to install the initscripts if you want to use systemd exclusively. Use

```
VIRTUAL-RUNTIME_initscripts = ""
```

to prevent the build system from installing the SysVinit initscripts.

A word of caution: some daemons may not yet have been adapted for use with systemd and therefore systemd service files are not available. If you come across such software, you may have to do the adaptation yourself. If you do so, please consider submitting your work to upstream.

7.4.5 Default Distribution Setup

The OE Core metadata layer provides default distribution setup through the file meta/conf/distro/defaultsetup.conf and a series of other files included by it (see Listing 7-13). It is not quite obvious how this default distribution setup is included into the build configuration, as this file is not included by distribution policy configuration files such as `poky.conf`, which we discussed earlier. Instead, the file is included by BitBake's main configuration file, `bitbake.conf`.

Knowing about `defaultsetup.conf` and understanding its settings is important because your own distribution policy configuration may extend or overwrite some of the default variable settings provided by it. If you do not set up the default distribution correctly, you may inadvertently lose important default settings, and your distribution build may fail or not yield the desired results.

Listing 7-13   Default Distribution Setup meta/conf/distro/defaultsetup.conf

```
include conf/distro/include/default-providers.inc
include conf/distro/include/default-versions.inc
include conf/distro/include/default-distrovars.inc
include conf/distro/include/world-broken.inc

TCMODE ?= "default"
require conf/distro/include/tcmode-${TCMODE}.inc

TCLIBC ?= "eglibc"
require conf/distro/include/tclibc-${TCLIBC}.inc

# Allow single libc distros to disable this code
TCLIBCAPPEND ?= "-${TCLIBC}"
TMPDIR .= "${TCLIBCAPPEND}"

CACHE = "${TMPDIR}/cache/${TCMODE}-${TCLIBC}${@['', '/' + \
        str(d.getVar('MACHINE', True))][bool(d.getVar('MACHINE', \
        True))]}${@['', '/' + str(d.getVar('SDKMACHINE', True))] \
        [bool(d.getVar('SDKMACHINE', True))]}"

USER_CLASSES ?= ""
PACKAGE_CLASSES ?= "package_ipk"
INHERIT_BLACKLIST = "blacklist"
INHERIT_DISTRO ?= "debian devshell sstate license"
INHERIT += "${PACKAGE_CLASSES} ${USER_CLASSES} ${INHERIT_DISTRO} \
            ${INHERIT_BLACKLIST}"
```

The file first includes three other files with default settings: `default-providers.inc`, `default-versions.inc`, and `default-distrovars.inc`. The names for these files are indicative of what the file content is providing.

The file `default-distrovars.inc` in particular provides default settings for `DISTRO_FEATURES`, `DISTRO_FEATURES_DEFAULT`, `DISTRO_FEATURES_LIBC`, and `DISTRO_FEATURES_LIBC_DEFAULT`. If you are going to set `DISTRO_FEATURES` in your own distribution policy configuration file, you need to pay attention that you do not inadvertently remove the default settings by overwriting the variable. A safe way of doing so is to use an assignment like

```
DISTRO_FEATURES ?= "${DISTRO_FEATURES_DEFAULT} ${DISTRO_FEATURES_LIBC} \
                    ${MY_DISTRO_FEATURES}"
MY_DISTRO_FEATURES = "<distro features>"
```

which includes all default settings and adds another variable to include additional distribution features as needed.

The configuration file `defaultsetup.conf` also sets the defaults for `TCMODE` and `TCLIBC` and includes their respective configuration files, as described earlier.

7.5 External Layers

For the examples in the preceding sections, we used software packages and package groups from the OE Core layer `meta` and the Yocto Project base layer `meta-yocto`.

With steadily increasing support and contributions to the Yocto Project and OpenEmbedded, a growing number of additional layers with hundreds of recipes for myriad software packages are now available. Many of them are cataloged on the OpenEmbedded website. If you are looking for a recipe to build a specific software package, chances are that someone has already done the work.

The OpenEmbedded website's metadata index[1] lets you search by layer, recipe, and machine. For example, searching for Java by layer gives you a list of the layers that provide Java. Searching for JDK by recipes gives you a list of all recipes that build JDK packages together with the layer that provides the recipe.

The metadata index also lets you filter for the supported Yocto Project release to see if a recipe or layer is compatible with that particular release. Once you find the layer containing the software package recipe you are looking for, all you need to do is download the layer, include its path into the `BBLAYERS` variable of the `conf/bblayers.conf` of your build environment, and add the desired software package to your image using one of the methods described earlier.

7.6 Hob

Hob is a graphical user interface for BitBake provided by the Yocto Project. It is one of the Yocto Project's subprojects and is maintained by the Yocto Project development team.

Why is it called Hob? In the early days of Hob, the three letters stood for *Human-Oriented Builder*. However, that does not really sound too appealing and now the name of the tool is commonly associated with *hob*, the British English word for cooktop. And that fits well into the scheme of BitBake and recipes.

With Hob you can conveniently customize your root filesystem images using your mouse rather than editing text files. If that's the case, why didn't we introduce Hob first rather than explain how to build your custom Linux distribution the "hard" way? There are a couple of reasons:

- You can do a lot with Hob, but not everything.
- Hob is a frontend to BitBake and your build environment. It manipulates files in your build environment, launches BitBake, and collects build results.

---

1. http://layers.openembedded.org

Understanding how this is done manually helps you understand what Hob does in particular if something goes wrong.

- Although Hob may hide some of the complexity, you still need to know the terminology and how certain variable settings influence your build results.

Using Hob is rather simple. First, set up a build environment and then launch Hob from inside it:

```
$ source oe-init-build-env build
$ hob
```

Hob launches and then verifies your build environment. After that check is completed, you see a screen similar to the one in Figure 7-1 (we already made choices for the machine and image recipe).

The Hob user interface is easy to understand:

- **Select a machine**: From the drop-down menu, choose the machine you want to build for. The list shows all the machines that are defined by any layer included with the build environment. Selecting the machine changes the MACHINE variable setting in the con/local.conf file.

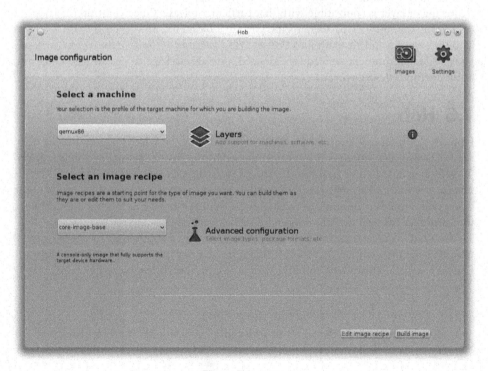

Figure 7-1   Hob

- **Layers**: Click this button to open a graphical editor that lets you include layers with and remove them from your build environment. Doing so modifies the `conf/bblayers.conf` file in your build environment.

- **Select an image recipe**: From this drop-down menu, you can choose the image that you want to build. This provides the image target to BitBake similar to running `bitbake <image-target>`. The menu contains image targets from all layers included with your build environment.

- **Advanced configuration**: Clicking on this button opens a menu that lets you select root filesystem types, packaging format, distribution policy, image size, and more, as outlined in Sections 7.3 and 7.4. Hob adds these options to the `conf/local.conf` file of the build environment.

- **Edit image recipe**: This button at the bottom of the screen lets you modify the image recipe by adding and/or removing packages and/or package groups. Doing so effectively modifies the `IMAGE_INSTALL` variable of the image target. You cannot, however, define new package groups from the Hob user interface. For that task, you have to write your package group recipe as explained in Section 7.1.6. But, of course, if you wrote your package recipe and included the layer it resides in with Hob, then you are able to select it from the package groups list.

- **Settings**: This button in the upper right corner of the user interface allows you to modify general settings contained in `conf/local.conf` such as parallelism, download directory, shared state cache, mirrors, and network proxies. Using the *Others* tab, you can add any variable to `conf/local.conf` and assign a value to it.

- **Images**: This button next to the *Settings* button in the upper right corner of the Hob user interface displays a list of previously built images. The list is created by parsing the `tmp/deploy/images/<machine>` subdirectories of the build environment. You can select an image from the list, run it if it is a QEMU image, or rebuild it.

- **Build image**: This button launches BitBake with the selected configuration and image target. The user interface switches to the *Log* tab of the build view from which you can follow the build process. This view has a major advantage over the BitBake output when started from the command line: not only do you see the tasks that are currently run but also the pending tasks and the ones that already have completed. If there are any build issues, warnings, or errors, they are logged underneath the *Issues* tab. There you can examine build issues and directly view the entire log file of a task without navigating through the build environment directory structure.

After the build finishes, Hob presents you with a summary page where you can view the created files in the file browser of your build system. You can also examine a summary log showing the run results for each task as well as any notes, warnings, or error messages. If you used Hob to build a root filesystem image and Linux kernel for the QEMU emulator, you can launch QEMU directly from Hob to verify your image by clicking on the *Run image* button in the lower right corner of the user interface. From the summary page, you can also make changes to your configuration and run a new build.

Whether you prefer Hob over configuring your build environment, customizing your target images, and launching BitBake manually is entirely up to you. Hob is great for rapid prototyping and to quickly enable somebody who is not all that familiar with BitBake and the Yocto Project to build predefined root filesystem image targets. Hob does not allow you to create your own image recipes, nor can you create your own distribution policy files with it (or even edit them). For these tasks, you need to set up your own layer and create the necessary files and recipes manually.

From Yocto Project version 2.1 on, Hob is being deprecated in favor of the web-based Toaster, which we explore in detail in Chapter 13.

7.7 Summary

The largest building block of a Linux distribution is the user space that contains the various libraries and applications that provide the essential functionality of the system. This chapter presented the fundamental concepts on how the Poky build system creates root filesystem images and how you can customize them to meet your requirements.

- The OpenEmbedded build system's core images provide distribution blueprints that you can extend and modify.

- Core images can easily be extended by appending packages and package groups to the list contained in the variable IMAGE_INSTALL.

- The QEMU emulator is a convenient and quick way to test your root file before booting it on an actual device.

- Enabling the build history lets you track changes to your images and compare subsequent executions of the build process.

- Creating your own image recipes that build on core image recipes by including them provides you with more control over what packages your root filesystem image contains. Image recipes that directly inherit the core-image class let you build root filesystem images from scratch.

- Package groups are a mechanism to bundle multiple packages and reference them by a single name, which greatly simplifies image customization with the IMAGE_INSTALL variable. Poky provides a series of predefined package groups that organize common packages.

- The build system can produce root filesystem images in various output formats. Some of them can be written directly to storage media such as flash devices to boot a system.

- Setting up a distribution policy allows operating system configuration independent of the content of the root filesystem. It also provides the means to use an external toolchain with the build system and to change the C library.

- Hob is a graphical user interface for BitBake. Launched from within an initialized build environment, it allows configuring and building of root filesystem images without modifying files using a text editor.

Software Package Recipes

Chapter 7, "Building a Custom Linux Distribution," explored how to build your own custom Linux OS stacks and create root filesystems to boot them. For the examples in that chapter, we used software packages for which the recipes are provided as part of the default metadata layers that are included with the OpenEmbedded build system. The default packages give you operational Linux systems as a foundation for your own projects. They can be as simple and basic as a system that just boots to an interactive console but also as complex as a system with the X Window System (X11) providing a graphical user interface.

Unless you are building development boards for embedded Linux engineers, your device eventually requires you to add your own software packages to the operating system stack. Ideally, you want BitBake to build your software packages for you and be able to include them with the root filesystem using the methods we discussed in Chapter 7.

This chapter begins by presenting the structure of a recipe building a software package and describing the typical metadata used. We then show how to write recipes that build directly from C files, build with standard makefiles, build using CMake, and build with GNU Autotools. We then explain how the various build artifacts are split into different packages using package management systems. We conclude this chapter with a section on how to modify existing recipes with append files.

8.1 Recipe Layout and Conventions

The majority of recipes are intended to build software packages. Over the course of the continuing evolution of the Yocto Project/OpenEmbedded conventions, guidelines and best practices have been established on how to write recipes for software packages. They are not absolute rules, and you find many recipes, particularly legacy recipes, that do not strictly adhere to these guidelines. However, the community converges toward these best practices, and it makes good sense to follow them. You can find a recipe style guide on the OpenEmbedded website.[1]

8.1.1 Recipe Filename

Recipe filenames follow the convention `<packagename>_<version>-<revision>.bb` where `packagename` is the name of the software package the recipe builds. The underscore separates the version string from the package name, and the hyphen separates the version string from the revision. Do not use the underscore anywhere else in the recipe name, such as for delimiting parts of the package name. The use of hyphens is allowed for the package name as well as for the package version but should be avoided for the latter. The package revision must not contain hyphens. Examples of recipe names are

- `avahi_0.6.31.bb`
- `linux-yocto_3.14.bb`
- `wpa-supplicant_2.2.bb`

The fields `packagename`, `version`, and `revision` of the recipe filename are assigned by BitBake to the variables `PN`, `PV`, and `PR`, respectively.

A particular issue for the recipe filename arises when the package is fetched from a branch of a software configuration management (SCM) system and the version is not associated with a tag. In this case, recipes should be named `<packagename>_<scm>.bb` where `scm` is the name of the versioning system, such as `git`, `svn`, or `cvs`. The recipe should then set `PV` explicitly to `PV = "<version>+git${SRCREV}"` where `version` is the most recent release or tag point, and `SRCREV` points to the revision to fetch from the SCM. It is important that you follow the naming guidelines for recipe files, as package name, version, and revision are also used for the package management systems. Using incorrect recipe names could result in trouble with the package managers creating, installing, and maintaining package versions for the target root filesystems.

8.1.2 Recipe Layout

Recipes follow a standard layout to make recipe files more accessible and easier to understand. This layout can be broken up into several sections that logically group metadata. We explain the structure using the gettext recipe from `meta/recipes-core/gettext/gettext_0.18.3.2.bb`, shown in Listing 8-1.

---

1. http://openembedded.org/wiki/Styleguide

Listing 8-1   **Gettext Recipe gettext_0.18.3.2.bb**

```
# Descriptive Meta-data
SUMMARY = "Utilities and libraries for producing multi-lingual messages"
DESCRIPTION = "GNU gettext is a set of tools that provides a framework to help
other programs produce multilingual messages. These tools include a set of
conventions about how programs should be written to support message catalogs,
a directory and file naming organization for the message catalogs themselves,
a runtime library supporting the retrieval of translated messages, and a few
standalone programs to massage in various ways the sets of translatable and
already translated strings."
HOMEPAGE = "http://www.gnu.org/software/gettext/gettext.html"

# Package Manager Meta-data
SECTION = "libs"

# Licensing Meta-data
LICENSE = "GPLv3+ & LGPL-2.1+"
LIC_FILES_CHKSUM = "file://COPYING;md5=d32239bcb673463ab874e80d47fae504"

# Inheritance Directives
inherit autotools texinfo

# Build Meta-data
DEPENDS = "gettext-native virtual/libiconv expat"
DEPENDS_class-native = "gettext-minimal-native"
PROVIDES = "virtual/libintl virtual/gettext"
PROVIDES_class-native = "virtual/gettext-native"
RCONFLICTS_${PN} = "proxy-libintl"
SRC_URI = "${GNU_MIRROR}/gettext/gettext-${PV}.tar.gz \
           file://parallel.patch \
           "

PACKAGECONFIG[msgcat-curses] = "\
    --with-libncurses-prefix=${STAGING_LIBDIR}/..,\
    --disable-curses,ncurses,"

LDFLAGS_prepend_libc-uclibc = " -lrt -lpthread "

SRC_URI[md5sum] = "241aba309d07aa428252c74b40a818ef"
SRC_URI[sha256sum] =
"d1a4e452d60eb407ab0305976529a45c18124bd518d976971ac6dc7aa8b4c5d7"

EXTRA_OECONF += "--without-lispdir \
                 --disable-csharp \
                 --disable-libasprintf \
                 --disable-java \
                 --disable-native-java \
                 --disable-openmp \
                 --disable-acl \
                 --with-included-glib \
                 --without-emacs \
                 --without-cvs \
                 --without-git \
                 --with-included-libxml \
                 --with-included-libcroco \
                 --with-included-libunistring \
                 "
```

```
acpaths = '-I ${S}/gettext-runtime/m4 \
          -I ${S}/gettext-tools/m4'

# Packaging Meta-data
# these lack the .x behind the .so, but shouldn't be in the -dev package
# Otherwise you get the following results:
# 7.4M    Angstrom-console-image-glibc-ipk-2008.1-test-20080104-ep93xx.rootfs.tar.gz
# 25M     Angstrom-console-image-uclibc-ipk-2008.1-test-20080104-ep93xx.rootfs.tar.gz
# because gettext depends on gettext-dev,
# which pulls in more -dev packages:
# 15228   KiB /ep93xx/libstdc++-dev_4.2.2-r2_ep93xx.ipk
# 1300    KiB /ep93xx/uclibc-dev_0.9.29-r8_ep93xx.ipk
# 140     KiB /armv4t/gettext-dev_0.14.1-r6_armv4t.ipk
# 4       KiB /ep93xx/libgcc-s-dev_4.2.2-r2_ep93xx.ipk

PACKAGES =+ "libgettextlib libgettextsrc"
FILES_libgettextlib = "${libdir}/libgettextlib-*.so*"
FILES_libgettextsrc = "${libdir}/libgettextsrc-*.so*"

PACKAGES =+ "gettext-runtime gettext-runtime-dev gettext-runtime-doc"

FILES_${PN} += "${libdir}/${BPN}/*"

FILES_gettext-runtime = "${bindir}/gettext \
                         ${bindir}/ngettext \
                         ${bindir}/envsubst \
                         ${bindir}/gettext.sh \
                         ${libdir}/libasprintf.so* \
                         ${libdir}/GNU.Gettext.dll \
                         "
FILES_gettext-runtime_append_libc-uclibc = " ${libdir}/libintl.so.* \
                                             ${libdir}/charset.alias \
                                             "
FILES_gettext-runtime-dev += "${libdir}/libasprintf.a \
                     ${includedir}/autosprintf.h \
                     "
FILES_gettext-runtime-dev_append_libc-uclibc = " ${libdir}/libintl.so \
                                                ${includedir}/libintl.h \
                                                "
FILES_gettext-runtime-doc = "${mandir}/man1/gettext.* \
                             ${mandir}/man1/ngettext.* \
                             ${mandir}/man1/envsubst.* \
                             ${mandir}/man1/.* \
                             ${mandir}/man3/* \
                             ${docdir}/gettext/gettext.* \
                             ${docdir}/gettext/ngettext.* \
                             ${docdir}/gettext/envsubst.* \
                             ${docdir}/gettext/*.3.html \
                             ${datadir}/gettext/ABOUT-NLS \
                             ${docdir}/gettext/csharpdoc/* \
                             ${docdir}/libasprintf/autosprintf.html \
                             ${infodir}/autosprintf.info \
                             "

# Task Overrides, Prepends and Appends
do_install_append() {
    rm -f ${D}${libdir}/preloadable_libintl.so
}
```

```
do_install_append_class-native () {
        rm ${D}${datadir}/aclocal/*
        rm ${D}${datadir}/gettext/config.rpath
        rm ${D}${datadir}/gettext/po/Makefile.in.in
        rm ${D}${datadir}/gettext/po/remove-potcdate.sin
}

# Variants / Class Extensions
BBCLASSEXTEND = "native nativesdk"
```

We reformatted this recipe slightly and included comments to outline the metadata sections we are discussing. Gettext is a fairly comprehensive recipe that includes most of the metadata you may encounter in a recipe. However, not all recipes are that complex. Most are actually rather simple because building their respective software packages can be carried out entirely by the various classes without any major modifications.

The following discussion explains the sections of a recipe and the metadata that they typically contain.

Descriptive Metadata

Descriptive metadata provides information about the recipe and the software package it builds.

- **SUMMARY**: A one-line (up to 80 characters long), short description of the package.

- **DESCRIPTION**: An extended (possibly multiple lines long), detailed description of the package and what it provides.

- **AUTHOR**: Name and e-mail address of the author of the software package (not the recipe) in the form of AUTHOR = "Santa Claus <santa@northpole.com>". This can be a list of multiple authors.

- **HOMEPAGE**: The URL, starting with http://, where the software package is hosted.

- **BUGTRACKER**: The URL, starting with http://, to the project's bug tracking system.

Package Manager Metadata

The metadata in this section provides additional information for the package management systems used primarily for the maintenance of the package database. Not all package management systems support these settings, however.

- **SECTION**: The category the software package belongs to. Package management tools use this category to organize the packages. Although the categories are not strictly standardized and the various mainstream Linux distributions define their own lists, a list of commonly used categories has evolved. Examples for common sections or categories are app, audio, base, devel, and libs.

- **PRIORITY**: Priorities are used to tell the package management tools whether a software package is required for a system to operate, is optional, or eventually conflicts with other packages. Priorities are utilized only by the Debian package manager dpkg and the Open Package Manager opkg. The priorities are

  - **standard**: Packages that are standard for any Linux distribution, including a reasonably small but not too limited console-mode system

  - **required**: Packages that are necessary for the proper function of the system

  - **optional**: Packages that are not necessary for a functional system but for a reasonably usable system

  - **extra**: Packages that may conflict with other packages from higher priorities or that have specialized requirements

Licensing Metadata

The metadata of this section allows the build system to automatically track open source licensing requirement. This information is mandatory for all recipes. We address the details of license management with the Yocto Project in Chapter 12, "Licensing and Compliance."

- **LICENSE**: The name of the license (or licenses) used for this software package. In most cases, only a single license applies, but some open source software packages employ multiple licenses. These can be dual licenses allowing the user of a package to choose one of several licenses or multiple licenses where parts of the software package are licensed differently. Dual licenses are specified by concatenating the license names with the pipe symbol (|). Multiple licenses are specified by concatenating the license names with the ampersand (&) symbol. The build system also supports complex logical license "arithmetic," such as GLv2 & (LGPLv2.1 | MPL-1.1 | BSD).

- **LIC_FILES_CHECKSUM**: This variable allows tracking changes to the license file itself. The variable contains a space-delimited list of license files with their respective checksums. After fetching and unpacking a software package's source files, the build system verifies the license by calculating a checksum over the license file, or portions thereof, and comparing it with the checksum provided.

Inheritance Directives and Includes

This section contains the inherit directives for the recipe to inherit functionality from classes. It can also contain include and/or require statements to insert other files directly at the location of the statement. The position in the recipe file does not matter for inheritance, but it may be important for including files. Included files can set variables that you may want to override in your recipe.

Build Metadata

We call the metadata in this section *build metadata* because it provides settings required to build the software package, such as URIs; declares dependencies; and defines the provisions.

- **PROVIDES**: Space-delimited list of one or more additional package names typically used for abstract provisioning.
- **DEPENDS**: Space-delimited list of names of packages that must be built before this package can be built.
- **PN**: The package name. The value of this variable is derived by BitBake from the base name of the recipe file. For most packages, this is correct and sufficient. Some packages may need to adjust this value. For example, the cross-toolchain applications—for instance, gcc-cross—have the target architecture appended to their names.
- **PV**: The package version, which is derived by BitBake from the base name of the recipe file. For all but packages that directly build from source repositories, this value is correct and sufficient. For those that build from SCM, Section 8.1.1 explains how to set PV correctly.
- **PR**: The package revision. The default revision is r0. In the past, BitBake required you to increase the revision every time the recipe itself has changed to trigger a rebuild. However, the new signature handlers now calculate the signature of recipe metadata including functions. The build system now entirely relies on the signatures for rebuilding.

  For correct package naming, it may still be necessary to increase the value of PR so that package managers can correctly maintain databases for package upgrades. Previously, maintenance was accomplished by using the PRINC variable. However, this approach has proven to be error prone, so PRINC has been deprecated and replaced with the *PR service*. PR service is a revision server that calculates PR on the basis of signatures.[2]
- **SRC_URI**: Space-delimited list of URIs to download source code, patches, and other files from.
- **SRCDATE**: The source code date. This variable applies only when sources are retrieved from SCM systems.
- **S**: The directory location in the build environment where the build system places the unpacked source code. The default location depends on the recipe name and version: ${WORKDIR}/${PN}-${PV}. The default location is appropriate for virtually all packages built from archives. For packages directly built from SCM, you need to set this variable explicitly, such as ${WORKDIR}/git for GIT repositories.

---

2. PR service is disabled by default. For more information and how to enable it, see the PR service wiki at https://wiki.yoctoproject.org/wiki/PR_Service.

- **B**: The directory location in the build environment where the build system places the object created during the build. The default is the same as S: ${WORKDIR}/${PN} -${PV}. Many software packages are built *in tree* or *in location*, placing the objects inside the source tree. Recipes building packages with GNU Autotools, the Linux kernel, and cross-toolchain applications separate source and build directories.

- **FILESEXTRAPATHS**: Extends the build system's search path for additional local files defined by FILESPATH. This variable is most commonly used for append files in the form FILESEXTRAPATHS_prepend := "${THISDIR}/${PN}", which causes the build system to first look for additional files in a subdirectory with the name of the package of the directory where the append file is located before looking in the other directories specified by FILESEXTRAPATHS.

- **PACKAGECONFIG**: This variable allows enabling and disabling features of a software package at build time. You define features as quadruples of lists in the form of

```
PACKAGECONFIG[f1] = "--with-f1,--wo-f1,build-deps-f1,rt-deps-f1"
PACKAGECONFIG[f2] = "--with-f2,--wo-f2,build-deps-f2,rt-deps-f2"
PACKAGECONFIG[f3] = "--with-f3,--wo-f3,build-deps-f3,rt-deps-f3"
```

The quadruples are delimited by commas. Their order is of significance:

1. Extra arguments added to the configuration list of the configure script (EXTRA_OECONF) if the feature is enabled

2. Extra arguments added to EXTRA_OECONF if the feature is disabled

3. Additional build dependencies added to DEPENDS if the feature is enabled

4. Additional runtime dependencies added to RDEPENDS if the feature is enabled

To enable a feature, you can either create an append file or do so in a configuration file:

- **Append file**: Create an append file in your own layer and name it <packagename> .bbappend where packagename is the name of the recipe you want to append. Inside your append file, you can then entirely redefine the variable by overwriting it with PACKAGECONFIG = "f2 f3" or you can preserve previously set values with PACKAGECONFIG_append = " f2 f3".

- **Configuration file**: You can simply add the variable to a configuration file such as local.conf or a distribution configuration file using PACKAGECONFIG_ pn-<packagename> = "f2 f3" or PACKAGECONFIG_append_pn-<packagename> = " f2 f3".

Both methods are identical in their result.

- **EXTRA_OECONF**: Additional configure script options.

- **EXTRA_OEMAKE**: Additional options for GNU Make.

- **EXTRA_OECMAKE**: Additional options for CMake.

- **LDFLAGS**: Options passed to the linker. The default setting depends on what the build system is building: TARGET_LDFLAGS when building for the target, BUILD_LDFLAGS when building for the build host, BUILDSDK_LDFLAGS when building an SDK for the host. You typically won't overwrite this variable entirely but instead will add options to it.

- **PACKAGE_ARCH**: Defines the architecture of the software package. By default, this variable is set to TUNE_PKGARCH when building for the target, to BUILD_ARCH when building for the build host, and to "${SDK_ARCH}-${SDKPKGSUFFIX}" when building an SDK. The defaults are typically adequate unless your software package is entirely dependent on a specific machine rather than on the machine's architecture. In this case, set PACKAGE_ARCH = "${MACHINE_ARCH}" inside the recipe.

Packaging Metadata

The metadata section of a recipe defines how the build output is packaged into different packages using the package manager. Packaging happens after the software has been built and installed into a root filesystem structure local to the package's build directory. We introduce the variables here and discuss the details in a following section.

- **PACKAGES**: This variable is a space-delimited list of packages that are created during the packaging process. The default value of this variable is "${PN}-dbg ${PN}-staticdev ${PN}-dev ${PN}-doc ${PN}-locale \${PACKAGE_BEFORE_PN} ${PN}". The list is processed from left to right, meaning that the leftmost package is created first and the rightmost last. The order is important, since a package consumes the files that are associated with it. If two or more packages consume the same files, only the first package processed contains the files. Recipes typically add extra packages to the front of the list.

- **FILES**: The FILES variable defines lists of directories and files that are placed into a particular package. The build system defines default file and directory lists for the default packages, such as FILES_${PN}-dbg = "<files>", where files is a space-delimited list of directories and files that can contain wildcards. If your recipe adds extra packages to the list in PACKAGES, you need to define FILES for that package, too. Your recipe may produce objects not typically found in the default packages that you would like to add to a standard package. In that case, you would append a list with those files to FILES.

- **PACKAGE_BEFORE_PN**: This variable lets you easily add packages before the final package name is created. You can easily see how this works. In the default list of PACKAGES, the content of the PACKAGE_BEFORE_PN variable is expanded before the final package PN. Simply add your packages to the variable: PACKAGE_BEFORE_PN = "${PN}-examples". Of course, you also have to define the FILES list for the examples package.

- **PACKAGE_DEBUG_SPLIT_STYLE**: This variable determines how to split binary and debug objects when the ${PN}-dgb package is created. There are three variants:
  - **".debug"**: The files containing the debug symbols are placed in a .debug directory inside the directory where the binaries are installed on the target. For example, if the binaries are installed in /usr/bin, the debug symbol files are placed in /usr/bin/.debug. This option also installs the source files in .debug, which is the default behavior.
  - **"debug-file-directory"**: Debug files are placed under /usr/lib/debug on the target, separating them from the binaries.
  - **"debug-without-src"**: This variant is the same as .debug, but the source files are not installed.
- **PACKAGESPLITFUNCS**: This variable defines a list of functions that perform the package splitting. The default, defined by package.bbclass, is PACKAGESPLITFUNCS ?= "package_do_split_locales populate_packages". Recipes can prepend to this variable to run their own package-splitting functions before the default ones are run.

Task Overrides, Prepends, and Appends

In this section recipes override, prepend, or append to tasks to redefine, change, or extend the default behavior.

Variants/Class Extensions

This section simply contains the BBCLASSEXTEND variable to create variants such as a native or SDK build of the package.

Runtime Metadata

This metadata section defines runtime dependencies.

- **RDEPENDS**: A list of packages that this package depends on at runtime and that must be installed for this package to function correctly. The variable applies to the packages being built, and hence you need to define it conditionally on the particular package. For example, if the development package depends on Perl to operate correctly, you need to specify RDEPENDS_${PN}-dev += "perl", which tells the build system to create this package dependency in the package manager's manifest.
- **RRECOMMENDS**: Similar to RDEPENDS but indicates a weak dependency, as these packages are not essential for the package being built. They do, however, enhance usability. Package managers install these packages if they are available but do not fail if not.
- **RSUGGESTS**: Similar to RRECOMMENDS but even weaker in the sense that package managers do not install these packages even if they are available. They only provide the information that installing these packages may be beneficial.

- **RPROVIDES**: Package name alias list for runtime provisioning. The package's own name is always implicitly part of that list. As for all of the runtime metadata that controls package creation, you need to use conditional assignment: `RPROVIDES_${PN} = "alias1 alias2"`.

- **RCONFLICTS**: List of names of conflicting packages. A package manager does not install this package if not all of the conflicting packages are removed prior to installation. As for all of the runtime metadata that controls package creation, you need to use conditional assignment: `RCONFILCTS_${PN} = "conflicting-package-name"`.

- **RREPLACES**: List of names of packages this package replaces. The package manager uses this variable to determine which other packages this package replaces. If the packages can coexist, then the package manager does install this package even if the other packages in this list are installed. If the packages cannot coexist, then this package must also set the RCONFLICTS variable to include those packages. As for all of the runtime metadata that controls package creation, you need to use conditional assignment: `RCONFILCTS_${PN} = "conflicting-package-name"`.

The build system supports versioned dependencies:

```
RDEPENDS_${PN} = "<package> (<operator> <version>)"
```

where the operator is one of =, <, >, <=, or >=. For example

```
RDEPENDS_${PN} = "gettext (> 0.16)"
```

You can use versioned dependencies with RDEPENDS, RRECOMMENDS, RSUGGESTS, RCONFILCTS, and RREPLACES.

8.1.3 Formatting Guidelines

Formatting guidelines for source code, BitBake recipes, and classes are essentially source code. Their purpose is to create a consistent format and look across all artifacts so that someone who is trying to work with the Yocto Project and OpenEmbedded can learn and understand quickly. Guidelines also ease reviewing contributions by maintainers.

OpenEmbedded has established a style guide[3] that establishes the ground rules for formatting recipes, classes, and configuration files:

- **Assignments**
  - Use a single space on each side of the assignment operator.
  - Use quotes only on the right hand side of the assignment:
    ```
    VARIABLE = "VALUE"
    ```

- **Continuation**
  - Continuation is used to split long variable lists, such as SRC_URI, for better readability.
  - Use the line continuation symbol (\).

---

3. http://openembedded.org/wiki/Styleguide

- Do not place any spaces after the line continuation symbol.
- Indent successive lines up to the level of the start of the value.
- Use spaces instead of tabs for indentation, since developers tend to set their tab sizes differently.
- Place the closing quote on its own line.

```
VARIABLE = "\
            value1 \
            value2 \
        "
```

- **Python Functions**
  - Use four spaces per indent; do not use tabs.
  - Python is rather finicky about indentation. Never mix spaces and tabs.
- **Shell Functions**
  - Use four spaces per indent; do not use tabs.
  - Some layers, such as OECore, use tabs for indentation for shell functions. However, it is recommended that you use four spaces for new layers to stay consistent with Python functions.
- **Comments**
  - Comments are allowed and encouraged in recipes, classes, and configuration files.
  - Comments must start at the beginning of the line using the # character.
  - Comments cannot be used inside of a continuation.

Even if you do not intend to submit patches or contribute recipes or layers to Open-Embedded or the Yocto Project, following these simple guidelines makes it much easier for you and your organization to maintain your own recipes, classes, and configuration files.

8.2 Writing a New Recipe

Writing a new recipe for a software package and adding it to your build is an essential task when working with the OpenEmbedded build system. It may be daunting at first, but it is not as hard as it might seem. Most of the complexity is covered by the various classes. Figure 8-1 shows a step-by-step approach to writing recipes.

The workflow for creating recipes pretty much resembles the BitBake process for building packages that we discussed in Chapter 3, "OpenEmbedded Build System." That, of course, is not by accident. When creating a new recipe, you add, step by step, the necessary metadata for each process step. The workflow is also not as linear as depicted but typically an iteration of making additions or changes to the recipe and then testing the changes. Since the outcome of a previous step influences subsequent steps, it is important to get each step right. Sometimes an issue with running a process step, such as *compile*, may be related to a problem in one of the preceding steps, such as *configure*.

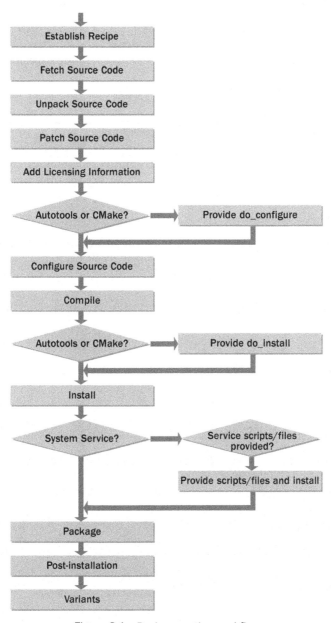

Figure 8-1   Recipe creation workflow

Before writing a new recipe, we recommend that you look for a recipe that some-one else has already written and that meets, or at least comes close to meeting, your requirements. The OpenEmbedded metadata index[4] is a good start for your search. You may find recipes that you can modify to fit your needs. However, that approach may not work well if you are writing a recipe for your own software packages. In that case, starting from an established recipe and trying to modify it may require more effort than creating a recipe from scratch or from a recipe skeleton.

The following sections detail each workflow step for creating a recipe from scratch.

8.2.1 Establish the Recipe

Even if you are creating only a single recipe, we always recommend that you place it into one of your own layers or create a new layer for it. Why? Very seldom does a project remain simple. Most projects grow over time, since you will be adding to them. Establishing a structure by using your own layers greatly simplifies maintenance down the road. If you do not already have a layer to place your recipe into, you can easily create one using the yocto-layer tool:

```
$ yocto-layer create mylayer
```

The tool interactively walks you through creating a layer and also offers to create a sample recipe for you. You can start from the sample recipe or from the skeleton shown in Listing 8-2.

Listing 8-2 **Skeleton Recipe**

```
SUMMARY = ""
DESCRPTION = ""
AUTHOR = ""
HOMEPAGE = ""
BUGTRACKER = ""
```

Create the skeleton recipe inside your layer. BitBake locates the recipes inside your layer according to the setting of the BBFILES variable in the conf/layer.conf file inside your layer. BBFILES defines a search pattern for recipe files. It is typically set to

```
BBFILES += "${LAYERDIR}/recipes-*/*/*.bb \
            ${LAYERDIR}/recipes-*/*/*.bbappend"
```

You could, of course, change the search pattern for your own layer, but using the above default makes good sense, as all OpenEmbedded/Yocto Project layers use it. Consequently, the yocto-layer tool creates the conf/layer.conf file with this setting for BBFILES.

For example, if you are creating a recipe for an application that is called *myapp*, you would want to place the recipe in the directory recipes-apps/myapp.

---

4. http://layers.openembedded.org

The name of your recipe must adhere to the naming conventions discussed in Section 8.1.1 and should at least be <packagename>_<version>.bb, such as myapp_1.0.bb.

8.2.2 Fetch the Source Code

The first thing a recipe does is fetch the source code. Consequently, a recipe must provide the SRC_URI variable to tell the build system where to fetch the sources from and what protocol to use. Fetching is carried out by the do_fetch task.

For most of the typical open source upstream downloads, the source files are provided as compressed archives. These archives can be fetched using the standard file transfer protocols, as we saw in Chapter 3 when we discussed the BitBake fetchers in detail. For example,

```
SRC_URI = "http://ftp.gnu.org/gnu/hello/hello-2.9.tar.gz"
```

fetches the source archive for the GNU Hello World program. Using hardcoded version numbers in SRC_URI, however, makes the recipe less portable. It is recommended to use PV instead:

```
SRC_URI = "http://ftp.gnu.org/gnu/hello/hello-${PV}.tar.gz"
```

When fetching source archives, the build system requires you to provide MD5 and/or SHA256 checksums to verify whether the archive has been downloaded correctly. You can specify the checksum directly as part of SRC_URI, but because these checksums tend to be somewhat unwieldy, we recommend that you give your archive a name in the SRC_URI and specify the checksum separately:

```
SRC_URI = "http://ftp.gnu.org/gnu/hello/hello-${PV}.tar.gz;name=archive"
SRC_URI[archive.md5sum] = "67607d2616a0faaf5bc94c59dca7c3cb"
SRC_URI[archive.sha256sum] = \
"ecbb7a2214196c57ff9340aa71458e1559abd38f6d8d169666846935df191ea7"
```

Doing so makes SRC_URI easier to maintain and also works better with when SRC_URI contains multiple URIs.

Fetching source code directly from an SCM is also common practice. The build system supports virtually all common SCM systems. The SCM most frequently used with open source software today is Git. Fetching from an SCM does not require checksums but typically requires a revision or tag to check out:

```
SRC_URI = "git://git.lttng.org/lttng-ust.git;branch=stable-2.5 \
           file://lttng-ust-doc-examples-disable.patch \
           "
SRCREV = "ce59a997afdb7dc8af02b464430bb7e35549fa66"
```

Many recipes also require files to be fetched locally from the build host. Commonly, these are integration patches, configuration files, and more:

```
SRC_URI = "git://git.lttng.org/lttng-tools.git;branch=stable-2.5 \
           file://runtest-2.4.0.patch \
           file://run-ptest \
           "
```

Using the `file://` protocol specifier instructs the build system to look for files on the build host. The paths are relative to the paths specified by FILESPATH. The variable typically contains multiple paths. The first path with a matching file is used. By default, the directory list in FILESPATH includes BP (base package name and version), BPN (base package name), and files. All of these are assumed to be subdirectories to the directory where the recipe is located.

8.2.3 Unpack the Source Code

After fetching, the source code needs to be unpacked. Unpacking is required only if the source code was downloaded as a source archive. If it was fetched from an SCM, unpacking is not necessary, as the files can be checked out individually from the repository. The do_unpack task takes care of the unpacking. It can handle virtually all common archiving and compression schemes.

The source code is unpacked into the directory specified by the variable S. The build system expects the source archive to contain a directory tree with a single top-level or root directory with the name ${BP} or ${BPN}-${PV}. Using the GNU Hello example, the `hello-2.9.tar.gz` archive must unpack into a single directory called `hello-2.9`. This is a convention that most open-source packages follow. For packages for which this is not the case, you need to set S in your recipe explicitly. For instance, for an archive that does not have a top-level directory, you need to set S to

```
S = "${WORKDIR}/${BP}"
```

What exactly you need to set S to depends on how the source code is packaged. It may eventually be necessary to append the do_unpack task to rename or copy a directory or to copy and move directory contents.

You also need to set S explicitly if your recipe is fetching source code from an SCM. In that case, S is typically set to ${WORKDIR}/<scm>, where <scm> is the name of the SCM. For Git, you would set

```
S = "${WORKDIR}/git"
```

After you set up your new recipe for fetching and unpacking, it is a good idea to run it and verify that the sources get downloaded and unpacked correctly:

```
$ bitbake -c fetch <myrecipe>
$ bitbake -c unpack <myrecipe>
```

lets you run the fetch and unpack tasks individually. If you just run the unpack task and the fetch task has not yet been run, BitBake automatically runs it because unpack is dependent on fetch.

After the fetch task has completed, you should find the source archive in the download directory specified by DL_DIR. For fetches from an SCM, the download directory contains a subdirectory with the name of the SCM to which the remote repositories have been cloned or checked out.

After running the unpack task, you should be able to find the unpacked sources in the source directory S.

8.2.4 Patch the Source Code

If your SRC_URI contains any patches—that is, files that end in .patch or .diff—then the do_patch task automatically applies these patches to the unpacked source code using the Quilt tool.

The build system expects that patches can be applied with the -p1 option, meaning that the first directory level is stripped off. If your patch needs multiple directory levels stripped off, you need to provide the striplevel option with a number as part of SRC_URI of the patch. If your patch needs to be applied in a specific subdirectory that is not provided inside the patch file itself, you can add the patchdir option to SRC_URI:

```
SRC_URI = "http://downloads.tld.com/pub/package-1.2.tar.gz \
           file://patch-1.patch;striplevel=3 \
           file://patch-2.diff;patchdir=src/common \
           "
```

You should place patches as well as any other locally fetched files in a subdirectory next to the recipe that is either named the same as the base name of the recipe BPN, named the base name plus the version number BP, or named files. For instance, if the name of your recipe is foo_2.3.1.bb, then the name of the directory can either be foo, foo-2.3.1, or files. Using foo instead of simply files helps with organizing the patches for different recipes. Using foo-2.3.1 instead of just foo allows separating patches for different versions of the foo recipe.

8.2.5 Add Licensing Information

All recipes are required to provide licensing information by setting the variables LICENSE and LIC_FILES_CHKSUM. Both variables are mandatory; otherwise, the build system rejects the recipe and does not build it.

- **LICENSE**: The name of the license used for this software package. In most cases, only a single license applies, but some open source software packages employ multiple licenses. These can be dual licenses that allow the user of a package to choose one of several licenses or multiple licenses where parts of the software package are licensed differently. Dual licenses are specified by concatenating the license names with the pipe symbol (|). Multiple licenses are specified by concatenating the license names with the ampersand (&) symbol. The build system also supports complex logical license "arithmetic," such as GLv2 & (LGPLv2.1 | MPL-1.1 | BSD).

- **LIC_FILES_CHKSUM**: This variable allows tracking changes to the license files itself. The variable contains a space-delimited list of license files with their respective checksums. After fetching and unpacking a software package's source files, the build system verifies the license by calculating a checksum over the license file, or portions thereof, and comparing it with the checksum provided.

Licenses listed by LICENSE can have any name as long as the name does not contain any spaces or the characters &, |, (, and). For standard licenses, we recommend that you use the names of the license files in `meta/files/common-licenses` or the license names from the `SPDXLICENSEMAP` attributes in `meta/conf/licenses.conf`.

If the source package provides the actual license in a file, such as `COPYING`, `LICENSE`, or a similar file, you should specify it in `LIC_FILES_CHKSUM`:

```
LIC_FILES_CHKSUM = "file://COPYING;md5=<md5sum>"
```

Some software packages using standard open source licenses may simply state the name and version of the license but may not include the license file itself. In that case, use the license files provided in `COMMON_LICENSE_DIR`:

```
LIC_FILES_CHKSUM = \
    "file://${COMMON_LICENSE_DIR}/MIT;md5=0835ade698e0bcf8506ecda2f7b4f302"
```

If you do not have the MD5 checksum of the license file, there is no need for you to calculate it manually. Just leave the `md5` parameter open, and the build system fails with an error message providing the checksum, which you then can copy and paste into your recipe.

8.2.6 Configure the Source Code

Building software packages commonly depends on the build system and the build environment, such as development tools and dependencies on other software packages and libraries. This is particularly the case when cross-building for different architectures. To make source packages portable so that they can be built on a variety of build systems with different build environments as well as for a large number of target systems, developers provide means to configure the source code and its build system.

In the simplest case, this configuration is carried out by setting environment variables that the source code's build system uses for its *makefiles* and/or *build scripts*. Unfortunately, this approach is not very user friendly, as someone who wants to build the software package needs to understand the variables and what they are intended to do in order to be able to provide the correct settings. Different developers also tend to name variables differently, which adds to the complexity. While there are some agreed-on common denominators—for example, `CC` as the variable for the C compiler, `CPP` for the C++ compiler, and `LD` for the linker—developers may still define other variables that you may need to address.

To mitigate the problem, build systems were developed that make source code portable in a standardized form. The two most common ones are GNU Autotools and CMake. Both are designed to simplify porting of source code and make configuration user friendly by providing automated tools for source code configuration. These tools determine the necessary configuration by matching a configuration file that is shipped with the source code to the actual build system and build environment configuration and then set the required variables based on the outcome.

As a first step, you need to determine what other software packages the package you are writing the recipe for depends on. Typically, the software package's documentation should provide you with this information. You need to add these packages to the DEPENDS variable so that BitBake can build these packages first to fulfill the dependencies.

Second, you need to determine whether the software package you are building uses a source configuration system.

- **GNU Autotools**: Your software package uses GNU Autotools if it contains a configure.ac file. This file contains a list of macros for detecting compilers, looking for specific header files, testing for libraries, and much more. The autoconf tool creates a shell script from this file called configure that then performs the actual tests. GNU Autotools build on top of the traditional Make native system for building software packages. After the configure script has completed successfully, it creates the makefile.

  If your software package uses GNU Autotools, then all you have to do is inherit the autotools class. This class provides the do_configure task, and in most cases, you do not have to modify the configuration any further.

  However, some software packages may still require you to make adjustments to the configuration. For this purpose, the OpenEmbedded build system provides the variable EXTRA_OECONF allowing you to add or overwrite configuration settings.

- **CMake**: Your software package uses CMake if it contains a CMakeLists.txt file. This file contains configuration directives. CMake is used in conjunction with native build systems such as Make.

  If your software package uses CMake, then all you have to do is inherit the cmake class. This class provides the do_configure task, and in most cases, you do not have to modify the configuration any further.

  If you do need to make adjustments to the configuration, the OpenEmbedded build system provides the variable EXTRA_OECMAKE for passing any required configuration options.

- **Other**: If your source package does not contain a configure.ac or CMakeLists.txt file, then it is using some other method of configuration by directly passing environment variables to the build system, which typically is Make. If that is the case, you may have to write your own do_configure task to apply the correct settings. In simpler cases, it may be sufficient to set the EXTRA_OEMAKE variable to pass the settings.

At this point, you should run the configure task and check its log file to ensure that the configuration succeeded and the correct options have been passed. The log also tells you if you are missing any required dependencies from the DEPENDS variable or if options have been enabled that you might not want.

8.2.7 Compile

Now your recipe is ready to compile the source code. Run the compile task and see if compilation succeeds. If it does, there is nothing else you need to do for this step. However, if compilation fails, you need to analyze the log file for the cause. The most common failures at this point are parallel build failure, host leakage, and missing headers or libraries:

- **Parallel Build Failure**: Using multiple threads for Make is enabled by default for all packages by the PARALLEL_MAKE variable in conf/local.conf of your build environment. Sometimes, this can cause race conditions, which manifest in intermittent failures. Commonly, compilation fails because an artifact could not be found that should have been created. These failures are hard to track down because upon inspection you may find that the artifact indeed has been created; however, the issue is that part of the build process has been executed in the wrong order.

  As a workaround, you can set PRALLEL_MAKE = "" (empty string) in the recipe. This setting turns off parallel building for just this recipe. It, of course, slows down building your software package. If you want to resolve the issue and allow parallel building, you may need to do further debugging and eventually apply a patch to change the order of the build process.

- **Host Leakage**: This issue is related to building for the target or when building an SDK. The problem occurs when the build process references header files, libraries, or other files from the host system rather than from the cross-build environment. The root cause in virtually all cases is the use of absolute paths such as /usr/include, /usr/lib, and so forth. Host leakage is reported by the QA tools, including Swabber. You should be able to easily spot these issues from the QA messages and by analyzing the log files and then create a patch to resolve them.

- **Missing Headers or Libraries**: If compilation fails because the compiler cannot find header files or libraries from other software packages, then the root cause typically is that these packages have not been declared in the DEPENDS variable, or the dependency exists but the path to the files is incorrect, and it was not detected by the configure step.

  Adding the dependency to DEPENDS resolves the issue in most cases. However, it may not manifest itself immediately. Commonly, you start out with a build environment that has already been used to build a target root filesystem. In many cases, the dependencies may already have been built for other software packages before you begin adding the recipe for your new package, causing the dependency to be fulfilled albeit not declared in DEPENDS. For that case, it is advisable to test with a fresh build environment.

  On rare occasions, you may need to adjust paths to header files and libraries of dependencies by setting the variables STAGING_BINDIR, STAGING_INCDIR, STAGING_DATADIR, STAGING_BASELIBDIR, and so on.

8.2.8 Install the Build Output

After the software package is built, the do_install task copies build artifacts such as binaries, libraries, header files, configuration files, and documentation files into a filesystem hierarchy that mirrors the root filesystem of the target device. The files are copied from the S, B, and WORKDIR directories to the D directory, which is set to ${WORKDIR}/image. After installation, this directory contains a local root filesystem structure with all the subdirectories and files of the installed software package.

Since the packaging process collects the files from the installation directory D, you have to ensure that your software package has been installed correctly: all directories and files have been created in the right place of the root filesystem structure. Depending on how your software package is built, you may need to make adjustments to the installation process:

- **GNU Autotools and CMake**: If your software package is built using GNU Autotools or CMake, the autotools and cmake classes respectively provide a do_install task that is adequate for installing most software packages. You just need to verify that the do_install task completes without issues and that the directory structure inside D is correct.

  If you need to install additional files that have not been copied by the do_install task as provided by the class, you need to create a do_install_append function in your recipe that takes care of installing the remaining files. You must use install -d <source> <dest> to copy the files rather than cp or any other copy utility.

- **Make**: If your software package is built using just the Make build system without GNU Autotools or CMake, you need to create a do_install task in your recipe. The makefile most likely already contains an install target to copy the files. This target typically requires a destination directory, which is the root directory of the filesystem structure and can be set through a variable. What this variable is depends on the makefile. Typical examples are DESTDIR, PREFIX, and INSTALLROOT.

  The OpenEmbedded build system provides the function oe_runmake, which executes Make with a specified target. This function allows you to pass variables to the makefile. You simply use that function in your do_install task, as follows, assuming that the variable required by the makefile to pass the root installation directory is called PREFIX:

```
:
do_install() {
    oe_runmake install PREFIX=${D}
}
```

  If your makefile does not provide an install target, then see the next bullet for manual installation.

- **Manual Installation**: If your software package's build system does not provide an installation facility at all, you need to create a do_install task and use install -d <src> <dest> to install the required files:

```
do_install() {
    install -d ${B}/bin/hello ${D}${bindir}
    install -d ${B}/lib/hello.lib ${D}${libdir}
}
```

You can use the following variables for standard installation directories and concatenate them to D:

- `bindir = "/usr/bin"`

- `sbindir = "/usr/sbin"`

- `libdir = "/usr/lib"`

- `libexecdir = "/usr/lib"`

- `sysconfdir = "/etc"`

- `datadir = "/usr/share"`

- `mandir = "/usr/share/man"`

- `includedir = "/usr/include"`

To verify the installation of your software package, run the install task and check the D directory for the correct subdirectories and files.

8.2.9 Setup System Services

If your software package provides a system service that is supposed to be started when the system boots and to be stopped when it shuts down, then your recipe needs to set up system services for your software packages.

First, you need to verify whether your software package provides the necessary startup scripts and the install task copies them into the correct location. What these scripts need to contain and where they are installed depends on the service manager you are using. If your package does not provide the scripts or does not install them, then you have to add them and append the `do_install` task.

The build system supports the two service managers *SysVinit* and *systemd*:

- **SysVinit**: System V Init is the traditional service manager for UNIX-like systems. After the Linux kernel completes its initialization on boot, it spawns the `init` process, which then goes through the service scripts and starts the services according to run level and priority.

  The `do_install` task must install the service `start-stop-script` into the proper directory, typically `/etc/init.d`. Then the service needs to be enabled by creating links to the script from the resource control directories (`/etc/rc0.d` through `/etc/rc6.d`), so that the service can be started and stopped when the system enters the particular run level. This is accomplished by the `update-rc.d` class, which uses the `update-rc.d` tool that your recipe needs to inherit. The class does all the configuration work. All that is needed are three variables in the recipe to provide the necessary configuration to the class:

  - `INITSCRIPT_PACKAGES`: List of packages that contain the `init` scripts for this software package. This variable is optional and defaults to `INITSCRIPT_PACKAGES = "${PN}"`.

  - `INITSCRIPT_NAME`: The name of the `init` script.

- ▪ **INITSCRIPT_PARAMS**: The parameters passed to update-rc.d. This can be a string such as "defaults 80 20" to start the service when entering run levels 2, 3, 4, and 5 and stop it from entering run levels 0, 1, and 6.

  The manual page[5] for update-rc.d provides details about the tool and its usage.

- ▪ **systemd**: The System Management Daemon (systemd) was developed as a substitute for the aging SysVinit. In particular, it provides better prioritization and dependency handling between services and the ability to start services in parallel, which speeds up the boot sequence of the system. The systemd homepage[6] provides detailed information.

  The software package must provide the systemd service script, and the recipe must install it in the proper location, which is typically /lib/systemd/system. Then the recipe can configure the service by inheriting the systemd class and providing the following variables:

  - ▪ **SYSTEMD_PACKAGES**: List of packages that contain the systemd service files for the software package. This variable is optional and defaults to SYSTEMD_PACKAGES = "${PN}".

  - ▪ **SYSTEMD_SERVICE**: The name of the service file.

While your Linux system obviously can utilize only one system management service, you can write your recipe to support both. The classes and variables do not conflict, and the build system selects the correct settings from your recipe.

For more information on how to set up system services, see update-rc.d.bbclass and systemd.bbclass and consult the documentation for the respective system service manager.

8.2.10 Package the Build Output

At this point, all the necessary files of the software package are built and staged in the filesystem structure residing inside the destination directory D. The next step, carried out by the do_package task, is to collect the files and distribute them into packages for the package management systems.

Package Splitting

The process of grouping the build output into different packages is called *package splitting*. Most software packages produce many different artifacts of which, depending on your requirements, you may need only some to be installed in the root filesystem of your target device. Splitting packages to select only the artifacts you need helps you control the footprint of your system and also avoids the installation of binaries, libraries, debug information, and other files that could pose a security risk for your device.

---

5. www.tin.org/bin/man.cgi?section=8&topic=update-rc.d

6. www.freedesktop.org/wiki/Software/systemd

The two main variables that control package splitting are PACKAGES and FILES:

- **PACKAGES**: This variable is a space-delimited list of package names. The default value of this variable is defined in meta/conf/bitbake.conf is PACKAGES = "${PN} -dbg ${PN}-staticdev ${PN}-dev ${PN}-doc ${PN}-locale ${PACKAGE_BEFORE_PN} ${PN}". The do_package task processes the list from the left to the right, creating the leftmost package first and the rightmost last. The order is important, since a package consumes the files that are associated with it.

- **FILES**: The FILES variable defines lists of directories and files that are placed into a particular package. This variable is always used with conditional assignment, for example:

  FILES_${PN}-dbg = "<files>"

with files being a space-delimited list of directories and files that can contain wildcards to match portions for the directory structure of the destination directory D where the do_install task created the directories and installed the files.

The default settings for FILES for the default packages listed in PACKAGES are defined in meta/conf/bitbake.conf.

The default settings for PACKAGES and FILES cover the needs of most software packages. However, your software package may create additional artifacts and install them into directories not covered by the default settings. In other cases, although covered by the default settings, you may wish to further split packages, such as to create different packages for multiple binaries created. In both cases you need to add package names to PACKAGES and/or include the additional artifacts by adding to FILES. Listing 8-3 demonstrates how to customize packaging.

Listing 8-3   **Customizing Packaging**

```
SUMMARY = "Hello Universe Application"
DESCRPTION = "The ultimate hello extending beyond 'world'."
AUTHOR = "spacey@universetrotter.com"
HOMEPAGE = "http://universetrotter.com"
BUGTRACKER = "https://bugs.universetrotter.com"

PN = "hellouniverse"

# Other recipe stuff
# ...

PACKAGES =+ "graphics"
FILES_${PN}-graphics = "${datadir}/pixmaps/*"
FILES_${PN}-doc =+ "${datadir}/blurbs/*"

PACKAGE_BEFORE_PN = "examples"
FILES_${PN}-examples = "${datadir}/examples"
```

The example in Listing 8-3 prepends an additional package, named graphics, to PACKAGES and then sets FILES_${PN}-graphics to the filter. It also appends a filter to

`FILES_${PN}-doc` to collect documentation files from the nonstandard `${datadir}/blurb` directory and place them into the `doc` package.

The last package from the default list in `PACKAGES` is `${PN}`, which is the standard package. The associated definition for `FILES` essentially consumes all files and directories that have not yet been claimed by packages preceding it:

```
SOLIBS = ".so.*"
FILES_${PN} = "${bindir}/* ${sbindir}/* ${libexecdir}/* ${libdir}/lib* \
               {SOLIBS} ${sysconfdir} ${sharedstatedir} ${localstatedir} \
               ${base_bindir}/* ${base_sbindir}/* \
               ${base_libdir}/*${SOLIBS} \
               ${base_prefix}/lib/udev/rules.d $prefix}/lib/udev/rules.d \
               ${datadir}/${BPN} ${libdir}/${BPN}/* \
               ${datadir}/pixmaps ${datadir}/applications \
               ${datadir}/idl ${datadir}/omf ${datadir}/sounds \
               ${libdir}/bonobo/servers"
```

The BitBake syntax only allows you to prepend or append to a variable. However, if you need to insert packages right before the `${PN}` package, you can set the `PACKAGE_BEFORE_PN` variable and then use a conditional assignment to `FILES` to set the file filter, as shown in Listing 8-3.

The final two variables that control packaging are `PACKAGE_DEBUG_SPLIT_STYLE` and `PACKAGESPLITFUNCS`. The former gives you control over how to handle binary and debug objects. The latter lets you add your own functions for package splitting to your recipe. They are less common. We explained the basics in Section 8.1.2.

Packaging QA

The `insane` class adds plausibility and error checking to the packaging process. The class defines a list of checking functions that are invoked before, during, and after the packaging process, such as ownership and file/directory permissions, correct architecture for executables and libraries, dependencies of debug packages on non-debug packages, and so on. For a list of the functions, refer to the class itself or to the *Yocto Project Reference Manual*.[7]

You can use the variables `WARN_QA` and `ERROR_QA` to determine whether a QA function should create a warning message, which lets the build continue and succeed despite the warning, or an error message, which fails the build. You typically set these variables on a global level, either as outlined in the previous chapter in a distribution configuration or in `conf/local.conf` of your build environment.

If you need to disable a particular check for a recipe, you can use the `INSANE_SKIP` variable. For example,

```
INSANE_SKIP_${PN} += "dev-so"
```

skips the symbolic link check for dynamically loaded libraries. Typically, these links are useful only for development packages, but some software packages may need them to function properly.

---

7. www.yoctoproject.org/docs/1.6.1/ref-manual/ref-manual.html#ref-classes-insane

In addition to the automatic checks performed by the insane class, you can manu-ally verify correct package splitting. The directory ${WORKDIR}/packages-split contains separate directory structures for each package created.

Package Architecture

In general, the build system marks all packages to be specific to the target architecture. That convention is appropriate for most packages. There are two use cases in which you may need to adjust the package architecture:

- **Machine-Dependent Package**: If your package is dependent on the particu-lar machine it is built for, which is typically the case if it passes the setting of the MACHINE variable to the configuration script when executing the do_configure task, then you need to set your package architecture explicitly to

  PACKAE_ARCH = "${MACHINE_ARCH}

- **Architecture-Independent Package**: If your package applies to all architectures regardless of the machine it is built for—for example, if it is a fonts or scripts package—then your recipe needs to inherit the allarch class to mark the package correctly:

  inherit allarch

Even if you do not change the package architecture explicitly, we recommend that you try building your package for different architectures by doing multiple builds for different machines by setting the MACHINE variable in the conf/local.conf file of your build environment.

8.2.11 Custom Installation Scripts

Package management systems have the ability to run custom scripts before and after a package is installed, upgraded, or uninstalled. These scripts are included with the package, and the package management system executes them when they are invoked to carry out a particular action. The OpenEmbedded build system supports providing such scripts as part of the recipe. They are added to the recipe as functions. The package class picks up the functions and adds them to the respective package depending on the package management system. The mechanism is transparent to the package manage-ment system and is supported only for RPM, dpkg, and ipkg. Tar packaging does not support custom installation scripts. You can define the following four scripts:

- **pkg_preinst_<packagename>**: Preinstallation script that is run *before the package is installed*

- **pkg_postinst_<packagename>**: Postinstallation script that is run *after the package is installed*

- **pkg_prerm_<packagename>**: Pre-uninstallation script that is run *before the package is uninstalled*

- **pkg_postrm_<packagename>**: Post-uninstallation script that is run *after the package is uninstalled*

You need to replace <packagename> with the name of the package, which is one of the names listed in the PACKAGES variable. Specifying the package name allows you to conditionally apply scripts to certain packages.

Custom installation scripts are typically shell scripts. Listing 8-4 shows a skeleton for a postinstallation script for the main package ${PN}.

Listing 8-4   **Postinstallation Script Skeleton**

```
pkg_postinst_${PN}() {
#!/bin/sh
# shell commands go here
}
```

This script is executed after the package is installed. For the package to install successfully, the script must complete successfully. The script executes regardless of whether the package manager is run by the OpenEmbedded build system when creating the root filesystem or is run on the target. In some cases, you may want to run the script only when the package is installed on the target by executing the package manager on the target, or you may want to carry out different commands when installing on the target. Listing 8-5 shows a skeleton of how to accomplish that.

Listing 8-5   **Conditional Postinstallation Script Skeleton**

```
pkg_postinst_${PN}() {
#!/bin/sh
if [ x"$D" = "x" ]; then
    # shell commands for target execution
else
    # shell commands for build system execution
fi
}
```

The logic behind the skeleton script in Listing 8-5 is that the destination directory variable D is set in the context of the build system but not when the package manager is executed on the target.

8.2.12 Variants

All recipes build the software package for the target. If you want your recipe to build for the build host and/or for an SDK in addition to the target, you have to set the BBCLASSEXTEND variable:

- **native**: Build for the build host.
- **native-sdk**: Build for the SDK.

You may need to make adjustments to the recipe as necessary by conditionally setting or overriding variables when building variants.

8.3 Recipe Examples

This section provides examples of how to write recipes for building different types of software packages. These are purposely simple examples that you can put to the test right away using your own build environment. As always, we recommend that you create your own layer for it:

```
$ yocto-layer create mylayer
```

Have the tool create the sample recipe for you, or create the directory structure and files manually. The examples are applications, and we assume that they are placed inside the layer under meta-mylayer/recipes-apps/<appname>.

Do not forget to include your layer in your build environment by adding it to the BBLAYERS variable in conf/bblayers.conf of your build environment.

8.3.1 C File Software Package

This example illustrates how to write a recipe that directly builds a software package from its source files. While this technique is not commonly used, since virtually all packages use some sort of a build system, the example shows that the build system can be adapted to build any software package. Also, if you have the necessary compilers as part of your native builds, you are not limited to building source code that uses the C or C++ programming languages.

The source code for the example consists of two C source files and one C header file, which we have replicated in Listing 8-6.

Listing 8-6   **C File Software Package Source Code**

```
helloprint.h:
void printHello(void);

helloprint.c:
#include <stdio.h>
#include "helloprint.h"
void printHello(void) {
    printf("Hello, World! My first Yocto Project recipe.\n");
    return;
}

hello.c:
#include "helloprint.h"
int main() {
    printHello();
    return(0);
}
```

For the example, we assume that you create a compressed tar archive containing the three files named hello-1.0.tgz using the command

```
$ tar cvfz hello-1.0.tgz .
```

from within the directory where you created the three files. Then copy the tar file into the subdirectory meta-mylayer/recipes-apps/hello/hello-1.0.

Next, create the recipe shown in Listing 8-7 with the name hello_1.0.bb in meta-mylayer/recipes-apps/hello.

Listing 8-7   **Recipe to Build C File Source Package**

```
SUMMARY = "Simple Hello World Application"
DESCRIPTION = "A test application to demonstrate how to create a recipe \
               by directly compiling C files with BitBake."

SECTION = "examples"
PRIORITY = "optional"

LICENSE = "MIT"
LIC_FILES_CHKSUM = "\
    file://${COMMON_LICENSE_DIR}/MIT;md5=0835ade698e0bcf8506ecda2f7b4f302"

SRC_URI = "file://hello-1.0.tgz"

S = "${WORKDIR}"

do_compile() {
    ${CC} -c helloprint.c
    ${CC} -c hello.c
    ${CC} -o hello hello.o helloprint.o
}

do_install() {
    install -d ${D}${bindir}
    install -m 0755 hello ${D}${bindir}
}
```

The build system sets the variable CC automatically for the correct C compiler including all necessary flags for machine architecture, system root, tuning parameters, and more. The only other thing to note about this recipe is the setting of the variable S. Since S defaults to ${WORKDIR}/${PN}-${PV} but our tar archive does not contain a root directory with the package name and package version, the recipe has to adjust the setting for S so that the build system can find the source.

This recipe builds the application and also automatically creates the main package hello. All other packages are empty, since do_install only installs the hello application file.

8.3.2 Makefile-Based Software Package

For this example, we reuse the three source files from the previous example and add the makefile shown in Listing 8-8 to build the software package.

Listing 8-8   **Makefile**

```
CC=gcc
RM=rm

CFLAGS=-c -Wall
LDFLAGS=

DESTDIR=
BINDIR=/usr/bin

SOURCES=hello.c helloprint.c
OBJECTS=$(SOURCES:.c=.o)

EXECUTABLE=hellomake

.cpp.o:
        $(CC) $(CFLAGS) $< -o $@

all: $(SOURCES) $(EXECUTABLE)

$(EXECUTABLE): $(OBJECTS)
        $(CC) $(LDFLAGS) $^ -o $@

clean:
        $(RM) $(EXECUTABLE) *.o

install: $(EXECUTABLE)
        mkdir -p $(DESTDIR)/$(BINDIR)
        install -m 0755 $< $(DESTDIR)/$(BINDIR)
```

This is a typical albeit simple makefile that sets a couple of variables specifying the C compiler and a couple of flags. Using this makefile, you can build the software package on your host system. However, the makefile does not take cross-building into consideration.

Place this makefile into the same directory as the other three source files, and create a tar archive using

```
$ tar --transform "s/^\./hellomake-1.0/" -cvzf hellomake-1.0.tgz .
```

This command not only creates the compressed tar archive but also prefixes the files in the archive with the directory hellomake-1.0 to create the proper directory structure so that the recipe does not have to adjust the S variable. Copy the tar file into the subdirectory meta-mylayer/recipes-apps/hello/hellomake-1.0.

Then create the recipe shown in Listing 8-9 with the name hellomake_1.0.bb in meta-mylayer/recipes-apps/hellomake.

Listing 8-9   **Recipe to Build Makefile-Based Software Package**

```
SUMMARY = "Hello with Makefile"
DESCRIPTION = "A test application to demonstrate how to create a \
              recipe for makefile-based project."
```

```
SECTION = "examples"
PRIORITY = "optional"

LICENSE = "MIT"
LIC_FILES_CHKSUM = "\
    file://${COMMON_LICENSE_DIR}/MIT;md5=0835ade698e0bcf8506ecda2f7b4f302"

SRC_URI = "file://${P}.tgz"

EXTRA_OEMAKE = "'CC=${CC}' 'RANLIB=${RANLIB}' 'AR=${AR}' \
    'CFLAGS=${CFLAGS} -I${S}/. -DWITHOUT_XATTR' 'BUILDDIR=${S}'"

do_install () {
    oe_runmake install DESTDIR=${D} BINDIR=${bindir} SBINDIR=${sbindir} \
        MANDIR=${mandir} INCLUDEDIR=${includedir}
}
```

The function oe_runmake is executed by the do_compile task and invokes the Make tool with the makefile. You typically have to pass parameters for variable settings to the makefile by setting the EXTRA_OEMAKE variable. The variable provides mappings from the build system variables to the variables used by the makefile and additional parameters.

If you need to provide additional options to the CFLAGS variable, you must not override it because the build system uses it to pass cross-build settings to the compiler. Instead use

```
CFLAGS_prepend = "<flags>"
```

to add the additional options.

There is no need to override the do_compile task. The default task defined by base.bbclass executes oe_runmake, which in turn executes the Make tool, passing the EXTRA_OEMAKE variable to it.

You do, however, have to provide your own do_install task, since the default defined by base.bbclass does nothing. If your makefile provides an install target, then the task can simply invoke oe_runmake with parameters, as shown in the example. Otherwise, you have to write the installation explicitly, as shown by the previous example.

8.3.3 CMake-Based Software Package

CMake is an open source cross-platform build system to build, test, and package software. The CMake suite of tools uses platform- and compiler-independent configuration files to control and manage the build process. CMake creates native makefiles and even workspaces for various integrated development environments (IDEs).

The OpenEmbedded build system provides support for software packages using CMake with the cmake class. The class takes care of the configuration and build process, reducing most recipes to just the descriptive metadata, licensing information, source URIs, and inherit statement for the cmake class. Listing 8-10 shows the recipe for building Synergy—a client–server application that allows sharing of keyboard and mouse between multiple computers over a local network. Synergy uses CMake to control its build process. The recipe shown is replicated from the OpenEmbedded `meta-oe` layer.

Listing 8-10   Recipe to Build Synergy—`synergy_1.3.8.bb`

```
SUMMARY = "Synergy - control multiple computers with one keyboard and mouse"
HOMEPAGE = "http://synergy.googlecode.com"
LIC_FILES_CHKSUM = "file://COPYING;md5=9772a11e3569985855e2ce450e56f991"
LICENSE = "GPL-2.0"
SECTION = "x11/utils"

DEPENDS = "libx11 libxtst libxinerama"

SRC_URI = "http://synergy.googlecode.com/files/synergy-${PV}-Source.tar.gz"

SRC_URI[md5sum] = "3534c65ecfa6e47d7899c57975442f03"
SRC_URI[sha256sum] = \
    "0afc83e4ed0b46ed497d4229b2b2854e8d3c581a112f4da05110943edbfacc03"

S = "${WORKDIR}/${PN}-${PV}-Source"

inherit cmake

do_install() {
    install -d ${D}/usr/bin
    install -m 0755 ${S}/bin/synergy* ${D}/usr/bin/
}
```

8.3.4 GNU Autotools-Based Software Package

The GNU build system, commonly called *GNU Autotools*, has emerged as a de facto standard for developing applications that can be ported between UNIX-like systems.

Developers frequently criticize Autotools for being complex and cumbersome to use. However, writing portable applications that can be compiled on a vast number of different systems is a complex task, even more so for embedded systems. Autotools relieves developers from having to understand the details of the many different systems and where they differ but requires them to provide a potentially long list of configuration settings.

A software package that has been created with Autotools support significantly simplifies the task of building the package on different systems. Typically, all you need to do is run the `configuration` script and then build the package.

A large number of open source packages use Autotools for configuration. The OpenEmbedded build system provides great support through the `autotools` class, which in most cases pretty much reduces writing a recipe to providing the descriptive metadata, adding source URIs and license information, and inheriting the `autotools` class. Listing 8-11 shows a recipe that builds the nano editor package.

Listing 8-11   Recipe to Build the Nano Editor—`nano_2.3.1.bb`

```
SUMMARY = "GNU nano - an enhanced clone of the Pico text editor"
DESCRIPTION = "GNU nano - an enhanced clone of the Pico text editor"

HOMEPAGE = "http://www.nano-editor.org"
BUGTRACKER = "https://savannah.gnu.org/bugs/?group=nano"

SECTION = "console/utils"
PRIORITY = "optional"

LICENSE = "GPLv3"
LIC_FILES_CHKSUM = "file://COPYING;md5=f27defe1e96c2e1ecd4e0c9be8967949"

DEPENDS = "ncurses"

PV_MAJ = "${@bb.data.getVar('PV',d,1).split('.')[0]}"
PV_MIN = "${@bb.data.getVar('PV',d,1).split('.')[1]}"

SRC_URI = "\
   http://www.nano-editor.org/dist/v${PV_MAJ}.${PV_MIN}/nano-${PV}.tar.gz"

SRC_URI[md5sum] = "af09f8828744b0ea0808d6c19a2b4bfd"
SRC_URI[sha256sum] = "\
   b7bace9a8e543b84736d6ef5ce5430305746efea3aacb24391f692efc6f3c8d3"
inherit autotools gettext
RDEPENDS_${PN} = "ncurses"
```

This recipe does not contain any special settings for any of the steps. Everything is taken care of by the `autotools` class. The only things to note about this recipe are the following:

- In addition to `autotools`, the recipe also inherits the `gettext` class. This class facilitates building software packages with GNU gettext Native Language Support (NLS).

- Nano is a console application that uses the *ncurses* library. Hence, the recipe declares build time and runtime dependencies on it.

- To make recipes easier to update for newer versions of a software package, it is good advice not to directly write version numbers into `SRC_URI`. Since the nano editor's upstream source repository uses a partial version number in its path, the recipe splits the `PV` variable into its portions to create the version number.

To build the nano editor, simply create the recipe shown in Listing 8-11 with the name `nano_2.3.1.bb` in `meta-mylayer/recipes-apps/nano`, and launch BitBake.

8.3.5 Externally Built Software Package

In some cases, you may need the build system to include a software package that has been built by some other means, and you are provided with a package that contains only binaries, configuration files, documentation, and so forth. Since you do not have the source code, you cannot use a regular recipe that fetches the source code and then builds it.

The solution is to write a recipe that fetches the binary package, unpacks it, skips the configure and compile steps, installs the package components, and then repackages them for integration with the root filesystem for your target device.

Although this is not the most ideal process and can lead to compatibility issues, it may be the only way to seamlessly integrate such a package.

To integrate externally built software packages, the OpenEmbedded build system provides the bin_package class. The class uses the default do_fetch and do_unpack tasks to fetch and unpack it into the S directory. It skips the do_configure and do_compile tasks and defines a do_install task that simply copies the files from the S to the D directory. After copying, it creates a single package to contain all files by setting FILES_${PN} = "/".

Listing 8-12 shows a sample recipe using bin_package.

Listing 8-12 **Recipe using bin_package**

```
SUMMARY = "Package the Proprietary Software"
DESCRIPTION = "A sample recipe utilizing the bin_package class \
               to package the externally build Proprietary software \
               package."

LICENSE = "CLOSED"

SRC_URI = "file://proprietary-${PV}.rpm"

inherit bin_package
```

The bin_package class works without any adjustments if the original software package, after being extracted to the S directory, is laid out exactly as it should be laid out on the target.

If your software package requires a different layout on your target, or if you want to split it into different packages, you need to override the do_install task and set the FILES variable (at least FILES_{PN} but eventually others from the PACKAGES list) accordingly.

8.4 Devtool

In the preceding sections of this chapter, we walked through the process of writing recipes for your software packages, creating a layer for them, including the layer with a build environment, adding your package to an image target, building and finally deploying your image. A lot of these steps can be simplified through use of devtool.

Devtool is a suite of tools that assist you in round-trip development with the Open-Embedded build system. It is essentially like a Swiss army knife, providing the most commonly used tools in a single package. Using the `--help` option gives you a list of the devtool subcommands:

```
$ devtool -help
usage: devtool [--basepath BASEPATH] [--bbpath BBPATH] [-d] [-q]
               [--color COLOR] [-h]
               <subcommand> ...

OpenEmbedded development tool

optional arguments:
  --basepath BASEPATH  Base directory of SDK / build directory
  --bbpath BBPATH      Explicitly specify the BBPATH, rather than
                       getting it
                       from the metadata
  -d, --debug          Enable debug output
  -q, --quiet          Print only errors
  --color COLOR        Colorize output (where COLOR is auto, always,
                       never)
  -h, --help           show this help message and exit

subcommands:
  <subcommand>
    create-workspace   Set up a workspace
    deploy-target      Deploy recipe output files to live target machine
    undeploy-target    Undeploy recipe output files in live target machine
    build-image        Build image including workspace recipe packages
    add                Add a new recipe
    modify             Modify the source for an existing recipe
    extract            Extract the source for an existing recipe
    sync               Synchronize the source for an existing recipe
    update-recipe      Apply changes from external source tree to recipe
    status             Show workspace status
    reset              Remove a recipe from your workspace
    search             Search available recipes
    upgrade            Upgrade an existing recipe
    build              Build a recipe

Use devtool <subcommand> --help to get help on a specific command
```

8.4.1 Round-Trip Development Using Devtool

Devtool creates and maintains a workspace layer for you, which it automatically integrates with your current build environment. Before you can use devtool for your round-trip development, you need to source a build environment, as usual.

Creating a workspace Layer

The command

```
$ devtool create-workspace [layerpath]
```

creates a new workspace layer for you at the given layerpath. If you omit layerpath, devtool creates a layer called workspace at the current location. The created workspace layer includes a `conf/layer.conf` file. Devtool automatically adds the layer to the `conf/bblayers.conf` file of your current build environment unless you specify the `--create-only` option.

You have to use the `create-workspace` command only if you explicitly want to specify `layerpath`, as other devtool commands automatically create the `workspace` layer if one does not already exist for your current build environment.

You can only have one `workspace` layer maintained by devtool at a time for the same build environment. If you use the `create-workspace` command again with a build environment that already has a workspace, then devtool creates a new layer and modifies `conf/bblayers.conf` accordingly. However, it does not delete your previous workspace layer.

The file `conf/devtool.conf` contains the configuration settings for devtool, in particular the path to the `workspace` layer.

Adding a New Recipe to the `workspace` Layer

To add a new recipe for a software package to the `workspace` layer, use the command

```
$ devtool add <recipe-name> <source-path>
```

where `recipe-name` is the name of the recipe and `source-path` is the path to the source of the software package. If you did not explicitly create a `workspace` layer, devtool will implicitly create one called `workspace` when using the add command.

Devtool creates the recipe inside the workspace layer as `recipes/<recipe-name>/<recipe-name>.bb`. The `SRC_URI` variable inside the recipe is empty, as devtool creates an `append/<recipe-name>.bbappend` file with `EXTERNALSRC` set to the `source-path`. If devtool cannot find license information included with the package sources, it sets `LICENSE = "CLOSED"` and `LIC_FILES_CHKSUM = ""`, which allows the recipe to build even though there is no license information. Devtool also tries to figure out how to build the sources and set up the recipe accordingly. For software packages using CMake and Autotools, it includes the respective classes. For makefile-based software packages, it sets up stubs for the `do_configure()`, `do_compile()`, and `do_install()` tasks. Although devtool produces a working recipe in most case, you will probably need to adjust it to make it fully operational.

If you can access the package sources from a remote location, you can use

```
$ devtool add <recipe-name> <source-path> -f <source-uri>
```

to fetch the sources directly from `<src-uri>` and unpack them into your local `<source-path>`. For example,

```
$ devtool add nano sources/nano \
     -f http://www.nano-editor.org/dist/v2.5/nano-2.5.1.tar.gz
```

fetches the `nano-2.5.1.tar.gz` source tarball from the nano editor download site and extracts them to the `sources/nano` directory where it initializes a Git repository. It also creates the recipe `nano.bb`, shown in Listing 8-13, in `workspace/recipes/nano` (we only reformatted the content of the recipe to make it fit the page of the book).

Listing 8-13 **Recipe for the Nano Editor Created with Devtool**

```
# Recipe created by recipetool
# This is the basis of a recipe and may need further editing in order
# to be fully functional.
# (Feel free to remove these comments when editing.)
#
# WARNING: the following LICENSE and LIC_FILES_CHKSUM values are
# best guesses - it is your responsibility to verify that the values are
# complete and correct.
#
# NOTE: multiple licenses have been detected; if that is correct you
# should separate these in the LICENSE value using & if the multiple
# licenses all apply, or | if there
# is a choice between the multiple licenses. If in doubt, check the
# accompanying documentation to determine which situation is applicable.
LICENSE = "GPLv3 Unknown"
LIC_FILES_CHKSUM = " \
    file://COPYING;md5=f27defe1e96c2e1ecd4e0c9be8967949 \
    file://COPYING.DOC;md5=ad1419ecc56e060eccf8184a87c4285f"

SRC_URI = "http://www.nano-editor.org/dist/v2.5/nano-2.5.1.tar.gz"
SRC_URI[md5sum] = "f25c7da9813ae5f1df7e5dd1072de4ce"
SRC_URI[sha256sum] =
"e06fca01bf183f4d531aa65a28dffc0e2d10185239909eb3de797023f3453bde"

S = "${WORKDIR}/nano-2.5.1"

# NOTE: the following prog dependencies are unknown, ignoring: makeinfo
# NOTE: the following library dependencies are unknown, ignoring:
# ncursesw ncursesw ncurses curses curses magic z
# (this is based on recipes that have previously been built and packaged)
# NOTE: if this software is not capable of being built in a separate
# build directory from the source, you should replace autotools with
# autotools-brokensep in the inherit line
inherit pkgconfig gettext autotools

# Specify any options you want to pass to the configure script using
# EXTRA_OECONF:
EXTRA_OECONF = ""
```

Note that the variable SRC_URI is set to the URI specified with the -f (--fetch) option. Nevertheless, devtool creates the append file workspace/append/nano.bbappend, shown in Listing 8-14.

Listing 8-14 **External Source nano.bbappend**

```
inherit externalsrc
EXTERNALSRC = "/run/media/rstreif/YoctoDevelop/projects/kc/src/nano"

# initial_rev: c0516cb63fa0d376f81aec4e75a9c3cbd80823cb
```

The append file overrides the SRC_URI setting of the recipe, allowing you to modify the sources without needing to change the recipe.

Building the Recipe

After you have added your recipe, reviewed it, and eventually made some adjustments, you can build it using devtool:

```
$ devtool build <recipe-name>
```

which essentially calls bitbake <recipe-name> using all the settings from your build environment, including the parallelism option for make. You can disable parallel make by adding the -s (--disable-parallel-make) to the build command.

Deploying the Package to a Target System

Now you can deploy your freshly built package to a target system. The target system can be actual hardware or QEMU. The only requirement is that the target system must be running a Secure Shell (SSH) server. The command

```
$ devtool deploy-target <recipe-name> [user@]target-host[:destdir]
```

transmits all files installed into the root filesystem by the do_install() task. You can specify an alternative user name and a destination directory to which the files are copied.

Several options modify the behavior of the command:

- -n, --dry-run: This option lists the files to be deployed only without actually copying them to the target system.
- -s, --show-status: If you use this option, the command will display status and progress output.
- -c, --no-host-check: Skips the SSH host key verification.

Removing a Package from a Target System

Similar to deploy-target, you can use the command

```
$ devtool undploy-target <recipe-name> [user@]target-host
```

to delete files deployed with deploy-target from the target system. If you used destdir when deploying, devtool remembers it and removes the files from that directory.

The options for the undeploy-target command are the same as for the deploy-target command.

Building Images

With devtool, you also build images that include all the recipes from the workspace layer. The command

```
$ devtool build-image <image-name>
```

extends the image identified by <image-name> with the recipes from the workspace by adding them to IMAGE_INSTALL_append, and then starts BitBake to build the image.

Displaying Workspace Information

The command

```
$ devtool status
```

prints status information about the `workspace` layer.

8.4.2 Workflow for Existing Recipes

Commonly, you may need to create patches for software packages that have recipes defined in another layer. To accomplish this task, you typically have to retrieve the source code of the package, unpack it locally, and create an append file to use the local source code. After you make changes to your local source code, you need to create a patch, which you then add to the recipe. Devtool provides commands that greatly assist you with this workflow by taking care of the tedious tasks for managing the package source code and recipe.

Adding an Existing Recipe to the Workspace

The command

```
$ devtool modify -x <recipe-name> <source-path>
```

retrieves the source code for the package built by the recipe `<recipe-name>`, extracts it into the directory specified by `<source-path>`, and sets the source code up in a Git repository. The command does not copy the recipe from the original layer to your `workspace` layer but simply creates an append file to override `SRC_URI`.

For example, if you run the command

```
$ devtool modify -x sqlite3 src/sqlite3
```

from your build environment, it creates a source repository in `workspace/src/sqlite3` and the append file `workspace/append/sqlite3.bbappend`.

You can now make changes to the SQLite3 source code and build the package with the changes using

```
devtool build sqlite3
```

Updating the Recipe

Once you are happy with your changes, you commit them to the repository, as usual with Git:

```
$ git add .
$ git commit -s
```

Now you use devtool to create a patch from your commit and add it to the original recipe:

```
$ devtool update-recipe <recipe-name>
```

This command directly updates the recipe in the original layer. For our example with SQLite3, this means that devtool adds the patch to `poky/meta/recipes/sqlite/sqlite3` and modifies the recipe accordingly.

If you do not wish to modify the original layer but rather want to add an append file to another layer, use the command in the form

```
$ devtool update-recipe <recipe-name> -a <layer-dir>
```

where `<layer-dir>` is the path to the top-level directory of the layer you wish to add the append file to.

You always have to commit your changes to the repository first; otherwise, devtool ignores them and does not create a patch. You can use this behavior for creating a series of patches by committing changes subsequently.

8.5 Summary

Writing recipes seems hard at first but becomes easier with practice. There are literally thousands of recipes available for you to examine and learn from at the OpenEmbedded website. The layer index and the search function make it easy to find recipes that are already close to what you are trying to accomplish.

In this chapter we

- Explored the structure of recipes and discussed the typical variables
- Explained recipe naming and formatting conventions
- Provided step-by-step instructions on how to write your own recipes
- Showed examples for typical recipes
- Explained how to use devtool for rapid round-trip development and to comfortably work with existing recipes and the software packages they build

8.6 References

OpenEmbedded Metadata Layer Index, http://layers.openembedded.org/layerindex/branch/master/layers/

Yocto Project Documentation, https://www.yoctoproject.org/documentation/current

9

Kernel Recipes

In This Chapter

An embedded Linux project would not be an embedded Linux project without customizing the Linux kernel to fully support the hardware. Although it is not a microkernel architecture,[1] the Linux kernel is modular. Functionality can be either compiled into the Linux kernel or inserted into the kernel during runtime as loadable kernel modules. In the sense of modularity, the Linux kernel is similar to a microkernel architecture. However, unlike a microkernel in which device drivers and other kernel code that is not part of the kernel core are executed as separate but privileged processes, module and device driver code is always executed within the kernel context, which makes the Linux kernel a monolithic kernel. Because of this architecture, Linux modules have access to all kernel data structures, for the good or the bad, and do not need to use kernel interprocess communication (IPC) as a microkernel must. However, IPC is available for Linux kernel modules.

Whether you want to compile kernel functionality into the kernel or make it runtime loadable depends on various factors you need to consider for your project:

- **Availability as Kernel Module**: If functionality is provided by a kernel module, you have the choice between compiling the module code directly into the kernel or compiling it as a loadable module that can be loaded and unloaded at kernel

---

1. We do not go into the pros and cons of a microkernel architecture versus a monolithic kernel architecture here. Linus Torvalds had a very entertaining debate on the subject with Andrew Tanenbaum, the inventor of the Minix OS: https://groups.google.com/forum/?fromgroups=#!topic/comp.os.minix/wlhw16QWltI%5B1-25%5D. While the debate is far from being entirely objective and based on facts, it provides good insight into the advantages and disadvantages of both architectures.

runtime. If you choose to compile a kernel module into the kernel, it cannot be unloaded again during runtime. Some functionality, however, due to its technical nature, can never be loaded during runtime. If your project requires that functionality, you have to compile it into the kernel.

- **Kernel Footprint**: Less functionality compiled into the kernel means a smaller kernel that can be loaded quickly from storage media.

- **Boot Time**: A smaller kernel with fewer drivers compiled into the kernel means less initialization during kernel startup, which contributes to a faster boot time.

- **Hardware Support at Startup**: Because kernel modules are inserted into the Linux kernel after the kernel has launched user space, all hardware support that needs to be available during kernel boot, such as disks and eventually network hardware, must be compiled into the kernel. Alternatively, you can use an initial ramdisk (initrd) image to probe for the hardware, as most Linux desktop and server distributions do. Using initrd keeps the kernel more universal, but probing hardware requires more time.

- **Ability to Upgrade**: Hardware drivers may need upgrades after the embedded system has shipped. If a device driver is compiled into the kernel, the entire kernel must be upgraded, which is not possible without rebooting the system. If a device driver is loaded as a kernel module, the old module can be unloaded during runtime and the new module loaded to replace it.

In this chapter, we explain how to use the Linux kernel's configuration system with the Yocto Project to customize the kernel, the different ways of building the kernel with kernel recipes, how to add patches to the kernel, and how to build out-of-tree kernel modules.

9.1 Kernel Configuration

The Linux kernel provides its own configuration system, commonly called *kconfig*. Kconfig is essentially a configuration database organized in a tree structure. All configuration options are consolidated into a single file, .config, in the top-level directory of the kernel source tree. The kernel's build system uses that file to propagate the settings to all kernel source files. The dot as the first character of the filename makes this file a hidden file on UNIX systems. You have to use ls -a to actually see it in a directory listing. Although you can edit that file directly using a text editor, doing so is not recommended. It contains more than 5,500 configuration settings in a flat, line-by-line file, which may be one of the reasons the kernel developers decided to make .config a hidden file.

The .config file is typically created automatically either from a default platform configuration file or from an existing configuration for a particular system. If you want to edit it, the Linux kernel configuration system provides menu editors for it. These editors also recognize dependencies and interdependencies of configuration settings.

If you choose a configuration setting that depends on one or more other settings, the editor automatically selects those too if they are not already set.

9.1.1 Menu Configuration

If you have worked with the Linux kernel before and built it for a native environment, you are most likely familiar with the commands `make menuconfig`, `make xconfig`, and `make gconfig`. All of these commands launch a menu-based hierarchical editor that allows browsing, searching, and changing of configuration options.

The Yocto Project's kernel recipes provide the functionality of `make menuconfig` by invoking

```
$ bitbake -c menuconfig <kernel-recipe>
```

For example,

```
$ bitbake -c menuconfig virtual/kernel
```

launches the menu editor for the current kernel dependent on the machine settings.

For the menu editor to work, a valid configuration must be available. Therefore, you must have built the kernel at least once. That would typically be the case if you first built an entire image before making changes. However, if you do have a new kernel recipe and do not wish to wait for the kernel to build entirely before you can modify the configuration using the menu editor, you can use the `kernel_configme` command to run the kernel build process up to and including the configuration step that creates the .config file:

```
$ bitbake -c kernel_configme virtual/kernel
```

If you are using a graphical desktop environment for developing with the Yocto Project, launching the menu editor opens another terminal window. The `terminal` class, which provides the code for launching a terminal window, attempts to find a suitable terminal program based on the configuration of your system. On virtually all systems, the `terminal` class succeeds and presents a suitable terminal program. If the menu editor does not look correct, or if you prefer to use a different terminal type, you can override the automatic selection by explicitly setting the variable `OE_TERMINAL` in `conf/local.conf` of your build environment.

You can now use the menu editor to make changes to the kernel configuration. A simple example that can easily be tested with the QEMU emulator is to disable symmetric multiprocessing (SMP). The Yocto Project kernel configuration for QEMU enables this feature by default. From the submenu *Processor type and features*, deselect the entry *Symmetric multi-processing support*, then click *Save* and *Exit*.

The menu editor saves the changed configuration to the .config file inside the kernel build directory of the build environment. To apply the new configuration, you have to compile the kernel:

```
$ bitbake -C compile virtual/kernel
```

The capital -C invalidates the stamp for the shared state cache entry for the specified task and then runs the default task. In this case, it forces BitBake to build the kernel again, but without fetching the source code first. Since using the menu editor directly modifies the .config file inside the build directory, fetching the kernel sources again, which includes fetching the kernel configuration, would overwrite the new configuration.

You can now test the new configuration by launching QEMU:

```
$ runqemu qemux86 qemuparams="-smp 2"
```

The runqemu script launches QEMU in single-processor mode. Adding qemuparams="-smp 2" starts QEMU with two processor cores. After QEMU boots your Linux system, log in as root user and execute from the command line:

```
# cat /proc/cpuinfo | grep processor
```

Although QEMU provides two processor cores, only one processor is shown. You can perform the test again by re-enabling SMP using the menu editor. This time, the command shows two processors.

The menu editor is an excellent tool to quickly test new kernel configurations. However, since the modifications to the kernel configuration are written to the .config file inside the kernel build environment, those changes are not permanent. If you fetch the kernel source code again, delete the build environment, or use the cleanall command, your changes are lost.

You might think that before further modifying the Linux kernel configuration, you want to set CONFIG_LOCALVERSION[2] to a custom string to identify your modified kernel. However, that does not work because the build system sets CONFIG_LOCALVERSION through the configuration variable LINUX_VERSION_EXTENSION.

9.1.2 Configuration Fragments

Of course, you do not want to manually modify the kernel configuration with the menu editor every time you rebuild the kernel. For that purpose, the build system provides a mechanism to merge partial configuration, referred to as *configuration fragments*, into the .config file using a recipe. Figure 9-1 illustrates the configuration fragment concept.

Configuration fragments are files that contain one or more lines of kernel configuration settings as you find them in the .config file—for instance, CONFIG_SMP=n. You can then simply add those files to SRC_URI of the kernel recipe. Since the kernel recipe often is provided by a Yocto Project, OpenEmbedded, or board support package (BSP) layer, rather than modifying the recipe directly inside that layer, we recommend that you create your own layer and use an append file to the kernel recipe.

---

2. CONFIG_LOCALVERSION is the string that the command uname -r prints to the console.

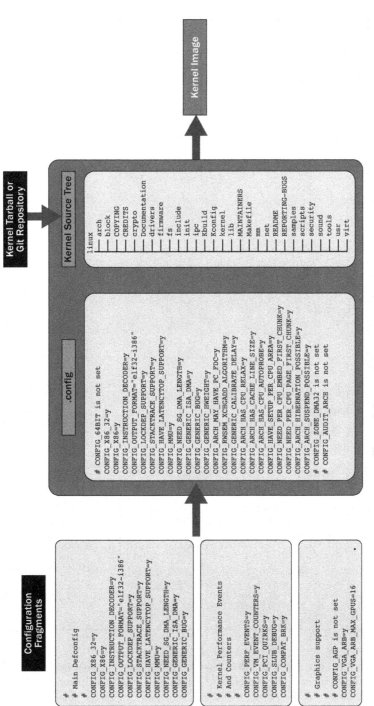

Figure 9-1 Configuration fragments

We explained creating layers in Chapter 3, "OpenEmbedded Build System." Using

```
$ yocto-layer create ypbook
```

from inside an initialized build environment creates the basic layer structure for you. Add your new layer to the BBLAYERS variable in conf/bblayers.conf of the build environment (see Listing 9-1).

Listing 9-1   **<builddir>/conf/bblayers.conf**

```
# LAYER_CONF_VERSION is increased each time build/conf/bblayers.conf
# changes incompatibly
LCONF_VERSION = "6"

BBPATH = "${TOPDIR}"
BBFILES ?= ""

BBLAYERS ?= " \
  ${HOME}/yocto/poky/meta \
  ${HOME}/yocto/poky/meta-yocto \
  ${HOME}/yocto/poky/meta-yocto-bsp \
  ${HOME}/yocto/build/meta-ypbook \
  "
BBLAYERS_NON_REMOVABLE ?= " \
  ${HOME}/yocto/poky/meta \
  ${HOME}/yocto/poky/meta-yocto \
  "
```

Now create the directory for the kernel append file and a subdirectory in it for the configuration fragment file:

```
$ mkdir -p recipes-kernel/linux
$ mkdir -p recipes-kernel/linux/files
```

Add the file smp.cfg and the kernel append file to the directory recipes-kernel/linux, as shown in Listing 9-2.

Listing 9-2   **Configuration Fragments**

```
recipes-kernel/linux/files/smp.cfg:
# Disable SMP
CONFIG_SMP=n

recipes-kernel/linux/linux-yocto_3.19.bbappend:
# Include kernel configuration fragment
FILESEXTRAPATHS_prepend := "${THISDIR}/files:"
SRC_URI += "file://smp.cfg"
```

The name of the kernel append file depends on the kernel version used by the build system when building virtual/kernel. You can find the name from the kernel build output. In our example, the kernel recipe is linux-yocto_3.19.bb. Therefore, the append file we create is `linux-yocto_3.19.bbappend`. For the fetcher to be able to find the file `smp.cfg`, the path to it needs to be added to the `FILESEXTRAPATH` variable. In our example, we simply put the file in the same directory with the kernel append file. The path of a recipe or recipe append file can be referenced by using the `THISDIR` variable.

Now you can rebuild the kernel with

```
$ bitbake -C fetch virtual/kernel
```

This time we explicitly want to fetch the kernel sources, which now include our configuration fragment. After BitBake completes building the kernel, you can test the result using QEMU.

For the preceding example, we manually created the file containing the configuration fragment. That fragment can become difficult to track if you are changing many configuration options, particularly if dependent settings are enabled automatically by the menu editor. Although the menu editor adds them automatically to the `.config` file, they have to be explicitly carried over to the configuration fragment.

To facilitate the task of creating configuration fragments, the build system provides the `diffconfig` command, which compares the old to the new configuration and creates the configuration fragment file. After editing the configuration with the menu editor, execute

```
$ bitbake -C diffconfig virtual/kernel
```

The command places the configuration fragment into `${WORKDIR}`.

After you have created your configuration fragment and added it to your recipe, you can use the configuration validation of the kernel tools to check your kernel configuration:

```
$ bitbake -C kernel_configcheck -f virtual/kernel
```

The `-C` option invalidates the shared state cache for `kernel_configcheck` to force running it even if BitBake executed it before. If there are any issues with your kernel configuration, the build system notifies you about the issues.

9.2 Kernel Patches

Applying patches to kernel sources with kernel recipes is no different from applying patches with recipes for regular software packages. If you already have a formatted patch file, simply provide the file and add it to `SRC_URI` of the append file to the kernel recipe.

To create patches yourself from modified kernel sources inside the kernel build directory, follow these steps that outline the workflow for a new kernel driver module.

1. **Change to the kernel source directory.** Change your working directory to the kernel source directory. The kernel source directory can be somewhat hard to find. However, as with any recipe, the variable `${S}` points to the source

directory. For kernel recipes, ${S} is set to ${STAGING_KERNEL_DIR}. To find the kernel source directory, use the command

```
$ bitbake -e virtual/kernel | grep STAGING_KERNEL_DIR
```

Then use the output to change to the directory. Alternatively, you can use

```
$ bitbake -c devshell virtual/kernel
```

which opens another terminal window in the kernel source directory.

2. **Add/modify kernel source files.** For this example, we add a simple device driver to the kernel. Edit/add the files, as follows:

```
drivers/misc/Kconfig (add to the end of the file):
config YP_DRIVER
  tristate "Yocto Project Test Driver"
  help
     This driver does nothing but print a message.

drivers/misc/Makefile (add to the end of the file):
obj-$(CONFIG_YP_DRIVER) += yp-driver.o

drivers/misc/yp-driver.c (add new file):
#include <linux/module.h>

static int __init yocto_testmod_init(void)
{
        pr_info("Hello Kernel from the Yocto Project!");
}

static void __exit yocto_testmod_exit(void)
{
        pr_info("Gone fishing. I'll be back!");
}

module_init(yocto_testmod_init);
module_exit(yocto_testmod_exit);

MODULE_AUTHOR("Rudolf Streif <rudolf.streif@gmail.com");
MODULE_DESCRIPTION("Yocto Project Test Driver");
MODULE_LICENSE("GPL");
```

3. **Stage and commit changes.** Yocto Project kernels are checked out from Git repositories. Therefore, you can simply use Git to create the patch:

```
$ git status
$ git add .
$ git commit -m "Added Yocto Project Driver"[3]
```

4. **Create the patch file.** Now use Git again to create from the top-level directory of the kernel sources to create the patch file

```
$ git format-patch -n HEAD^
```

which creates the file 0001-Added-Yocto-Project-Driver.patch file.

---

3. Alternatively, you may want to use git commit -s to include the signed-off-by message into the patch.

5. **Move the patch file to your layer.** Copy or move the patch file `0001-Added-Yocto-Project-Driver.patch` to the `recipes-kernel/linux/files` directory of the layer we created in the previous step.

6. **Create the configuration fragment.** Since we are adding a new driver, we need to enable it with a configuration fragment:

```
recipes-kernel/linux/files/yp-driver.cfg:
# Enable Yocto Project Driver
CONFIG_MISC_DEVICES=y
CONFIG_YP_DRIVER=y
```

7. **Add the configuration fragment and patch to the recipe.** Now we need to add the configuration fragment and the patch to the recipe append file we created in the previous step.

```
recipes-kernel/linux/linux-yocto_3.19.bbappend:
# Include kernel configuration fragment and patch
FILESEXTRAPATHS_prepend := "${THISDIR}/files:"
SRC_URI += "file://smp.cfg"
SRC_URI += "file://yp-driver.cfg"
SRC_URI += "file://001-Added-Yocto-Project-Driver.patch"
```

8. **Build the kernel.** Build the kernel with

```
$ bitbake -C fetch virtual/kernel
```

Now you can verify the result by running QEMU and looking for the driver's startup message in `dmesg`. After logging on as root, execute

```
# dmesg | grep "Hello Kernel"
```

The example shows how you can directly patch the kernel sources for any purpose. However, you need to patch the kernel sources directly for modules only if you want to compile them into the kernel. For modules that can be loaded during runtime, you can also compile the module out-of-tree. We explain how to do so in Section 9.4.

9.3 Kernel Recipes

The Poky reference distribution specifies how to build the Linux kernel, like any other software package, with recipes that provide the necessary instructions. The complexities of building and packaging the Linux kernel, particularly for cross-targets, are hidden by the kernel classes. The class `kernel.bbclass` is the main class, which inherits from various other classes. Kernel recipes inherit from `kernel`, which reduces developing kernel recipes to a few lines of code.

The Yocto Project maintains its own kernel infrastructure that comprises repositories for kernel sources and metadata such as configurations, configuration fragments, and patches. All of the Yocto Project kernels—that is, kernels that are used for the QEMU machines—and BSPs provided with Poky are built from that kernel repository. Many companies are using the Yocto Project kernel repository for their BSPs.

The following section details how to develop recipes for building the Linux kernel using any kernel tree. Section 9.3.2 explains the Yocto Project kernel infrastructure and how you can use it for your projects.

9.3.1 Building from a Linux Kernel Tree

There are various reasons you may not be able to use the Yocto Project kernel infrastructure and one of its kernel versions for your embedded project. Whatever the reason is, you can still take advantage of the tooling that the build system provides for building the Linux kernel.

We explain the process of building from an upstream Linux kernel tree using a recent kernel version directly from www.kernel.org. The mechanisms described apply to any upstream kernel tree, a kernel tree that you may have received from a hardware provider, or one that you are maintaining within your organization. The method described is the "traditional" kernel method that combines kernel sources with a configuration file, as shown in Figure 9-2.

You are responsible for providing a kernel configuration that matches your hardware and the kernel version. The kernel tree can be provided as a tarball, which you can

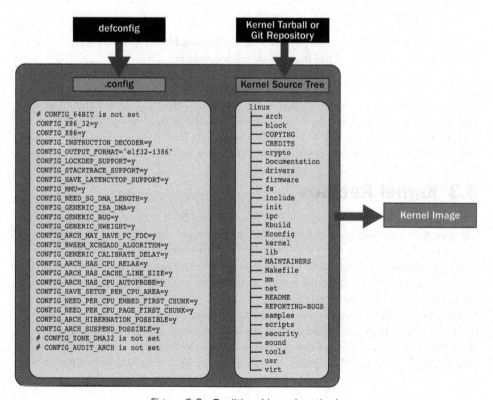

Figure 9-2 Traditional kernel method

download from www.kernel.org, or the kernel tree can be directly checked out from a Git repository.

Building from a Linux Kernel Tarball

Building from a tarball is the classic way of building a Linux kernel. This method has been supported by the OpenEmbedded build system from the beginning. Many custom kernel recipes are still using this method. Although it does not provide features such as configuration fragments as the newer kernel tooling does, many developers prefer it because of its simplicity and because it is very close to what kernel developers would typically use without the Yocto Project. Listing 9-3 shows a recipe that builds the kernel from a tarball retrieved from www.kernel.org.

Listing 9-3   **Linux Kernel from Tarball (`linux-ypbook_4.2.bb`)**

```
DESCRIPTION = "Linux Kernel from Tarball"
SECTION = "kernel"
LICENSE = "GPLv2"

inherit kernel

LIC_FILES_CHKSUM = "file://COPYING;md5=d7810fab7487fb0aad327b76f1be7cd7"

LINUX_VERSION ?= "${PV}"
LINUX_RC = "rc1"

SRC_URI = \
    "https://www.kernel.org/pub/linux/kernel/v4.x/testing/ \
     linux-${LINUX_VERSION}-${LINUX_RC}.tar.xz"
SRC_URI += "file://defconfig"

SRC_URI[md5sum] = "3e8331759af56ddd621528b2c7015ae1"
SRC_URI[sha256sum] = \
    "3c524ee0446b4ea8288708fa30acd28647317b9724f2d336052130e164c83f29"

S = "${WORKDIR}/linux-${LINUX_VERSION}-${PR}"

COMPATIBLE_MACHINE = "qemux86|qemux86-64"
```

Lines in the listing are broken for space and readability. In particular, `SRC_URI` must not contain any spaces or line breaks within the URI itself. The recipe inherits from the `kernel` class, which provides all the functionality for building the Linux kernel and keeps the recipe itself rather simple. For your own project, you may have to adjust the following variables:

- **`LIC_FILES_CHKSUM`**: Name of the license file and MD5 checksum. You may omit the checksum on your first attempt to build the recipe. The build system then complains about the missing checksum but computes it for you to copy into the recipe.
- **`LINUX_VERSION`**: The version number of the Linux kernel that the recipe is building.

- **LINUX_RC**: Linux release candidate.
- **SRC_URI**: Specifies the path to the Linux kernel tarball, which can be remote or local. Additionally, the variable must specify a defconfig file containing the kernel configuration.
- **SRC_URI[md5sum]**, **SRC_URI[sha256sum]**: Checksums for remote downloads. You may omit the checksums for your first attempt to build the recipe. The build system then complains about the missing checksums but computes them for you to copy into the recipe.
- **S**: Directory into which the kernel sources are unpacked. It must reflect the name of the source package.
- **COMPATIBLE_MACHINE**: A list of names for machines that are supported by this kernel. The names are separated by a pipe (|) symbol.

Save this recipe into `recipes-kernel/linux` of your layer. Also add a `defconfig` file to `recipes-kernel/linux`, or preferably, to `recipes-kernel/linux/linux-ypbook`. Doing so allows you to separate `defconfig` files for different kernels from each other.

Before you can start building the kernel with your new kernel recipe, set

```
PREFERRED_PROVIDER_virtual/kernel ?= "linux-ypbook"
```

in `conf/local.conf` of your build environment to tell the build system to use your new kernel recipe to build the Linux kernel. Now you are ready to launch the build with

```
$ bitbake linux-ypbook
```

After the build completes, test your new kernel with QEMU.

Building from a Linux Kernel Git Repository

If you are actively developing for the Linux kernel, you are probably doing so using Git. After all, Git was created by Linus Torvalds to support the development process of the Linux kernel community. When working with Git, it would be beneficial to be able to build the Linux kernel directly from a Git repository rather than from a tarball. Listing 9-4 shows a sample recipe on how to build the Linux kernel directly from Linus Torvalds's Git repository at www.kernel.org.

Listing 9-4   Linux Kernel from Git Repository (`linux-ypbook_git.bb`)

```
DESCRIPTION = "Linux Kernel from kernel.org Git Repository"
SECTION = "kernel"
LICENSE = "GPLv2"

require recipes-kernel/linux/linux-yocto.inc

LIC_FILES_CHKSUM = "file://COPYING;md5=d7810fab7487fb0aad327b76f1be7cd7"

LINUX_VERSION ?= "4.2"
LINUX_VERSION_EXTENSION ?= "-ypbook"
PV = "${LINUX_VERSION}+git${SRCPV}"
```

```
SRC_URI = \
    "git://git.kernel.org/pub/scm/linux/kernel/git/torvalds/linux.git;\
    protocol=git;nocheckout=1"
SRC_URI += "file://defconfig"

SRCREV = "d770e558e21961ad6cfdf0ff7df0eb5d7d4f0754"

COMPATIBLE_MACHINE = "qemux86|qemux86-64"
```

The recipe includes `linux-yocto.inc` from `meta/recipes-kernel/linux`. This include file is used by all Yocto Project kernel recipes and inherits from the `kernel` class and the `kernel-yocto` class. In addition to the functionality of the `kernel` class, the `kernel-yocto` class provides the tooling for building from a Git repository as well as other functionality such as configuration fragments. Adjust the variables of the recipe to meet your requirements:

- **LIC_FILES_CHKSUM**: Name of the license file and MD5 checksum. You may omit the checksum on your first attempt to build the recipe. The build system then complains about the missing checksum but computes it for you to copy into the recipe.

- **LINUX_VERSION**: The version number of the Linux kernel that the recipe is building.

- **PV**: A string concatenated from `${LINUX_VERSION}`, the literal `+git`, and the `${SRCPV}` variable, which contains the source code revision maintained by the source repository. This default setting is the convention, and you typically do not have to modify it for your own recipes.

- **SRC_URI**: Specifies the URI to the Git repository of the Linux kernel sources, which can be a local or remote repository. Additionally, the variable must specify a `defconfig` file containing the kernel configuration.

- **SRCREV**: The revision of the kernel sources.

- **COMPATIBLE_MACHINE**: A list of names for machines that are supported by this kernel. The names are separated by a pipe (|) symbol.

You store and build this recipe the same as you do the recipe for building from a tarball of the previous section.

Applying Configuration Settings and Patches

To apply kernel configuration settings, you add them to the `defconfig` file you provide with the kernel recipe. If you are using the Yocto Project kernel tooling by including `linux-yocto.inc` from `meta/recipes-kernel/linux`, you can use configuration fragments, as shown in Section 9.1.2. Using the Yocto Project kernel tooling is not limited to recipes building from Git repositories. You can use it with recipes that are building from Linux kernel tarballs, too. And of course, you can use the menu editor to test configuration changes first.

Patches are applied exactly as described in Section 9.2.

Using In-Tree Configuration Files

A kernel recipe that inherits from the `kernel-yocto` class can utilize a `defconfig` file that is included with the kernel sources, commonly referred to as *in-tree*, instead of providing a `defconfig` file with `SRC_URI += "file://defconfig"`, referred to as *out-of-tree*. A reason for doing so is that you may not want to maintain copies of `defconfig` configuration files in your layer but rather would like to use default configuration from the kernel tree. Configuration fragments then allow you to further customize the kernel configuration.

To specify an in-tree configuration file, add the following line to your kernel recipe:

```
KBUILD_DEFCONFIG_<KMACHINE> ?= "<defconfig file>"
```

where you replace `<KMACHINE>` with the name of the kernel machine and `<defconfig file>` with the name of the `defconfig` file inside the kernel tree. For example,

```
KBUILD_DEFCONFIG_beaglebone ?= "omap2plus_defconfig"
```

9.3.2 Building from Yocto Project Kernel Repositories

The Yocto Project maintains its own kernel infrastructure, which includes repositories for kernel sources and metadata and a powerful set of tools that assists with managing kernel sources and configuration data.

In the previous section, we demonstrated how to customize the kernel by providing `defconfig`, configuration fragments, and patches with the recipe. While this approach works well and is flexible, it separates the kernel sources from the configuration, making maintenance more difficult.

Using in-tree configuration solves the problem for `defconfig` but is less flexible, as only the default configuration can be provided that way. Additional configuration and patches still need to be provided with the recipe. In-tree configuration also requires porting the configuration to each new version of the Linux kernel.

Another problem is how to maintain and apply different kernel configurations and patches for different target hardware for the same kernel version as well as how to enable kernel features and add patches across multiple hardware platforms.

An ideal solution would move configuration and patches close to the kernel sources without being in-tree and provide tooling to flexibly choose patches and configuration for a large variety of target hardware. With the Yocto Project kernel infrastructure, the Yocto Project kernel developers have devised such a solution.

Yocto Project Kernel Infrastructure

For each version of the Linux kernel the Yocto Project kernel developers adopt, they create a repository. The Yocto Project Git server hosts the repositories.[4] Figure 9-3 depicts the basic structure of a Yocto Project kernel repository.

---

4. http://git.yoctoproject.org/

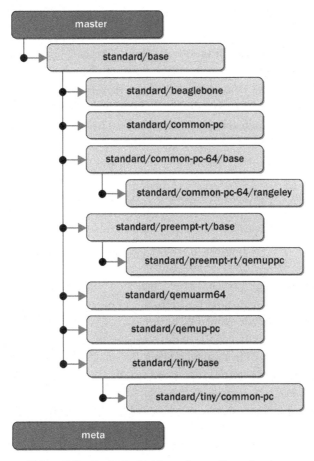

Figure 9-3   Yocto Project kernel repository structure

Each repository has multiple branches for the kernel sources and one branch for the metadata. Kernel source branches are either *base branches* or *BSP branches*. The base branches provide common functionality that is shared across the various BSP branches. The branches shown in Figure 9-3 (we omitted some of the BSP branches from the figure for clarity) are as follows:

- **Master Branch**: The master branch is a verbatim clone of the respective branch from www.kernel.org. This branch is maintained with updates from www.kernel.org. However, it remains pristine in the sense that it does not contain any Yocto Project adaptations. All base branches are derived from the master branch.
- **Base Branches**: Currently there are three base branches that are directly derived from the master. The base branches provide the foundation for the BSP branches.

Base branches typically require conflicting configurations, which is why they are separated.

- **Standard Base Branch (standard/base)**: This base branch is for a standard kernel configuration.

- **Real-Time Base Branch (standard/preempt-rt/base)**: This base branch is for real-time kernels. It applies the PREEMPT-RT patches to the kernel sources.

- **Tiny Base Branch (standard/tiny/base)**: This base branch configures a very compact Linux kernel.

- **BSP Branches**: There can be any number of BSP branches. BSP branches are derived from the base branches.

  - **Common PC (standard/common-pc)**: BSP branches with adaptations for 32-bit x86 architecture. There is one branch derived from standard base and one derived from tiny base.

  - **Common PC 64 (standard/common-pc-64/base)**[5]: BSP branch with adaptation for 64-bit x86 (x86_64) architecture.

  - **BeagleBone**: BSP branch for the BeagleBone board.

  - **Rangeley**: BSP branch for boards based on the Intel Atom Processor C2000 product family, code-named Rangeley.

  - **QEMU PPC**: BSP branches with adaptations for PowerPC emulation. There is one branch derived from standard base and one derived from real-time base.

  - **QEMU ARM 64**: BSP branch with adaptions for ARM 64-bit architecture (ARMv8-A).

- **Meta Branch**: This branch contains the metadata for the kernel source branches. This branch is not derived from any other branch but complements the kernel source branches by providing configuration and patches for them. Since this branch is independent, it is also referred to as an *orphan branch*.

The naming convention of the kernel source branches indicates the ancestry. The branch name of a BSP branch that inherits from standard/base begins with standard. Therefore, the standard/preempt-rt/base branch inherits from standard/base. So does standard/tiny/base. If the Yocto Project kernel developers make a change to standard/base, this change is merged into all branches that inherit from it.

Kernel branches and data from the meta branch are combined by the build system to create a valid kernel configuration. Figure 9-4 illustrates the principle.

---

5. In the author's opinion, this branch is named incorrectly. To be consistent with the branch naming convention, its name should actually be standard/common-pc-64, since this branch is not a base branch but a BSP branch for x86_64 architecture.

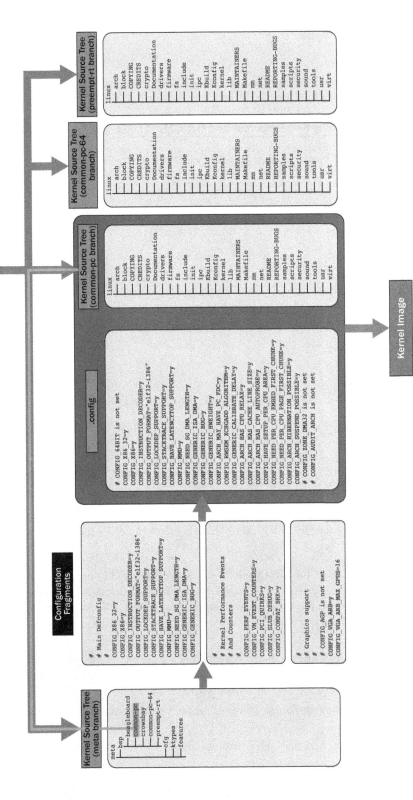

Figure 9-4   Yocto Project kernel infrastructure

Listing 9-5 shows the recipe for building a 3.14 real-time kernel. We chose this kernel recipe because it illustrates well how kernel sources and metadata are combined.

Listing 9-5   **Combining Kernel Sources and Metadata (`linux-yocto-rt_3.14.bb`)**

```
KBRANCH ?= "standard/preempt-rt/base"
KBRANCH_qemuppc ?= "standard/preempt-rt/qemuppc"

require recipes-kernel/linux/linux-yocto.inc

SRCREV_machine ?= "3428de71031ede23682dd0842b9cfc23ae465f39"
SRCREV_machine_qemuppc ?= "32c44a56a8218c3349f50d8151a10252d5e85dd1"
SRCREV_meta ?= "a996d95104b72c422a56e7d9bc8615ec4219ac74"

SRC_URI = "git://git.yoctoproject.org/linux-yocto-3.14.git; \
    bareclone=1;branch=${KBRANCH},meta;name=machine,meta"

LINUX_VERSION ?= "3.14.36"

PV = "${LINUX_VERSION}+git${SRCPV}"

KMETA = "meta"
KCONF_BSP_AUDIT_LEVEL = "2"

LINUX_KERNEL_TYPE = "preempt-rt"

COMPATIBLE_MACHINE = "(qemux86|qemux86-64|qemuarm|qemuppc|qemumips)"

# Functionality flags
KERNEL_EXTRA_FEATURES ?= "features/netfilter/netfilter.scc features/taskstats/
taskstats.scc"
KERNEL_FEATURES_append = " ${KERNEL_EXTRA_FEATURES}"
KERNEL_FEATURES_append_qemux86=" cfg/sound.scc cfg/paravirt_kvm.scc"
KERNEL_FEATURES_append_qemux86-64=" cfg/sound.scc"
```

We look at the variables in logical order rather than the order they appear in the recipe:

- **SRC_URI**: Specifies the URI to the Yocto Project kernel Git repository, in this case `linux-yocto-3.14.git`. Two branches are checked out through the `branch` parameter: the kernel source branch and the metadata branch. The `name` parameter assigns the name `machine` to the kernel source branch and the name `meta` to the metadata branch.

- **KBRANCH**: Provides the branch for the kernel sources. This variable is local to the recipe. The default value is `standard/preempt-rt/base`, which is conditionally overridden for the `qemuppc` machine with `standard/preempt-rt/qemuppc`.

- **SRCREV**: Specifies the source revisions for the kernel source and the metadata branches.

- **LINUX_VERSION**: Sets the Linux version number.

- **PV:** Sets the package version number. PV is derived by concatenating LINUX_VERSION with the literal +git and SRCPV.
- **LINUX_KERNEL_TYPE**: Sets the type of the kernel to be built according to the base kernel branches:
    - **standard**: Setting for all kernels built from standard/base and kernel branches derived from it other than the real-time and tiny kernels. LINUX_KERNEL_TYPE defaults to this value if it is not explicitly set.
    - **preempt-rt**: Setting for all real-time kernels built from standard/preempt-rt/base and kernel branches derived from it.
    - **tiny**: Setting for all tiny kernels built from standard/tiny/base and kernel branches derived from it.

    The kernel type set by LINUX_KERNEL_TYPE must match the kernel branch. For example, you must not use LINUX_KERNEL_TYPE = "preempt-rt" with KBRANCH = "standard/base".
- **KMETA**: Set the metadata branch name. The default is to provide the metadata in its own orphan branch called meta. Alternatively, the metadata can reside inside the kernel source tree in a directory called meta. In this case, KMETA is set to an empty string.
- **COMPATIBLE_MACHINE**: List of target machine names, separated by the pipe character (|), that this kernel can be used with.
- **KERNEL_FEATURES**: List of files containing kernel feature configurations.
- **KCONF_BSP_AUDIT_LEVEL**: The kernel-yocto class can detect and report incorrect kernel configurations. This variable sets what type of configuration errors to report:
    - **KCONF_BSP_AUDIT_LEVEL = "0"**: Do not report any configuration errors.
    - **KCONF_BSP_AUDIT_LEVEL = "1"**: Report configuration settings that were specified but not included in the final kernel.
    - **KCONF_BSP_AUDIT_LEVEL = "2"**: In addition to 1, report hardware settings that were specified in non-hardware configuration.
- **KMACHINE**: The name of the hardware machine as it is known to the Linux kernel. Every kernel recipe must set this variable. While it is not explicitly set in the recipe example, it is set by the include file linux-yocto.inc to equal the MACHINE variable, which is the name the machine is known by to the build system. In most cases this default is adequate. In cases where MACHINE does not accurately represent the machine name by which the Linux kernel knows the machine, the KMACHINE variable provides the mapping between the build system machine name and the kernel machine name.

    For instance, you provide your own target machine configuration and call it *excalibur*. The build system refers to this machine by its name, but technically excalibur is based on an Intel Core i7 64-bit CPU. The Linux kernel refers to this machine by the name of its CPU: intel-corei7-64. To tell the build system to build a kernel suitable for the Intel Core i7 CPU when you are asking it to build for excalibur, add KMACHINE_excalibur = "intel-corei7-64" to the kernel recipe.

Using the recipes provided with the build system, you can easily create your own kernel recipes that build Linux kernels from the Yocto Project kernel repositories. You can also clone the Yocto Project kernel repository and create your own BSP branch that inherits from one of the base branches to include drivers and other code specific to your machine. This approach allows you to benefit from the maintenance work that the Yocto Project kernel developers are doing on the base branches. When new security patches or other updates that are otherwise important for the particular kernel version are released by www.kernel.org, the Yocto Project kernel developers merge them into the base branches and test them. You can then cherry-pick and merge them into your own BSP branches.

Metadata Syntax

The data contained in the meta branch of the Yocto Project kernel repositories can be categorized into the following categories:

- **Configuration Fragment Files**: Configuration fragments are files that end in .cfg and contain kernel configuration settings, as described in Section 9.1.2.
- **Patch Files**: Patch files ending in .patch are applied to the kernel sources, as described in Section 9.2.
- **Description Files**: Files ending in .scc describe and aggregate configuration fragments and patches. Descriptions may also include other descriptions.

Description Files

Description files describe and aggregate configurations and patches and how they are included with the build of the Linux kernel. They use a scripting language consisting of these keywords:

- **define**: Set a variable.
- **kconf**: Apply a configuration fragment.
- **patch**: Apply a patch.
- **include**: Include another SCC file.
- **if [<condition>]; then <block> fi**: Conditionally execute <block> dependent on the evaluation of <condition>. The condition can contain variables that are set by other SCC files which include that file.

A collection description consists of a description file together with configuration fragment files and patch files. There are different categories of collection descriptions.

Configuration Collection Description

A metadata configuration collection description consists of one or more configuration files containing the Linux kernel configuration parameters together with a configuration description file that describes the collection of configuration fragments. Listing 9-6 shows a configuration collection description that enables extended firmware interface (EFI) support.

Listing 9-6 **Configuration Collection Description**

```
cfg/efi.cfg:
    # EFI Support
    # Dependencies
    CONFIG_PCI=y
    CONFIG_ACPI=y
    # Enable basic EFI support
    CONFIG_EFI=y
    CONFIG_EFI_STUB=y
    CONFIG_EFIVAR_FS=m

efi.scc:
    define KFEATURE_DESCRIPTION "Core EFI support"
    define KFEATURE_COMPATIBILITY arch
    kconf hardware efi.cfg
```

The configuration description file defines two variables:

- **KFEATURE_DESCRIPTION**: A short description that user tools can display to users
- **KFEATURE_COMPATIBILITY**: Compatibility of the configuration:
  - **board**: Compatible with specific boards
  - **arch**: Compatible with specific architectures
  - **all**: Compatible with all boards and architectures

The kconf directive is used to include the actual configuration fragment. The hardware keyword marks the configuration as enabling a hardware function, as opposed to the non-hardware keyword for general configuration. The distinction has no impact on the kernel build but is for the kernel configuration validation tools.

Patch Collection Description

Patch collection descriptions consist of at least one patch file together with an SCC file describing the collection of patches. If the patch or patches provide configurable kernel functionality, the collection description may also include a configuration file enabling them. Listing 9-7 shows the metadata collection description for a patch for ARM architecture.

Listing 9-7   **Patch Collection Description**

```
patches/arm.scc:
    # patches are for everyone, but the kconfig data is just for ARM builds.
    if [ "$KARCH" = "arm" ]; then
        kconf hardware arm.cfg
        include cfg/timer/hz_100.scc
    fi
    include v7-A15/v7-A15.scc
    patch arm-ARM-EABI-socketcall.patch
    patch vexpress-Pass-LOADADDR-to-Makefile.patch
```

The example shows how the patches are applied regardless of the architecture but are enabled only if the build architecture (KARM) is set to arm.

Feature Collection Description

Feature collection descriptions enable complex kernel features that may require the combination of many different configurations and patches and the inclusion of other collection descriptions. Listing 9-8 shows a feature collection description enabling a fictitious kernel test framework feature.

Listing 9-8   **Feature Collection Description**

```
features/testframework.scc:
    define KFEATURE_DESCRIPTION "Enable Kernel Test Framework"

    patch 0001-test-framework-core.patch
    patch 0002-test-framework-proc.patch

    include cfg/testframework-deps.scc
    kconfig non-hardware testframework.scc
```

Features provide a higher-level aggregation to enable certain functionality. In your kernel recipes, you would typically enable a feature described by a feature collection description by adding the relative path and name of the SCC file to the KERNEL_FEATURES variable.

Kernel Type Collection Description

Kernel type collection descriptions aggregate default configurations, patches, and features for the three different kernel types: standard, preempt-rt, and tiny. A kernel type collection description is essentially a feature collection description.

Kernel type collection descriptions are for separation purposes only. There is no link between LINUX_KERNEL_TYPE and these descriptions. To use them, a BSP collection description must explicitly include them.

BSP Collection Description

A BSP collection description aggregates configurations, patches, and features as required by a particular hardware platform. Listing 9-9 shows the BSP collection description for Intel's MinnowBoard for the standard kernel type.

Listing 9-9   **BSP Collection Description**

```
bsp/minnow/minnow-standard.scc:
    define KMACHINE minnow
    define KTYPE standard
    define KARCH i386

    include ktypes/standard
    include minnow.scc

    # Extra minnow configs above the minimal defined in minnow.scc
    include cfg/efi-ext.scc
    include features/media/media-all.scc
    include features/sound/snd_hda_intel.scc

    # The following should really be in standard.scc
    # USB live-image support
    include cfg/usb-mass-storage.scc
    include cfg/boot-live.scc

    # Basic profiling
    include features/latencytop/latencytop.scc
    include features/profiling/profiling.scc

    # Requested drivers that don't have an existing scc
    kconf hardware minnow-drivers-extra.cfg
```

All BSP collection descriptions must define KMACHINE, KTYPE, and KARCH for the
build system to identify the collection description suitable for the requirements defined
by a kernel recipe.

Kernel recipes express their requirements by setting the KMACHINE and KTYPE variables.
The build system matches KMACHINE and KTYPE of the BSP collection description to
KMACHINE and LINUX_KERNEL_TYPE set by the kernel recipe respectively to find the BSP
collection that provides the proper configuration for the kernel required by the recipe.

Metadata Organization

The metadata can be provided *in-recipe space* or *in-tree*. In-recipe space provisioning
means that collection descriptions, configuration fragments, and patches are provided
with the recipe. In-tree provisioning means that the metadata is provided in a branch,
typically meta, of the kernel repository.

In-Recipe Space Metadata

For in-recipe space provisioning, you place the files inside a directory hierarchy below
FILESEXTRAPATHS, as shown in Listing 9-10.

Listing 9-10   **In-Recipe Space Metadata**

```
meta-mylayer
└── recipes-kernel
    └── linux
        ├── linux-custom
```

```
|   ├── bsp-standard.scc
|   ├── bsp.cfg
|   └── standard.cfg
└── linux-custom_4.2.bb
```

To make the recipe aware of the configuration collection, you have to include the SCC file into SRC_URI by adding

```
SRC_URI += "file://bsp-standard.scc"
```

Since the name of the kernel recipe in the example is linux-custom_4.2.bb and FILESEXTRAPATH is automatically set to include ${THISDIR}/${PN}, BitBake finds the collection description.

In-Tree Metadata

In-tree metadata is stored inside the metadata branch, typically meta, that is part of the kernel repository, as shown by Listing 9-11.

Listing 9-11   **In-Tree Metadata**

```
meta
└── cfg
    └── kernel-cache
        ├── bsp-standard.scc
        ├── bsp.cfg
        └── standard.cfg
```

The path meta/cfg/kernel-cache is expected by the kernel tools and therefore mandatory. Below the kernel-cache directory, the metadata can be organized in any directory hierarchy, as is the case with the meta branch of the Yocto Project Kernel repositories. The structure of the meta branch of the Yocto Project Kernel repositories is shown in Listing 9-12.

Listing 9-12   **Yocto Project Kernel Repository meta Branch**

```
meta
└── cfg2
    └── kernel-cache
        ├── 00-README
        ├── arch
        |   ├── arm
        |   ├── mips
        |   ├── omap
        |   ├── powerpc
        |   └── x86
        ├── backports
        ├── bsp
        |   ├── arm-versatile-926ejs
        |   ├── beagleboard
        |   ├── beaglebone
```

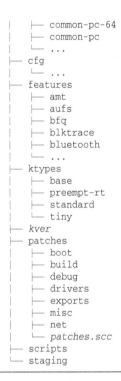

```
|   ├── common-pc-64
|   ├── common-pc
|   └── ...
├── cfg
|   └── ...
├── features
|   ├── amt
|   ├── aufs
|   ├── bfq
|   ├── blktrace
|   ├── bluetooth
|   └── ...
├── ktypes
|   ├── base
|   ├── preempt-rt
|   ├── standard
|   └── tiny
├── kver
├── patches
|   ├── boot
|   ├── build
|   ├── debug
|   ├── drivers
|   ├── exports
|   ├── misc
|   ├── net
|   └── patches.scc
├── scripts
└── staging
```

Collection descriptions, configuration fragments, and patches are organized into the subdirectories:

- **arch**: Feature collection descriptions for architectures
- **backports**: Patch collection descriptions for patches that back-port functionality from newer kernel versions
- **bsp**: BSP collection descriptions
- **cfg**: Configuration collection descriptions
- **features**: Feature collection descriptions enabling non-hardware features
- **ktypes**: Kernel type collection descriptions
- **patches**: Patch collection descriptions
- **staging**: Staging patches

The scripts directory contains tooling scripts, and the kver file contains the kernel version.

To apply in-tree metadata when building the Linux kernel with a kernel recipe, you have to add the collection description file to the KERNEL_FEATURES variable including its relative path. For example, to add the AUFS (Another Union File System) feature use

```
KERNEL_FEATURES_append = " features/aufs/aufs.cfg"
```

The variable KERNEL_FEATURES contains a space-delimited list of collection description files. Since _append does not add a space, you have add it explicitly. Do not assign a list of collection descriptions directly to KERNEL_FEATURES, as the build system populates it with its own list.

We explained earlier that the metadata branch is an orphan branch inside a kernel repository. An orphaned branch is a branch that is not related to any other branches of the repository. If you want to use your own kernel source repository with your own metadata branch, you have to create an orphan branch inside the repository:

```
$ cd <kernel repo>
$ git checkout --orphan meta
$ git rm -rf .
$ git commit –allow-empty -m "Create orphan meta branch"
$ mkdir -p meta/cfg/kernel-cache
```

You can now start adding metadata files to the new metadata branch. After adding and modifying files, you must commit them to the repository. Once you commit them, you need to adjust SRCREV_meta in your kernel recipe to the new commit hash; otherwise, the build system fetches an older version. Forgetting to do so is a common mistake leading to frustration.

Metadata Application

The build system gathers the correct metadata list by

- Matching KMACHINE and KTYPE of the BSP collection description to KMACHINE and LINUX_KERNEL_TYPE set by the kernel recipe respectively to find the BSP collection with all its includes
- Including any collection descriptions found in SRC_URI
- Evaluating the variable KERNEL_FEATURES

From this information, the kernel tools then create a consolidated .config file for the kernel configuration and a combined list of patches to be applied to the kernel sources.

Long-Term Support Initiative (LTSI) Kernels

The Yocto Project kernel developers pick the Linux kernels from upstream www.kernel.org based on a variety of criteria. One of them is long-term support. Typically, www.kernel.org releases a new kernel about every 90 days. Once a new kernel version has been released, the previous version it replaces no longer receives any updates. That can be problematic for embedded systems that may need patches for security and other selected improvements but cannot be upgraded to newer kernel versions.

To address this issue, a couple of companies have created the *Long-Term Support Initiative (LTSI)* under the auspices of the Linux Foundation.[6] LTSI picks certain Linux

---

6. http://ltsi.linuxfoundation.org/what-is-ltsi

kernel versions and maintains them with patches and ports cherry-picked features from newer kernel versions into them for a period of two years from the original kernel release date.

The Yocto Project has teamed up with LTSI, and the Yocto Project kernel developers always select LTSI kernels for the Yocto Project kernels. Every LTSI kernel does eventually become a Yocto Project kernel. However, not every Yocto Project kernel is an LTSI kernel, since the Yocto Project kernel developers typically select additional kernel versions between the LTSI releases.

If you choose a Yocto Project kernel that is also an LTSI, you receive the benefit of a kernel that is maintained for up to three years from its original release date.

9.4 Out-of-Tree Modules

The easiest way to build kernel modules is, of course, in-tree. The module's source code has been integrated into the Linux kernel source tree, and it becomes just a matter of enabling the module through a configuration parameter, as long as the module is set up correctly for the kernel's kconfig configuration facilities.

However, that is not always an option. You may have received the module's source code as a source package, which is not uncommon with device drivers provided by hardware vendors. Even for your own modules, you may choose to build them out-of-tree rather than integrating their source code into the Linux kernel source tree. For that purpose, the build system provides the module class, which contains most of the logic for building out-of-tree modules.[7]

9.4.1 Developing a Kernel Module

If you do write your own kernel module, you are of course in charge of the source files. This allows you to write the makefile, so that the module class can use it directly without any modifications to the compilation and installation functions in the recipe.

The Yocto Project provides a simple example for a module consisting of one C source file, a license file, and the makefile together with a corresponding recipe to build it. You can find this example at

```
poky/meta-skeleton/recipes-kernel/hello-mod
```

The recipe is straightforward. We replicated it in Listing 9-13 for your convenience.

Listing 9-13 **Module Recipe (`hello-mod_0.1.bb`)**

```
SUMMARY = "Example of how to build an external Linux kernel module"
LICENSE = "GPLv2"
LIC_FILES_CHKSUM = "file://COPYING;md5=12f884d2ae1ff87c09e5b7ccc2c4ca7e"
```

---

7. Nevertheless, if possible, always try to submit your kernel modules upstream to the Linux kernel sources. Once upstream, your module gets "automatically" maintained by the kernel community from kernel version to kernel version.

```
inherit module

PR = "r0"
PV = "0.1"

SRC_URI = "file://Makefile \
           file://hello.c \
           file://COPYING \
           "

S = "${WORKDIR}"

# The inherit of module.bbclass will automatically name module packages
# with "kernel-module-" prefix as required by the oe-core build
# environment.
```

As you do for any recipe, you have to provide SUMMARY, LICENSE, LIC_FILES_CHKSUM, and SRC_URI. For the example, the latter simply includes the three files, which are provided in-recipe space. Of course, if you have a more complex module, you would structure and package the source files. The example also sets PV, which, strictly speaking, is redundant because the build system derives it from the name of the recipe file. The recipe inherits the build logic from the module class and also sets S to ${WORKDIR}, as the fetcher directly copies the source files there.

That is all there is to the recipe, because the makefile, replicated in Listing 9-14, adheres to the build target and parameter conventions of the module class.

Listing 9-14   **Module Makefile (`Makefile`)**

```
obj-m := hello.o

SRC := $(shell pwd)

all:
        $(MAKE) -C $(KERNEL_SRC) M=$(SRC)

modules_install:
        $(MAKE) -C $(KERNEL_SRC) M=$(SRC) modules_install

clean:
        rm -f *.o *~ core .depend .*.cmd *.ko *.mod.c
        rm -f Module.markers Module.symvers modules.order
        rm -rf .tmp_versions Modules.symvers
```

This is a typical, albeit simple, Linux kernel module makefile. The module class expects a default target (all) and an install target named modules_install. Kernel modules must be built from within the kernel source tree. Hence, the variable KERNEL_SRC is passed with the -C parameter. The module class sets KERNEL_SRC to STAGING_KERNEL_DIR, which contains the location where the build system keeps the kernel sources. The parameter M[8] tells the kernel build system that an out-of-tree kernel module is being built. M must be set to the module's source directory.

Listing 9-15   **Module Class (`poky/meta/classes/module.bbclass`)**

```
DEPENDS += "virtual/kernel"

inherit module-base kernel-module-split

addtask make_scripts after do_patch before do_compile
do_make_scripts[lockfiles] = "${TMPDIR}/kernel-scripts.lock"
do_make_scripts[deptask] = "do_populate_sysroot"

module_do_compile() {
        unset CFLAGS CPPFLAGS CXXFLAGS LDFLAGS
        oe_runmake KERNEL_PATH=${STAGING_KERNEL_DIR}       \
                KERNEL_SRC=${STAGING_KERNEL_DIR}           \
                KERNEL_VERSION=${KERNEL_VERSION}           \
                CC="${KERNEL_CC}" LD="${KERNEL_LD}" \
                AR="${KERNEL_AR}" \
                ${MAKE_TARGETS}
}

module_do_install() {
        unset CFLAGS CPPFLAGS CXXFLAGS LDFLAGS
        oe_runmake DEPMOD=echo INSTALL_MOD_PATH="${D}" \
                KERNEL_SRC=${STAGING_KERNEL_DIR} \
                CC="${KERNEL_CC}" LD="${KERNEL_LD}" \
                modules_install
}

EXPORT_FUNCTIONS do_compile do_install

# add all splitted modules to PN RDEPENDS, PN can be empty now
KERNEL_MODULES_META_PACKAGE = "${PN}"
FILES_${PN} = ""
ALLOW_EMPTY_${PN} = "1"
```

We replicated the module class in Listing 9-15 because understanding the class helps when writing kernel modules and their recipes.

- The class sets `virtual/kernel` as a build dependency, which ensures that the kernel has been built before the build system attempts to build the module.
- It inherits from `module-base`, which defines a `make_scripts` task to build the kernel scripts before building the module. It adds that task after the `patch` task and before the `compile` task. The Linux kernel source tree contains several tools that are built for the host system. Some modules require these tools; however,

---

8. In makefiles of older kernel modules, you may also find the variable SUBDIRS, which is kept for backwards compatibility.

STAGING_KERNEL_DIR does not contain the binary versions of these tools. The build
system removes the binaries from STAGING_KERNEL_DIR before packaging the kernel sources for the target. The reason is that tools built for the host system do not
apply to the target, which of course means that the tools have to be built again for
building modules after the kernel has been packaged.

- The kernel-module-split class takes care of the packaging of the kernel module.
  The main package is prefixed with kernel-module-. For our hello-mod example,
  kernel-module-hello-mod package contains the actual kernel module binary.

- Besides KERNEL_SRC the class passes KERNEL_PATH to the makefile in the module_
  do_compile task. Passing both variables takes care of the two variable names for
  the kernel source directory most commonly used in module makefiles. The class
  also passes the commands for the compiler (CC), the linker (LD), and the archiver
  (AR) from the variables KERNEL_CC, KERNEL_LD, and KERNEL_AR, which of course
  contain the proper cross-toolchain versions for the target architecture.

- When running the module_do_install task, the class passes DEPMOD=echo to the
  makefile. Since virtually all modules are intended to be built and installed on a
  host system, the install target typically calls the depmod utility to create the symbol
  maps. That, of course, is not appropriate when building a module on a host system
  for a different target system. Hence, depmod is replaced with echo, which simply
  produces a log output.

When using the Yocto Project to build a third-party module, you may have to
override the module_do_compile and/or the module_do_install tasks to match the
parameters.

9.4.2 Creating a Recipe for a Third-Party Module

Typically, out-of-tree kernel modules are delivered with a makefile for building the
module natively; that is, for the build system. A look at the makefile can tell you if and
how you need to adapt the recipe to build the kernel module. Here are some items to
watch for:

- **Kernel Source Directory**: To make the process simple for users, module developers commonly build logic into the makefile to automatically detect the location
  of the kernel sources. This works fine when building for the host system but does
  not work for a Yocto Project build environment. Hence, you need to look for a
  variable that is used for the kernel source directory, such as KSRC, KERNEL_PATH, or
  KERNEL_SRC, and eventually assign it in your recipe.

- **Build Targets**: Most kernel module makefiles define a default build target that
  compiles the module. This target is invoked if no target is explicitly passed to the
  makefile, which is the default for the module_do_compile task. This works just
  fine for most cases.

- **Install Target**: The `module` class expects the install target to be `modules_install`, which is kernel development convention. However, many modules just use `install`.

- **Subdirectory Structure**: If the makefile is not located on the top-level directory of the module source package but in a subdirectory containing the sources, you have to adjust the `S` variable accordingly.

- **License File**: The build system expects the license file on the top-level directory of the module source package. If that is not the case, your recipe has to copy it there. Add a `do_configure_prepend` to your recipe for copying the license file.

Listing 9-16 shows the recipe to build the Linux driver for the Intel PCI-E 40 Gigabit Network Connections[9] as an example.

Listing 9-16   **Recipe for Intel PCI-E 40 Linux Driver**

```
SUMMARY = "Base Driver for the Intel(R) XL710 Ethernet Controller Family"

LICENSE = "GPLv2"
LIC_FILES_CHKSUM  = "file://COPYING;md5=d181af11d575d88127d52226700b0888"

inherit module

PR      = "r0"

# Point SRC_URI to SDK tarball
SRC_URI = "file://${TOPDIR}/../i40e-1.2.46.tar.gz"

do_configure_prepend() {
    # license file is expected to be in ${S}
    cp ${WORKDIR}/${P}/COPYING ${S}
}

module_do_compile() {
        unset CFLAGS CPPFLAGS CXXFLAGS LDFLAGS
        oe_runmake KSRC=${STAGING_KERNEL_DIR}    \
                BUILD_KERNEL=${KERNEL_VERSION}     \
                KVER=${KERNEL_VERSION}      \
           INSTALL_MOD_PATH="${D}" \
                CC="${KERNEL_CC}" LD="${KERNEL_LD}" \
                AR="${KERNEL_AR}" \
                ${MAKE_TARGETS}
}

module_do_install() {
        unset CFLAGS CPPFLAGS CXXFLAGS LDFLAGS
        oe_runmake DEPMOD=echo INSTALL_MOD_PATH="${D}" \
                BUILD_KERNEL=${KERNEL_VERSION}     \
                KSRC=${STAGING_KERNEL_DIR} \
```

9. You can find the source package for the driver at https://downloadcenter.intel.com/download/24411/Network-Adapter-Driver-for-PCI-E-40-Gigabit-Network-Connections-under-Linux-.

```
                      KVER=${KERNEL_VERSION}     \
                      CC="${KERNEL_CC}" LD="${KERNEL_LD}" \
                      install
}

S = "${WORKDIR}/${P}/src"
```

For many modules, you can adjust the defaults from the `module` class in your recipe to build the module. This is the preferred method, as you do not have to patch the module source code. However, there may be modules for which you have to provide patches to be able to build the module. For such modules, provide the patches in-recipe space and add them to `SRC_URI`.

9.4.3 Including the Module with the Root Filesystem

The final step is to include the module with the root filesystem image for the target. The vast majority of modules are for hardware drivers, which of course means that including them into the root filesystem is only valuable if the target hardware is accordingly equipped. For this purpose, the build system provides the following variables, which are typically set in a machine configuration file:[10]

- **MACHINE_ESSENTIAL_EXTRA_RDEPENDS**: A list of machine-specific packages that are required for the image to build. Any module packages you are adding to this variable have to be built before the build system can create the image. Because it is a *machine-essential* variable, packages in the list are considered essential for the machine to boot. The variable is evaluated by all images that are based on `packagegroup-core-boot`.

- **MACHINE_ESSENTIAL_EXTRA_RRECOMMENDS**: A list of machine-specific packages recommended for the machine, similar to the previous variable, but the build process does not depend on them. That means even if the packages in this list are not present, the image builds successfully. Packages in this list are also *machine essential*, which means they are required for the machine to boot. What sounds like a contradiction makes sense for modules that may be compiled into the Linux kernel rather than be provided as module packages.

- **MACHINE_EXTRA_RDEPENDS**: A list of machine-specific packages required for the image to build. However, compared to `MACHINE_ESSENTIAL_EXTRA_RDEPENDS`, these packages are not essential for the machine to boot. The variable is evaluated by all images that are based on `packagegroup-base`.

- **MACHINE_EXTRA_RRECOMMENDS**: A list of machine-specific packages recommended for the machine but not essential to boot the machine.

---

10. We discuss machine configurations in the following chapter when we discuss Yocto Project board support packages.

For example, add

```
MACHINE_EXTRA_RDEPENDS += "kernel-module-<module name>"
```

to your machine definition file to include the kernel module in your image.

You may wonder whether you could add the module to the IMAGE_INSTALL variable in the image recipe. That is, of course, possible but only recommended if the module is not dependent on machine-specific hardware features.

9.4.4 Module Autoloading

The build system can configure automatic but static module loading using /etc/modules-load.d and /etc/modprobe.d on your target system. While it is usually a better idea that you rely on automatic module loading provided by *udev* on the basis of hardware identification and similar triggers, there may be use cases for which static module loading at boot time makes sense.

When using systemd and systemd-modules-load.service, the variable KERNEL_MODULE_AUTOLOAD specifies a list of modules that need to be loaded at boot time:

```
KERNEL_MODULE_AUTOLOAD += "module1 module2 module3"
```

For each module listed, the build system creates a file with the name of the module and ending in .conf in /etc/modules-load.d containing the name of the module to load. The lexicographical order of the files determines the load order of the modules.

To provide configuration parameters for modules through /etc/modprobe.d, you use the variables KERNEL_MODULE_PROBECONF and module_conf_<module_name>. Like KERNEL_MODULE_AUTOLOAD, KERNEL_MODULE_PROBECONF is simply a list of module names. For each item in KERNEL_MODULE_PROBECONF, the build system expects a module_conf_<module_name> variable, which specifies the module configuration as expected by modprobe. For example, for a fictitious module named foofighter that requires two configuration variables, use

```
KERNEL_MODULE_PROBECONF += "foofighter"
Module_conf_foofighter = "options foofighter foo=1 bar=2"
```

You typically place these settings in the recipe for your module.

9.5 Device Tree

Simply put, device tree is a data structure describing a hardware platform. Rather than hardcoding every detail of devices and their configuration, such as I/O addresses, memory address space, interrupts, and more, into the kernel sources, a data structure is passed to the kernel at boot time. The *device tree compiler (DTC)* compiles device trees from their human-readable hierarchical format into a binary format commonly referred to as *flattened device tree (FTD)*.

The OpenEmbedded build system provides support for building the FTD from device tree source files using the DTC. Device tree source files end in .dts. Files containing the FTB end in .dtb. In this section, we explain how to build device trees for a given platform or machine with the build system.[11]

Device trees are platform or machine specific, as they describe the hardware configuration of the platform. They are built as part of a kernel recipe. For this to work, the kernel recipe must include either

```
require recipes-kernel/linux/linux-dtb.inc
```

or

```
require recipes-kernel/linux/linux-yocto.inc
```

as the latter includes the former.

Now you have to tell the build system what device tree to build for your platform by setting the variable KERNEL_DEVICETREE to the name of the FTD for your platform. For example,

```
KERNEL_DEVICETREE = "am335x-bone.dtb am335x-boneblack.dtb"
```

instructs the build system to generate the FTD files for the BeagleBone (White) and BeagleBone Black. The best place for this variable is the machine configuration file, which contains all the machine-specific settings.

9.6 Summary

In this chapter, we focused on building the Linux kernel and kernel modules with the Yocto Project.

- With menu configuration and configuration fragments, the build system provides tooling that allows for fast round-trip testing and integration of kernel configuration.

- Patches to the kernel source code are applied in exactly the same way as for any other software package.

- In its simplest form, the Linux kernel can be built directly from kernel tree sources, either from source tarballs or Git repositories, by providing in-recipe space or in-tree configuration.

- The Yocto Project maintains its own Linux kernel infrastructure consisting of repositories containing the kernel sources as well as configuration metadata and patches. The Yocto Project kernel tooling allows for flexible configuration using metadata features.

- The Yocto Project kernel infrastructure provides maintained kernel sources for the three base configurations—standard, real-time, and tiny—from which specific branches for BSPs can be derived.

---

11. If you are looking for information on how device trees are structured and how to develop a device tree for your platform, refer to www.devicetree.org and http://elinux.org/Device_Tree.

- The Yocto Project adopts LTSI kernels providing continuous support for multiple years, which is particularly beneficial for embedded projects.
- Through the `module` class, the build system supports convenient building of out-of-tree kernel modules.

9.7 References

Linux Kernel Build System, Documentation/kbuild/kbuild.txt

Yocto Project Linux Kernel Development Manual, www.yoctoproject.org/docs/1.8/kernel-dev/kernel-dev.html

10

Board Support Packages

The preceding chapters laid the foundation for building custom a Linux system with the Yocto Project tools. We used the software system emulator QEMU for testing. In this chapter, we take it one step further and demonstrate how the build system supports creating Linux kernel and root filesystem images for actual hardware.

Hardware support is provided by *board support packages* (BSPs). If you are familiar with embedded system development, you have most likely heard the term *BSP* before. However, regardless of having the same name, Yocto Project BSPs are substantially different from the, let's say, more traditional BSP for the typical embedded system.

We begin by explaining the philosophy behind Yocto Project BSPs and why Yocto Project BSPs are different from traditional BSPs. Then we use a BSP to build a system for an embedded evaluation board, put that system on that board, and finally boot the board. At the end of this chapter, we outline how you can create a Yocto Project BSP for your own hardware.

10.1 Yocto Project BSP Philosophy

In general, a BSP is a specific adaptation of a given operating system for given hardware, such as an embedded device board. BSPs are typically provided by semiconductor and board vendors to their customers so that the customers can build, load, and run the operating system on the vendor's hardware.

Traditional BSPs typically comprise these items:

- **Documentation**: We put documentation first because any BSP should contain documentation that describes the content of the BSP, provides information on the specific hardware the BSP supports, and includes instructions on how to use the BSP to build the operating system for the hardware, to transfer the operating system image to the hardware, and to boot the hardware. In addition, documentation may include information on how you can adapt the BSP to hardware that is similar to the reference hardware the BSP supports.

- **Development Tools**: Commonly, the vendors include at least a toolchain with compiler, assembler, linker, and archiver. The toolchain matches the supported device and the source code. Some BSPs may even include a software development kit (SDK) and eventually an integrated development environment (IDE), such as Eclipse, which make development for the target hardware even more convenient.

- **Operating System Source Code and Binaries**: Some BSPs go as far as to include the entire source code for the operating system if the operating system is open source. If it is proprietary, only source code necessary to compile device drivers and application software, such as header files and statically linked libraries, may be included. All other operating system files are provided as binaries. Since operating system sources and binaries are potentially large, it is common that the provided development tools use the vendor's repositories and download sites to obtain the source code and binaries as necessary when building the system.

- **Source Code Patches**: If the hardware targeted by the BSP requires special device drivers, configuration, or other modules on top of the base operating system software packages, the BSP may provide them. Alternatively, it is not uncommon that the vendor has already patched the operating system sources so that the BSP does not need to include any patches.

- **Filesystem Images**: A BSP may also include entire filesystem images for the supported hardware, which is very convenient, as it helps in bringing up the target and provides a reference when building your own system.

A BSP that includes everything from documentation to filesystem images makes it very convenient for users to get started with the BSP quickly, as most of the dependencies are resolved by what is contained in the BSP. However, long-term maintenance can sometimes become a challenge, particularly if the vendor does not provide regular updates. We still see many vendor BSPs for system-on-chips (SoC) and development boards that use Linux kernel version 2.6.

This becomes a problem if an embedded project wants to utilize one of those SoCs together with other hardware that is supported only by newer kernel versions. If the SoC vendor does not provide an update for the BSP for a later Linux kernel, you as a system engineer face the task of either porting the BSP to a newer kernel version or back-porting device support into the older kernel version supported by the BSP. Both approaches have potential pitfalls.

Porting the BSP to a later Linux kernel version may become rather difficult for a BSP with an unknown history: When did the vendor branch the upstream sources? What modifications have been applied?

Back-porting a device driver, on the other hand, may be impossible if the device driver relies on features that are only available in the newest Linux kernels.

The Yocto Project takes a different approach for BSPs:

- Yocto Project BSPs are not standalone like the traditional BSPs. They rely on the base metadata layers such as OpenEmbedded Core (`meta`) and possibly other layers.

- Yocto Project BSPs do not include a build system or any development tools. They are provided by the Yocto Project itself and created during the build process.

- Yocto Project BSPs do not include any source code other than recipes and eventually patches.

- Yocto Project BSPs are concerned only with components that are specific to the particular hardware.

Essentially, a Yocto Project BSP is nothing but a specialized metadata layer that includes additions and modifications to the core layers for the support of the target hardware. All Yocto Project BSPs depend at least on the OE Core metadata layer.

Yocto Project BSPs limit the maintenance of the BSP to the packages the BSP adds and the ones for the underlying layers that it modifies. All other maintenance work lies with the underlying layers. This approach, of course, means that a specific version of a Yocto Project BSP is bound to the particular versions of the underlying layers it depends on. If an underlying layer changes—for example, if the `meta` layer drops the support for a particular kernel version—then the BSP must be adapted. However, this maintenance work is typically much less than maintaining a traditional BSP.

Maintenance effort for Yocto Project BSPs is further reduced by the Poky build system's dependency handling. Most packages are not dependent on the particular target hardware. The dependency handling provided by conditional variable overrides ensures that recipes building packages dependent on the hardware, such as the Linux kernel, receive the proper information about the target hardware and its architecture.

10.1.1 BSP Dependency Handling

The BSP dependency handling of the build system not only eases maintenance effort but also enables BSPs to easily be exchanged for each other, almost literally by changing a single line in a configuration file. This is a huge benefit for system builders like you. It enables you to build exactly the same root filesystem for one board today and for another one that may even use an SoC with a completely different architecture the next day. We refer to this feature as the *orthogonality* of Yocto Project BSPs. Although the term is not entirely correct in the mathematical sense of *orthogonal*,[1] users can swap one BSP for the next without worrying about any changes to the rest of the build system.

It is worth it to have a quick look at how the build system handles target-specific dependencies, as they can commonly be found in recipes that are dependent on the hardware configuration.

In Chapter 4, "BitBake Build Engine," Section 4.4.2, we discussed BitBake's conditional variable assignment mechanism using the variable OVERRIDES. This mechanism is the backbone of the build system's dependency handling for BSPs. The variable OVERRIDES contains a comma-delimited list of override conditions with increasing priority from left to right. The Poky reference distribution sets the variable to this expression:[2]

```
OVERRIDES="${TARGET_OS}:${TRANSLATED_TARGET_ARCH}:build-${BUILD_OS}: \
    pn-${PN}:${MACHINEOVERRIDES}:${DISTROOVERRIDES}: \
    ${CLASSOVERRIDE}:forcevariable"
```

For a particular target, the variables inside the expression are expanded accordingly. For example, for an 64-bit X86 Qemu target,

```
OVERRIDES="linux:x86-64:build-linux:pn-core-image-minimal: \
    qemuall:qemux86-64:poky:class-target:forcevariable:libc-glibc"
```

the BSP-specific settings are provided by the variable MACHINEOVERRIDES, which for the example expands to qemuall:qemux86-64.

Essentially, there are two settings: qemuall and qemux86-64. The former provides an override for all QEMU machines, while the latter provides it specifically for the 64-bit x86 emulation. The latter has higher priority, as it is listed after the former. If a particular variable requires a machine-dependent setting, it is just a matter of appending the machine override to the variable. For example,

```
KERNEL_FEATURES_append_qemux86-64=" cfg/sound.scc"
```

adds a configuration description to KERNEL_FEATURES if the target build is for qemux86-64.

BSPs frequently use conditional variable assignments like the preceding one in recipes and append files to tweak the recipe for the particular target.

For the remaining sections of this chapter, unless we explicitly state otherwise, we refer to the *Yocto Project Board Support Package (Yocto Project BSP)* simply as *BSP* to make the text more legible.

---

1. Orthogonal in mathematics means that two dimensions are entirely independent from each other. That is not true, of course, for the build system, as target-dependent variable settings provided by a BSP override the standard settings of the build system. From a user's point of view, without looking at the details of the BSP, it looks as if BSP and build system were independent.

2. You can obtain this information by executing bitbake -e core-image-minimal | grep OVERRIDES in your build environment.

10.2 Building with a BSP

A BSP simply is a metadata layer that contains a machine definition in the form of a configuration file with the name of the machine ending in .conf. Machine configuration files are located inside the conf/machine subdirectory of the BSP layer. To use a BSP, you have to add it to the BBLAYERS variable in the conf/bblayers.conf file of your build environment. You then have to set the MACHINE variable inside the conf/local.conf file of your build environment to the name of the machine you want to build for.

Technically, we have implicitly been using a BSP for our qemux86 builds throughout the preceding chapters. You can find the machine definitions for qemux86 in the OE Core metadata layer of your build system at poky/meta/conf/machine/qemux86.conf. The OE Core metadata layer provides machine definitions for a variety of emulated machines for different architectures: qemuarm, qemuarm64, qemumips, qemumips64, qemuppc, qemux86, and qemux86-64. Providing machine definitions essentially qualifies the layer as a BSP layer.

The Yocto Project also includes its own BSP layer for actual hardware machines: meta-yocto-bsp. This layer is by default included in BBLAYERS of every build environment created with oe-init-build-env. It provides machine definitions for the Texas Instruments BeagleBone[3] board, the Ubiquity Networks EdgeRouter,[4] the Freescale MPC8351E-RDB Reference Platform,[5] and generic 32-bit and 64-bit x86 platforms.

Building for any of these target platforms is simple. The file conf/local.conf already contains the MACHINE settings for them. You just need to uncomment the one you wish to build for.

Of course, this is only a very limited list of hardware platforms. The Yocto Project metadata includes them for convenience and test purposes. There are many other BSPs available from SoC, board vendors, and the community for a large variety of hardware. We look into the details of how to find and utilize external BSPs in Section 10.2.2.

10.2.1 Building for the BeagleBone

The BeagleBone is a development board based on the Texas Instruments AM335x ARM Cortex-A8 SoC. Hardware and software are open designs, created and supported by the BeagleBoard.org Foundation,[6] a US-based nonprofit organization with the goal "to provide education in and promotion of the design and use of open-source software and hardware in embedded computing."

There are multiple variants of the BeagleBone, the original BeagleBone (White), the BeagleBone Black, and now the BeagleBone Green. They can easily be distinguished

---

3. http://beagleboard.org/bone

4. https://www.ubnt.com/edgemax/edgerouter

5. http://www.nxp.com/files/32bit/doc/fact_sheet/MPC8315ERDBFS.pdf

6. http://beagleboard.org/about

by the respective colors of their printed circuit boards (PCBs). The BeagleBone Black uses a more powerful version of the AM3358 SoC with 1 GHz of clock speed, provides 512 MB of RAM (twice the RAM of the original BeagleBone), and also offers 2 GB (4 GB on the revision C model) of on-board embedded multimedia card (eMMC) storage. In addition, the BeagleBone Black costs only a little more than half the price of the original board. However, the Black version does not have a USB-to-serial converter for the system console on board. The serial system console is necessary to interact with the system when running a Yocto Project build, as the boards do not have a display.[7] The BeagleBone Green is based on the BeagleBone Black but removes the onboard high-definition multimedia interface (HDMI) connector to make room for two connectors carrying I²C signals to easily interface with Grove sensors offered by Seeed Studios.[8]

Building the BeagleBone Images

To build a Linux system for the BeagleBone with the OpenEmbedded build system, simply uncomment the line

```
MACHINE = "beaglebone"
```

in conf/local.conf of your build environment (and eventually comment out any other MACHINE settings you have used previously). It does not matter that you have used the same build environment before for building systems for a qemux86, a machine that is based on x86 architecture. However, if you prefer to keeps things separate, you can of course create a new build environment by sourcing oe-init-build-env. If you do, make sure that you set DL_DIR and SSTATE_DIR to the directories you previously used. It saves you a lot of time downloading shared source packages and re-creating build artifacts that are shared between the architectures.

Now start your build with

```
$ bitbake -k core-image-minimal
```

Once the build completes, you can find the images for the bootloader, Linux kernel, and root filesystem in the tmp/deploy/images/beaglebone subdirectory inside your build environment. The Poky build system neatly separates the images for different machines into their own directories so that they cannot get mixed up.

Now what do you do with these images?

Understanding the BeagleBone Boot Process

To be able to boot the target hardware, you need to understand how your target hardware, in our case the BeagleBone, boots its operating system. The BeagleBone boots from its

---

7. It is not uncommon for embedded systems to have no display, as they may be used for purposes that do not require a display, such as in industrial control. Although a display can be added to the BeagleBone (via a cape or HDMI), the designers decided not to do so but to leave the hardware architecture open and extensible.

8. www.seeedstudio.com/wiki/Grove_System

external SD card in a specific way. You can find this information on BeagleBone.org. We
summarize it here:

1. After power-on-reset (POR), the BeagleBone's SoC loads and runs a stage 0
   bootloader from its on-board ROM.

2. The stage 0 bootloader accesses a file called MLO, which must be located in the
   first sectors of the first partition on the SD card. MLO is a stage 1 bootloader
   that is provided by U-Boot's secondary program loader (SPL) functionality.

3. The U-Boot SPL MLO configures the off-chip memory of the BeagleBone and
   then loads the file u-boot.img, which is the full U-Boot bootloader. U-Boot is
   the stage 2 bootloader in this process.

4. U-Boot then loads the Linux kernel image into memory and passes control on to
   the Linux kernel. U-Boot by default expects the kernel image uImage in the
   /boot directory of the second partition on the SD card. The second partition contains a Linux ext3 filesystem with the entire root filesystem for the BeagleBone.

5. The Linux kernel then begins its boot process, mounts the root filesystem as
   instructed by the kernel command line provided by the bootloader, and finally
   launches the first user space process.

The SD card requires a specific layout with two partitions: a small FAT boot partition and a Linux partition containing the root filesystem. The Linux partition for the
root filesystem can be any file system supported by Linux, such as ext3 and ext4. The
file README.hardware in the top directory of the Poky build system describes how to
create the partitions and format them.

Creating a Boot SD Card

You can accomplish partitioning and formatting an SD card for booting the BeagleBone
manually by following the instructions and using the commands fdisk, mkfs.vfat, and
mkfs.ext3. However, automating the process with a little script is much more convenient. Listing 10.1 shows a script for partitioning and formatting an SD card for the
BeagleBone.

Listing 10-1   **Script for Partitioning and Formatting a BeagleBone SD Card**

```
# (c) bbonesd.sh, 2015, Rudolf J Streif
#!/bin/sh

echo "Partitioning and formatting SD card for BeagleBone"

# test for the most common problems
test "$(id -u)" != "0" \
    && echo "You need to be 'root' to run this script." \
    && exit 1
test -z "$1" && \
    echo "No disk device specified." \
    && exit 1
```

```
test "$1" = "/dev/sda" \
    && echo "OOPS - System disk specified: ${1}" \
    && exit 1

# be sure before continuing
echo "Are you sure that you want to format ${1}? Type YES to proceed."
read RESPONSE
test "$RESPONSE" != "YES" && echo "Exiting." && exit 1

# now do the job
DRIVE=$1
if [ -b "$DRIVE" ] ; then
        dd if=/dev/zero of=$DRIVE bs=1024 count=1024
        SIZE=`fdisk -l $DRIVE | grep Disk | awk '{print $5}'`
        echo DISK SIZE - $SIZE bytes
        CYLINDERS=`echo $SIZE/255/63/512 | bc`
        echo CYLINDERS - $CYLINDERS
        {
                echo ,9,0x0C,*
                echo ,200,0x83,-
                echo ,,0x83,-
        } | sfdisk -D -H 255 -S 63 -C $CYLINDERS $DRIVE
        if [[ $1 == '/dev/sd'* ]] ; then
                mkfs.vfat -F 32 -n "beagboot" ${DRIVE}1
                mkfs.ext3 -L "beagroot" ${DRIVE}2
        else
                mkfs.vfat -F 32 -n "beagboot" ${DRIVE}p1
                mkfs.ext3 -L "beagroot" ${DRIVE}p2
        fi
fi
echo Done.
```

After you insert an SD card into your development system, determine the device with the dmesg command:

```
$ dmesg
[ 4389.803854] sd 9:0:0:1: [sdf] 15278080 512-byte logical blocks: \
    (7.82 GB/7.28 GiB)
[ 4389.822434]  sdf: sdf1
```

In this example, the SD card has been recognized as /dev/sdf, so you need to invoke the script with

```
$ sudo ./bbonesd.sh /dev/sdf
```

The script works with SD cards recognized as SCSI drives (/dev/sd*, typically, when connected via a USB card reader) and also with SD recognized as memory block devices (/dev/mmcblk*, typically, when inserted into a card slot of a computer).

Now that we partitioned and formatted the SD card, we need to copy the bootloader and root filesystem to their respective partitions. The following assumes that the boot partition is mounted on /media/beagboot and the root partition is mounted on /media/beagroot. If your system mounts them to different mount points, you need to make adjustments accordingly. From the top-level directory of your build environment, change to the directory with the images for the Beaglebone:

```
$ cd tmp/deploy/images/beaglebone
```

Copy the bootloader files to the boot partition:

```
$ sudo cp MLO /media/beagboot
$ sudo cp u-boot.img /media/beagboot
```

Extract the root filesystem and kernel modules into the root partition:

```
$ tar x -C /media/beagroot -f core-image-minimal.tar.bz2
$ tar x -C /medai/beagroot -f modules-beaglebone.tgz
```

Copy the kernel image and device tree files to the /boot directory of the root partition:

```
$ cp zImage /media/beagroot/boot
$ cp zImage-am335x-bone.dtb /media/beagroot/boot/am335x-bone.dtb
$ cp zImage-am335x-boneblack.dtb /media/beagroot/boot/am335x-boneblack.dtb
```

Copying and extracting the files may take a while. Even when the last command returns, the process may not yet be completed, as Linux provides write buffers for disk operations. Use

```
$ sync
```

to flush all the buffers and wait for the command to return before unmounting and removing the SD card. If you use umount from the command line, it waits for the filesystem buffers to be flushed before unmounting, as sync is called by umount before the filesystem is actually unmounted.

Now you are ready to boot your BeagleBone board.

Booting the BeagleBone

To boot your BeagleBone board and to follow its boot process, you need to provide power for it and connect its console serial port to your development system. If you call the original BeagleBone (White) your own, booting is very straightforward. If you own a BeagleBone Black, you need to take a couple of extra steps.

Connecting the BeagleBone (White)

To connect a BeagleBone (White) to your development computer, you need a USB cable with a USB A plug on one end and a mini USB plug on the other. The former plugs into your development computer, and the latter plugs into the mini USB port on the underside of the BeagleBone (White). The USB cable provides power as well as the serial connection between the BeagleBone's console port and your development system. Since the BeagleBone (White) ships with the USB cable, there is no additional hardware required.

Before you connect the board, insert the SD card into the SD card slot of the BeagleBone (White).

Connecting the BeagleBone Black

Connecting the BeagleBone Black is a little bit more difficult because this board does not have a built-in serial-to-USB converter. You need an external serial-to-USB converter cable, which is not provided with the BeagleBone Black. These cables are commonly referred to as *FTDI* cables after the company Future Technology Devices International Ltd. that produces the converter chips and the cables.

The BeagleBone Black has a 6-pin, single-in-line 0.1-inch pitch connector on its top side. This is the connector for its serial console port. To connect to it, you need a serial-to-USB converter cable with a USB A connector on one end and the 6-way, single-in-line connector on the other. You also need to pay attention to the signal levels of the BeagleBone Black's serial console port, which are 3.3V. There are also cables for 5V signal levels. Using a 5V cable with the BeagleBone could damage your board's CPU. The correct cable is an FTDI TTL-232R-3V3. You can find it on FTDI's website.[9] Most component distributors carry these cables.

To connect the cable to the board, set it topside-up with the Ethernet and 5V power connectors to the left. The black wire of the cable's connector goes to the leftmost pin of the board's connector. That pin is also marked with a little white dot on the board.

The serial-to-USB converter cable does not provide power to the BeagleBone. You can either connect a 5V power supply capable of providing at least 1.2A (or 6W) to the barrel connector, or you can use a USB A to mini USB cable. In most cases, the latter may be easier because the BeagleBone Black ships with such a cable. The USB cable connects to the mini USB port on the bottom side of the BeagleBone Black.

Setting Up a Terminal Emulator

To interact with the BeagleBone via serial connection, you need a terminal emulation program. There are a couple of choices for Linux. We recommend *Minicom*. Virtually any Linux distribution provides Minicom through its package repository. If it is not yet installed on your system, install it using your distribution's package manager.

All current Linux systems recognize the FTDI serial-to-USB converters as ttyUSB devices. After you plug your BeagleBone into a USB port of your development computer, the device node /dev/ttyUSB0[10] is created by the Linux kernel. The Linux kernel protects device nodes from access by regular users. The /dev/ttyUSB devices are owned by root but also typically belong to the dialout user group. For Minicom to be able to access the device while running under your user account, you need to add yourself to the dialout user group:

```
$ sudo usermod -a -G dialout <username>
```

where you replace <username> with your actual user name. You need to log out and log in again for the change to take effect.

---

9. www.ftdichip.com/Products/Cables/USBTTLSerial.htm

10. Unless you have more than one serial-to-USB converter connected to your development system, in which case there are multiple /dev/ttyUSB devices, and you have to find out which one connects to your BeagleBone.

Now connect your BeagleBone to your computer and launch Minicom in setup mode:[11]

```
$ sudo minicom -s
```

At this point, you should see Minicom's setup menu. Select the *Serial port setup* menu option and change the settings:

- Serial Device to /dev/ttyUSB0
- Bps/Par/Bits to 115200 8N1
- Hardware Flow Control to No (if necessary)
- Software Flow Control to No (if necessary)

Exit from the *Serial port setup* menu by pressing *Enter*, and then select *Save as dfl* from the main setup menu. Finally, exit from Minicom.

Now launch Minicom again with

```
$ sudo minicom -o -w
```

The -o option tells Minicom not to send any modem initialization strings to your BeagleBone, and the -w option turns on line wrap for long lines.

Now you are connected to the console of your BeagleBone. If your board is a BeagleBone (White), it probably has already booted. If you hit *Enter* on your keyboard, you should see a Linux login prompt similar to this one:

```
Poky (Yocto Project Reference Distro) 1.8+snapshot-20150720 beaglebone \
    /dev/ttyO0
beaglebone login:
```

If your board is a BeagleBone Black, you may just see the U-Boot prompt when you hit *Enter*. The reason for this is that the BeagleBone Black has internal eMMC storage, while the BeagleBone (White) does not. By default, the BeagleBone Black boots first from its internal eMMC. To temporarily tell it to boot from the SD card, follow these steps:

- Unplug power from the board (mini-USB or 5V barrel connector depending on what you are using).
- Press and hold the *USER/BOOT* button on the board (the small button to the upper-right on the top side of the board when Ethernet and 5V power connector are facing to the left).
- Plug in power again while still holding the *USER/BOOT* button until the first messages from U-Boot appear in your Minicom window. You can then release the button.

Your BeagleBone boots and eventually shows the Linux login prompt.

---

11. Running Minicom in setup mode requires root privileges.

You can permanently change the boot order from internal eMMC to SD card by issuing these commands from the U-Boot command prompt:

```
mmc dev 1
mmc erase 0 512
```

This erases the content from internal eMMC.

From the Linux command prompt, you can log in to your system running on the BeagleBone.

Congratulations, you have successfully created a Yocto Project image for an embedded board and used it to boot the board.

10.2.2 External Yocto Project BSP

The Internet of Things and the Maker Movement are driving the demand for inexpensive computer hardware. Professional developers and hobbyists[12] alike are looking for development boards that they can use for designs and prototypes and integrate with their projects. A steadily increasing number of boards is available built around a large variety of SoCs. The vast majority uses silicon that is based on ARM architecture, but x86, x86_64, xScale, and PowerPC can also be found. The Raspberry Pi has set a new benchmark for a low-cost embedded computer capable of running a full Linux OS stack. Other boards have followed suit, and many of them set you back only as much as a good dinner in a decent restaurant.

Popular Development Boards

Table 10-1 shows, in alphabetical order, some of the more popular development boards capable of running Linux. They all provide various low-speed I/O interfaces that are readily accessible via pin headers. For some of them, expansion boards are available that directly plug on to the headers. Expansion boards offer anything from parallel I/O with LED status and relays to analog-to-digital (ADC) and digital-to-analog (DAC) converters to stepper motor drivers for robotic applications and much more.

The table presents only a small selection of development boards at the time of the writing of this book. With every new generation of SoC, new boards come to the market almost simultaneously.

Finding the Yocto Project BSP for Your Board

Once you have decided on the board for your next development project, where do you find development boards supported by Yocto Project BSP? A good starting point is the website for the board itself. In many cases, you can find links to the Yocto Project or to a community providing hardware support.

---

12. We do not distinguish professional developers and hobbyists based on their skills but rather whether they are working on embedded systems as part of their job or as a hobby.

Table 10-1   **Popular Development Boards**

Board	CPU/Memory	I/O	Graphics	Homepage Yocto Project BSP
BeagleBoard-xM	TI DM3730 ARM Cortex-A8, 720 MHz 512 MB RAM MicroSD card slot	USB hub USB OTG 10/100 BaseT McBSP DSS I2C UART LCD McSPI PWM JTAG Camera	DVI-D S-Video	www.beagleboard.org git://git.yoctoproject.org/ meta-ti -b dora
BeagleBone	TI AM3358 ARM Cortex-A8, 720 MHz 256 MB RAM MicroSD card slot	USB 2.0 client USB 2.0 host 10/100 BaseT 4× UART 8× PWM LCD GPMC MMC1 2× SPI 2× I2C ADC 2× CAN 4 timers FTDI USB	No	www.beagleboard.org git://git.yoctoproject.org/ meta-yocto -b fido
BeagleBone Black	TI AM3358 ARM Cortex-A8, 1 GHz 512 MB RAM 2 GB RAM (Rev C) MicroSD card slot eMMC	USB 2.0 client USB 2.0 host 10/100 BaseT 4× UART 8× PWM LCD GPMC MMC1 2× SPI 2× I2C ADC 2× CAN 4 Timers	HDMI	www.beagleboard.org git://git.yoctoproject.org/ meta-yocto -b fido

Continues

Table 10-1   **Popular Development Boards (*Continued*)**

Board	CPU/Memory	I/O	Graphics	Homepage Yocto Project BSP
CubieBoard 2	AllWinnerTech SOC A20, ARM Cortex-A7, dual core 1 GB RAM 3.4 GB NAND Flash MicroSD card	USB 2.0 host USB 2.0 OTG 10/100 BaseT Infrared I2C SPI CSI/TS FM-IN ADC CVBS SPDIF-OUT	Mali 400 HDMI RGB LVDS	www.cubieboard.org https://github.com/linux-sunxi/meta-sunxi
CubieTruck (CubieBoard 3)	AllWinnerTech SOC A 20, ARM Cortex-A7, dual core 1 GB/2GB RAM MicroSD card	USB 2.0 host USB 2.0 client 10/100 BaseT SATA 2.0 Infrared I2C SPI CSI/TS FM-IN TV-IN ADC CVBS SPDIF	Mali 400 HDMI	www.cubieboard.org https://github.com/linux-sunxi/meta-sunxi
Edison	SoC with Intel Atom dual core, dual-threaded CPU at 500 MHz and a 32-bit Intel Quark microcontroller 1 GB LPDDR3 4 GB eMMC	WiFi a/b/g/n dual-band Bluetooth 4.0 2× UART 2× I2C 1× SPI 1× I2S 40× digital I/O USB 2.0 OTG	No	www.intel.com/content/www/us/en/do-it-yourself/edison.html
Galileo	Intel Quark SoC X1000, 400 MHz, 32-bit, single core 256 MB RAM-disk MicroSD card	USB 2.0 host USB 2.0 client 10/100 BaseT PCI Express 2.0 JTAG 2× UART 20× digital I/O ADC SPI	No	www.intel.com/content/www/us/en/embedded/products/galileo/galileo-overview.html git://git.yoctoproject.org/meta-intel-gallileo -b dizzy

Table 10-1   **Popular Development Boards (Continued)**

Board	CPU/Memory	I/O	Graphics	Homepage Yocto Project BSP
MinnowBoard Max	Intel Atom E38xx SoC, 1.33 GHz, dual core 1 GB/2 GB RAM 8 MB SPI Flash MicroSD card slot	USB 3.0 host USB 2.0 host UART 10/100/1000 BaseT I2C SPI	Intel HD graphics HDMI	www.minnowboard.org/ meet-minnowboard-max git://git.yoctoproject.org/ meta-intel -b fido
ODROID-XU4	Samsung Exynos 5422 ARM Cortex A-15, quad core 2 GB RAM MicroSD card slot	USB 3.0 host USB 2.0 host 10/100/1000 BaseT	Mali T628 HDMI	www.hardkernel.com https://github.com/akuster/ meta-odroid
Raspberry Pi 2 B	Broadcom BCM2836, ARM Cortex-A7, 900 MHz, quad core 1 GB RAM MicroSD card	USB 3.0 host 10/100 BaseT CSI camera port DSI display port 40 GPIO	HDMI	https://www.raspberrypi.org/ products/raspberry-pi-2-model-b git://git.yoctoproject.org/ meta-raspberrypi
WandBoard	Freescale i.MX6, ARM Cortex-A9, single, dual, quad core 512 MB RAM (single) 1 GB RAM (dual) 2 GB RAM (quad) MicroSD card slot	USB 3.0 host USB 3.0 OTG 10/100/1000 BaseT Audio SPDIF Optical Camera Interf. SATA (quad)	Vivante GC880 Vivante GC320 HDMI	www.wandboard.org git://github.com/Freescale/ meta-fsl-arm-extra.git

The Yocto Project maintains a searchable BSP[13] page on its website with an overview of the boards and BSPs that are hosted on Yocto Project repositories. These BSPs are provided by organizations, commercial and open source, that support the Yocto Project through resources and development work.[14]

Some are listed as Yocto Project Compatible, a status that functions as a recognition by the Yocto Project of organizations who support the project. Yocto Project Compatible does not imply that layers without that status are incompatible, only that those layers listed as Yocto Project Compatible have gone through a vetting process and are supported by a Yocto Project member organization.

---

13. https://www.yoctoproject.org/downloads/bsps

14. The word *free* in free and open source software (FOSS) pertains to freedom, not to cost. Organizations seeking Yocto Project Compatible certification support the project with resources for development and infrastructure.

The Yocto Project Git repository[15] hosts many BSP layers, including ones that are not officially Yocto Project certified. The list of BSP layers includes the following:

- **meta-fsl-arm**: BSP layer for Freescale platforms using SoC based on ARM architecture.

- **meta-fsl-ppc**: BSP layer for Freescale platforms using SoC based on PowerPC architecture.

- **meta-intel**: Compound BSP layer for Intel platforms based on x86 and x86_64 architectures. This layer contains multiple sublayers for the actual platforms.

- **meta-intel-galileo**: BSP layer for Intel Galileo platform support.

- **meta-intel-quark**: BSP layer for Intel Quark platform support.

- **meta-minnow**: BSP layer for the original MinnowBoard (not the MinnowBoard Max, which is supported by meta-intel).

- **meta-raspberrypi**: BSP layer for Raspberry Pi 1 and Raspberry Pi 2 devices.

- **meta-renesas**: BSP layer for Renesas devices.

- **meta-ti**: BSP layer for Texas Instruments devices, including extended hardware support for the BeagleBone that is not provided by meta-yocto-bsp.

- **meta-xilinx**: BSP layer for Xilinx devices.

- **meta-zynq**: BSP layer for Zynq devices.

And last but not least, the OpenEmbedded website[16] provides a searchable layer index that includes many BSPs provided by various communities. The search function allows searching by machine name and lists layers that provide support for that machine. Sometimes, multiple BSP layers for the same machine are available, which may differ in the level of support they are providing for the board.

Building with an External Yocto Project BSP

Yocto Project BSPs are layers, and building with them is as easy as 1-2-3:

1. Include the BSP layer with your build environment by adding its path to the BBLAYERS variable in conf/bblayers.conf.

2. Assign the machine from the BSP you want to build for to the MACHINE variable in conf/local.conf.

3. Choose an image target and start your build—for instance, bitbake -k core-image-minimal. It is good advice to start with a small image, just capable of booting to the console command line, such as core-image-minimal or core-image-base. If that works, you can test a larger image such as core-image-sato

---

15. http://git.yoctoproject.org
16. http://openembedded.org/wiki/Main_Page

or start building your own custom image recipe. Some BSPs contain their own image targets, which are a good starting point too.

When using Yocto Project BSPs, you need to pay attention that the BSP version matches the version of the OpenEmbedded build system. BSPs commonly extend recipes from the core layers of OE Core with bbappend files. If the versions do not match, there is a chance that versions of individual recipes that are extended by the BSP do not match the versions found in the core layers. If that happens, BitBake issues an error message for the individual recipe, but the root cause is not always obvious.

The Yocto Project developers use code names for the major releases: Dora for 1.5, Daisy for 1.6, Dizzy for 1.7, Fido for 1.8, and Jethro for 2.0. Although you can download tarballs for the releases from the Yocto Project website,[17] we recommend that you check out the releases from the Yocto Project Git repository. Using the Git repository makes it easy to keep track of the versions and even switch between versions. For example, if you are looking to use the meta-ti layer instead meta-yocto-bsp to build for the BeagleBone simply clone the matching branches from the poky and meta-ti repositories:

```
$ git clone git://git.yoctoproject.org/poky -b fido
$ git clone git://git.yoctoproject.org/meta-ti -b fido
```

There is another thing you should be aware of: while BSPs typically do not interfere with each other, there are BSPs, such as meta-yocto-bsp and meta-ti, that have an overlap in machine definitions (in this case beaglebone). To avoid the conflict, you must include only one or the other BSP layer with BBLAYERS. In general, it is good advice to include only one BSP layer with a build environment at the same time.

10.3 Inside a Yocto Project BSP

Yocto Project BSPs are specialized BitBake layers. As such, they follow the conventions for layers, as discussed in Chapter 3, but also include items that are characteristic for BSP layers. Listing 10-2 depicts the generic BSP layer layout.

Listing 10-2   **Yocto Project BSP Layer Layout**

```
meta-<bspname>
├── LICENSE
├── MAINTAINERS
├── README
├── README.sources
├── binary
│   ├── <bootable-image-1>
│   ├── <bootable-image-2>
│   ├── ...
│   └── <bootable-image-n>
├── conf
│   ├── layer.conf
```

---

17. https://www.yoctoproject.org/downloads

```
|   ├── machine
|   |   ├── <machine-1>.conf
|   |   ├── <machine-2>.conf
|   |   ├── ...
|   |   └── <machine-m>.conf
├── classes
|   ├── class-<1>.bbclass
|   ├── class-<2>.bbclass
|   ├── ...
|   └── class<m>.bbclass
├── recipes-bsp
|   ├── formfactor
|   |   ├── formfactor_0.0.bbappend
|   |   └── formfactor
|   |       ├── machine-1
|   |       |   └── machconfig
|   |       ├── machine-2
|   |       |   └── machconfig
|   |       ├── ...
|   |       └── machine-m
|   |           └── machconfig
|   ├── <package a>
|   |   ├── <package a>_<version 1>.bb
|   |   └── <package a>_<version 2>.bb
|   ├── <package b>
|   |   ├── <package b>_<version 1>.bb
|   |   └── <package b>_<version 2>.bb
|   ├── ...
|   └── <package z>
├── recipes-core
|   ├── images
|   |   ├── core-image-1.bb
|   |   ├── core-image-2.bb
|   |   ├── ...
|   |   └── core-image-n.bb
|   └── ...
├── recipes-graphics
|   ├── <package a>
|   |   ├── <package a>_<version 1>.bb
|   |   └── <package a>_<version 2>.bb
|   ├── <package b>
|   |   ├── <package b>_<version 1>.bb
|   |   └── <package b>_<version 2>.bb
|   ├── ...
|   └── <package z>
├── recipes-kernel
|   ├── linux
|   |   ├── linux-yocto_<version 1>.bbappend
|   |   └── linux-yocto_<version 2>.bbappend
└── recipes-<category x>
    └── ...
```

The majority of this structure is pure convention. However, the build system expects certain directories and files to be named specifically and in specific locations. Like any layer, the top-level directory of the layer is named meta-<layername>, where layername is the name of the BSP.

10.3.1 License Files

License files are located at the top-level directory of the BSP. They can have any name, but names such as LICENSE, EULA, and COPYING typically are used.

License files are optional in the sense that the build system does not look for them and enforce their presence. Nevertheless, we strongly recommend that you provide a license file when writing your own BSP. Providing a license file gives users of your BSP certainty on what they can and cannot do with the BSP.

10.3.2 Maintainers File

The maintainers file contains information on who the developers are who are responsible for maintaining the BSP. This file is optional, and maintainer information commonly is included in the top-level README file. If a BSP has multiple, possibly many, maintainers, it makes good sense to provide this information in a separate file.

10.3.3 README File

A Yocto Project–compliant BSP must include a README file in the top-level directory of the BSP. This file should, at a minimum, include the following information:

- A section describing the BSP and the hardware that it targets.
- A section detailing all the dependencies for this BSP layer. Typically, these are other layers such as meta and meta-yocto. Virtually all BSPs depend on the OE Core metadata layer meta. Although it seems somewhat obvious, it is good practice to include it in the list of dependencies.
- A section providing guidelines for asking questions, reporting bugs, and submitting patches. This information makes it easier for both users and maintainers to communicate and collaborate.
- If not provided by a separate file, a section about the developers maintaining the BSP.
- Instructions on how to use the BSP to build binary images for the target hardware.
- Instructions on how images built with the BSP can be installed on the target hardware and how to boot the target hardware.
- Instructions on how to use prebuilt binary images contained in the binary directory of the BSP if such images are provided by the BSP.
- A section containing information on any known bugs or issues that users of the BSP should be aware of when using the BSP.

The more detailed the information inside the README file is, the easier it is for users of the BSP to successfully include the BSP with their projects and use the target hardware.

10.3.4 `README.sources` File

This file provides information on where users can find the source files that are used to build the bootable images in the binary directory. Commonly, these are the metadata layers that have been used to create the images. This seems redundant with the dependency information in the `README` file. However, it is not, as the build environment used to build the images may have included other optional but not required layers.

10.3.5 Prebuilt Binaries

A BSP may include prebuilt bootable image binaries in the `binary` subdirectory. While including bootable images is optional, it assists users of the BSP in bringing up the target hardware with a known good image. Together with the information in the `README.sources` file, users can more easily debug issues that they may have with images they built themselves by comparing them to the prebuilt ones. Of course, adding prebuilt image binaries can increase the size of the BSP tremendously.

10.3.6 Layer Configuration File

Like any layer, a BSP must include the layer configuration file `conf/layer.conf`. For a BSP, this file is no different from a layer configuration file used by a regular layer. The boilerplate file is shown in Listing 10-3.

Listing 10-3   **Layer Configuration File for a BSP**

```
# We have a conf and classes directory, add to BBPATH
BBPATH .= ":${LAYERDIR}"

# We have a recipes directory, add to BBFILES
BBFILES += "${LAYERDIR}/recipes-*/*/*.bb \
            ${LAYERDIR}/recipes-*/*/*.bbappend"

BBFILE_COLLECTIONS += "bsp"
BBFILE_PATTERN_bsp = "^${LAYERDIR}/"
BBFILE_PRIORITY_bsp = "6"

LAYERDEPENDS_bsp = "<deplayer>"
```

To use this boilerplate, you have to substitute `bsp` for the actual name of the layer (without `meta-`). If the BSP layer depends on other layers, such as a common layer used for multiple BSPs, the layer configuration file sets the `LAYERDEPENDS_bsp` variable to a space-delimited list of layers.

10.3.7 Machine Configuration Files

The machine configuration file is what distinguishes a BSP layer from a regular layer. A BSP layer contains at least one but can have any number of machine configuration files in the conf/machine subdirectory for the different hardware targets supported by the BSP. Machine configuration files are named <machinename>.conf. You select your desired machine target by setting the MACHINE variable in conf/local.conf of your build environment to the name of the machine configuration file without the .conf ending.

Machine configuration files include settings to select and configure software packages that are built by recipes contained in the BSP or in other metadata layers in general. A typical example is the Linux kernel type and version that the BSP uses for the particular machine. The machine configuration file contains settings for PREFERRED_PROVIDER_virtual/kernel and PREFERRED_VERSION_virtual/kernel to select kernel type and version respectively.

Machine configuration files commonly also include tuning parameters for the particular CPU architecture the target hardware is using. Those parameters and other parameters that are shared between multiple machines are typically separated into their own files. These files are included in the machine configuration file by the require directive.

10.3.8 Classes

A BSP may contain custom classes in the classes subdirectory. Frequently these are image classes that assemble the bootable binary images in a certain way the target hardware expects them. Such image classes and the images that they build make it easier to create bootable media from the images.

10.3.9 Recipe Files

Any BSP contains a number of recipe files to either build software packages specific to the BSP and/or to extend recipes for packages from other layers using .bbappend files. Recipe files of a BSP are organized in recipes-<category>/<package> subdirectories exactly the same way as in any other metadata layer. Following are the more common recipes you find in BSP layers:

- **BSP-Specific Recipe Files (recipes-bsp)**: Miscellaneous recipes specific for the BSP. Commonly, you find *bootloader* and *formfactor* metadata files in a directory structure beneath recipes-bsp.

  Formfactor files provide information to the build system regarding whether the target machines use keyboard, touchscreen, mouse, and so on.

- **Core Support Files (recipes-core)**: In the directory recipes-core you typically find recipes for binary images for the target hardware as well as adaptations to other core recipes such as init-scripts, systemd, udev, and more.

- **Display Support Files (recipes-graphics)**: In the directory recipes-graphics you find recipes related to display support if the target hardware of the BSP has specific graphics requirements. Typically, these are configuration recipes for the X11 server or the Wayland/Weston compositor.

- **Linux Kernel (`recipes-kernel`)**: The directory `recipes-kernel` and its subdirectories contain recipes and configuration files pertaining to the Linux kernel.
  Commonly, these are `.bbappend` files to add kernel configuration fragments to
  kernel recipes in the `meta` core layer and/or kernel patches. Some BSPs provide
  their own kernel recipes, which build the Linux kernel from their own repositories. We discussed Linux kernel configuration and the various parameter settings
  at length in Chapter 9, "Kernel Recipes."
- **Other Recipes (`recipes-*`)**: A BSP may add its own recipes and/or extend recipes from other layers as required by the target hardware. These you can find in
  their respective recipe subdirectories inside the BSP layer.

It entirely depends on the BSP and the target hardware it supports which recipes it
provides.

10.4 Creating a Yocto Project BSP

If you are developing your own hardware, you want to create a Yocto Project BSP
to provide full support for it. Principally, you can take one of the following three
approaches for creating a Yocto Project BSP:

- **Create Manually**: You can start by creating an empty layer using the `yocto-layer`
  script and then populate directories and files for your BSP manually.
- **Copy from Existing BSP Layer**: If the hardware that your BSP targets is similar to hardware from another BSP, you can copy that layer and make adjustments
  to meet the requirements of your target hardware.
- **Use the Yocto Project BSP Tools**: The Yocto Project provides a couple of
  tools that simplify the task of creating a BSP. They are interactive and allow
  setting common BSP parameters by responding to a series of questions. The tools
  then create a skeleton for your BSP, and you then can fill in the missing details.

Creating a BSP manually from scratch is the most tedious approach, as it requires
you to add files and directories yourself. In virtually all cases, using the Yocto Project
BSP tools is the better option because it allows you to interactively tailor your BSP
layer. Copying from an existing BSP is a good alternative if your target hardware is
close to the hardware supported by that BSP. You could also extend the other BSP and
make it a dependency for your BSP. That approach avoids duplication but requires you
to maintain your BSP when changes are made to the other BSP your BSP depends on.

10.4.1 Yocto Project BSP Tools

There are two tools to assist you with creating a Yocto Project BSP: `yocto-bsp` and
`yocto-kernel`. The former, you guessed it, assists in creating the BSP layer, and the
latter assists in configuring the Linux kernel. Both tools have several subcommands.

Invoking the tool without specifying the subcommand results in printing the help message with the list of available subcommands.

The tools are located in the poky/scripts directory of the Poky reference distribution. You have to source the oe-init-build-env script to use the tools. However, you do not have to create your BSP inside your build environment. Once you have sourced the script, you change directories to where you would like to set up your BSP.

The yocto-bsp Tool

Invoking yocto-bsp or yocto-bsp help provides you with information about the available subcommands:

```
$ yocto-bsp
ERROR:root:No subcommand specified, exiting
Usage:

  Create a customized Yocto BSP layer.

  usage: yocto-bsp [--version] [--help] COMMAND [ARGS]

  Current 'yocto-bsp' commands are:
    create              Create a new Yocto BSP
    list                List available values for options and BSP properties

  See 'yocto-bsp help COMMAND' for more information on a specific command.


Options:
  --version     show program's version number and exit
  -h, --help    show this help message and exit
  -D, --debug   output debug information
```

The tool has two subcommands: create and list. Invoking the tool with yocto-bsp <subcommand> --help prints further information on the particular subcommand.

Subcommand yocto-bsp list

The subcommand yocto-bsp list shows information only. Currently, that is information on the supported kernel architectures:

```
$ yocto-bsp list karch
Architectures available:
    i386
    mips64
    arm
    powerpc
    mips
    x86_64
    qemu
```

For each kernel architecture, there are several properties available that the tool sets when creating the BSP. For instance,

```
$ yocto-bsp list x86_64 properties
```

shows a list of all properties in JSON format available for x86_64 architecture. When you are creating a BSP for x86_64, the tool interactively walks through these properties asking you for the setting it should apply.

You can dump the output of the list subcommand into a file by specifying the `-o <filename>` or `--outfile <filename>` parameters:

```
$ yocto-bsp list x86_64 properties -o x84_64.prop
```

The dump in the file is also in JSON format.

Subcommand `yocto-bsp create`

You create a BSP by invoking `yocto-bsp create <bsp-name> <karch>`, where you replace `<bsp-name>` with the name for your BSP (without `meta-`) and `<karch>` with the desired kernel architecture. The subcommand accepts several optional parameters:

- **`-o <outdir>` or `--outdir <outdir>`**: Without this parameter, the tool creates the BSP in the current directory with the name `<bsp-name>`. To create it in a different directory, use the `-o` or `--outfile` option. Unfortunately, if you use one of these options, you have to provide the entire path of the BSP and not just the base path, as the tool does not use `<bsp-name>` in that case.

- **`-i <properties-file>` or `--infile <properties-file>`**: These parameters cause the tool to read the settings for the various properties from a file rather than interactively asking for them. The file must be in JSON format.

- **`-c codedump` or `--codedump`**: Rather than running the BSP creation, dump the code to the file `bspgen.out`. Use this option if you like to know what the tool does to create the BSP without actually creating it.

- **`-s` or `-skip-git-check`**: These parameters check for access to a remote Git repository. Provide this option to spare a little time when creating the BSP.

We walk through the generation of a BSP in Section 10.4.2.

The `yocto-kernel` Tool

The `yocto-kernel` tool provides functionality for listing, adding, and removing configuration settings, features, and patches to the BSP's kernel recipe. It interactively creates the kernel configuration fragment, feature, and patch collections discussed in Chapter 9. Like the `yocto-bsp` tool, the `yocto-kernel` tool has a list of subcommands that you can print with the `--help` option:

```
$ yocto-kernel --help
Usage:

 Modify and list Yocto BSP kernel config items and patches.

 usage: yocto-kernel [--version] [--help] COMMAND [ARGS]
```

```
Current 'yocto-kernel' commands are:
  config list      List the modifiable set of bare kernel config options
                   for a BSP
  config add       Add or modify bare kernel config options for a BSP
  config rm        Remove bare kernel config options from a BSP
  patch list       List the patches associated with a BSP
  patch add        Patch the Yocto kernel for a BSP
  patch rm         Remove patches from a BSP
  feature list     List the features used by a BSP
  feature add      Have a BSP use a feature
  feature rm       Have a BSP stop using a feature
  features list    List the features available to BSPs
  feature describe Describe a particular feature
  feature create   Create a new BSP-local feature
  feature destroy  Remove a BSP-local feature

See 'yocto-kernel help COMMAND' for more information on a specific
command.

Options:
  --version     show program's version number and exit
  -h, --help    show this help message and exit
  -D, --debug   output debug information
```

To use the yocto-kernel tool, you must have sourced your build environment. Then execute the command from within the build environment. The majority of the subcommands take the name of a BSP as parameter. This BSP must be included in the BBLAYERS variable of conf/bblayers.conf in your build environment.

Managing Linux Kernel Configuration Options

The config subcommands allow simple management of the kernel configuration options:

- **yocto-kernel config list <bsp>**: List all configuration fragments for the Linux kernel used by the BSP <bsp>.

- **yocto-kernel config add <bsp> CONFIG_<parameter>=[y|n|m]**: Add a configuration fragment that modifies the kernel configuration option <parameter>:

  - y (yes): Turn the parameter on.

  - n (no): Turn the parameter off.

  - m (module): Build the kernel module (applicable only to kernel modules).

- **yocto-kernel config rm <bsp> CONFIG_<parameter>**: Remove the configuration fragment for the kernel configuration option <parameter>.

You can provide more than one configuration item for the config add and config rm subcommannds.

Managing Kernel Patches

You can manage patches for your BSP using the patch subcommands:

- **yocto-kernel patch list <bsp>**: List all patches for the Linux kernel used by the BSP <bsp>.

- **yocto-kernel patch add <bsp> /path/to/patchfile.patch**: Copy the patch patchfile.patch from the provided path to recipes-kernel/linux/files inside the BSP layer <bsp>, and add it to SRC_URI of the kernel recipe.

- **yocto-kernel patch rm <bsp> patchfile.patch**: Remove the patch patchfile .patch from recipes-kernel/linux/files inside the BSP <bsp>, and remove it from SRC_URI of the kernel recipe.

You can provide more than one patch for patch add and patch rm subcommands at a time.

Managing Kernel Features

Similar to kernel configuration options and patches, you can manage features with the feature subcommands:

- **yocto-kernel features list <bsp>**: Lists all the kernel features that are locally available to the BSP <bsp>. These are feature files ending in .scc that are in the BSP in recipes-kernel/linux/files.

- **yocto-kernel feature list <bsp>**: List all kernel features currently used by the BSP <bsp>.

- **yocto-kernel feature create <bsp> featurefile.scc "Feature Description" \capabilities CONFI_parameter=[y|n|m] /path/to/patchfile.patch**: Create a new local feature for the BSP <bsp> named featurefile.scc using "Feature Description" as the description, and add the kernel configuration parameters and patches listed after capabilities.

- **yocto-kernel feature add <bsp> featurefile.scc**: Add the local feature featurefile .scc to the kernel feature list of the BSP <bsp>. The feature must have previously been created with yocto-kernel feature create.

- **yocto-kernel feature rm <bsp>**: Remove one or more features from the list of kernel features of the BSP <bsp>. The tool lists the features and then prompts for the ones to be removed. This command does not delete the feature from BSP, it just removes it from the kernel's feature inclusion list.

- **yocto-kernel feature destroy <bsp> featurefile.scc**: Delete the feature from the local list of features of the BSP <bsp>. This command does delete the feature file, configuration fragments, and patches from the BSP.

The feature subcommand is a convenient way of managing the features included with the kernel without manually modifying the feature files and modifying SRC_URI of the recipe.

10.4.2 Creating a BSP with the Yocto Project BSP Tools

Now it is time to put it all together and use the Yocto Project BSP tools to create a basic BSP. Our BSP is for an information kiosk device. The device uses an Intel Core i7 CPU, has HDMI graphics output on board, and is connected to a multitouch touchscreen for a great user experience. As a test platform for our device, we use the MinnowBoard Max and connect a multitouch touchscreen with HDMI and USB inputs to it. We also want our BSP to identify itself with an entry in the kernel log when starting up. For that purpose, we developed a simple device driver, which is essentially the same as the one shown in Chapter 9, Listing 9-3. We just changed the message texts to "Yocto Project Book Kiosk BSP: init" and "Yocto Project Book BSP: exit." Simply follow the steps from Section 9.2 to create the patch.

The following steps outline the workflow to create your BSP, which we call ypbkiosk:

1. **Initialize the build environment.** To create a BSP with the Yocto Project BSP tools, you need a build environment:

   ```
   $ source /path/to/poky/oe-init-build-env kiosk
   ```

   Set the build environment variables DL_DIR and SSTATE_DIR in conf/local.conf.

2. **Create the BSP layer.** For the sake of simplicity, we create our new BSP layer inside the build environment. The command

   ```
   $ yocto-bsp create ypbkiosk x86_64
   ```

   starts the interactive process to create a BSP layer called ypbkiosk for a machine ypbkiosk with x86_64 architecture. The tool now asks a couple of questions about the features we want to use for our BSP:

   - Would you like to use the default (3.19) kernel? (y/n) [default: y] *y*
   - Do you need a new machine branch for this BSP (the alternative is to re-use an existing branch)? (y/n) [default: y] *n*
   - Please choose a machine branch to base this BSP on: [default: standard/ common-pc-64/base] *7 (or Enter for default)*
   - Do you need SMP support? (y/n) [default: y] *y (or Enter for default)*
   - Which machine tuning would you like to use? [default: tune_core2] *2 (Corei7 tuning optimization)*
   - Do you need support for X? (y/n) [default: y] *y (or Enter for default)*
   - Please select an xserver for this machine: [default: xserver_i915] *4 (fbdev xserver support)*
   - Does your BSP have a touchscreen? (y/n) [default: n] *y*
   - Does your BSP have a keyboard? (y/n) [default: y] *y (or Enter for default)*

   After you respond to the last question, the BSP tool sets up the BSP and exits with New x86_64 BSP created in meta-ypbkiosk.

3. **Enable the touchscreen driver.** For our kiosk BSP, we need the multitouch touchscreen driver enabled in the Linux kernel. The driver's configuration setting is CONFIG_HID_MULTITOUCH. We use the Yocto Project kernel tool to add a configuration fragment that enables the driver:

```
$ yocto-kernel config add ypbkiosk
CONFIG_HID_MULTITOUCH=y
Added item:
        CONFIG_HID_MULTITOUCH=y
```

The tool adds the setting to ypbkiosk-user-config.cfg in meta-ypbkiosk/
recipes-kernel/linux/files.

4. **Add the BSP driver patch.** We are adding the BSP driver patch as a feature.
The feature applies the patch and also adds the configuration setting to enable it:

```
$ yocto-kernel feature create ypbkiosk ypbbspmsg.scc \
 "Yocto Project Book BSP Message" capabilities \
 CONFIG_YP_DRIVER=y 0001-Yocto-Project-Book-Kiosk-BSP-Message.patch
Added feature:
   features/ypbbspmsg.scc
$ yocto-kernel feature add ypbkiosk features/ypbbspmsg.scc
Added features:
 features/ypbbspmsg.scc
```

The first command, yocto-kernel feature create, creates the feature and adds
it to the BSP. However, it is not yet included with the kernel build, which is
accomplished by the second command, yocto-kernel feature add.

5. **Build the image.** Now that we have created the BSP with the desired kernel
configuration, we can start building the image:

```
$ bitbake -k core-image-sato
```

We are using the core-image-sato image target, which provides us with a
graphical user interface for testing.

6. **Copy the image to a bootable medium.** We are using the MinnowBoard
Max as the test target system for our kiosk. The board boots from a USB memory stick. Copy the image to the memory stick:

```
$ dd if=tmp/deploy/images/ypbkiosk/core-image-sato-ypbkiosk.hddimg \
    of=/dev/<usbstickdevice>
```

You need to replace <usbstickdevice> with the name of the device node, which
you can find with the dmesg command after plugging the USB stick into your
development system.

7. **Boot the target.** The MinnowBoard Max has a UEFI BIOS with a shell. After
you plug the USB memory stick into the board and turn it on, the MinnowBoard
Max launches the shell. The filesystem on the memory stick is recognized as fs0.
At the shell prompt, enter fs0:, and at the next prompt, bootx64. The Minnow-
Board Max should then boot into the Sato user interface. If you have a touchscreen connected to your board, you should be able to use it. You can also open
a terminal and look for the BSP message.

The two Yocto Project BSP tools yocto-bsp and yocto-kernel provide a straightforward way to create BSP layers. With only a few interactive steps, they set up the

core framework with the necessary directories and files for a basic BSP that you then can further customize. Managing kernel configuration options, patches, and features becomes a simple task with the yocto-kernel tool. There is no need to modify recipes and other files manually.

10.5 Tuning

If you examine the machine configuration file ypbkiosk.conf we created in the previous section, notice the following two lines:

```
DEFAULTTUNE = "corei7-64"
require conf/machine/include/tune-corei7.inc
```

The first line selects the CPU architecture and *application binary interface (ABI)* tune used by the build system. The second line provides the detailed toolchain settings, such as GCC compiler flags, for the particular tune.

CPU architectures may provide backwards compatibility, meaning that you could potentially use the tune for an earlier version of the architecture with a CPU using a newer generation of the architecture, which is what you want to create a kernel that runs on multiple architectures. However, by doing so you are not, of course, getting the benefits of the extended instruction set and functionality of the newer architecture generation. This hierarchy of CPU architecture generations is reflected by the hierarchy of the tuning files. It is particularly visible with Intel x86 architecture:

- **tune-corei7.inc**: Tunes for the Intel Core i7 CPU generation with 64-bit extensions and MMX, SSE, SSE2, SSE3, SSSE3, SSE4.1, and SSE4.2 instruction set support. Based on tune-core2.

- **tune-core2.inc**: Tunes for the Intel Core2 CPU generation with 64-bit extensions and MMX, SSE, SSE2, SSE3, and SSSE3 instruction set support. Based on tune-586.

- **tune-i586.inc**: Tunes that enable Intel i586 specific processor optimization. Based on arch-x86.

- **arch-x86**: Core architecture definitions for Intel x86 32-bit, x86 64-bit, and x32 architectures.

You can find the tune files in the conf/machine directory and subdirectories thereof of the OE Core metadata layer meta.

The DEFAULT_TUNE variable selects the TUNE_FEATURES for a particular CPU architecture. The build system uses DEFAULT_TUNE and TUNE_FEATURES to determine the settings for the following:

- **TUNE_ARCH**: The canonical architecture for the GNU toolchain for a specific CPU architecture. TUNE_ARCH is closely related to TARGET_ARCH, as the BitBake configuration file (meta/conf/bitbake.conf) assigns TARGET_ARCH = "${TUNE_ARCH}".

- **TUNE_PKGARCH**: The package architecture as it is known to the packaging system to define the correct architecture, ABI, and tuning of the output packages.
- **TUNE_ASARGS**: Assembler flags for the particular tuning architecture.
- **TUNE_CCARGS**: Compiler flags for the particular tuning architecture.
- **TUNE_LDARGS**: Linker flags for the particular tuning architecture.

The build system validates the tuning settings for their compatibility, particularly for conflicting ABI settings.

Each tune is added to the list of available tunes represented by the variable AVAILTUNES. You can use the command

```
$ bitbake -e | grep AVAILTUNES
```

to obtain the list for your current configuration. For example, with the settings provided by our ypbkioks.conf machine configuration, you will see:

```
$ bitbake -e  | grep AVAILTUNES
# $AVAILTUNES [10 operations]
AVAILTUNES=" x86 x86-64 x86-64-x32 i586 core2-32 core2-64 core2-64-x32 \
            corei7-32 corei7-64 corei7-64-x32"
```

In detail:

- **x86**: Intel x86 32-bit architecture with 32-bit ABI
- **x86-86**: Intel x86 64-bit architecture with 64-bit ABI
- **x86-64-x32**: Intel x86 64-bit architecture with 32-bit ABI
- **i586**: Intel i586 32-bit architecture with 32-bit ABI
- **core2-32**: Intel Core2 32-bit architecture with 32-bit ABI
- **core2-64**: Intel Core2 64-bit architecture with 64-bit ABI
- **core2-64-x32**: Intel Core2 64-bit architecture with 32-bit ABI
- **corei7-32**: Intel Core i7 32-bit architecture with 32-bit ABI
- **corei7-64**: Intel Core i7 64-bit architecture with 64-bit ABI
- **corei7-64-x32**: Intel Core i7 64-bit architecture with 32-bit ABI

Tunes for other CPU architectures provide similar configurations for CPU architecture and ABI.

10.6 Creating Bootable Media Images

Images created by the OpenEmbedded build system cannot always be used directly on storage media to create a bootable system. We saw that when we created our first image for the BeagleBone. Additional steps were necessary to partition and format the SD card and then copy files and images to the various partitions. Boot images depend on the target platform as well as on the storage hardware and media used. An SD may require a different image format than an HDD. To facilitate the process of creating bootable images that can be transferred directly to storage media, the OpenEmbedded build system provides the *OpenEmbedded Image Creator (wic)*.[18]

The wic tool creates bootable images from the artifacts created by the build system. For the `wic` command to work correctly, it has to be run from within the context of a build environment, as usual, sourced by `oe-init-build-env`.

wic uses *kickstart files* ending in .wks that instruct the tool what images to create and how to create them. A set of kickstart files ships with the build system. To obtain a list of the built-in images, use

```
$ wic list images
```

wic is intended to be extensible. The wic kickstart files describe the steps necessary to create the disk image. The wic *source plugins* contain the code that wic executes for the various steps. To list the available source plugins, use

```
$ wic list source-plugins
```

We show how kickstart files and source plugins play together when we look at kickstart files in more detail.

wic has two operational modes:

- **Raw Mode**: You have to specify the parameters required by the kickstart file at the wic command line.
- **Cooked Mode**: wic uses the current MACHINE setting of your build environment to determine the options.

Raw mode provides more flexibility and gives you more control over the image creation process, while Cooked mode is easier to use. Both modes are essentially invoked the same way:

```
$ wic create <kickstart_file> [options]
```

The options determine whether wic runs in Raw mode or Cooked mode. We explain the two modes and what options you can use with either one of them in the next two sections. If you are using a kickstart file from the list shown by `wic list images`, you do not have to provide the .wks extension.

Before you can put wic to use, you need to build a couple of tools for your development host using the build system:

```
$ bitbake parted-native dosfstools-native mtools-native
```

You do not need to run wic as root. As a matter of fact, you should not. wic does not write any storage media: it creates images for them, which you can then copy to the media.

---

18. You may ask why the tool is called *wic* instead of *oeic* (OpenEmbedded Image Creator). Try saying the diphthong *oeic* quickly and you will notice that it sounds more like *wic*.

10.6.1 Creating an Image with Cooked Mode

In Cooked mode, only two parameters are required to create an image with wic:

```
$ wic create <kickstart_file> -e <image_target> [options]
```

where

- `<kickstart_file>` is the OpenEmbedded kickstart file. You can use one of the canned kickstart files that are provided with wic, or you can provide your own.
- `<image_target>` is the name of the build system image target, such as `core-image-base` or `core-image-sato` or any of your own images.

All other settings are determined by wic from the build environment, in general, and the MACHINE setting in `conf/local.conf` in particular.

With Cooked mode, these additional options are available:

- **-o PATH, --outdir=PATH**: The path to the location of the final image.
- **-c COMPRESSOR, --compress-with=COMPRESSOR**: The compression utility to use to compress the final image. wic supports gzip, bzip2, and xz as COMPRESSOR.
- **-f IMAGE, --build-rootfs=IMAGE**: Use BitBake IMAGE to build the root filesystem image before creating the media image.
- **-D, --debug**: Display detailed debug information about the creation process. It shows the exact command sequence and helps troubleshooting problems.
- **-s, --skip-build-check**: Skip the build check step, which is a simple sanity checker to verify whether the build environment has been sourced correctly.

For example,

```
$ wic create bootimg-efi -e core-image-base
```

creates an image to boot with an *extended firmware interface (EFI)* BIOS that can be transferred directly to a bootable media.

A fair warning: just because you can create an image with wic using a kickstart file does not automatically mean that this image will boot on your target system. You need to make sure that you choose the right kickstart file that matches your target system. If in the preceding example the machine configuration were MACHINE = "beaglebone", wic would indeed create an image with a boot partition for EFI. However, it would not boot on a BeagleBone board, since the BeagleBone does not have an EFI BIOS.

10.6.2 Creating an Image with Raw Mode

When using wic in Raw mode, you have to provide the necessary parameters on the command line:

```
$ wic create <kickstart_file> [options]
```

where `<kickstart_file>` is the OpenEmbedded kickstart file, which can be one of the kickstart files provided with wic or one that you created yourself. The options are as follows:

- **-r ROOTFSDIR, --rootfs-dir=ROOTFSDIR**: The path to the root filesystem for the target on the development host.

- **-b BOOTIMGDIR, --bootimg-dir=BOOTIMGDIR**: The path to bootloader artifacts, such as the `EFI` or `syslinux` directories or U-Boot files.

- **-k KERNELDIR, --kernel-dir=KERNEL_DIR**: The path to the Linux kernel.

- **-n NATIVE_SYSROOT, --native-sysroot=NATIVE_SYSROOT**: The path to the native tools such as parted, the DOS filesystem tools, and so on. These can be the tools built by the OpenEmbedded build system or tools provided by your development host.

- **-o PATH, --outdir=PATH**: The path to the location of the final image.

- **-c COMPRESSOR, --compress-with=COMPRESSOR**: The compression utility to use to compress the final image. wic supports gzip, bzip2, and xz as `COMPRESSOR`.

- **-f IMAGE, --build-rootfs=IMAGE**: Use BitBake `IMAGE` to build the root filesystem image before creating the media image.

- **-D, --debug**: Display detailed debug information about the creation process. It shows the exact command sequence and helps troubleshooting problems.

In its simplest form, you have to call wic in Raw mode, as follows:

```
$ wic create bootimg-efi -r <ROOTFSDIR> -b <BOOTIMGDIR> -k <KERNELDIR>
```

The example assumes that you have filesystem tools installed on your development host.

When using Cooked mode with the `-e <image_target>` option, wic automatically determines the various options from the build environment by running `bitbake -e <image_target>`:

- -r, --rootfs-dir: IMAGE_ROOTFS

- -k, --kernel-dir: STAGING_KERNEL_DIR

- -n, -- native-sysroot: STAGING_DIR_NATIVE

- -b, --bootimg-dir: Empty; the source plugins for the various bootloaders need to determine this.

Unless you are using the `-f` (`--build-rootfs`) option, you do not have to source a build environment in Raw mode.

10.6.3 Kickstart Files

As we saw, the command

```
$ wic list images
```

provides a list of the available kickstart files. The actual kickstart files are located in `poky/scripts/lib/wic/canned-wks`.

Listing 10-4 shows a kickstart file for creating an image with a vfat boot partition and an ext4 root filesystem partition for an SD card suitable for the BeagleBone.

Listing 10-4   **SD Card Image (sdimage-bootpart.wks)**

```
# short-description: Create SD card image with a boot partition
# long-description: Creates a partitioned SD card image. Boot files
# are located in the first vfat partition.

part /boot --source bootimg-partition --ondisk mmcblk --fstype=vfat
    --label boot --active --align 4 --size 16
part / --source rootfs --ondisk mmcblk --fstype=ext4 --label root
    --align 4
```

The part directive instructs wic to create a partition. The first parameter is the mount point of the partition—in this kickstart file, /boot for the boot partition and / for the root filesystem. The source parameter specifies the source plugin to use to create the partition, bootimg-partition for the boot partition and rootfs for the root filesystem partition. The remaining parameters determine the partition characteristics, which we explain in detail shortly.

Listing 10-5 shows a kickstart file to create an image for booting a system with a legacy PC BIOS.

Listing 10-5   **Legacy PC BIOS Boot Image (directdisk.wks)**

```
# short-description: Create a 'pcbios' direct disk image
# long-description: Creates a partitioned legacy BIOS disk image that the
# user can directly dd to boot media.

part /boot --source bootimg-pcbios --ondisk sda --label boot -active \
    --align 1024
part / --source rootfs --ondisk sda --fstype=ext4 --label platform \
    --align 1024

bootloader --timeout=0 --append="rootwait rootfstype=ext4 \
                         video=vesafb vga=0x318 console=tty0"
```

In this example, the boot partition uses the source plugin bootimg-pcbios, which creates a Syslinux boot partition. The bootloader directive instructs Syslinux to boot the kernel immediately (--timeout=0) and to pass the parameters specified by append to the Linux kernel.

Listing 10-6 shows an example of a kickstart file creating an image for booting a system with EFI BIOS.

Listing 10-6   **EFI BIOS Boot Image (mkefidisk.wks)**

```
# short-description: Create an EFI disk image
# long-description: Creates a partitioned EFI disk image that the user
# can directly dd to boot media.
```

```
part /boot --source bootimg-efi --sourceparams="loader=grub-efi" \
    --ondisk sda --label msdos --active --align 1024

part / --source rootfs --ondisk sda --fstype=ext4 --label platform \
    --align 1024

part swap --ondisk sda --size 44 --label swap1 --fstype=swap

bootloader --timeout=10 --append="rootwait rootfstype=ext4 \
    console=ttyPCH0,115200 console=tty0 vmalloc=256MB \
    snd-hda-intel.enable_msi=0"
```

In this example, the boot partition is created using the `bootimg-efi` source plugin using the EFI Grub bootloader. In addition to the boot and root filesystem partitions, a swap partition is created. The bootloader directive instructs Grub to wait for 10 seconds (`timeout=10`) before booting the Linux kernel and to pass the parameters specified by append to the Linux kernel.

10.6.4 Kickstart File Directives

You can easily create your own kickstart files either from scratch or by copying one of the canned files. If you create your own kickstart files inside the directory `poky/scripts/lib/wic/canned-wks`, then they are known to wic and you do not have to provide a path and extension. The disadvantage is that you are modifying the build system sources, which makes updates a little harder. In any case, you may want to consider submitting your kickstart files to the Yocto Project. They can be of use for others too.

Kickstart files currently contain only two directives: `partition` and `bootloader`. Each directive takes a defined set of parameters. The source plugins providing the functionality need to understand the parameters.

`partition` Directive

The `partition` directive `part` creates a partition on a media. The format is

```
Part <mountpoint> <options>
```

The `<mountpoint>` determines where the partition is mounted. It can be either

- **`/path`**: Partition mount-point path—for instance, /, /usr, /opt, /home, and so on.
- **`swap`**: Partition is a swap partition.

The `<options>` provide the necessary information on how to create the partition:

- **`--source`**: Determines the source of the data that populates the partition.

    If you do not use this option, wic creates an empty partition, and you have to provide at least `--size`. If you want wic to format the partition with a filesystem, you need to provide `--fstype`.

If you use `--source rootfs`, wic creates a root filesystem partition with sufficient space for the root filesystem provided by the -r (`--rootfs-dir`) parameter. You also need to provide the `--fstype` to determine the filesystem type.

- **`--size`**: The minimum partition size in MB. You must provide this parameter if you do not use `--source`. You can provide this parameter with `--source` if you want to create a larger partition than determined by the root filesystem content (see also `--extra-space` and `--overhead-factor`).

- **`--ondisk`**: Create the partition on a particular device.

- **`--ondrive`**: Same as `--ondisk`.

- **`--fstype`**: Filesystem type to format the partition with. Supported filesystem types are ext2, ext3, ext4, btrfs, squashfs, and swap.

- **`--fsoptions`**: String of options that will be written to `/etc/tstab`. The string needs to be enclosed in quotes. If you do not specify this parameter, it is set to "defaults".

- **`--label`**: Partition label.

- **`--active`**: Mark partition as the boot partition.

- **`--align`**: Start the partition on an *n* kB boundary.

- **`--no-table`**: Create, format, and populate the partition but do not add it to the partition table.

- **`--extra-space`**: Add additional space (in MB) to the partition. The default value is 10 MB.

- **`--overhead-factor`**: Multiply the size of the partition, which is either provided by `--size` or determined from the content of the root filesystem directory specified by -r (`--rootfs-dir`), with this factor. The factor must be greater than or equal to 1. The default value is 1.3.

- **`--part-type`**: Specifies the globally unique identifier (GUID) for the type of the partition for use with a GUID partition table (GPT).[19]

- **`--use-uuid`**: Generate a random Linux UUID for the partition

- **`--uuid`**: Specify a Linux UUID for the partition.

`bootloader` Directive

The `bootloader` directive provides the configuration for the bootloader:

```
bootloader --timeout=<timeout_in_seconds> --append="<kernel_parameters>
```

---

19. For information on GPT, see https://wiki.archlinux.org/index.php/GUID_Partition_Table and https://en.wikipedia.org/wiki/GUID_Partition_Table#Partition_type_GUIDs.

The directive takes only two parameters:

- **`--timeout`**: Time in seconds the bootloader waits before booting the default option. This parameter is used with bootloaders that display a list of boot options to the user.

- **`--append`**: String of parameters enclosed in quotes that are passed to the Linux kernel.

10.6.5 Plugins

Plugins provide for easy extensibility of wic functionality. They are written in Python. Currently, there are two types of plugins: *imager* and *source*. You can find the plugins in the directory `poky/scripts/lib/wic/plugins`. Each plugin type has its own subdirectory.

The imager plugins install an entire system into a file that contains a partition table and one or more partitions that are formatted with filesystems. The output of an imager plugin is a file that can be transferred directly to a media. All imager plugins inherit from the `ImagerPlugin` Python class. There currently is only one imager plugin, the `DirectPlugin`, which is used to create all images.

The source plugins create partitions of particular types from specific sources. They are used with the `part` directive in kickstart files. Source plugins inherit from the `SourcePlugin` Python class.

The file `poky/scripts/lib/wic/pluginbase.py` defines the core plugin classes `ImagerPlugin` and `SourcePlugin`.

Currently, user extension is restricted to source plugins only. To create your own source plugin, write a Python source file containing the plugin class. You can place the file into the directory `poky/scripts/lib/wic/plugins/source`, or you can place it into your own layer in the directory `meta-mylayer/scripts/lib/wic/plugins/source`. The exact path below the root directory of the layer is important; otherwise, wic cannot locate the plugin.

To write your own source plugin, you derive it from the base source plugin class `SourcePlugin` and implement the functions to carry out the tasks, as shown in Listing 10-7.

Listing 10-7   **Source Plugin**

```
class MyPartitionPlugin(SourcePlugin):
    name = 'mypartition'

@classmethod
def do_prepare_partiton(cls, part, ...)
    ...

@classmethod
def do_configure_partition(cls, part, ...)
    ...
```

```
@classmethod
def do_install_disk(cls, part, ...)
    ...

@classmethod
def do_stage_partition(cls, part, ...)
    ...
```

Your own source plugin always must set the name attribute to a unique name. This is the name under which the source plugin is known to wic. It is the name you use with the --source parameter of the part directive, for example:

```
part / --source mypartition <options>
```

Depending on your source plugin, you need to implement one or more of the methods that wic calls at various stages of the partition creation process:

- **do_configure_partition()**: Called before do_prepare_partition() and used to create configuration files for the partition, such as bootloader configuration files.

- **do_stage_partition()**: Called before do_prepare_partition() and used to tailor the partition content provided by the source.

- **do_prepare_partition()**: Called to populate the content into the partition. This method creates the partition image that is then incorporated into the disk image.

- **do_install_disk()**: Called if additional steps need to be performed after do_prepare_partition() before the partition can be incorporated with the final disk image.

A source plugin at least implements the do_prepare_partition() method, as it is the method that actually populates the partition content from the content sources rootfs-dir, kernel-dir, and bootimg-dir. The values of these parameters are passed to the method so that the plugin can access the respective directories. If your source plugin does not implement a particular method, the superclass method is used instead. For all four methods, superclass methods do nothing but log a debug message.

10.6.6 Transferring Images

After wic completes the creation of an image, you can simply transfer it to an SD card or USB stick or whatever other media you built your image for:

```
$ sudo dd if=<image_file> of=/dev/<device>
```

wic provides you with the name and location of the image file after creating it. By default, the output directory is /var/tmp/wic/build.

Since you are writing the image file directly to a device, you must execute the command with root privileges. This is potentially dangerous, as specifying the wrong device can wipe out devices and partitions on your development host. Always double-check that you are using the correct device name. It is always a good idea to use dmesg immediately after inserting the media to find the correct device name.

10.7 Summary

Yocto Project BSPs provide the adaptation layer to support many different hardware platforms with the same core build system.

- Unlike traditional embedded BSPs, Yocto Project BSPs are not standalone. They require the OE Core and possibly other metadata layers.
- Yocto Project BSPs do not contain toolchains or development tools. These are provided by the core layers.
- Yocto Project BSPs are BitBake layers that are included with a build environment by adding their path to the BBLAYERS variable in the conf/bblayers.conf file of the build environment.
- A Yocto Project BSP must define at least one machine configuration file that provides the target platform-specific settings.
- A Yocto Project BSP may add its own recipes and/or append recipes from other layers to adapt building of packages to the requirements of the target hardware.
- Yocto Project BSPs can easily be swapped for each other without touching configuration settings other than the MACHINE variable in the conf/local.conf file of the build environment.
- Since Yocto Project BSPs contain only target-specific adaptation of the build system, maintenance is greatly reduced.
- Yocto Project BSPs follow a specific layout.
- The yocto-bsp tool allows quick creation of a basic BSP that is compliant with the BSP conventions.
- The yocto-kernel tool simplifies the management of Linux kernel configuration options, patches, and features.
- The OpenEmbedded Image Creator (wic) greatly simplifies the creation of bootable images that can directly be transferred to various media. wic can be extended through kickstart files and source plugins.

10.8 References

Yocto Project Board Support Package (BSP)Developer's Guide, www.yoctoproject.org/docs/1.8/bsp-guide/bsp-guide.html

Application Development

In This Chapter

In the chapters leading up to this one, we learned how to use the Yocto Project to build Linux OS images, how to customize those images, and how to adapt them to a particular hardware through board support packages (BSPs). Devices comprising hardware, an operating system stack, and a bunch of other open-source software packages do not make a product. Eventually, you want to develop your own software packages providing the end-user functionality for your device, build them, and deploy them to the device. For that task, you need a software development environment for your target system that is commonly found in what is referred to as *application development toolkit (ADT)* or *software development kit (SDK)*. The Yocto Project uses both terms and typically refers to an ADT as an SDK that has been installed by the ADT installer from package feeds pulled from a web server and to SDK as an SDK that has been created with the build system. The actual toolkits provide the same functionality, as the package feeds for the ADT have previously been created with the build system.

Using the Yocto Project build system, you can build an ADT that matches your target system yourself. You can then use the ADT environment to develop and build applications for your device.

In this chapter, we explore what a Yocto Project ADT is made up of as well as how you can build and use it.

11.1 Inside a Yocto Project ADT

So what exactly are you getting with a Yocto Project ADT? A complete application development environment consisting of the following:

- **Cross-Development Toolchain**: The ADT cross-development toolchain comprises a cross-compiler, cross-linker, cross-debugger, and a set of other tools used for application development.

- **System Roots**: An ADT contains two system roots: one for the development host, which contains the cross-development toolchain and other tools, and one for the target, which is an entire root filesystem for the target that also contains the development packages with header files, libraries, and more.

- **QEMU Emulator**: Together with a kernel and a root filesystem image, QEMU provides for testing of your user space applications without the actual hardware. You can develop applications for the target even before the hardware is available.

- **Environment Setup**: Scripts for setting up the environment on your development host for cross-development with the ADT are provided.

- **Yocto Project Eclipse Plugin**: The plugin is for the popular Eclipse IDE[1] to integrate an ADT.

- **Profiling Tools**: Various user space tools for profiling applications on your target system are included with an ADT. The set of tools includes the following:

  - **LatencyTOP**: LatencyTOP[2] is a tool to measure and resolve latency issues in applications for Linux systems that impact the user experience, such as audio and video skips during media playback, delayed response to user input on desktop interfaces, and more, even if your system has plenty of CPU power.

  - **PowerTOP**: Power management is paramount for virtually all embedded systems, particularly if they are running on batteries. PowerTOP[3] is a diagnostic tool to measure power consumption and trace it into applications, libraries, routines, and code fragments.

  - **OProfile**: OProfile[4] is a systemwide profiling tool for Linux systems, capable of profiling running code by adding only minimal overhead. It consists of a Linux kernel driver and a daemon for collecting sample data for the target system, as well as several offline tools to analyze the sample data on a host system.

---

1. https://www.eclipse.org
2. http://git.infradead.org/latencytop.git
3. https://01.org/powertop
4. http://oprofile.sourceforge.net

- **Perf**: Perf[5] is a Linux profiling tool that uses Linux kernel performance counters for collecting data on various hardware and software events, such as CPU cycles, instructions, interrupts, cache references, and many more.
- **System Tap**: System Tap[6] is infrastructure and instrumentation for gathering information about a running Linux system. System Tap scripts allow tracing virtually any system event by placing probes.
- **Linux Trace Toolkit—Next Generation (LTTng)**: LTTng[7] is an open source tracing framework for Linux systems that provides instrumentation to identify system events, extraction of identified events with little overhead, and tools for investigation and analysis.

The components included with an ADT provide application developers with all the necessary tools to write user space applications in C and C++ using the Linux and middleware APIs. These can be GNU Make–based, GNU Autotools–based, or CMake-based applications. After initializing the ADT environment, you can use the command-line to cross-build your applications.

Many application developers, however, prefer the convenience and productivity of an integrated development environment (IDE) that allows them to edit, build, and debug their applications from within a graphical user interface. For that purpose, the Yocto Project offers a plugin for the popular and extensible Eclipse IDE. The plugin integrates an ADT with the many tools available for Eclipse, namely, with the Eclipse C/C++ Tooling (CDT). The Yocto Project Eclipse plugin also provides on-target remote application execution and debugging through the Eclipse Target Communication Framework (TCF). Via TCF, you can directly deploy an application binary to your target device, run it on the target device, and interact with it from within the Eclipse IDE. You can also remotely run your application inside the GNU Debugger (GDB) server (gdbserver) on your target. The GDB cross-debugger, started by Eclipse on your development host, connects to the gdbserver on your target, allowing you to control the debug session from the Eclipse IDE, including but not limited to setting breakpoints, stepping through your code, and inspecting variables.

Developing applications for embedded systems does not stop with writing the code then debugging and deploying it, but commonly involves optimization for performance, power consumption, and more. The profiling tools, of which all but System Tap integrate with the Eclipse IDE, can be integrated with the ADT and added to a target root filesystem to assist you with analyzing your applications.

The following sections walk you through the process of building an ADT, installing it, using it for command-line development, and integrating it with the Eclipse IDE

---

5. https://perf.wiki.kernel.org

6. https://sourceware.org/systemtap

7. http://lttng.org

for developing, building, and on-target debugging for a complete round-trip development experience.

11.2 Setting Up a Yocto Project ADT

You can set up an ADT in various ways:

- **Download the ADT Installer**: Download the ADT installer tarball from the Yocto Project download site,[8] unpack it, configure it for your target, and then run it. The ADT installer then downloads the appropriate cross-toolchain, root filesystems, and more from the Yocto Project download site and installs them on your development system. This method is the most convenient for setting up an ADT, but it uses a prebuilt system root image, which most likely does not match your target image.
- **Build the ADT Installer**: Use a Yocto Project build environment to build the ADT installer tarball yourself rather than downloading it. After that, it is the same as for downloading the ADT Installer.
- **Build a Toolchain Installer to Create an ADT**: Using your target build environment, you create a toolchain installer that includes cross-toolchain and target system root that exactly match your target system with all the development packages for the software packages that you may have added to your custom system image.

The first two methods are explained in detail by the *Yocto Project Application Developer's Guide.*[9] In this chapter, we focus on the third method, creating a toolchain installer for a target using the build environment.

11.2.1 Building a Toolchain Installer

If you already have a build environment for your target system, potentially including a BSP and other layers, you can use it to build a toolchain installer with all the software components that you added to a custom root filesystem image. For our example, we are using the build environment and BSP layer for our kiosk project from the previous chapter.

Our BSP layer `meta-ypbkiosk` currently does not contain a custom image target. Listing 11-1 shows the image recipe for it.

Listing 11-1   **Custom Image Recipe (ypbkiosk-image-sato.bb)**

```
DESCRIPTION = "Custom image for the Yocto book Kiosk, which is based \
               on core-inmage-sato. We only replaced the Dropbear SSH \
               server with the OpenSSH server, which is necessary for \
               the ADT, and added tar.bz2 to the image types built."
```

---

8. http://downloads.yoctoproject.org/releases/yocto/yocto-2.0/adt-installer
9. www.yoctoproject.org/docs/1.8/adt-manual/adt-manual.html

```
IMAGE_FEATURES += "splash package-management x11-base \
                  x11-sato ssh-server-openssh hwcodecs"

LICENSE = "MIT"

inherit core-image

IMAGE_INSTALL += "packagegroup-core-x11-sato-games"

IMAGE_FSTYPES += "tar.bz2"
```

Create the directory `recipes-core/images` inside the `meta-ypbkiosk` layer, and add the recipe file `ypbkiosk-image-sato.bb` of Listing 11-1 to it.

Now build the toolchain installer by executing

```
$ bitbake -c populate_sdk ypbkiosk-image-sato
```

after sourcing the build environment. Also make sure that the `MACHINE` variable in `conf/local.conf` of your build environment is set to `MACHINE = "ypbkiosk"`. The build system derives the proper architecture settings for the toolchain from this variable.

The `populate_sdk` task applies to all image targets and creates a toolchain for the image target honoring all the other settings such as `MACHINE`, `EXTRA_IMAGE_FEATURES`, and so forth. Once the task completes, it places the toolchain installer in `tmp/deploy/sdk` of the build environment. The toolchain installer is a single executable file ending in `.sh`. It is part shell script installer and part payload that contains the actual toolchain with host and target system roots. If you open the file and look at its contents, you find the text `MARKER:`, which separates the script from the payload.

Besides being convenient for distribution, the purpose of this single-file configuration is to make the toolchain entirely self-contained, meaning that all binaries are linked against their own copy of libc, which results in no dependencies on the host system. Since the installation path of the toolchain is not known at build time (you can install it anywhere on your system), and the pointer to the dynamic loader cannot be altered dynamically, the shell script portion takes care of the relocation.

The architecture for the development host for which the toolchain is built is determined by the configuration variable `SDKMACHINE`. This variable is automatically set to the architecture of the host the build system is running on when creating the toolchain installer. If you wish to build the toolchain for a different development host architecture than the one you are using to build the toolchain, then you can set the `SDKMACHINE` variable explicitly in the `conf/local.conf` file of your build environment. The only architectures currently supported for building are `i686` (x86 32-bit) and `x86_64` (x86 64-bit).

11.2.2 Installing the Toolchain

Installation of the toolchain is now rather simple:

```
$ cd tmp/deploy/sdk
$ ./poky-glibc-x86_64-ypbkiosk-image-sato-corei7-64-toolchain-2.0.sh
```

The actual toolchain installer file may be different dependent on your setup. The toolchain installer by default installs the toolchain into the /opt/poky/<version> directory. You can provide a different directory if you wish.

A feature of the toolchain installer is that you can create different installers for any machine with any architecture and install them into the same directory. The build system creates only one set of cross-canadian toolchain binaries[10] per architecture and the toolchain installer separates the target system roots into different directories. This is possible because details describing the target hardware can be passed as options to the compiler. Those options are set up by the environment script by assigning variables such as CC, LD, and more.

Listing 11-2 shows the layout of the toolchain installation directory obtained with tree -L 3.

Listing 11-2   **Toolchain Installation Directory Layout**

```
/opt/poky/2.0
├── environment-setup-corei7-64-poky-linux
├── environment-setup-cortexa8hf-vfp-neon-poky-linux-gnueabi
├── site-config-corei7-64-poky-linux
├── site-config-cortexa8hf-vfp-neon-poky-linux-gnueabi
├── sysroots
│   ├── corei7-64-poky-linux
│   │   ├── bin
│   │   ├── boot
│   │   ├── dev
│   │   ├── etc
│   │   ├── home
│   │   ├── lib
│   │   ├── media
│   │   ├── mnt
│   │   ├── proc
│   │   ├── run
│   │   ├── sbin
│   │   ├── sys
│   │   ├── tmp
│   │   ├── usr
│   │   └── var
│   ├── cortexa8hf-vfp-neon-poky-linux-gnueabi
│   │   ├── bin
│   │   ├── boot
│   │   ├── dev
│   │   ├── etc
│   │   ├── home
│   │   ├── lib
│   │   ├── media
│   │   ├── mnt
│   │   ├── proc
```

---

10. *Cross-canadian* means that the build system running on the architecture defined by HOST_ARCH creates a toolchain to run on the architecture defined by SDKMACHINE, which in turn can build software for a system running on the architecture defined by TARGET_ARCH. Potentially, this involves three different architectures. However, most commonly, SDKMACHINE and HOST_ARCH are the same.

```
|   |   ├── run
|   |   ├── sbin
|   |   ├── sys
|   |   ├── tmp
|   |   ├── usr
|   |   └── var
|   └── x86_64-pokysdk-linux
|       ├── etc
|       ├── lib
|       ├── sbin
|       ├── usr
|       └── var
├── version-corei7-64-poky-linux
└── version-cortexa8hf-vfp-neon-poky-linux-gnueabi
```

Files and subdirectories can be categorized into the following:

- **Environment Setup**: The `environment-setup-*` scripts set the toolchain configuration for the various architectures. If you want to use a particular toolchain, you need to source the respective script, similar to sourcing the `oe-init-build-env` script when setting up a Yocto Project build environment.

- **Site Configuration**: The site configuration files `site-config-*` contain configuration settings when developing software packages utilizing GNU Autotools.

- **System Roots**: The `sysroots` subdirectory contains a subdirectory with the system root for each target architecture and the host architecture. In the example, the subdirectory `x86_64-pokysdk-linux` is the system root for the host, which contains the cross-toolchains. In addition, the example contains a target system root for Intel Core i7 used for the MinnowBoard Max and a target system root for ARM Cortex A8 used for the BeagleBone.

- **Version Files**: The `version-*` files contain version information about the toolchain versions.

One final note about building a toolchain installer: by default, the toolchains created build only dynamically linked binaries. If you want to build statically linked binaries, you need to make sure to include the packages containing the static libraries with your system root. You can achieve this by adding them to the `IMAGE_INSTALL` variable. This example adds the glibc static libraries:

```
IMAGE_INSTALL_append = " glibc-static"
```

Add this line to `conf/local.conf`, and add any other static libraries you require.

11.2.3 Working with the Toolchain

To put a Yocto Project toolchain to work with your project, you first have to initialize the environment using the appropriate script. For our example with the kiosk, it is

```
$ source environment-setup-corei7-64-poky-linux
```

The toolchain initialization scripts are sourced exactly like the build environment setup script.

If you look inside the script, you notice that it sets a series of environment variables that are assigned by the script (listed here in alphabetical order, not in the order as they appear in the script):

- **AR**: Minimal command and options for ar to maintain static libraries.
- **ARCH**: Architecture of the target system.
- **AS**: Minimal command and options to run the cross-assembler for the target system.
- **CC**: Minimal command and options to run the C cross-compiler for the target system.
- **CCACHE_PATH**: Ccache[11] is a compiler cache for C, C++, Objective-C, and Objective-C++ compilers. It caches intermediate compiler output in a directory during a build and reuses it, if nothing has changed, on subsequent builds. It can significantly speed up build time on subsequent builds. The first build is slower because the cache is created. Ccache works only with GNU Compiler Collection (GCC) compilers and compilers with similar behavior. The script adds the path to the cross-toolchain to tell ccache where to find the toolchain binaries. By default, ccache stores the cache files in ${HOME}/.ccache. If you want to change the location, you also need to set the CCACHE_DIR environment variable. The script does not do that.
- **CFLAGS**: Flags for the C cross-compiler.
- **CONFIG_SITE**: Site configuration for GNU Autotools.
- **CONFIGURE_FLAGS**: Flags for the GNU Autotools configure command.
- **CPP**: Minimal command and options to run the C preprocessor for the target system.
- **CPPFLAGS**: Flags for the preprocessor.
- **CXX**: Minimal command and options to run the C++ cross-compiler for the target system.
- **CXXFLAGS**: Flags for the C++ cross-compiler.
- **GDB**: Minimal command and options to run the GNU Debugger for the target system.
- **KCFLAGS**: Flags for compiling the Linux kernel.
- **LD**: Minimal command and options to run the cross-linker for the target system.
- **LDFLAGS**: Flags for the cross-linker.

---

11. http://ccache.samba.org

- **NM**: Minimal command and options for `nm` to examine binary files (executables, object files, libraries) and display meta information stored inside them, in particular, the symbol tables.

- **OBJCOPY**: Minimal command and options for `objcopy` to copy and translate object files.

- **OBJDUMP**: Minimal command and options for `objdump` for displaying various information about object files.

- **OECORE_ACLOCAL_OPTS**: Options for the `aclocal` command, which is part of GNU Autotools Autoconfig.

- **OECORE_DISTRO_VERSION**: Version number for the toolchain.

- **OECORE_NATIVE_SYSROOT**: Path to the host system root.

- **OECORE_TARGET_SYSROOT**: Path to the target system root.

- **PATH**: Adds the path to the `/usr/bin` directory inside the host system root to the search path for executable files of your development system so that the cross-toolchain commands can be found and executed.

- **PKG_CONFIG_SYSROOT** and **PKG_CONFIG_PATH**: Paths to the target package configuration used by `pkg-config`.

- **PYTHONHOME**: Path to the Python interpreter included in the host system root.

- **RANLIB**: Minimal command and options for `ranlib` to add and update files in static libraries.

- **SDKTARGETSYSROOT**: The path to the target system root containing the development packages. This variable is passed to the cross-toolchain commands such as compiler, linker, and so forth.

- **STRIP**: Minimal command and options for the `strip` command to strip symbols from binaries.

- **TARGET_PREFIX, CROSS_COMPILE**: Toolchain binary prefix for the cross-toolchain tools.

Many of these environment variables are standard variables, as they are used by makefiles for building applications. When you are developing your own applications for your target system, make use of these variables in the makefiles you are writing. These variables are also used by the build system in recipes, which means you do not have to override them with EXTRA_OEMAKE.

Before we go into more details of writing applications, let us build a simple program consisting of just one C file, as in Listing 11-3.

Listing 11-3   **Calculate Fibonacci Series (`fibonacci.c`)**

```
#include <stdio.h>

int main()
{
   int n, first = 0, second = 1, next, c;
```

```
printf("Enter the number of terms: ");
scanf("%d",&n);

printf("First %d terms of Fibonacci series are:\n", n);

for (c = 0 ; c < n ; c++)
{
    if (c <= 1)
        next = c;
    else
    {
        next = first + second;
        first = second;
        second = next;
    }
    printf("%d\n",next);
}

return 0;
}
```

Create this file in any directory of your development system. Then initialize the toolchain and build the application:

```
$ source environment-setup-corei7-64-poky-linux
$ ${CC} fibonacci.c -g -o fibonacci
```

The second command cross-compiles fibonacci.c for our kiosk target system using the toolchain environment. We added the -g option to add debug symbols. If you try to execute the application on your development host, you most likely see output similar to this:

```
$ ./fibonacci
bash: ./fibonacci: /lib/ld-linux-x86-64.so.2: bad ELF interpreter: \
   No such file or directory
```

That is no surprise, as your application is dynamically linked to the glibc library for our target, which is almost certainly different from the library on your development system.

11.2.4 On-Target Execution

If you have a MinnowBoard Max with the Linux OS stack that we built in the previous chapter ready, copy the executable to the target. You can do this via memory stick or, more conveniently, via network using scp:

```
$ scp fibonacci root@<target_ip>:/usr/bin/fibonacci
```

Replace <target_ip> with the IP address of your MinnowBoard Max. You can now execute the program on the target either using the target's console or establishing a connection via ssh:

```
$ ssh root@<target_ip>
root@ypbkiosk:~# fibonacci
Enter the number of terms: 10
First 10 terms of the Fibonacci series are:
0
1
...
root@ypbkiosk:~#
```

11.2.5 Remote On-Target Debugging

Troubleshooting and fixing bugs is your daily bread as a software developer. The tool of choice is a debugger that lets you control and examine the status of a running program as well as analyze a program after it crashes, commonly referred to as *post-mortem* debugging. The Yocto Project provides GDB[12] as a package for the target as well as a package with a cross-version for the development host. Like any cross-development tool, a cross-debugger runs on a development host using one architecture while being able to debug binaries, executables, and libraries that have been compiled for another.

We already included the target package by including `tools-debug` in the variable `EXTRA_IMAGE_FEATURES` in `conf/local.conf`. The cross-version is automatically included with the SDK.

You can directly run GDB on the target using

```
root@ypbkiosk:~# gdb /usr/bin/fibonacci
```

GDB launches, starts our Fibonacci program, and halts it at the first instruction. From here, you can use GDB commands to control the running program, in GDB terms referred to as the *inferior*, display program variables, and much more, using the GDB command line.

However, debugging directly on the target is not always possible. Targets with memory and disk constraints may not be able to store and load the debugging information of the binaries or the program being processed. Furthermore, GDB needs to locate and process information such as function and variable names, variable values, and stack traces, requiring you to use an executable that contains debug information on the target, also referred to as a *non-stripped binary*. In addition, to be able to inspect your program's source code within GDB while debugging, you need to copy all of the program's source files to the target. That is straightforward with a program as simple as our Fibonacci example, but it can get rather cumbersome with a program that is built from many different source files.

To overcome these limitations, you can use remote debugging with gdbserver. Gdbserver is not a debugger but a server process that runs on the target and controls the debugged program or inferior. Gdbserver does not load and process any debug information about the debugged program but instead relays all information back to a GDB running on a development host. The GDB on the development host sends control

---

12. https://www.gnu.org/software/gdb

commands to the gdbserver on the target to start or stop the inferior, set breakpoints, read and write target variables, step through the program, and more. Since all the processing for debugging is done by GDB on the development host, only binaries with debug symbols are required on the target.

If you want to debug libraries that you use with your program, you need to install the debug packages of these libraries on the target by including them in the IMAGE_INSTALL variable of your target image. By convention, all debug packages end in -dbg. If you want to include the debug packages of all packages installed by your target images, you can add dbg-pkgs to EXTRA_IMAGE_FEATURES in conf/local.conf.

If you do include the debug packages of all the packages, be aware that the size of your target root filesystem image will increase considerably due to the source files being part of the *-dbg packages. You can instruct the build system not to include the source files into the debug packages by setting the PACKAGE_DEBUG_SPLIT_STYLE variable to debug-without-src in the conf/local.conf file of your build environment. Since this variable controls the packaging behavior for all packages globally, it will cause a rebuild of the entire target system.

Because the GDB on the development host is responsible for loading and processing all the debugging information, it must have access to the *non-stripped* binaries—that is, the executable and all libraries compiled with the -g option and without any optimizations. The binaries on the target can be stripped but must not be compiled with optimizations.

GDB and gdbserver communicate with each other using a command interface over a network, or alternatively, a serial, connection. You first launch gdbserver on the target with the debugged program and then start GDB on your development host, instructing it to connect to the gdbserver on your target.

Launching Gdbserver on the Target

For remote debugging, you need gdbserver installed on your target. You can directly install the gdbserver package in your target image, but using the tools-debug image feature is more convenient.[13]

Launch gdbserver on your target, either directly on a console or remotely via Secure Shell (SSH), for example, for our Fibonacci program, using

```
root@ypbkiosk:~# gdbserver localhost:2345 /usr/bin/fibonacci
Process /usr/bin/fibonacci created; pid = 810
Listening on port 2345
```

Gdbserver will not exit until the debugged process terminates. Port number 2345 is the default port for GDB and gdbserver. You can change the port if you wish.

Launching GDB on the Development Host

To debug the running process on your target, you need to launch the cross-debugger and instruct it to connect to gdbserver on your target. From the directory where you

---

13. We recommend using tools-debug over directly installing the gdbserver package, as it only requires a change to conf/local.conf rather than modifying the image recipe.

have built the Fibonacci application, source the environment setup script as you did earlier in Section 11.2.3, and launch the debugger:

```
$ source environment-setup-corei7-64-poky-linux
$ ${GDB} fibonacci
GNU gdb (GDB) 7.9.1
...
Reading symbols from fibonacci...done.
(gdb)
```

We omitted some of the initial output of GDB for clarity. After going through its initialization, GDB displays its command prompt (gdb). Instruct GDB to connect to gdbserver on your target:

```
(gdb) target remote <target_ip>:2345
Remote debugging using <target_ip>:2345
...
(gdb)
```

Replace <target_ip> with the IP address of your target system. If you specified a different port for gdbserver, you will have to specify the same port here. On your target system, you should see gdbserver respond to the connection:

```
Remote debugging from host <host_ip>
```

Now you are ready to start your debugging session on your development host. Typing *continue* will run the program on your target. When the inferior process on the target terminates, gdbserver running on the target will terminate too. However, GDB on your development host will continue to run. You can restart gdbserver on the target and then reconnect GDB.

Unless you are a die-hard command-line developer, using GDB and its command line may not be your thing. There are many graphical frontends available for GDB. One of them is the trusted *Data Display Debugger (DDD)*[14] provided by the GNU Project. DDD can easily be installed with a package management system of any Linux distribution. DDD has a basic but functional user interface without any frills, as shown in Figure 11-1.

DDD by default uses the host GDB installed on your development system. You can instruct DDD to use the cross-debugger from the Yocto Project SDK:

```
$ source environment-setup-corei7-64-poky-linux
$ ddd --debugger ${GDB}
```

DDD does not offer a button or menu item to connect to a remote gdbserver. You have to enter the target remote command manually into the GDB command window at the bottom of DDD.

The Eclipse IDE also provides a very comfortable graphical frontend to GDB. We explain how to integrate Eclipse with the Yocto Project and the use of the debugger in Section 11.4.

---

14. https://www.gnu.org/software/ddd

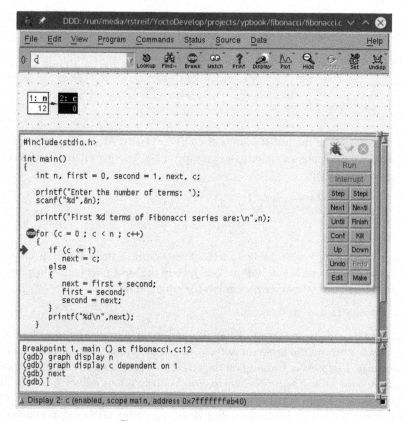

Figure 11-1   DDD user interface

Debugging Standard Libraries

If you are looking to trace into standard libraries installed on your target with GDB, you need to tell GDB where to find the debug information and source files for the libraries. The SDK installs all of the debug packages, including the source files in the SDK system root, for the target platform on your development host—for example, /opt/poky/2.0/sysroots/corei7-64-poky-linux for the SDK for our MinnowBoard Max.

You can instruct GDB to use a system root by typing

```
(gdb) set sysroot /opt/poky/2.0/sysroots/corei7-64-poky-linux
(gdb) set substitute-path /usr/src/debug \
      /opt/poky/2.0/sysroots/corei7-64-poky-linux/usr/src/debug
```

GDB will then use this system root to look for debug information and source files. Entering these settings repeatedly again when starting GDB is rather tedious. Therefore, you can add the statements to a .gdbinit file. You can place this file either in your home directory, in which case the settings will apply to all projects, or in the project directory, in which case it will apply only to the current project when you start GDB from within that directory. If you do use a local .gdbinit file in a project directory, you still need a .gdbinit file in your home directory containing the lines

```
set auto-load safe-path /
set auto-load local-gdbinit on
```

GDB's default security policies only allow autoloading initialization files from the user's home directory. These settings also allow autoloading from the current directory.

11.3 Building Applications

Any nontrivial application consists of potentially many source files that are compiled and linked into libraries and/or executable program files. The environment setup of the toolchain makes it rather simple to develop makefile-based and GNU Autotools–based applications.

11.3.1 Makefile-Based Applications

For makefile-based projects, it is best not to set any environment variables, such as CC, AS, LD, and CFLAGS, inside the makefile, as the settings for those variables are established by the initialization script for the toolchain environment. In general, you do not want to set or provide any toolchain flags that pertain to a particular architecture directly, as they may limit the ability to compile the project on different architectures. The toolchain environment, as well as the Yocto Project build environment, provide all architecture-dependent settings.

Listing 11-4 shows a simple makefile to build our project to compute the Fibonacci series.

Listing 11-4 **Makefile for Fibonacci Series Project**

```
# Makefile for the Fibonacci Application

# Files
SOURCES=fibonacci.c
OBJECTS=$(SOURCES:.c=.o)
EXEC=fibonacci

# Define extra flags here
EXTRACFLAGS=-ansi

all: $(SOURCES) $(EXEC)

$(EXEC): $(OBJECTS)
        $(CC) $(CFLAGS) $(EXTRACFLAGS) $(OBJECTS) -o $@

%.o : %.c
        $(CC) $(CFLAGS) $(EXTRACFLAGS) -c $<
```

```
install:
        install $(EXEC) $(DESTDIR)/usr/bin

clean:
        rm -rf *.o $(EXEC)
```

Of course, it is still a rather simple project, but it illustrates the concepts of using the variables set by the environment and providing any additional configuration settings via separate variables.

11.3.2 Autotools-Based Applications

We talked about GNU Autotools and writing recipes for autotooled software packages in Chapter 8, "Software Package Recipes." The toolchain environment provides all the necessary settings to build autotooled packages, including site configuration files. GNU Autotools makes applications portable between different UNIX-like systems by detecting the system configuration. That detection does not work correctly when working in a cross-development environment: the Autotools would detect the development host configuration rather than the proper configuration for the target. Providing the target configuration to Autotools is the purpose of the site configuration files.

To illustrate the process of using the toolchain with an autotooled project, we are going to build the GNU Hello application:

```
$ source environment-setup-corei7-64-poky-linux
$ wget http://ftp.gnu.org/gnu/hello/hello-2.10.tar.gz
$ tar xvf hello-2.10.tar.gz
$ cd hello-2.10
$ aclocal ${OECORE_ACLOCAL_OPTS} -I m4
$ autoconf
$ autoheader
$ automake -a
$ ./configure ${CONFIGURE_FLAGS}
$ make
```

The first four steps are self-explanatory: we set up the environment, then download the source package for the GNU Hello application, unpack it, and change into the unpacked source directory.

We then run `aclocal` to automatically generate the `aclocal.m4` files based on `automake` macros. These macros are collected from directories added through the `-I` option. The `OECORE_ACLOCAL_OPTS` adds those for the toolchain configuration, while `-I m4` includes the local `m4` directory of the source.

Running `autoconf`, `autoheader`, and `automake` then create the configuration inputs, header template, and makefile template used by `configure`.

After that, the local configure script is executed to determine the build configuration and generate the makefile. The environment variable `CONFIGURE_FLAGS` provides host and target configuration settings for cross-compilation.

And last but not least, running `make` builds the application.

11.4 Eclipse Integration

Development with command-line tools, editors, cross-toolchains, makefiles, scripts, and more, has long been the daily routine of embedded developers as the development of IDEs with graphical user interfaces for embedded systems has been lagging behind their counterparts for native development. Application developers working on native applications for operating systems for personal computers commonly have the choice between a variety of different IDEs for their platforms to best meet their requirements. Embedded developers have had to work with what silicon vendors or third-party toolchain companies offered for a particular hardware and software platform, which, in many cases, was not much. Using Linux for embedded systems development has broadened the choice of development tools for embedded developers.

One of these choices, but not the only one, is *Eclipse*. Eclipse, originally developed by IBM for Java development,[15] is an IDE that can be extended through plugins to serve many different development purposes and to integrate various tools in a common framework following standardized workflows. Behind the scenes, Equinox,[16] an implementation of the core Open Services Gateway Initiative (OSGi)[17] framework specification, provides the plumbing for plugins to be installed and integrated into Eclipse and to communicate with each other. In OSGi terminology, plugins are commonly referred to as *bundles*, software packages that can be installed in an OSGi framework and provide services to other bundles.

Although Eclipse was originally developed as an IDE for the Java programming language, it has been extended to support many other programming languages, among them Ada, C/C++, Cobol, Erlang, Fortran, Haskell, JavaScript, Lua, Perl, PHP, Python, Ruby, Scala, and many more; interface with a range of SCM such as Git, Perforce, Subversion, and others; and integrate with a growing list of tools. One of those is the Yocto Project Eclipse plugin that integrates Yocto Project toolchains and much more.

11.4.1 Installing the Eclipse IDE

Eclipse installation packages are released preconfigured for a particular task, such as Eclipse IDE for Java Developers, Eclipse IDE for Java EE Developers, Eclipse IDE for C/C++ Developers, and so forth. You can find a complete list on the Eclipse download site.[18] For the integration with the Yocto Project, Eclipse IDE for C/C++ Developers is the best choice, as it already includes the core components required by the plugin:

- C/C++ Development Tools
- Eclipse Git Team Provider
- Remote System Explorer (RSE)

---

15. The original Eclipse code base stems from the IBM VisualAge IDE.

16. www.eclipse.org/equinox

17. www.osgi.org

18. www.eclipse.org/downloads

The Yocto Project Eclipse plugin requires a matching version of Eclipse. For Yocto Project 2.0 (Jethro), the Eclipse versions for which a plugin is available are Juno, Kepler, and Luna. You can always find which version of Eclipse you need to install on the Yocto Project Eclipse website.[19]

Virtually all mainstream Linux distributions offer Eclipse for installation from their package repositories. These may work, but before installing any of them, you need to verify that a matching version for the Yocto Project is provided, and you most likely need to install the three plugins listed above separately.[20] If there is no matching version offered by your distribution, or if you prefer a manual installation, you need to use an installation package from the Eclipse site:

1. **Install Java**: Eclipse is a Java application and requires at least a Java Runtime Environment (JRE)[21] to run. Eclipse works with OpenJDK as well as with Oracle Java. Linux distributions typically provide OpenJDK for installation from the package repositories. Simply use your distribution's package manager to install Java and verify the installation with

   ```
   $ java -version
   openjdk version "1.8.0_40"
   OpenJDK Runtime Environment (build 1.8.0_40-b25)
   OpenJDK 64-Bit Server VM (build 25.40-b25, mixed mode)
   ```

2. **Install Eclipse**: Download the proper version of the Eclipse IDE for C/C++ Developers for your development host system. In our example, this is eclipse-cpp-luna-SR2-linux-gtk-x86_64.tar.gz, suitable for any 64-bit x86-based Linux system. The installation package is a simple compressed tarball that you can extract into any directory on your system (we use /opt, which, however, requires root access):

   ```
   $ cd /opt
   $ sudo tar xvf \
       ~/Downloads/eclipse-cpp-luna-SR2-linux-gtk-x86_64.tar.gz
   ```

   Now start the Eclipse IDE:

   ```
   $ /opt/eclipse/eclipse &
   ```

   Eclipse first shows a dialog for selecting a location for its workspace. The default ~/workspace is adequate unless you would like to use a different directory.

3. **Install Standard Eclipse Plugins**: You need to install a couple of standard plugins that are provided through the Eclipse download site. To install those, first select *Install New Software...* from the *Help* menu of the Eclipse workbench. Then, from the *Work with:* combo-box, choose the download site that matches your version of Eclipse (for Eclipse Luna, that is *Luna—http://download.eclipse.org/releases/luna*).

---

19. https://www.yoctoproject.org/tools-resources/projects/eclipse-ide-plug

20. Eclipse Git Team Provider is not strictly necessary for the Yocto Project Eclipse plugin but is recommended.

21. You can, of course, also use a Java Development Kit (JDK) that includes the JRE.

Now you can select the various plugins for installation (if any of the following items are not shown, they are already installed):

a. Expand the list *Mobile Device Development* and select the following:

- C/C++ Remote Launch (Requires RSE Remote System Explorer)
- Remote System Explorer End-user Runtime
- Remote System Explorer User Actions
- Target Management Terminal (Core SDK)
- TCF Remote System Explorer add-in
- TCF Target Explorer

b. Expand the list *Linux Tools* and select

- Linux Tools LTTng Tracer Control

c. Expand the list *Programming Languages* and select

- C/C++ Autotools Support
- C/C++ Development Tools

Complete the installation and restart Eclipse.

4. **Install Eclipse Yocto Plugin**: We are installing the plugin from the Yocto Project download site.

a. After Eclipse has started again, select *Install New Software...* from the *Help* menu, and click on *Add...* in the *Work with:* area. Enter *http://downloads.yocto-project.org/releases/eclipse-plugin/2.0/luna* in the *Location:* field and a meaningful name, such as *Yocto Project*, in the *Name:* field.

b. Select the check boxes next to

- Yocto Project ADT Plug-in
- Yocto Project BitBake Commander Plug-in
- Yocto Project Documentation plug-in

Complete the installation by accepting the license agreement, and restart Eclipse.

Your Eclipse installation is now ready for integration with a Yocto Project ADT.

11.4.2 Integrating a Yocto Project ADT

We are now integrating the ADT that we set up in Section 11.2 with Eclipse and the Yocto Project Eclipse plugin. The process is split into the following steps:

1. Configuring the cross-toolchain options
2. Configuring the target options

The configuration options you choose in the following steps become the default settings for all projects you develop with the Yocto Project plugin. Each new project you create inherits these settings, and you can adjust them later individually for each project. For the configuration steps described in the following sections, you first need to

1. Select *Preferences* from the *Window* menu to show the Preferences dialog.

2. Choose *Yocto Project ADT* from the list to show the configuration screen.

The configuration screen is divided into the following sections:

- **Cross-Development Profiles**: You can create multiple profiles with different settings for your Yocto Project ADT development. The profile named *Standard Profile* is the default, which is applied to all new projects unless you choose a different profile when creating the project. You cannot remove the *Standard Profile*. Leave the selection to *Standard Profile*.

- **Cross Compiler Options**: This section configures the cross-toolchain.

  - **Toolchain Type**: You have the choice between

    - **Standalone Prebuilt Toolchain**: This option is for application developers who have been provided with a prebuilt and packaged Yocto Project toolchain, which they have installed on their development system.

    - **Build System Derived Toolchain**: Use this option if you want to use the toolchain from a Yocto Project build environment.

    Since we built a toolchain with the Yocto Project and installed it on our development system, select the first option.

  - **Toolchain Root Location**: This option is the path that points to the toolchain installation location. This path depends on the Toolchain Type:

    - **Standalone Prebuilt Toolchain**: Point the path to the location where you installed the toolchain. In our example, that is /opt/poky/2.0.

    - **Build System–Derived Toolchain**: If you intend to use a build system–derived toolchain, point the path to the top directory of your build environment.

  - **Sysroot Location**: This option is the path to the location where the system root for your target resides. For our kiosk project using the MinnowBoard Max, this is /opt/poky/2.0/sysroots/corei7-64-poky-linux.

- **Target Options**: This section configures the target you want to use with your Eclipse setup. There are two choices:

  - **QEMU**: Choose this option if you intend to use the QEMU emulator to test your applications. If you are using QEMU, you also have to provide a kernel to which you may pass additional options.

  - **External-HW**: This option is for external hardware, which is what we are using.

Click *Apply* to have the Yocto Project plugin verify your settings and to save the configuration, and click *OK* to dismiss the dialog. Eclipse and the Yocto Project plugin are now ready for application development.

11.4.3 Developing Applications

The Yocto Project Eclipse plugin provides project templates for developing C/C++ applications using CMake and GNU Autotools. The build files, such as the makefile, are created with environment settings that meet the requirements of the build system's `cmake.bbclass` and `autotools.bbclass` classes. Hence, writing recipes that build the projects that you have developed with Eclipse and a Yocto Project cross-toolchain is as simple as providing `SRC_URI` and inheriting the respective class.

You can also develop applications that just use a makefile without CMake or Autotools. However, you have to set the Eclipse environment for the cross-toolchain manually. Hence, we recommend that you stick to one of the provided project templates. Whether you choose to build your project with CMake or with Autotools depends on the requirements of your project and, of course, your personal preferences.

Start creating your new project by launching Eclipse and selecting *New > Project...* from the *File* menu. From the *New Project* dialog box, expand the *C/C++* folder and choose either *C Project* or *C++ Project*. The following examples build a simple Hello World–style project using identical source code, so it does not make any difference whether you choose C Project or C++ Project. For the examples, we choose C Project.

The next dialog box lets you select the type of project you want to create. The choices

- Yocto Project ADT Autotools Project
- Yocto Project ADT CMake Project

are provided by the Yocto Project Eclipse plugin and include the templates that integrate with the Yocto Project cross-toolchain.

Developing a CMake-Based Application

Starting from the project dialog, follow these steps to create your project:

1. **C Project Page**: Expand the folder *Yocto Project ADT CMake Project*, and from the list choose *Hello World C CMake Project*. This creates a simple project with one C file containing a main function, CMake files, and so on. Alternatively, you can choose *Empty Project*, but then you have to create all the files manually. Enter a name in the field *Project Name* at the top, and leave *Use default location* checked. The project name must not contain any special characters or spaces. Click *Next*.

2. **General Settings Page**: If you wish, enter your author information. You may also leave the page blank. The information you enter here is automatically added to a header in the source files. Click *Next*.

3. **Select Configurations Page**: The Debug configuration is selected by default. If you click *Advanced Settings*, the project properties dialog opens up. The item *Yocto Project Settings* contains the ADT settings with cross-development profiles, cross-compiler options, and target options. The fields are prefilled with the settings we entered earlier. You can override these settings by choosing *Use project specific settings*. You can come back to this dialog at any time after your project has been created by choosing *Properties* from the Eclipse *Project* menu. Click *Finish*.

4. **C/C++ Perspective**: Depending on your current Eclipse state, the *Open Perspective* prompt may appear asking you if you want to change to the *C/C++ Perspective*. Confirm opening the *C/C++ Perspective*. Eclipse calls its different environments *perspectives*. Depending on your Eclipse installation, there are perspectives for Java, C/C++, Debug, and many more. You can switch between perspectives from the Eclipse *Window* menu or use the buttons in the upper right corner of the Eclipse window. Each perspective can have multiple different *views* that are displayed in the workbench area of the perspective. On the left side, you see the *Project Explorer* view showing the project structure and the files of your project. If you want to edit a file, double-click on its name in the Project Explorer, which loads it into the built-in editor.

You can now comfortably perform all development tasks from within the C/C++ perspective, including building the project with the Yocto Project ADT cross-toolchain and system root for your target. Either

- Select *Build Project* from the Eclipse *Project* menu, or
- Right-click on the project name in the *Project Explorer* and select *Build Project*.

During the build process, which of course is rather quick for this simple project, the *Console* view shows the output of the various build steps. If there are any build errors, Eclipse switches to the *Problems* view. If the build was successful, Eclipse shows the binary files under *Binaries* in the Project Explorer.

Developing an Autotools-Based Application

Creating and building an Autotools-based application is not much different from a CMake-based application. Once again, starting from the project dialog, follow these steps to create your project:

1. **C Project Page**: Expand the folder *Yocto Project ADT Autotools Project*, and from the list choose *Hello World ANSI C Autotools Project*. Enter a name in the field *Project Name* at the top, and leave *Use default location* checked. The project name must not contain any special characters or spaces. Click *Next*.

2. **Basic Settings Page**: If you wish, enter your author information and choose the license. This dialog is slightly different from *General Settings* for the CMake project, but it serves a similar purpose. Click *Next*.

3. **Select Configurations Page**: This dialog is exactly the same as for the CMake project. Click *Finish*.

4. **C/C++ Perspective**: After completion, Eclipse either directly switches to the C/C++ perspective or asks you before doing so depending on your current Eclipse state.

Building an Autotools-based application involves two steps that you can execute from within the C/C++ perspective:

- **Configure**: Right-click on the project name in the Project Explorer, and select *Reconfigure Project*. This invokes the `autogen.sh` script, which in turn executes `libtoolize`, `aclocal`, `autoconf`, `autoheader`, `automake`, and `configure`, similar to what we did on the command line in Section 11.3.2.

- **Build**: Right-click on the project name in the Project Explorer, and select *Build Project*.

You can follow the steps in the *Console* view. After a successful build, Eclipse shows the binary files under *Binaries* in the Project Explorer.

11.4.4 Deploying, Running, and Testing on the Target

Integration of the Yocto Project ADT toolchain with Eclipse makes creating and building CMake-based and GNU Autotools–based projects as simple as a couple of mouse-clicks in the graphical user interface. You still have to write the code, of course, but the tedious mechanics are taken care of. Deploying, running, and testing your application on the target system, however, is still a matter of copying binary files manually to the target.

This is where Eclipse's TCF adds the missing link for a complete round-trip development experience. TCF enables copying the binary files to the target system, remotely running executable applications on the target system, and even remotely debugging applications on the target system directly from within Eclipse.

TCF is a lightweight but extensible network protocol mainly for, but not limited to, communication with embedded devices, or targets. It is designed as a framework for tools on a development system to interact with services on the target using a standardized communication layer that is independent of a particular transport such as TCP/IP, serial wire connection, SSH tunnel, and so forth. While TCP/IP is the standard communication channel, other protocols are available and can be added. TCF uses JSON for data marshalling and also supports automatic discovery of targets and services on targets. At its core, TCF consists of a plain C implementation of an extensible agent running on the target and a Java client API. The latter is integrated with various Eclipse tools but can also be used in standalone applications.

Preparing the Target for Remote Control

To be able to use Eclipse with TCF to remotely deploy, run, test, and debug applications we need to prepare the target root filesystem by installing the required components.

The Yocto Project provides a set of image features which makes this task rather easy and straightforward. All you have to do is add the features `tools-debug` and `eclipse-debug` to the `EXTRA_IMAGE_FEATURES` in the `conf/local.conf` file of your build environment:

```
EXTRA_IMAGE_FEATURES = "debug-tweaks tools-debug eclipse-debug"
```

Then rebuild the image:

```
$ bitbake -k ypbkiosk-image-sato
```

and deploy it to the MinnowBoard Max target system, as explained in the previous chapter. After rebooting the board, you can verify that the TCF agent is running by executing on the target:

```
# ps | grep tcf-agent
699 root       668m S    /usr/sbin/tcf-agent -d -L- -l0
931 root       4412 R    grep tcf-agent
```

Of course, your output is most likely slightly different, but the line containing /usr/sbin/tcf-agent indicates that the TCF agent is running on the target. Your target is now ready to accept TCF connections from your Eclipse workbench.

Before you can set up a TCP connection from the Eclipse workbench on your development system to your target system, both systems need to be connected to the same local network. Our ypbkiosk-image-sato is derived from the default core-image-sato, which includes networking support with Dynamic Host Configuration Protocol (DHCP). All you have to do is connect your MinnowBoard Max target to the same router as your development system. You may want to use a separate router and an additional network port on your development system if the IT department of your organization does not allow you to connect your target system to the organization's network.

Using the Eclipse Target Explorer

With the Target Explorer, you can inspect your target system from the Eclipse workbench. You can browse the target's filesystem, list running processes as well as terminate them and attach a debugger to them, and create application launch configurations.

The Target Explorer uses TCF's discovery mechanism, which is very handy, as you do not have to find out your target's IP address manually.[22] The TCF discovery mechanism scans your local network for TCF agents listening on its default port 1534. Follow these steps to set up a connection to your target with the Target Explorer:

1. **Open the Target Explorer Perspective**: From the Eclipse *Window* menu, select *Open Perspective*, and from the submenu, select *Other...* From the list of perspectives in the dialog, select *Target Explorer*. Eclipse automatically switches to the Target Explorer perspective with a *System Management* tab on the left side.

---

22. Not that it is very hard to run `ifconfig` on the target system, but it requires a serial terminal or a screen and a keyboard.

2. **System Management Tab**: The System Management tab contains a list with three folders: *Favorites*, *Connections*, and *Neighborhood*. If you have never used Target Explorer before, the *Favorites* folder is empty, and the *Connections* folder has one entry called *Create New Connection...* The *Neighborhood* folder, however, shows an entry for each TCF agent the discovery mechanism has found on the local network in the form of *TCF Agent <ip address>*.

3. **Setting Up the Connection**: Right-click on the TCF Agent with the IP address you want to connect to and select *Connect* from the menu. Eclipse opens the *New Connection* dialog. The fields of the dialog are prefilled with the connection parameters the discovery mechanism has detected. All you need to do is give the connection a meaningful *Connection Name*. After you click *Finish*, Eclipse connects to the TCF agent on the target and opens a tab for the new connection.

4. **Connection Tab**: Depending on the connection status, the Connection tab has multiple subtabs that are shown on the bottom:

   a. **Details (Overview)**: Shows the connection details. The fields can be modified only if the connection is closed.

   b. **Source Paths**: Search path for source files when attaching the debugger to a process. By default, these are paths on the target, but paths on the development host can be added.

   c. **Launches**: Allows creation of launch configurations to run applications installed on the target. Standard input (stdin), standard output (stdout), and standard error (stderr) are redirected via TCF to eclipse so that you can interact with the running application.

   d. **Processes**: List of processes running on the target. The list is retrieved from the target when you click on the subtab. You can load it again by clicking on the *Refresh* button in the upper right corner.

   e. **File System**: Lets you explore the filesystem on the target. You can create new folders and files, move them, delete them, copy them, and rename them. You can also search for folders and files on the target.

If you have developed native applications (that is, applications that can be executed on the development system itself) with Eclipse before, you know that you can execute and debug them directly from the development environment within Eclipse, for instance, the C/C++ or Java perspective, after compiling them. With TCF, you can do the same on the target. It requires a few configuration steps, which we explain in the next sections.

Running Applications on the Target

Through Eclipse's *Run Configurations*, you can set up environments for executing applications. You create and manage your environments using a dialog you launch by selecting *Run Configurations...* from Eclipse's *Run* menu. On the left side of the dialog, Eclipse shows a list with the various run configuration types, and underneath each type, a list with predefined configurations. To create a run configuration to execute our C/C++ application on the remote target, you choose *C/C++ Remote Application* and then click on the *New* button in the upper left corner above the list.

1. **Name**: Eclipse fills in a name for your run configuration based on the current project. Accept the default if it meets your requirements, or enter a new name.

2. **Main Tab**:

   a. **Connection**: Create a new connection by clicking *New...*

      i. Select *TCF* from the list and click *Next >*.

      ii. Enter the IP address of your target board or a host name if you have a local DNS in the *Host Name* field.

      iii. Enter a name for your connection in the field *Connection Name*.

      iv. Enter a *Description* if you wish.

      v. Click *Finish* to create the connection and dismiss the dialog.

   b. **Project**: Eclipse automatically fills in the name of your current project. If that is not the project you want, choose a different project using the *Browse...* button.

   c. **Build configuration**: Eclipse automatically chooses the current configuration of the project. You may override it by choosing a different one from the list.

   d. **C/C++ application**: A project can potentially build more than one application. Use *Search Project...* to select the correct executable.

   e. **Remote absolute file path for C/C++ application**: This field contains the absolute path and name of the application on the target. Eclipse copies the application to that path. You can choose a different name than the name of the executable file created by the Eclipse build process. Use *Browse...* to select the path on the target and then append a name, such as /usr/bin/hello.

   f. **Commands to execute before application**: In this field you can enter additional commands to execute on the target before Eclipse launches the application. Leave it blank.

   g. **Skip download to target path**: Do not check this box. You want Eclipse to download your application to the target every time so that your latest changes are applied.

3. **Arguments Tab**: If your application requires command-line arguments, you can enter them into the *Program Arguments* field.

4. **Common Tab**: General settings for the run configuration are accessed through the *Common* tab. The default settings are appropriate in most cases. If you would

like Eclipse to store your application's output, check *File* and provide a path and name for the file to store the output.

Click *Apply* and then *Run* on the bottom of the dialog to launch your application on the target. If it is the first time Eclipse uses this connection to run an application on that target, it presents you with a dialog asking for a *User ID* and *Password* for the user account under which to execute the application. Enter *root* as the *User ID* and leave *Password* empty, as a standard Yocto Project image has only a *root* user account with no password.

Watch the Console window inside Eclipse as Eclipse first builds your application, then transfers it to the target, and finally executes it. The Console window should show output similar to the following:

```
root@ypbkiosk:/#
echo $PWD'>'
/>
root@ypbkiosk:/# /usr/bin/hello;exit
Hello World!
logout
```

Eclipse and TCF only redirect standard input (`stdin`), standard output (`stdout`), and standard error (`stderr`) from the target to a terminal inside Eclipse. If your target application is a graphical application, its output is displayed on a screen connected to the target hardware. In general, this makes sense because you would want to test your application with a local screen.

Debugging Applications on the Target

Similar to Run Configurations for executing applications on a target, Eclipse provides Debug Configurations for debugging applications on a target. For debugging, an application or program is launched from within the context of the debugger. The debugger then controls and monitors the execution of the program and provides access to variables, stack, dynamic storage, file pointers, and more, used by the program.

Remote debugging requires a debugger that is capable of executing a program on the target while controlling and monitoring it from a different system, the development host, via a connection link such as a network or serial connection. The GDB, which is the standard debugger for Linux systems, has a matching server, the gdbserver, for remote debugging. The GDB running on the host system communicates with gdbserver on the target system via a network connection using TCP or via serial connection.

It is useful to understand the principal Eclipse workflow for remote debugging, as it uses a combination of TCF and the communication protocol used by the debugger:

1. Eclipse downloads the application to the target system via TCF.

2. Eclipse launches gdbserver on the target with the application to be debugged via TCF by executing a command similar to `gdbserver host:2345 <program> <arguments>`. The parameter `host:2345` indicates to use a TCP connection on port 2345 (the gdbserver default port), `<program>` is the application that Eclipse

downloaded in the previous step, and `<arguments>` are, if provided, command-line arguments passed to the application.

3. Eclipse starts GDB on the development system or host and switches to the Debug perspective.

4. Eclipse instructs GDB, through its GDB/MI interface, to connect to the gdbserver running on the target using the command `target remote <target>:2345`, where `<target>` is the hostname, if DNS is available, or the IP address of the target.

5. GDB starts the application on the target and automatically holds execution at the first instruction of the `main()` function.

6. You can now control and monitor the application with GDB on the target via the graphical user interface provided by Eclipse's Debug perspective.

GDB provides multiple command interpreters and command infrastructure through which users and other applications can interact with it:

- **GDB/CLI**: The console or command-line interpreter that is commonly used by users. It provides a simple command infrastructure in human-readable form. This is the default interpreter.

- **GDB/MI**: The machine interpreter typically used by other programs, such as Eclipse and other frontends to GDB. There are two versions of GDB/MI: mi1 and mi2. The latter is the current version.

All GDB interpreters use `stdin` to accept commands, `stdout` for information and data output, and `stderr` for error messages. Eclipse uses the latest GDB/MI version, mi2.

Creating a debug configuration is not much more difficult than creating a run configuration. As a matter of fact, if you already created a run configuration for your application, Eclipse uses it as a starting point. From the Eclipse *Run* menu, select *Debug Configurations...* to open the configuration editor. The dialog looks pretty much the same as the Run Configurations dialog. On the left side, you have your list of application types. If you created a run configuration as described in the previous section, Eclipse most likely already highlighted that configuration in the list and is showing the configuration details on the right.

The tabs Main, Arguments, and Common let you view and edit the same information as their respective counterparts of the Run Configurations dialog. We explained those in the previous section. The tabs *Debugger* and *Source* are new:

- **Debugger Tab**: This is where you configure the GDB:

  - **Stop on startup at**: If checked and a function name is provided in the field next to it, GDB sets a breakpoint at the first instruction of the provided function. On startup, GDB executes the program until it reaches the breakpoint. The default setting is to halt execution at the `main()`. If you are debugging a complex program and you are not interested in what is happening in the beginning of the program, set it to a different function.

- **Main Subtab**: General settings for GDB:

  - **GDB Debugger**: This setting is for the path and name of the GDB debugger. This information should already be filled out correctly by the Yocto Project plugin to point to the cross-debugger for the platform.

  - **GDB Command File**: This setting points to the project command file for GDB. The debugger reads this file on startup. The filename is typically .gdbinit and is located inside the Eclipse project directory.

  - **Non-stop Mode**: If checked, this setting allows you to debug stopped threads of a multithreaded program while other threads are running freely.

  - **Enable Reverse Debugging**: With this setting checked, you can step and continue backwards through a program. Normally, you can only step and continue in the order of the program's flow. This GDB functionality is still limited to certain architectures and platforms and is not generally available for remote debugging.

  - **Force Thread List Update on Suspend**: This setting automatically updates the thread information in the Eclipse Debug perspective when a thread hits a breakpoint.

  - **Automatically Debug Forked Processes**: Typically, the GDB debugger attaches to the main process. If that process creates child processes, GDB continues debugging the main process. Newer versions of GDB can attach to forked processes. Enable this option to have GDB automatically also attach to child processes.

  - **Tracepoint Mode:** For some applications, particularly real-time applications, it is not feasible to use breakpoints and inspect variables because suspending the program alters the timing characteristics. That is where a developer can use tracepoints to have GDB automatically collect and report data. In *Normal* mode, tracepoints are inserted into the program as traps; in *Fast* mode, they are inserted as jumps. Jump tracepoints are not supported on all platforms and under all conditions. The *Automatic* mode leaves the decision to the debugger.

- **Shared Libraries Subtab**: In this subtab, you can add directory paths to additional shared libraries into the text box. The standard shared libraries are known and loaded by default. If you want to debug shared libraries, you need to check the *Load Shared Library Symbols Automatically* option.

- **Gdbserver Settings Subtab**: Path and name of the gdbserver executable on the target are shown in this subtab. The default is gdbserver, which is sufficient for Yocto Project target images, as the gdbserver is in the default PATH. Port number is the TCP port to be used for communication between GDB running on the host and gdbserver running on the target. The default is 2345.

- **Source Tab**: When stepping through a program, the debugger needs to show you the source so that you effectively can trace your program. For that purpose, the debugger needs to be able to locate and load the source files. The paths added to the list in Source Lookup Path serve that purpose. Eclipse adds the project paths by default. If you need to debug any shared libraries, you must add their paths to that list to be able to see their sources.

Accept your modifications by clicking *Apply*, and then launch the debugger by clicking *Debug*. Eclipse starts the debugger and switches to the Debug perspective. Execution halts at the first instruction of the main() function. You can now step through the code, set breakpoints, and examine variables of the program running on the target as you would do with a program running in the debugger locally.

Tracing Library Functions

You can use the debugger to trace into functions of shared libraries, such as C library libc. However, the debugger cannot display the source code because it has no information on where to locate it. When building the SDK, the build system automatically adds the debug and source packages with the system roots for all installed packages, including standard shared libraries. To tell the debugger where to find the source files, we have to add the necessary information to the .gdbinit file located in the project directory of the Eclipse workspace (Listing 11-5).

Listing 11-5   **GDB Startup File .gdbinit**

```
set sysroot /opt/poky/2.0/sysroots/corei7-64-poky-linux
set substitute-path /usr/src/debug \
    /opt/poky/2.0/sysroots/corei7-64-poky-linux/usr/src/debug
```

Listing 11-5 shows an example of the .gdbinit file that sets the paths for GDB to locate the source files for library debugging for an SDK installed in /opt/poky/2.0:

- **set sysroot**: Specifies the local directory that contains the copies of the libraries that are installed on the target. This paths enables the debugger to locate and load the libraries and their symbols. This is the path to the Yocto Project SDK installed on your development system.
- **set substitute-path**: Specifies a substitution rule for the debugger to find the source files for the libraries. Standard executables and libraries compiled for Linux systems record their compilation directory with a path prefix as /usr/src/debug. The substitute-path command causes GDB to replace the first path fragment with the second when locating the source files.

Unfortunately, Eclipse does not provide any means to give GDB configuration settings such as, but not limited to, the ones shown previously for cross-debugging. However, you can modify the .gdbinit file using Eclipse's text editor. Since the file is a hidden file on Linux/UNIX systems, the Eclipse Project Explorer does not show it by default. Click the down arrow in the menu next to the title Project Explorer, and then select *Customize View...* from the menu. Then remove the checkmark next to *.* resources*. Alternatively, you can give the *GDB Command File* in the *Debug Configuration* dialog a different filename so that it is not a hidden file (no dot leading the filename).

11.5 Application Development Using an Emulated Target

Many embedded projects are combined efforts of hardware and software engineering. The actual target hardware, or even early engineering samples, may not be available for software development well into the development cycle. To shorten the development cycle, you may want to commence software development on application software early in the project in parallel with the hardware development. One approach is to use inexpensive development boards such as the BeagleBone, MinnowBoard Max, Wandboard, and others that resemble your project's target hardware. Another approach is to use target emulation. Target emulation also has the advantage that application developers do not have to deal with embedded hardware because they can build and test their applications using their development system.

The Yocto Project uses QEMU for target emulation. We have used QEMU throughout this book for testing our various Yocto Project system builds. Now we illustrate how to use QEMU for application development with a Yocto Project SDK and Eclipse.

11.5.1 Preparing for Application Development with QEMU

We need two things for application development with an emulated target:

- Linux kernel and root filesystem for QEMU
- ADT to match the former

Both, of course, we build with the build system. We already have the build environment that we used to create the image for our kiosk project with the MinnowBoard Max. We just need to change the machine from ypbkiosk to QEMU machine. It makes good sense to use an emulated machine whose core architecture is similar to the actual hardware target. Since the MinnowBoard Max is equipped with a 64-bit x86 CPU, we choose qemux86-64 as the machine. Change the MACHINE variable in conf/local.conf of the build environment to qemux86-64, and launch BitBake with

```
$ bitbake -k ypbkiosk-image-sato
```

to build the Linux kernel and the ypbkiosk-image-sato root filesystem image. Once the build completes, create the matching SDK with

```
$ bitbake -c populate_sdk ypbkiosk-image-sato
```

Once that has finished, install the ADT, as explained in Section 11.2.2. You can safely install the ADT in the same /opt/poky/<version> directory, as toolchain, system roots, and setup scripts are uniquely named and separated from each other.

Extracting the Root Filesystem

Eclipse launches QEMU with a root filesystem exported from the development host via *Network File System (NFS)*. To set up the root filesystem for QEMU and NFS, we need to extract and prepare the root filesystem that we created during the previous step. The ADT includes a script that performs all the necessary work.

1. Change directory to the ADT installation:

   ```
   $ cd /opt/poky/<version>
   ```

2. Source the QEMU ADT environment:

   ```
   $ source environment-setup-core2-64-poky-linux
   ```

3. Change directory to sysroots:

   ```
   $ cd sysroots
   ```

4. Extract the root filesystem from the build environment:

   ```
   $ runqemu-extract-sdk \
   /<path-to-build-environment>/tmp/deploy/images/qemux86-64/\
   ypbkiosk-image-sato-qemux86-64.tar.bz2 \
   core2-64-poky-linux
   ```

5. Copy the Linux kernel image from the build environment:

   ```
   $ cp /<path-to-build-envrionment>/bzImage-qemux86-64.bin \
   core2-64-poky-linux/boot
   ```

For NFS, your development system must have *rpcbind*, the Universal Address to RPC Program Number Mapper, installed. Depending on your system's configuration, you may need to install it using your system package manager, for instance, on Ubuntu sudo apt-get install rpcbind. Furthermore, for user space NFS, rpcbind is required to run in *insecure mode*, allowing calls to SET and UNSET from any host. To enable insecure mode, you need to add the -i option to the rpcbind startup configuration. On Ubuntu, add -i to the OPTIONS variable in the file /etc/init.d/rpcbind and restart rpcbind with sudo service rpcbind restart.

Integrating with Eclipse

Now we need to integrate our ADT and the root filesystem extracted for QEMU with Eclipse.

Open the *Preferences* dialog from the Eclipse *Window* menu, click *Yocto Project ADT*, and create a new cross-development profile for application development with QEMU following these instructions:

1. **Cross Development Profiles**: Your *Standard Profile* from the Cross Development Profiles list should reflect the settings we used in the previous sections for the MinnowBoard Max. Save the Standard Profile as *MinnowBoard Max* and then change the selection back to Standard Profile.

2. **Cross Compiler Options**: Keep the settings for *Standalone Pre-built Toolchain* and *Toolchain Root Location*. Click on *Browse...* next to Sysroot Location, and browse to `/opt/poky/<version>/sysroots/core2-64-poky-linux`, which is the location where we extracted the root filesystem to. From the Target Architecture list, choose `core2-64-poky-linux`.

3. **Target Options**: Select QEMU and browse to the location we copied the Linux kernel to: `/opt/poky/<version>/sysroots/core2-64-poky-linux/boot/bzImage-qemux86-64.bin`.

Eclipse is now ready for application development with QEMU.

11.5.2 Building an Application and Launching It in QEMU

You can now create a new application project as described in Section 11.4.3. After creating the project, right-click on its name in the Project Explorer and select *Yocto Project Settings* at the bottom of the list. From *Cross Development Profiles*, choose the *QEMU* profile, and click *Apply*. Your project now uses the cross-toolchain for QEMU to compile and debug.

To execute and debug your application, you first need to start QEMU. From the Run menu in Eclipse select External Tools. The first entry of the submenu is the QEMU integration that we just created: `qemu_core2-64-poky-linux`. Click on it, and Eclipse launches a terminal window in which it starts QEMU. QEMU itself starts in a second window.

Use Run Configurations and Debug Configurations to deploy, execute, and debug your application on the emulated target using TCF and GDB/gdbserver, as explained in Section 11.4.4.

11.6 Summary

Operating system stacks and middleware form the foundation for devices. Applications and user software create the value for end users. Yocto Project Application Development Toolkits (ADTs) provide application developers with the necessary tools to build, test, and deploy applications for their target devices.

- A Yocto Project ADT comprises cross-development toolchains, system roots for the hardware target devices and emulated targets, QEMU emulator, test and profiling tools, and integration scripts for convenient development environment setup.

- The build system creates ADTs to match the target device by including the exact toolchain used to build the device's Linux OS stack and by packaging the device's root filesystem image.

- ADT cross-development tools can be used directly from the command line for traditional development and for integration with build tools. Setup only requires sourcing of script that sets the necessary environment variables.

- Integration of an ADT with the Eclipse IDE provides access to the cross-development tools from the convenience of a graphical user interface.

- Eclipse's Target Communication Framework (TCF) allows deployment, execution, and debugging to actual target hardware as well as to an emulated target directly from the IDE.

11.7 References

Yocto Project Application Developer's Guide, www.yoctoproject.org/docs/2.0/adt-manual/adt-manual.html

Yocto Project Development Manual, www.yoctoproject.org/docs/1.8/dev-manual/dev-manual.html

Licensing and Compliance

A fully functional Linux OS stack comprises many hundreds, possibly thousands, of open source software packages. These software packages are released by their authors under the terms and conditions of a rather large variety of open source licenses. Virtually all of these licenses require that end users are given access to the license texts to inform them about their rights and potential duties when using the software. As a system builder who is building an entire system from many different open source software packages, you are required to collect all the license information and provide it to the users of your system. In addition to providing the license information, some open source licenses, particularly the GNU General Public License (GPL) licenses, require you to provide the source code that you used to build the binaries of the software packages. Collecting, managing, and providing license information and source code can be a time-consuming task. The Yocto Project greatly simplifies this task by providing a set of tools that take care of the tedious aspects of open source license and source code management.

12.1 Managing Licenses

For any software product, it is common practice to include an *End-User License Agreement (EULA)* with the product that informs users about their rights and duties when using the product. This process is simple and straightforward if all of the code that is included with the product has been entirely developed by the organization or individual who is shipping the product. Just provide and include the proprietary license agreement with the product and have the customer accept the agreement when installing the software on a computer system. That has been the standard practice for any software for personal computers. However, matters are substantially different if

- The software product contains software components, such as libraries, from other providers

- The software product is built using open source software packages
- The software product is provided together with hardware as part of an embedded system

All of the above are true for a Linux OS stack for an embedded device. While it is not a requirement that end users explicitly accept open source licenses for the software packages included with a product, they must be made aware that the product was built using open source software. License texts and information on how to obtain the source code must be made available to the end users.

License and source code information can be included with the device or provided by other means. For example, on Android devices, you can access license information from the *Legal Information* item in the *About Device* menu of the *Settings* app. License information and text can be stored on the device, or alternatively, in particular for connected devices, accessed through hypertext links directing the end user to a website where the license information can be shown. That is convenient for devices with a user interface at least capable of displaying text. For devices without such capabilities, license information can be provided with the user documentation, on the manufacturer's website, and so on.

Managing licenses for your product is not a trivial task. The Yocto Project includes over 170 common license schemes. The majority of them are open source licenses, but there are also some commercial licenses included for some software packages. Some developers of open source software use their own licenses, which can further complicate matters, since they may not be legally sound. The *Open Source Initiative (OSI)* examines licenses in a license review process for their compliance with the *Open Source Definition*.[1] OSI lists about 70 open source licenses on its website that have passed the organization's license review process and are approved as compliant with the Open Source Definition.[2]

Further complicating the issue is that a single open source project can actually use multiple license schemes. Following are common examples:

- Libraries for which one licensing scheme applies to the source code of the library and any work derived from it, such as bug fixes and enhancements, and another licensing scheme applies to the use of the library by other software components through its APIs. For instance, GnuTLS uses GPLv3+ for the sources and LGPLv2.1+ for the use of the library by other components.
- Packages that comprise multiple components that are licensed individually by different schemes. That scheme is commonly found in packages that provide a plugin mechanism. An example is media frameworks where plugins for encoders and decoders can be licensed differently from the framework itself, and other encoders/decoders, such as Free Lossless Audio Codec (FLAC).

---

1. http://opensource.org/osd
2. http://opensource.org/licenses/alphabetical

The Yocto Project assists with managing licenses in several ways:

- License tracking
- Common licenses
- Commercially-licensed packages
- License deployment

We examine these in the following sections.

12.1.1 License Tracking

All recipes must set the LICENSE variable to a list of source licenses that apply to the software package the recipe builds. The license information for the software package itself may be, and in virtually all cases is, different from the license for the recipe. The latter is typically specified in the LICENSE file of the layer. You must not confuse the two.

The LICENSE variable may contain a single license designation or a list of multiple license designations if the software package is covered by multiple licenses:

- If there is a choice of licenses, separate the license designations with the pipe (|) symbol: for instance, LICENSE = "LGPLv2.1+ | GPLv3".
- If multiple licenses cover different parts of the package sources, separate the license designations with the ampersand (&) symbol: for instance, LICENSE = "MPLv2 & LGPLv2.1".

License designations can be any text string but must not contain any white-space characters. For standard licenses, use the names of the common license files in meta/files/common-licenses or use the *Software Package Data Exchange (SPDX)* license flag names defined in meta/conf/licenses.conf as license designations. SPDX[3] is a standard format for license information created and maintained by the SPDX Working Group of the Linux Foundation.

Unless LICENSE is set to the special license designation CLOSED (LICENSE = "CLOSED"), a recipe must also set the variable LIC_FILES_CHKSUM to enable license tracking.

The author or copyright holder of a software package may change the license itself, such as from GPLv2 to GPLv3, or may modify the license text from one version of the software package to the next.[4] It is important that a build system can track such changes and show a notice, so that you as the system builder can take action on whether or not you want to adopt the new package version with the updated license. The LIC_FILES_CHKSUM variable, which is evaluated by the license class, provides a flexible mechanism

---

3. https://spdx.org/

4. In fact, newer versions of many software packages, particularly the ones provided by GNU, for which earlier versions have been licensed under the terms and conditions of GPLv2, are now licensed under the newer GPLv3.

for tracking license changes. The following example shows the various ways to specify `LIC_FILES_CHKSUM` in a recipe:

```
LIC_FILES_CHKSUM = "file://COPYING;md5=wwww \
                    file://header.h;beginline=7;endline=34;md5=xxxx \
                    file://source.c;beginline=10;md5=yyyy \
                    file://license3.txt;endline=46;md5=zzzz"
```

The variable contains a space-delimited list of license files that contain the license text. The build system computes an MD5 checksum over the license text and compares it to the value provided by the `md5` parameter. If neither the parameter `beginline` nor the parameter `endline` is provided, the entire file is considered as the license text. That approach works well with separate license files commonly named `COPYING` or `LICENSE`. Sometimes, license information is provided as part of a source file, such as a C header or similar file. In that case, only a portion of the file contents actually represents the license information. You can specify that portion by setting the parameters `beginline` and `endline` to the line number where the license text begins or ends respectively.

The build system by default searches for the license files in the directory specified by the variable `S`, which is the directory where the source code is unpacked. You can explicitly provide directory information by adding directory paths:

```
LIC_FILES_CHKSUM = "file://src/header.h;beginline=7;endline=34;md5=xxxx \
                    file://${WORKDIR}/license.txt;md5=yyyy"
```

The first line locates the file `header.h` containing the license information relative to `S` in `${S}/src`, while the second lines refers to the variable `WORKDIR` to locate the file `license.txt`.

12.1.2 Common Licenses

The OpenEmbedded Core metadata layer includes files with the license texts for common licenses in the directory `meta/files/common-licenses`. This directory is referenced by the variable `COMMON_LICENSE_DIR`. You can use this variable and the common license filename for `LIC_FILES_CHKSUM`, such as

```
LIC_FILES_CHKSUM = "\
file://${COMMON_LICENSE_DIR}/GPL-2.0;md5=801f80980d171dd6425610833a22dbe6"
```

However, we recommend doing so only if the source package does not actually contain the license text but just a reference to the common license in a file. In that case, we also recommend that you include the file containing the reference with `LIC_FILES_`
`CHKSUM`. The reason is that simply using the common license file effectively disables the license-tracking mechanism. Changes to the license information inside the package sources may go unnoticed by the build system, as the recipe uses the common license file.

You can provide your own license directory, or directories if more than one, for the build system to search by adding them to the `LICENSE_PATH` variable:

```
LICENSE_PATH += "/path/to/my/licenses"
```

This variable may contain a list of directories separated by space characters. The build system adds the path(s) of the variable to the path provided by COMMON_LICENSE_DIR.

12.1.3 Commercially Licensed Packages

Some software packages, while open source, are licensed using commercial licenses or special license terms and conditions not compliant with open source licensing. Recipes building such software packages flag the special licensing requirements by setting the variable LICENSE_FLAGS: for example, LICENSE_FLAGS = "commercial".

The LICENSE_FLAGS variable can contain any string, but as soon as a recipe sets the variable, the build system does not build the software package unless it is explicitly enabled.

To enable a particular license flag, you add it to the LICENSE_FLAGS_WHITELIST variable. The variable contains a space-delimited list of license flags. The build system matches the license flag set by the recipe to the list of license flags in LICENSE_FLAGS_ WHITELIST. Before doing so, however, it appends the package name PN to the license flag defined in LICENSE_FLAGS of the recipe. For example, for a recipe building the hello package containing

```
LICENSE_FLAGS = "commercial"
```

the variable effectively becomes

```
LICENSE_FLAGS = "commercial_hello"
```

You can now specifically enable the hello recipe by setting

```
LICENSE_FLAGS_WHITELIST = "commercial_hello"
```

or enable all recipes using the commercial license flags, including hello, by setting

```
LICENSE_FLAGS_WHITELIST = "commercial"
```

This matching scheme gives you fine control over which packages you want to enable building. You can drive this further by explicitly specifying package name PN and package version PV in the LICENSE_FLAGS setting of your recipe. Consider the recipe building the hello package to contain

```
LICENSE_FLAGS = "commercial_${PN}_${PV}"
```

which allows you to enable only a particular version of the hello recipe, such as version 1.0, by using

```
LICENSE_FLAGS_WHITELIST = "commercial_hello_1.0"
```

You specify the LICENSE_FLAGS_WHITELIST variable in the conf/local.conf file of your build environment, or even better, in a distribution configuration file such as conf/distro/mydistro.conf of a custom layer.

12.1.4 License Deployment

When building a target, the build system places the license information into the `${TMPDIR}/deploy/licenses` directory inside the build environment. For every recipe the build system builds, it creates a subdirectory in `${TMPDIR}/deploy/licenses`:

- If the recipe builds a software package, the subdirectory has the name of the recipe and contains the license files.

- If the recipe builds an image target, such as `core-image-minimal`, the subdirectory has the name of the image recipe with an added timestamp, for example, `core-image-minimal-20150817224402`. The directory contains two files: `package.manifest` and `license.manifest`. The former is an alphabetically sorted flat list with the names of all packages contained in the image. The latter is an alphabetically sorted list of the same packages with information about package name, package version, recipe name, and license details.

- If the recipe is for a package group, the build system creates the subdirectory with the name of the package group, but there are no files inside the subdirectory.

If you are looking to deploy the licensing information into the root filesystem image for your target system

- Setting the variable `COPY_LIC_MANIFEST = "1"` copies the file `license.manifest` into the root filesystem to `/usr/share/common-licenses/license.manifest`.

- Setting the variable `COPY_LIC_DIRS = "1"` copies the license directories to `/usr/share/common-licenses`.

You specify these variables in `conf/local.conf` of your build environment, or even better, in a distribution configuration file such as `conf/distro/mydistro.conf` of a custom layer.

12.1.5 Blacklisting Licenses

By setting the variable `INCOMPATIBLE_LICENSE` to a space-separated list of license designations, you can exclude recipes from the build. Packages for which their respective recipes do not provide alternatives to the listed licenses are not built. For example, setting

```
INCOMPATIBLE_LICENSE = "GPL-3.0 LGPL-3.0 AGPL-3.0"
```

effectively excludes all packages licensed under these licenses from the build, unless there are license alternatives, which could be an earlier version using a different license or a package providing similar functionality. The preceding example represents the setting with which the Yocto Project team tests this functionality. Although you can use other settings, you might be required to handle dependencies yourself by either removing them or providing alternatives to produce a functional system.

12.1.6 Providing License Manifest and Texts

A common requirement for open source licenses is that you have to provide license information. Using

```
COPY_LIC_MANIFEST = "1"
```

copies the license manifest to the target image into the directory /usr/share/common-licenses/license.manifest. The license manifest contains a list of all open source software packages installed on the target with their respective licenses.

Using

```
COPY_LIC_DIRS = "1"
```

also copies the license texts to the target image into the directory /usr/share/common-licenses for all packages installed on the target. COPY_LIC_DIRS can be used only in conjunction with COPY_LIC_MANIFEST; otherwise, setting the variable has no effect.

For target systems that have a user interface capable of displaying license manifest and license texts, including them with the target image simplifies this part of open source license compliance significantly. If your embedded target does not have a user interface or does not have enough storage space to hold license manifest and texts, you need to provide the information in an alternative way, such as printed information or a page on your organization's website.

12.2 Managing Source Code

Some open source licenses explicitly require you to provide the source code you used to build the software stack for your target system to the end users of your system. Providing the source code is part of the compliance management activities you have to perform, and you should consider the necessary tasks before you create the final image for your target system.

The simplest way to provide the source code is to provide the entire download directory DL_DIR. However, there are a couple of issues with this approach:

- The size of the entire download directory can be rather large. It also contains the sources for packages that you typically do not deploy in a released image, such as the toolchain sources. There are also files in the download directory that you never deploy, namely the *.done files that indicate whether a source package has successfully been downloaded. Furthermore, the download directory includes subdirectories containing unpacked repositories for sources that have been directly retrieved from source control management (SCM) systems.

- The download directory does not contain any patches that are provided with a recipe. To provide sources that an end user can use to build the binaries, you would need to include those patches manually.

- Most important, the download directory also contains source packages and/or repositories for closed source and/or proprietary software packages, which you do not want to release to end users.

A better way of providing source code is offered by the `archiver` class, which gives you flexibility to control what source code you want to provide and in what form you want to provide it. You enable the source archiving with the `archiver` class by adding the class to the `INHERIT` variable to the `conf/local.conf` file in your build environment:

```
INHERIT += "archiver"
```

You control what and how the `archiver` class does its job by setting several variables and variable flags:

- `ARCHIVER_MODE[src]` is a flag that controls how the source code is archived:
  - `ARCHIVER_MODE[src] = "original"` archives source package and patches separately.
  - `ARCHIVER_MODE[src] = "patched"` archives the source package with the patches applied. This is the default setting.
  - `ARCHIVER_MODE[src] = "configured"` archives the source package with the patches applied and configured.
- `ARCHIVER_MODE[diff] = "1"` archives the patches between the `do_unpack` and the `do_patch` tasks.
- `ARCHIVER_MODE[diff-exclude]` is a space-delimited list of files and directories of patches that you want to exclude from `ARCHIVER_MODE[diff]`. The default setting is `ARCHIVER_MODE[diff-exclude] = ".pc autom4te.cache patches"`.
- `ARCHIVER_MODE[dumpdata] = "1"` includes a file containing the environment data for a particular package, similar to `bitbake -e <recipe>`. The default setting is `ARCHIVER_MODE[dumpdata] = "0"`.
- `ARCHIVER_MODE[recipe] = "1"` includes the recipe (.bb file including any .bbappend) and any include files. The default setting is `ARCHIVER_MODE[recipe] = "0"`.
- `ARCHIVER_MODE[srpm] = "1"` outputs the sources as source RPM (SRPM) files in addition to the compressed tar archive. The `ARCHIVER_MODE[src]` flag applies to the SRPM as well. The default setting is `ARCHIVER_MODE[srpm] = "0"`.

In addition to the various `ARCHIVER_MODE` flags, the `archiver` class allows filtering for licenses and for what recipe types the package sources is archived:

- `COPYLEFT_LICENSE_INCLUDE` is a space-delimited list of licenses for which the source code is archived. Wildcards for license designations are allowed. For example, `COPYLEFT_LICENSE_INCLUDE = "GPL* LGPL*"` includes the sources for all packages licensed under any version of GPL and LGPL. The default setting is `COPYLEFT_LICENSE_INCLUDE = ""`.
- `COPYLEFT_LICENSE_EXCLUDE` is a space-delimited list of licenses that are explicitly excluded from source archiving. For example, `COPYLEFT_LICENSE_EXCLUDE = "CLOSED Proprietary"` explicitly excludes all software packages with closed

or proprietary licensing from source archiving. The default setting is `COPYLEFT_LICENSE_EXCLUDE = ""`.

- `COPYLEFT_TARGET_TYPES` is a space-delimited list of recipe types for which source archiving is enabled. Possible recipe types are
  - **target**: Archive sources for all packages built for the target
  - **native**: Archive sources for all packages built for the build host
  - **nativesdk**: Archive sources for all packages that are built for the host SDK
  - **cross**: Archive sources for all cross-build packages
  - **crosssdk**: Archive sources for all cross-build SDK packages
  - **cross-canadian**: Archive sources for all cross-canadian packages

  The default setting is to include all of the above recipe types.

Because both `COPYLEFT_LICENSE_INCLUDE` and `COPYLEFT_LICENSE_EXCLUDE` are set to empty strings by default, the `archiver` class does not perform any license filtering. At a minimum, you probably want to set `COPYLEFT_LICENSE_EXCLUDE` to exclude any of your proprietary software packages. Rather than doing that in the `conf/local.conf` file of the build environment, we recommend setting it in a distribution policy file such as `conf/distro/mydistro.conf` of a custom layer, so that enabling the `archiver` class will by default exclude your proprietary software packages when building your target distribution.

To further limit the size of your source deployment, consider setting `COPYLEFT_TARGET_TYPES = "target"` in the `conf/local.conf` file or the distribution policy configuration file.

The archiver class copies source package output it creates to the `${TMPDIR}/deploy/sources` directory. It organizes the packages in subdirectories by architecture and then by package name. You can override the default output directory by setting the variable `DEPLOY_DIR_SRC`.

12.3 Summary

Compliance management for open source software packages according to license requirements of their respective licenses is an important task that a system builder has to perform. Due to the increased popularity of Linux and open source for embedded devices and software products in general, multiple organizations such as the *Free Software Foundation*[5] and the *Software Freedom Conservancy*[6] are actively monitoring whether companies offering products containing open source software are meeting compliance requirements of the various open source licenses, particularly the GPL. If these organizations discover a failure of a company to comply with the license requirements,

---

5. www.fsf.org

6. https://sfconservancy.org

they ask the company to remedy the situation. If a company does not take action, these organizations potentially file a lawsuit against the company on behalf of the author of the software package in question.

As permissive as open source licenses are, they are legally binding documents and as such enforceable by law. It is best to avoid any issues by staying on top of the compliance requirements and plan the proper release of license texts and source code before shipping a product.

In this chapter we discussed

- License management by tracking licenses with recipes, creating commercially licensed packages and their respective recipes, and collecting and deploying license information.

- Source code management with the `archiver` class, which provides a convenient way of controlling source code archiving based on licenses and recipe types.

12.4 References

Yocto Project Development Manual, www.yoctoproject.org/docs/1.8/dev-manual/dev-manual.html

Advanced Topics

In This Chapter

In this chapter, we discuss select topics that facilitate using the Yocto Project in team and production environments. One of the strengths of the Yocto Project build system is that it can be easily deployed on individual development systems of software and build engineers. The features discussed in this chapter extend the build system's capabilities, enabling you to share resources and track build results necessary for team development and for requiring reproducibility, consistency, and repeatability in the production environment.

13.1 Toaster

Toaster is a graphical user interface to the build system. Unlike Hob, which is a native application, Toaster is a web interface accessed via web browser. Because it is a web interface, Toaster is suitable for deployment on remote systems in build farms or cloud services.

Similar to Hob, Toaster allows you to configure, launch, and monitor builds. Toaster also offers functionality to search and add metadata layers and recipes to your build. Since Yocto Project version 1.8 Fido, Hob has officially been deprecated by the Yocto Project team and development has stopped in favor of Toaster.

Working with Toaster is slightly more complex than working with Hob, as it requires additional setup for the web server environment. Toaster uses the Django[1] web framework. Django is a high-level web framework written entirely in Python. Django employs *object-relational mapping (ORM)* with database-backed object storage. Toaster uses ORM to store build statistics and other data in a database allowing easy comparison between subsequent builds. The database system can be any relational database management system

---

1. https://www.djangoproject.com

(RDBMS) supported by Django. By default, for local use, Toaster uses SQLite for the sake of simplicity. For deployment on a remote build server, the use of an actual RDBMS such as MySQL, MariaDB, or PostgreSQL is recommended.

In the following sections, we discuss the two Toaster operational modes, setup for local development in both modes, Toaster configuration, and setup of a production build system with Toaster.

13.1.1 Toaster Operational Modes

You can run Toaster in either *Analysis* mode or *Build* mode.

Analysis Mode

In Analysis mode, Toaster attaches to an existing build environment that you have previously created with `oe-init-build-env`. In this mode, you start building images directly using the `bitbake` command. Toaster then collects build statistics and other information, stores them in the database, and makes them available for browsing and viewing through its web interface. You need to start Toaster first before launching your build through BitBake.

In Analysis mode, Toaster provides the following functionality:

- Detailed information on the image that was built including recipes and packages
- Manifest of what packages were installed into the image
- Ability to browse the directory structure of the image
- Build configuration including variable settings
- Examination of error, warning, and log messages to facilitate debugging
- Information on task execution and shared state usage
- Dependency explorer
- Performance information such as build time, time per task, CPU usage, and more

Build Mode

In Build Mode, Toaster creates build environments and manages the configuration, BitBake execution, and data collection and analysis tasks of the Analysis mode. You interact with Toaster only through its web interface. You can select your image, configure the target machine and other aspects of builds, and start builds from the Toaster interface. You do not interact directly with BitBake as you do when Toaster is in Analysis mode.

In Build mode, Toaster provides the following functionality in addition to the functionality of Analysis mode:

- Browse layers and add layers to the build configuration.
- Select target images, target machine, and distribution policies.
- Inspect and set configuration variables.
- Execute builds.

In Build mode, Toaster offers configuration and execution functionality on par with Hob. Configuring images by adding packages to them is not as convenient with Toaster, as it requires you to edit the IMAGE_INSTALL_append variable from the Toaster user interface. With Hob, it was simply a matter of checking a checkbox. Compared to Hob, Toaster offers more detailed build analysis and statistics.

13.1.2 Toaster Setup

Toaster is based on the Django web framework and therefore requires additional Python packages to be installed before you can use it. You can find the list of packages in the file bitbake/toaster-requirements.txt in the root directory where you have installed the build system—for instance, /home/myname/poky. You can use this file directly to install the required Python packages.

You can install those packages either directly into the Python library directories of your build host or you can use a *Python virtual environment*. A Python virtual environment creates a Python sandbox based on the original Python setup on your build host. This is particularly useful if you are concerned about conflicting package versions. We strongly recommend using a Python virtual environment.

Setting Up a Python Virtual Environment

You set up a Python virtual environment with the virtualenv command, which all Linux distributions provide as a package. If it is not already installed on your build host, you can install it with

```
$ sudo dnf install python-virtualenv
```

for Fedora or Red Hat systems, or with

```
$ sudo apt-get install python-virtualenv
```

for Ubuntu systems.

Then you can create a Python virtual environment with

```
$ virtualenv pvenv
```

The command creates a new Python virtual environment in a directory called pvenv at the current location. It then copies all the necessary files from your build host's Python environment to the new virtual environment. It is irrelevant where on your build host you create your Python virtual environment.

Before you can use your Python virtual environment, you have to activate it with

```
$ source pvenv/bin/activate
(pvenv) $
```

To indicate that you are working with a Python virtual environment, your command prompt is prefixed with the name of the virtual environment in parentheses, in our example (pvenv).

You have to execute all operations related to Toaster, including the installation of the required Python packages, from within an active Python virtual environment; otherwise, your build host uses its default Python environment.

To exit a Python virtual environment, you type

```
(pvenv) $ deactivate
```

while within the Python virtual environment.

Installing the Toaster Requirements

From within the Python virtual environment, executing

```
(pvenv) $ pip install -r bitbake/toaster-requirements.txt
```

installs the required Python packages, including Django, into the Python virtual environment.

Now your build host is ready for local Toaster development.

13.1.3 Local Toaster Development

In local deployment mode, Toaster uses Django's built-in web server rather than integrating with an external web server, and it uses SQLite instead of an RDBMS. That greatly simplifies installation and configuration. However, it does not scale for workgroup use and remote deployment. For a scalable deployment, you want to consider using a Toaster production setup, as described in Section 13.1.5.

Local Toaster Development in Build Mode

While within the active Python virtual environment, change to the root directory of your build system installation, for example,

```
(pvenv) $ cd /home/myname/poky
```

Then launch Toaster with

```
(pvenv) $ bitbake/bin/toaster
```

If it is the first time you launch Toaster, it initializes the database, reads layer and build system configuration, and performs a series of other initial setup tasks. Once setup is complete, Toaster prints

```
Starting webserver...
Webserver address: http://0.0.0.0:8000/
Starting browser...
Toaster is now running. You can stop it with Ctrl-C
```

The default web browser of your build host should launch automatically, showing the Toaster landing page. If the web browser does not start automatically, open your preferred web browser and, in the navigation bar, enter

```
http://localhost:8000
```

You can now create a Toaster project, configure it, and build it.

Local Toaster Development in Analysis Mode

If you like to use Toaster with an existing build environment and control the build process directly by invoking BitBake, first source the build environment from within the Python virtual environment:

```
(pvenv) $ source /home/myname/poky/oe-init-build-env tbuild
```

Then, from within the build environment, launch Toaster:

```
(pvenv) $ source /home/myname/poky/bitbake/bin/toaster
```

You can now run BitBake builds as usual, for example:

```
(pvenv) $ bitbake -k core-image-base
```

To monitor progress during build and to view build statistics and more after the build has completed, point your browser to:

```
http://localhost:8000
```

To stop Toaster, enter

```
(pvenv) $ source /home/myname/poky/bitbake/bin/toaster stop
```

from within the Python virtual environment, which terminates all Toaster processes.

13.1.4 Toaster Configuration

Toaster operation can be configured and administrated through command-line options, environment variables, and the Django administrative user interface.

Setting a Different Port

By default, Toaster listens on port 8000 on all network interfaces of your build host. To change the port, start Toaster in Build mode with the webport argument, as follows:

```
(pvenv) $ /home/myname/poky/bitbake/bin/toaster webport=5000
```

Alternatively, you can start Toaster in Analysis mode with the webport argument:

```
(pvenv) $ source /home/myname/poky/bitbake/bin/toaster webport=5000
```

Toaster then listens on the provided port on all network interfaces.[2]

Setting the Toaster Directory for Build Mode

In Build mode, Toaster stores the build environment and clones of additional layers from remote repositories in a directory defined by the environment variable TOASTER_DIR. Inside that directory, Toaster creates the directory build, which contains the build

---

2. If you are familiar with Django, you may know that Django allows you not only to set the port but also specify the network interface. The latter is currently not possible with Toaster.

environment; the directory _toaster_clones, which contains the cloned layers; and the database toaster.sqlite, which stores the configuration and build data. By default, TOASTER_DIR is set to the current directory from where Toaster is started.

The only way to set the Toaster directory is to launch Toaster from a different directory. Toaster then creates a new database as well as build and layer directories.

Administrating the Django Framework

The Django web framework, on top of which Toaster is built, provides an administrative user interface that gives you direct access to the ORM stored in the database. To use the user interface, you first have to create a Django superuser. From within the Python virtual environment, execute

```
(pvenv) $ /home/myname/poky/bitbake/lib/toaster/manage.py createsuperuser
```

The command launches the Django administrative utility, which first prompts you for the following items:

- User name for the superuser (mandatory)
- E-mail address (optional)
- Password (required; you have to enter it twice for verification)

After Django creates the superuser, you can launch Toaster as usual with

```
(pvenv) $ /home/myname/poky/bitbake/bin/toaster
```

and then access the administrative user interface by entering

```
http://localhost:8000/admin
```

into your browser's navigation bar. From the administrative user interface, you can browse the Toaster ORM, add new database entries, and more.

If you start Toaster from different directories, each directory contains its own toaster.sqlite database. For each of these Toaster environments, you have to create the superuser individually.

Toaster administration provides access to the following categories:

- **Auth**: Authentication category that defines users and user groups. A local Toaster configuration does not make use of this functionality other than for the superuser. Toaster environments for production use this functionality to share Toaster instances with remote and multiple users to control access.

- **Bldcontrol**: Build control category that contains information about the build environments used by Toaster. One Toaster instance can potentially control multiple build environments on the same build host or on different build hosts over the network. For local development, there is typically only one build environment.

- **Orm**: Object-relational model category that contains information on BitBake versions, layer sources, Yocto Project releases, and Toaster settings. The latter contains various BitBake variables that you can set via the Toaster user interface by clicking on *BitBake variables* in the *Project Configuration* screen.

Typically, you do not need to access the ORM directly but can use the Toaster user interface for configuration purposes.

13.1.5 Toaster Production Deployment

A production deployment of Toaster allows sharing of the instance with multiple as well as remote users. To scale to the loads of multiple users accessing the Toaster service, Toaster uses an external web server instead of the Django built-in web server and an RDBMS instead of SQLite. A production deployment is typically also set up in Build mode rather than Analysis mode. Build mode, as we have seen, allows users to create Toaster projects and launch builds directly from the web user interface.

The web server of choice for a Django production deployment is Apache. As for the RDBMS, you have the choice between MySQL and PostgreSQL. Which you choose may depend on your preferences and prior experience. For this example, we choose MySQL.

Virtually all Linux distributions have replaced MySQL with MariaDB.[3] MariaDB is a drop-in replacement for MySQL that is maintained by the original developers of MySQL. Even though package managers of Linux distributions may still use *mysql* in package names, they actually install MariaDB.

Preparing the Production Host

To prepare your production system for Toaster setup, perform the following steps:

1. Install the prerequisites for the Yocto Project build system, as described in Chapter 2, "The Yocto Project."

2. Install Apache web server, MySQL (MariaDB) with development libraries, Python virtual environment, and the Apache Python module.

   a. On Ubuntu systems:

      ```
      $ sudo apt-get install apache2 libapache2-mod-wsgi mysql-server \
          virtualenv libmysqlclient-dev
      ```

   b. On Fedora or Red Hat systems:

      ```
      $ sudo dnf install httpd mod_wsgi python-virtualenv mysql-server \
          mysql mysql-devel
      ```

3. Start the Apache web server.

   a. On Ubuntu systems:

      ```
      $ sudo service apache2 start
      ```

---

3. https://mariadb.org

b. On Fedora or Red Hat systems:

```
$ sudo systemctl start httpd
```

Validate whether the web server is running by pointing your browser to the production host. You should see a default web page, depending on your distribution.

4. Start the database server.

a. On Ubuntu systems:

```
$ sudo service mysql start
```

b. On Fedora or RedHat systems:

```
$ sudo systemctl start mariadb
```

5. By default, MySQL (MariaDB) does not have a root password set. To set the root password for the first time, execute

```
$ mysqladmin -u root password <rootpassword>
```

6. Validate that you can log in to the MySQL (MariaDB) server:

```
$ mysql -u root -p
```

The database server should prompt you for the password that you set in the previous step and then show the command prompt.

7. Prepare the MySQL database for Toaster:

```
$ mysql -u root -p
mysql> CREATE USER 'toaster'@'localhost' identified by 'password';
mysql> CREATE DATABASE toaster;
mysql> GRANT all on toaster.* to 'toaster'@'localhost';
mysql> exit
```

Your production host is now ready for installation and configuration of Toaster.

Toaster Installation and Configuration

For production configuration, Toaster, which is part of the Poky build system, ideally is installed into the document root of the Apache web server, which allows for simpler application of the Apache access rule hierarchy. Typically, that directory is /var/www. You may install into a different directory, but you then need to adjust the Apache configuration accordingly. Perform the following steps to install and configure Toaster on your production host:

1. Create a directory in the web server document root directory and install the Poky build system. We are using /var/www/toaster as the installation directory and the Jethro branch of Poky:

```
$ sudo mkdir /var/www/toaster
$ cd /var/www/toaster
$ sudo git clone git://git.yoctoproject.org/poky
$ cd poky
$ sudo git checkout jethro
```

2. Install Python packages required by Toaster and by the Django web frame-work to access the MySQL database. We recommend using a Python virtual environment again to isolate the Toaster setup from the production host's Python setup.

```
$ cd /var/www/toaster
$ sudo virtualenv pvenv
$ source pvenv/bin/activate
$ sudo pip install -r poky/bitbake/toaster-requirements.txt
$ sudo pip install mysql
$ sudo pip install MySQL-python
```

3. Configure Toaster by editing configuration sections in the file /var/www/toaster/poky/bitbake/lib/toaster/toastermain/settings.py as follows:

   a. Modify the DATABASES section for MySQL:

   ```
   DATABASES = {
   'default': {
       'ENGINE': 'django.db.backends.mysql',
       'NAME': 'toaster',
       'USER': 'toaster',
       'PASSWORD': 'password',
       'HOST': 'localhost',
       'PORT': '3306',
     }
   }
   ```

   For database NAME, USER, and PASSWORD, use the values from step 7 of the previous section. Remove the HOST and PORT settings to use UNIX domain sockets to access the MySQL server, which is the default.

   b. Change the SECRET_KEY to a unique key:

   ```
   SECRET_KEY = 'secretkey'
   ```

   You can use OpenSSL to create an arbitrary key. The following command creates a base64-encoded key that is 16 characters long:

   ```
   $ openssl rand -baes64 16
   ```

   c. Change STATIC_ROOT to

   ```
   STATIC_ROOT = '/var/www/toaster/static/'
   ```

   Both Django and Toaster use statically served files such as HTML and JavaScript files that need to be served by the Apache web server. These files are collected and copied into this directory.

   d. Enable Build mode by changing BUILD_MODE to

   ```
   BUILD_MODE = True
   ```

4. Create database schema, load default data, and collect the statically served files:

```
$ cd /var/www/toaster/poky
$ ./bitbake/lib/toaster/manage.py syncdb
$ ./bitbake/lib/toaster/manage.py migrate
```

```
$ TOASTER_DIR=`pwd` TOASTER_CONF=./meta-yocto/conf/toasterconf.json\
    ./bitbake/lib/toaster/manage.py checksettings
$ sudo ./bitbake/lib/toaster/manage.py collectstatic
```

A couple of explanations concerning the steps are in order:

- The syncdb and migrate commands create the database schema. They also install Django's authentication system, which asks you if you want to create a superuser for access to the administrative user interface. We recommend doing so at this time. Alternatively, you can create a superuser at a later time, as described earlier in the section "Administrating the Django Framework."

- The checksettings command loads the Toaster configuration data from the file poky/meta-yocto/conf/toasterconf.json. This file contains the default configuration as well as information on layer sources. The TOASTER_DIR environment variable determines where Toaster creates the build environment. Using pwd, as in the preceding example, places the build environment into the /var/www/toaster/ poky directory, which may not be desirable because the build environment gets quite large. You can specify a different directory—just make sure that it exists and is writable by the user who will be running the Toaster builds.

- The collectstatic command retrieves the statically served files, as described earlier. Unlike the other commands, you have to run collectstatic with root privileges unless you change permissions on the static directory.

Web Server Configuration

This step integrates Toaster with the Apache web server. You need a *Web Server Gateway Interface (WSGI)* configuration file in the Apache configuration directory of your production host.

On Ubuntu and Debian systems, create the file

```
/etc/apache2/conf-available/toaster.conf
```

On Fedora and Red Hat systems, create the file

```
/etc/httpd/conf.d/toaster.conf
```

with the content of Listing 13-1.

Listing 13-1 **WSGI Configuration (toaster.conf)**

```
Alias /static /var/www/toaster/static
    <Directory /var/www/toaster/static>
            Order allow,deny
            Allow from all
            Require all granted
    </Directory>

WSGIDaemonProcess toaster_wsgi \
    python-path=/var/www/toaster/poky/bitbake/lib/toaster: \
    /var/www/toaster/pvenv/lib/python2.7/site-packages
WSGIProcessGroup toaster_wsgi
```

```
WSGIScriptAlias / \
    "/var/www/toaster/poky/bitbake/lib/toaster/toastermain/wsgi.py"
```

If you changed the location of the Poky installation and/or the Python virtual environment from the example, make sure that you adjust them accordingly in the `WSGIDaemonProcess` setting.

On Ubuntu and Debian systems, you need to explicitly enable the WSGI module and the Toaster configuration with

```
$ sudo a2enmod wsgi
$ sudo a2enconf toaster
```

That step is not required on Fedora and Red Hat systems.

Finally, you need to restart the Apache web server. On Ubuntu and Debian systems, use

```
$ sudo service apache2 restart
```

On Fedora and Red Hat systems, use

```
$ sudo systemctl restart httpd
```

Now enter the hostname or IP address of your production host into the navigation bar of your web browser, and you should see the Toaster landing page. If you get an error message, consult the Apache web server's log files in `/var/log/apache2` on Ubuntu and Debian systems or `/var/log/httpd` on Fedora and Red Hat systems, for detailed information on the root cause of the error.

Installing the Build Runner Service

The build runner service needs to be running to execute builds. The service creates a Yocto Project build environment with the configuration settings for `bblayers.conf` and `local.conf` and executes BitBake with the provided image target. To start the build runner service, use

```
$ source /var/www/toaster/pvenv/bin/activate
(pvenv) $ /var/www/toaster/poky/bitbake/lib/toaster/mangage.py runbuilds
```

You may wrap that into a simple shell script to simplify execution, as shown in Listing 13-2.

Listing 13-2 Toaster Build Runner Shell Script (`toasterbuildrunner.sh`)

```
#!/bin/sh
# Launch Toaster Build Runner on a production host
pushd /var/www/toaster
source ./pvenv/bin/activate
./poky/bitbake/lib/toaster/manage.py runbuilds
```

Do not run the build runner service as root. The build runner service executes itBake, and BitBake refuses to run with root privileges. Make sure that the user running the build runner service has full access to the directory you specified with TOASTER_DIR when installing and configuring Toaster.

Now you can launch builds from the Toaster web user interface.

Maintaining Your Toaster Production Instance

To keep your Toaster production instance up to date at all times, you regularly need to update the layer source information in the database. This ensures that you always have access to the latest layers and recipes. To load the latest layer information into the Toaster database, use the command

```
$ /var/www/toaster/poky/bitbake/lib/toaster/manage.py lsupdates
```

To update your production toaster instance to a later version of the Yocto Project, use

```
$ cd /var/www/toaster/poky
$ git pull
$ git checkout <branch>
$ TOASTER_DIR=`pwd` TOASTER_CONF=./meta-yocto/conf/toasterconf.json \
    ./bitbake/lib/toaster/manage.py checksettings
$ sudo ./bitbake/lib/toaster/manage.py collectstatic
```

Running checksettings populates the database with updated release and layer information from the toasterconf.json file. Executing collectstatic ensures that user interface updates are made available to the web server. After updating, make sure that you restart the web server.

13.1.6 Toaster Web User Interface

The Toaster web user interface provides the following functionality:

- **Project Management**: Create, configure, and view Toaster projects. A Toaster project is similar to a build environment that you create from the command line by sourcing oe-init-build-env. Toaster creates and manages the build environments for you. For a project, you select the Yocto Project release that you want to use to build your project with.

- **Build Configuration**: Within a Toaster project, you can configure machine, distribution, and other settings as you would by editing the conf/local.conf file of a build environment. The Toaster user interface provides direct access to common configuration variables, such as DISTRO, IMAGE_FSTYPES, IMAGE_INSTALL_append, PACKAGE_CLASSES, and SDKMACHINE. You can add other variables as you wish. However, some variables are precluded. These are variables that affect the configuration of the build host and variables that set paths to where build artifacts are stored such as SSTATE_DIR and TMPDIR.

- **Layer Management**: The Toaster user interface allows you to add and remove layers to your project. You can also browse a list of available layers. The three layers meta, yocto, and yocto-bsp are by default included in a project and are checked out automatically from the Poky repository. Information about layers from the OpenEmbedded Layer Index is obtained directly from the web and shown in the Toaster user interface. You can add those layers to your project by a simple click of a button. These layers are checked out from the OpenEmbedded Layer repositories on demand. In addition, you can import your own layers from Git repositories. You need to ensure that the layers you are importing are compatible with the Yocto Project release you have chosen for your project.

- **Image Targets**: Toaster identifies and lists the image targets from the various available layers. If an image target is available from a layer that is already included with your build configuration, then you can build it directly by clicking a *Build recipe* button next to the image target. Otherwise, click the *Add layer* button to add the layer to your build configuration. If a layer is dependent on other layers, Toaster informs you about the dependencies and includes them automatically.

- **Package Recipes**: Toaster maintains a list of all recipes of all layers, whether already included with your build or not. A search function assists in finding a particular recipe. For example, entering *jdk* into the search bar lists all recipes that provide the Java JDK. With the click of a button, you can add the layer containing the recipe and build it. However, building a recipe does not automatically add it to IMAGE_INSTALL. You have to do this explicitly by editing the IMAGE_INSTALL_ append variable from the BitBake variables screen.

- **Build Log**: You can directly view and examine trace, warning, and error messages from the Toaster user interface. You can also download the build log from Toaster to your local machine.

- **Build Statistics and Performance Information**: Toaster collects build statistics such as overall build time, time per task, CPU usage, and disk I/O.

- **Image Information**: Toaster collects and presents information on what software packages have been built and included with your image. You can browse the structure of your image from the Toaster user interface and view dependency relationships between recipes and packages.

While Toaster allows you to select and build a particular recipe and include it with your image, you cannot directly choose a specific version of a recipe to build if a layer provides more than one for it. Typically, as we have seen earlier, the build system chooses the latest version of a recipe. For instance, if the latest version of the Linux Yocto kernel is 4.1 but you would like to build version 3.9, you need to add

```
PREFERRED_VERSION_linux-yocto = "3.9%"
```

to the variable configuration in the Toaster user interface.

The Yocto Project Toaster team has produced a series of instructional videos covering the various aspects of Toaster. You can find these videos on www.youtube.com. Simply enter *Yocto Project Toaster* into the YouTube search bar.

13.2 Build History

A rather large collection of recipes and configuration files processed by the build system determines what software packages are built, how they are built, how they depend on each other, and ultimately, what the completed output artifacts consist of. Those output artifacts include, but are not limited to, binary packages, the kernel and root filesystem images, and the software development kit (SDK). With so many factors influencing a build, maintaining repeatability and consistency between builds and the ability to track and audit changes is a strong requirement.

Consider the upgrade of a software package to a newer version. What seems simple enough could have major consequences if that software package depends on a newer version of a library that is shared with many other packages. In that case, building the new version of the software package automatically pulls in the newer version of the library, which could cause problems for other software packages if that library is not backwards-compatible.

The build system's *build history* function provides automated support for maintaining the build quality by recording essential information about package, images, and SDK build; storing them in files; and committing those files into a Git repository to create a traceable history. Build history is implemented by the buildhistory class that is universally inherited by all recipes. Its behavior is controlled by a couple of configuration variables that let you define where the build history is stored, from what build artifacts to collect information, and more.

13.2.1 Enabling Build History

Build history is disabled by default. You have to enable it by adding it to the INHERIT variable in the conf/local.conf file of your build environment:

```
INHERIT += "buildhistory"
BUILDHISTORY_COMMIT = "1"
```

The first statement enables the buildhistory class, which collects the build information for all recipes. The second statement enables committing all changes to the build history to a Git repository. If you are interested in gathering information only on your last build then, you can disable committing to a Git repository by setting BUILDHISTORY_COMMIT = "0".

Build history is additive, meaning that information is collected only on recipes and their tasks that have run during the build process. That implies that if you are looking for a complete build history, you have to enable it for your build environment before you start building for the first time.

13.2.2 Configuring Build History

You can tune the behavior of build history through a set of configuration variables:

- **BUILDHISTORY_DIR**: This variable specifies the path to the directory where the buildhistory class stores the build history information. The default setting is BUILDHISTORY_DIR ?= "${TOPDIR}/buildhistory. If BUILDHISTORY_COMMIT is enabled, the buildhistory class creates a Git directory in that location. Use this variable to relocate the build history.

- **BUILDHISTORY_COMMIT**: This variable controls whether the build history is committed to a local Git repository residing in BUILDHISTORY_DIR. When used for the first time on an existing build history, the buildhistory class initializes the Git repository in BUILDHISTORY_DIR. After every completed BitBake run, the changes to the build history are committed to the repository. If you want to track changes to the build history, set BUILDHISTORY_COMMIT = "1". The default setting is BUILDHISTORY_COMMIT ?= "0".

- **BUILDHISTORY_COMMIT_AUTHOR**: When using a Git repository to track build history changes over time, the variable provides a Git user name for the commits to the repository. Git requires the format of the value for the variable to be in the form of name <email@domain>. The default setting for the variable is BUILDHISTORY_COMMIT_AUTHOR ?= "buildhistory <buildhistory@${DISTRO}>. The setting of this variable has no effect unless BUILDHISTORY_COMMIT is set to "1".

- **BUILDHISTORY_FEATURES**: The buildhistory class collects analysis data for different categories:
  - **image**: Analysis data of the content of images including the installed packages.
  - **package**: Analysis data of the content of the individual packages.
  - **sdk**: Analysis data of the content of SDKs.

  You can specify any combination of these as a space-separated list. The default value is BUILDHISTORY_FEATURES ?= "image package sdk".

- **BUILDHISTORY_IMAGE_FILES**: This variable specifies a space-separated list of paths to files installed in a root filesystem image so that you can track their content. That is particularly useful for system and application configuration files. The default setting is BUILDHISTORY_IMAGE_FILES ?= "/etc/passwd /etc/group", which allows you to track changes to user and group entries. The buildhistory class uses the cp command to copy the files from the image root to the build history directories. You can use wildcards for the last segment of the path to copy multiple files with a single entry in the variable. However, subdirectories are not copied recursively. For example, using BUILDHISTORY_IMAGE_FILES = "/etc/*" copies all files in /etc but not the subdirectories. You need to specify those explicitly.

- **BUILDHISTORY_PUSH_REPO**: When using a Git repository to track the changes, which is strongly recommended, you can optionally specify a remote Git repository to push the build history to a Git repository server after it has been committed to the local repository. For BUILDHISTORY_PUSH_COMMIT to work, the variable BUILDHISTORY_COMMIT must be set to 1. The default setting for the variable is BUILDHISTORY_PUSH_REPO ?= "".

13.2.3 Pushing Build History to a Git Repository Server

In addition to tracking build history with a local Git repository on the build host, pushing all changes to a Git repository is an important tool for ensuring build quality and maintaining history. Although setup is mostly straightforward, we have dedicated this section to the topic because there are some important things to consider.

To demonstrate the setup, we use the public GitHub repository server.[4] We do not recommend using GitHub for this purpose, but it provides a simple way of testing the functionality because setting up a Git repository server is outside of the scope of this book. Before you can use GitHub, you have to create a GitHub account, which is free of charge for accounts that host only public repositories. The GitHub website explains the process very well. Then, using the GitHub web user interface, create an empty Git repository—for instance, *yp_buildhistory*. Do not create any files, and do not do an initial commit to the repository. The first commit comes from the Yocto Project build.

Although you can freely read and clone any public repository on GitHub, pushing changes to a repository requires authentication. The build system uses Secure Shell (SSH) to push changes made to the local build history Git repository to a remote Git server. When using SSH, GitHub requires *public key infrastructure (PKI)* keys for authentication. PKI consists of a public and a private key pair. You create the key pair on your build host and upload the public key to GitHub. GitHub provides good instructions on how to accomplish that task.[5] When creating SSH keys, you have the option to protect the private key with a passphrase. Doing so is not recommended if you plan to do automated builds with the Yocto Project, as the build system stops execution and asks for the passphrase to be entered.

Once you have set up a GitHub account, added a public SSH key to your account, and created a repository, you need to set up build history for your build environment. As usual, that configuration is done by setting the variables in conf/local.conf, as shown in Listing 13-3.

Listing 13-3 **Build History Configuration (`conf/local.conf`)**

```
#
# Build History Configuration
#
INHERIT += "buildhistory"
BUILDHISTORY_COMMIT = "1"
BUILDHISTORY_COMMIT_AUTHOR = "Santa Claus <santa.claus@northpole.com>"
BUILDHISTORY_DIR = "${TOPDIR}/../../yocto/buildhistory"
BUILDHISTORY_IMAGE_FILES = "/etc/passwd /etc/group"
BUILDHISTORY_PUSH_REPO = "git@github.com:sclaus/yp_buildhistory.git master"
```

---

4. https://github.com

5. https://help.github.com/articles/generating-ssh-keys

The URL used for BUILDHISTORY_PUSH_REPO is of course dependent on the setup of the remote repository. Specifying a branch, in the case of the example master, is optional but requires that the branch already exists in the remote repository, which is not the case for an empty repository. Using branches and explicitly specifying them is strongly recommended with multiple build environments pushing build history to the same remote repository, which allows for using different branches per build environment. BitBake variable expansion applies to BUILDHISTORY_PUSH_REPO as it does to any other variable. That means that you can use variables such as ${DISTRO} to specify the branch.

As the build system always commits changes in the build history to the master branch, you have to create and switch to that branch in the local build history Git repository manually using

```
$ git checkout -b <branchname>
```

After that, you can use branchname in BUILDHISTORY_PUSH_REPO.

13.2.4 Understanding the Build History

The build history is stored underneath BUILDHISTORY_DIR as a specific structure consisting of directories and files (see Listing 13-4).

Listing 13-4   **Build History Structure**

```
$ tree -L 3 buildhistory
buildhistory/
├── metadata-revs
├── images
│   ├── qemux86_64
│   │   └── glibc
│   │       └── core-image-base
│   │           ├── build-id.txt
│   │           ├── depends.dot
│   │           ├── depends-nokernel.dot
│   │           ├── depends-nokernel-nolibc.dot
│   │           ├── depends-nokernel-nolibc-noupdate.dot
│   │           ├── depends-nokernel-nolibc-noupdate-nomodules.dot
│   │           ├── files-in-image.txt
│   │           ├── image-files
│   │           ├── image-info.txt
│   │           ├── installed-package-names.txt
│   │           ├── installed-package-sizes.txt
│   │           └── installed-packages.txt
│   └── ypbkiosk
│       └── glibc
│           └── core-image-minimal-initramfs
│               ├── build-id.txt
│               ├── depends.dot
│               ├── depends-nokernel.dot
│               ├── depends-nokernel-nolibc.dot
│               ├── depends-nokernel-nolibc-noupdate.dot
│               ├── depends-nokernel-nolibc-noupdate-nomodules.dot
│               ├── files-in-image.txt
```

```
│                   │         ├── image-files
│                   │         ├── image-info.txt
│                   │         ├── installed-package-names.txt
│                   │         ├── installed-package-sizes.txt
│                   │         └── installed-packages.txt
│                   └── ypbkiosk-image-sato
│                       ├── build-id.txt
│                       ├── depends.dot
│                       ├── depends-nokernel.dot
│                       ├── depends-nokernel-nolibc.dot
│                       ├── depends-nokernel-nolibc-noupdate.dot
│                       ├── depends-nokernel-nolibc-noupdate-nomodules.dot
│                       ├── files-in-image.txt
│                       ├── image-files
│                       ├── image-info.txt
│                       ├── installed-package-names.txt
│                       ├── installed-package-sizes.txt
│                       └── installed-packages.txt
├── metadata-revs
├── packages
│   ├── all-poky-linux
│   │   ├── adwaita-icon-theme
│   │   │   ├── adwaita-icon-theme
│   │   │   │   ├── latest
│   │   │   │   ├── latest.pkg_postinst
│   │   │   │   └── latest.pkg_postrm
│   │   │   ├── adwaita-icon-theme-cursors
│   │   │   │   ├── latest
│   │   │   │   ├── latest.pkg_postinst
│   │   │   │   └── latest.pkg_postrm
│   │   │   ├── adwaita-icon-theme-hires
│   │   │   │   ├── latest
│   │   │   │   ├── latest.pkg_postinst
│   │   │   │   └── latest.pkg_postrm
...
│   ├── core2-64-poky-linux
│   │   ├── acl
│   │   │   ├── acl
│   │   │   │   ├── files-in-package.txt
│   │   │   │   └── latest
│   │   │   ├── acl-dbg
│   │   │   │   ├── files-in-package.txt
│   │   │   │   └── latest
│   │   │   ├── acl-dev
│   │   │   │   ├── files-in-package.txt
│   │   │   │   └── latest
│   │   │   ├── acl-doc
│   │   │   │   ├── files-in-package.txt
│   │   │   │   └── latest
...
└── sdk
    └── poky-glibc-x86_64-hagw-image-base-corei7-64
        └── hagw-image-base
            ├── files-in-sdk.txt
            ├── sdk-info.txt
            ├── host
            │   ├── depends.dot
            │   ├── installed-package-names.txt
```

```
|   ├── installed-package-sizes.txt
|   └── installed-packages.txt
└── target
    ├── depends.dot
    ├── installed-package-names.txt
    ├── installed-package-sizes.txt
    └── installed-packages.txt
```

At the top level are subdirectories for the categories enabled through BUILDHISTORY_
FEATURES. The subdirectories for *image* and *package* features are always present after a
successful build. The subdirectory for the *sdk* feature is created and populated only after
you have built an SDK with -c populate_sdk. In addition, the top-level directory of
the build history contains the file metadata-revs that contains the revision information
for the metadata layers used by the build system when the build was produced.

Build History Image Information

Build history image information is categorized by machine as the images in the ${DEPLOY_
DIR}/images directory. Beneath that is a subdirectory with the name of the C library used.
Unless you are building with a different C library, the name of that subdirectory is glibc.
Inside the C library subdirectory, the build system creates a subdirectory for each image
target, for instance, core-image-base. Inside the image target subdirectory are various
files and directories containing the information about the image:

- **build-id.txt**: Build configuration used, including BitBake version, build host,
  metadata layer version, and more

- **depends.dot**: Full dependency graph in textual DOT format representation, that can
  be rendered by Graphviz or other software capable of interpreting DOT format

- **depends-nokernel.dot**: Same as previous but without kernel dependencies

- **depends-nokernel-nolibc.dot**: Same as previous but without C library
  dependencies

- **depends-nokernel-nolibc-noupdate.dot**: Same as previous but without update
  dependencies

- **depends-nokernel-nolibc-noupdate-nomodules.dot**: Same as previous but without
  kernel module dependencies

- **files-in-image.txt**: List of all files in the image, essentially the output of find
  / ! -path . -printf "%M %-10u %-10g %10s %p\n" of the root filesystem

- **image-files**: Subdirectory containing the files specified by
  BUILDHISTORY_IMAGE_FILES

- **image-info.txt**: List of variables with their variables directly influencing the content and the size of the image

- **installed-package-names.txt**: Alphabetically sorted list with the names of all
  packages installed in the image

- **installed-package-sizes.txt**: List of all packages installed in the image ordered by size from largest to smallest package

- **installed-packages.txt**: Alphabetically sorted list with the full package filenames of all packages installed in the image

The image-info.txt file with its summary overview of settings provides a useful starting point for tracking changes in image contents. Among the variables stored in the file are IMAGE_CLASSES, containing a list of classes used to create the image; and IMAGE_INSTALL, IMAGE_FEATURES, and ROOTFS_POSTPROCESS_COMMAND, which are directly involved in compiling the content of a root file system.

Build History Package Information

Build history for packages is organized into subdirectories by architecture and includes packages created for the build host as well as for the target. The architecture subdirectories are the same as used inside ${BASE_WORKDIR}.

Each package has its own subdirectory containing a file named latest and subdirectories for every installation package created during the package splitting process. The package top-level latest file contains the package version (PV) and package revision (PR) information, the list of build dependencies (DEPENDS), and the list of installation packages created (PACKAGES). If the package was created from sources fetched from a version control system such as Git, the directory also contains the file latest_srcrev, which contains a list with the source revisions for the branches used.

Each of the installation package subdirectories contains one or more files with information on the package:

- **latest**: List of variables and their values determining the package contents during build. This list includes PV, PR, RPROVIDES, RDEPENDS, FILES, and an entry PKGSIZE with the total package size in kilobytes.

- **files-in-package.txt**: List of all files contained in the package with their paths and sizes.

- **latest.pkg_***: Files that contain any commands performed by the package manager prior to or after carrying out a particular command, such as install, update, or remove.

The source revision information contained in a package's latest_srcrev is important when you are looking to fix source revisions for packages that use AUTOREV to automatically retrieve the latest revision from a repository branch. You can use the script buildhistory-collect-srcrevs to gather the source revisions from the build history in a format that you can directly use in a configuration file such as conf/local.conf or a distribution policy file. For each package obtained from a version control system source, the script produces a line in the form of

```
SRCREV_pn-<packagename> = "<versiontag>"
```

By default, the script produces output only for the packages that are using AUTOREV unless you use -a or --report-all to the command line when invoking the script.

Specifying SRCREV_pn-<packagename> in a configuration does not prevent the variable being overridden by append files to a recipe or elsewhere in the build configuration. To prevent overriding, forcevariable must be added:

```
SRCREV_pn-<packagename>_forcevariable = "<versiontag>"
```

The script can automatically add forcevariable when -f or --forcevariable is added to the command line.

Build History SDK Information

When an SDK target is processed by the build system, build history collects information on the content of the SDK. Multiple SDKs are separated into subdirectories by distribution and image target. Because SDKs are built for the build host as well as for the target, the build history contains information for each of them. The build history directory for an SDK contains the following:

- **files-in-sdk.txt**: A list of files included in the SDK. This list is for the build host and for the target.
- **sdk-info.txt**: List of configuration variables and their values that determine the content of the SDK as well as an entry for the size of the SDK:
  - **DISTRO**: Distribution policy.
  - **DISTRO_VERSION**: Version string of the distribution.
  - **SDK_NAME**: Name string of the SDK.
  - **SDK_VERSION**: Version string of the SDK.
  - **SDKMACHINE SDK**: Machine information.
  - **SDKIMAGE_FEATURES**: List of image features used to build the SDK root filesystem, typically dev-pkgs and dbg-pkgs.
  - **SDKSIZE**: Size of the SDK.
- **host** and **target**: Directories containing files with information on the host and target SDK. These files are created in both directories:
  - **depends.dot**: Full dependency graph in textual DOT format representation that can be rendered with Graphviz or other software capable of interpreting DOT format.
  - **installed-package-names.txt**: List with package names installed in the SDK in alphabetical order.
  - **installed-package-sizes.txt**: List with package names and the sizes of the packages installed in the SDK, ordered from largest to smallest package.
  - **installed-packages.txt**: Alphabetically sorted list with the full package file-names of all packages installed in the SDK.

13.3 Source Mirrors

In Chapter 4, "BitBake Build Engine," Section 4.5, we discussed how the build system accesses and downloads sources and how *mirror sites* can be used to set up alternative download locations without modifying SRC_URI inside recipes.

Setting up your own mirror site makes good sense for various reasons:

- Avoid downloading multiple gigabytes of source packages from the Internet for teams with many developers.
- Ensure that all developers of a team are building from the same sources for consistency and repeatability.
- Control source package versions for product delivery.

13.3.1 Using Source Mirrors

We have seen that after checking whether a source package is available from the local download directory, as specified by the DL_DIR, the build system first uses the mirror sites specified by the variable PREMIRRORS for remote access to source packages. The variable contains a list of tuples delimited by a newline character that specify regular expressions for the key to match the SRC_URI. Each key represents a scheme for a particular protocol, such as FTP, HTTP, HTTPS, Git, and so on. You can of course specify the PREMIRRORS variable directly yourself in the conf/local.conf file of your build environment. However, more conveniently, you can use the own-mirrors class and the variable SOURCE_MIRROR_URL. As Listing 13-5 shows, the own-mirrors class contains nothing more than an assignment of the PREMIRRORS variable.

Listing 13-5 **own-mirrors Class**

```
PREMIRRORS() {
cvs://.*/.*        ${SOURCE_MIRROR_URL}
svn://.*/.*        ${SOURCE_MIRROR_URL}
git://.*/.*        ${SOURCE_MIRROR_URL}
gitsm://.*/.*      ${SOURCE_MIRROR_URL}
hg://.*/.*         ${SOURCE_MIRROR_URL}
bzr://.*/.*        ${SOURCE_MIRROR_URL}
p4://.*/.*         ${SOURCE_MIRROR_URL}
osc://.*/.*        ${SOURCE_MIRROR_URL}
https?$://.*/.*    ${SOURCE_MIRROR_URL}
ftp://.*/.*        ${SOURCE_MIRROR_URL}
}
```

The class essentially does all the work for you by assigning the variable SOURCE_MIRROR_URL to all of the protocol schemes supported by the build system's fetchers. All you have to do is inherit the own-mirrors class and set the SOURCE_MIRROR_URL variable to your own mirror site in the conf/local.conf file of your build environment:

```
SOURCE_MIRROR_URL ?= "file:///path/to/directory/"
INHERIT += "own-mirrors"
```

The example uses the `file:` scheme to directly access file systems which can be local or any type of remote file system such as Network File System (NFS). Alternatively, you can use `ftp:`, `http:`, and `https:` schemes for the build system to access your mirror site. For team development, it may also make sense to use your distribution policy rather than the local build environment configuration to set your own mirrors.

Using the `own-mirrors` class with `SOURCE_MIRROR_URL` or setting `PREMIRRORS` directly does not prevent the build system from accessing other download sources such as `SRC_URI` of recipes or *postmirrors* specified by `MIRRORS`. However, for product development, it is essential that the build system does not inadvertently fetch any source packages from uncontrolled locations. Disabling postmirrors can be achieved simply by setting `MIRRORS` to an empty string; however, globally disabling `SRC_URI` in recipes is not possible.

Using

```
BB_NO_NETWORK = "1"
```

disables network access for fetching from any download source, including the ones specified by `PREMIRRORS`. This works fine if you intend to use only the `file:` scheme for your mirror site. However, for a setup useful for team development with automated build and quality assurance, you want to enable fetching from controlled mirror sites using FTP, HTTP, or HTTPS protocols without the risk of inadvertently fetching source packages from the Internet. You can achieve this be restricting access to `PREMIRRORS` only by setting

```
BB_FETCH_PREMIRRORONLY = "1"
```

In addition, or alternatively, you can restrict network access to specific hosts. The variable `BB_ALLOWED_NETWORKS` specifies a white-space delimited list of hosts from which the build system is allowed to fetch source packages:

```
BB_ALLOWED_HOSTS = "server1.acme.com server2.acme.com"
```

This example allows fetching from the server1 and server2 belonging to the acme.com domain. Basic wildcard matching is provided against the beginning of host names: for instance

```
BB_ALLOWED_HOSTS = "*.acme.com"
```

allows fetching from any host belonging to the acme.com domain.

When using `BB_ALLOWED_HOSTS`, hosts listed in the mirror variables `PREMIRRORS` and `MIRRORS` are simply skipped, and a log message is recorded. Accessing a `SRC_URI` with a host that is not contained in `BB_ALLOWED_HOSTS` results in an error.

Using `BB_ALLOWED_HOSTS` in conjunction with the `own-mirrors` class and `SOURCE_MIRROR_URL` or directly with `PREMIRRORS` allows you to utilize network protocol schemes while preventing the build system from accessing any download sites that are not listed in `BB_ALLOWED_HOSTS`. Adding hosts listed in `BB_ALLOWED_HOSTS` to `SOURCE_MIRROR_URL` or `PREMIRRORS` results in sources being fetched only from authorized hosts. If a source package is missing on the mirror sites, the build system tries to retrieve it by using `SRC_URI` from the recipe. That results in a failure, as the upstream host in `SRC_URI` is not listed by BB_ALLOWED_HOSTS. That is exactly the behavior you would want because it notifies you of any attempt to access sources from uncontrolled sites.

13.3.2 Setting Up Source Mirrors

How to set up a source mirror is up to you. You have to decide if you want to mount a filesystem export from the source mirror on your build host and use the file: scheme or if you would rather set up an HTTP/HTTPS or FTP server. In any case, you have to download the source packages once using the build system and then copy them from the download directory specified by DL_DIR to your mirror host.

Sources that are directly checked out from remote source repositories such as Git, Apache Subversion (SVN), Perforce, and so on, are placed into the download directory as trees. That makes them unsuitable for simple copies to the mirror site that later can be accessed via file:, ftp:, http:, or https: schemes. Using

```
BB_GENERATE_MIRROR_TARBALLS = "1"
```

in the conf/local.conf file of your build environment causes the build system to create tarballs from repository trees that you then can easily copy to your mirror site together with the other source packages. For performance reasons, BB_GENERATE_MIRROR_TARBALLS is disabled by default.

Following a few simple steps lets you set up your own source mirror:

1. Set up your build environment and enable BB_GENERATE_MIRROR_TARBALLS.

2. Start a build with bitbake -c fetchall <target>, where <target> is any comprehensive image target such as core-image-sato.

3. Copy all the source tarballs contained in the download directory to your mirror host.

4. Set up a build environment to inherit own-mirrors and point SOURCE_MIRROR_URL to your new mirror. You can disable BB_GENERATE_MIRROR_TARBALLS.

5. Start a build to test fetching from your new mirror.

6. Fine-tune your setup by setting BB_NO_NETWORK or BB_ALLOWED_HOSTS as required.

13.4 Autobuilder

The *Yocto Project Autobuilder* is an automated build system based on the open source continuous integration framework *Buildbot*.[6] Buildbot is an extensible framework for automating software builds, quality assurance, and release processes.

Buildbot is implemented in Python using the *Twisted Python*[7] event-driven networking engine. Buildbot is a job scheduling system: it queues jobs, monitors resources

---

6. http://buildbot.net

7. https://twistedmatrix.com/trac

necessary to execute jobs, executes jobs when the resources become available, and reports the results.

A Buildbot deployment typically comprises at least one *controller* and a collection of *workers*. The controllers monitor source code repositories, schedule the jobs, coordinate the workers, and report results of the job execution. Controllers provide a web user interface for users to interact with the system. Workers can be deployed either on the same system as a controller or on separate systems, which makes Buildbot a distributed build engine. Controllers dispatch *builders* to the workers, which execute them and report the results back to the controllers.

Buildbot configuration is done through Python scripts, which can be as simple as setting configuration variables. However, full Python functionality is available, allowing dynamic generation of configuration through Python code.

The Yocto Project Autobuilder extends Buildbot with a set of standard builders for Yocto Project targets. The Yocto Project build infrastructure uses Autobuilder for nightly builds, continuous integration, and release builds. You can access the Yocto Project Autobuilder via its front page at https://autobuilder.yoctoproject.org. Unless you have a login to the Yocto Project Autobuilder, you cannot schedule and execute builds yourself, but you can look at the current status of the latest builds and the build history. You can also download builds of images for various machines, Eclipse plugins, and many more, directly from the publish directory[8] of the Yocto Project Autobuilder.

The Yocto Project build team has packaged Autobuilder with setup and execution scripts, which make it a matter of minutes to get an instance of Autobuilder running on your own system.

13.4.1 Installing Autobuilder

A basic installation and configuration of Autobuilder with one controller and one worker running on the same host can be done in three simple steps:

```
$ git clone git://yoctoproject.org/yocto-autobuilder
$ cd yocto-autobuilder
$ source yocto-autobuilder-setup
```

That's it. The yocto-autobuilder-setup script produces a lot of output, some of which you should note:

- **Client–Server Password**: This is the password that workers use to identify themselves with the controller. This password is used in the controller configuration file yocto-controller/controller.cfg and in the worker configuration file yocto-worker/buildbot.tac.

- **User Name and Password**: The script creates a user name and password for the web user interface and stores them in the file yocto-autobuilder/.htpasswd. The password is stored in encrypted form, so you need to make a note of the password.

---

8. http://autobuilder.yoctoproject.org/pub

If you forget or lose your password, you can create a new one and write it to the password file with

```
$ cd yocto-autobuilder
$ ./bin/htpasswd -b .htpasswd <username> <password>
```

Make sure that you use the `./bin/htpasswd` command provided with Autobuilder and not the one that is installed on your system.

- **Environment Variables**: The script adds Autobuilder paths to the environment variables `PYTHONPATH` and `PATH` and sets the variable `YOCTO_AB_CONFIG` and prints their values to the console. You can copy and paste the settings into your `.bashrc` file, or you can source the script every time you want to use Autobuilder. Sourcing the script again is safe. It detects previous settings, such as existing configuration and password files, and does not overwrite them.

Now you can start Autobuilder with

```
$ ./auto-start-autobuilder both
```

which starts a controller and a worker on the same node. The script takes the following arguments:

- **both**: Start controller and worker.
- **controller**: Start the controller only.
- **worker**: Start the worker only.

To stop Autobuilder, use the `yocto-stop-autobuilder`, which takes the same arguments as the start script.

After starting Autobuilder, point your web browser to

```
localhost:8010
```

which takes you to the Autobuilder landing page. From there, you can log into Autobuilder using your user name and password.

Click the *Builders* link, which takes you to a list of all the configured builders. Click one, such as *nightly-x86-64*. To force start a builder outside its regular schedule, click the *Force Build* button. Once the builder is started, you can watch its progress in the *Waterfall* view.

13.4.2 Configuring Autobuilder

Autobuilder configuration is done through a series of configuration files. These are not BitBake configuration files. That means you do not have BitBake variable expansion at your disposal.

Autobuilder Global Configuration File

The file `config/autobuilder.conf` is the global Autobuilder configuration file. The file is divided into sections. Each section is introduced by the section name in square brackets. Each section contains one or more configuration variables. Section names and variable names are mostly self-explanatory. Here we discuss the parameters you most commonly would want to adjust.

- **[GitSettings]**: Handling of Git repositories.
  - **OPTIMIZED_GIT_CLONE**: If set to True, Git repositories get moved to a temporary storage location after use rather than being deleted from within Autobuilder. That speeds up the build process but requires external cleanup of the obsolete directories with a cronjob. The default setting is True. However, this setting can be rather disk-space intensive. If your workers are low on disk space, you may want to consider disabling this setting.
  - **OGIT_TRASH_DIR**: Directory to which obsolete Git repositories get moved.
  - **OGIT_MIRROR_DIR**: Directory to which to clone Git repositories.
  - **OGIT_TRASH_CRON_TIME**: Cronjob settings for cleaning up obsolete Git repositories.
  - **OGIT_TRASH_NICE_LEVEL**: Priority level for the cleanup task.
- **[BuildHistorySettings]**: Whether Autobuilder should collect build history and where to store it.
  - **BUILD_HISTORY_COLLECT**: If set to True, Autobuilder collects the build history.
  - **BUILD_HISTORY_DIR**: Directory where the build history is stored.
  - **BUILD_HISTORY_REPO**: Remote repository for the build history.
- **[ErrorReportSettings]**: Whether Autobuilder collects, stores, and publishes reports on errors encountered by Autobuilder.
  - **ERROR_REPORT_COLLECT**: If set to True, Autobuilder collects error reports.
  - **ERROR_REPORT_EMAIL**: E-mail address to which error reports are sent.
- **[PublishSettings]**: If and where to publish build artifacts.
  - **PUBLSIH_BUILDS**: If set to True, Autobuilder publishes images and package feeds to MACHINE_PUBLISH_DIR, QEMU_PUBLISH_DIR, RPM_PUBLISH_DIR, DEB_PUBLISH_DIR, and IPK_PUBLISH_DIR, which are subdirectories of BUILD_PUBLISH_DIR.
  - **PUBLISH_SOURCE_MIRROR**: If set to True, Autobuilder publishes the source files to be used for a source mirror to SOURCE_PUBLISH_DIR.
  - **PUBLISH_SSTATE**: If set to True, Autobuilder publishes the shared state cache to SSTATE_PUBLISH_DIR.
- **[BuildSettings]**: Settings for the conf/local.conf file of the build environments used by the worker.
- **[QAEmail]**: E-mail addresses to which Autobuilder should send e-mail about build results.

Typically, you probably want to adjust directories for build artifacts and other data you need to keep. The default settings store all files in /tmp/yocto-autobuilder, which is lost when the system reboots.

Controller Configuration File

The file yocto-controller/controller.cfg contains the configuration settings for the controller. This file uses Python syntax. All configuration is stored in a dictionary named BuildmasterConfig. These are Buildbot configuration settings that are explained in detail by the Buildbot documentation at http://docs.buildbot.net. We cover the most important ones here:

- **c['debugPassword']**: If set, you can use the Buildbot debug client to connect to the controller.

- **c['title']**: Title that appears on top of the Autobuilder web page.

- **c['titleURL']**: URL that is embedded in the title (typically matches c['buildbotURL']).

- **c['buildbotURL']**: URL, host, and port that Autobuilder's web server listens to.

- **c['workers']**: List of workers that are recognized by the controller. Each worker must have a unique name and a password it uses to authenticate itself with the controller. Worker name and password must match the respective values of the worker configuration.

- **c['workerPortnum']**: TCP port number the controller listens on for worker connections. The port number must match the port number of the worker configuration.

- **c['status']**: List of status targets to which Autobuilder publishes build status reports. Buildbot offers a variety of status targets, such as web pages, e-mail senders, and Internet Relay Chat (IRC) bots. The Buildbot documentation contains the details on how to configure the various status targets.

- **c['db']**: Database that Autobuilder uses to store its status information. The default is a SQLite database. Other databases, including MySQL and PostgreSQL, can be configured. The Buildbot documentation explains the details. For performance reasons, you would want to use an RDBMS rather than SQLite for productions systems.

You can set other configuration options in the file, such as c['multiMaster'], which allows using multiple controllers to create even more scalable build factories.

Worker Configuration File

The file yocto-worker/buildbot.tac contains the worker configuration. This file also uses Python syntax. These are the settings you need to adjust to create a distributed system:

- **buildmaster_host**: Host name or IP address of the host the controller is running on.

- **port**: The port number the controller listens on for worker connections. The value must match c['workerPortnum'] of the controller configuration.

- **workername**: Unique name for the worker. The value must match the name of the worker in c['workers'] of the controller configuration.

- **passwd**: The password for authentication with the controller. The value must match the password used for the worker in c['workers'] of the controller configuration.

Buildset Configuration

The Autobuilder root directory contains multiple directories whose names all begin with buildset-. A buildset in Buildbot lingo is a series of steps that are executed in the order defined by the buildset. Listing 13-6 shows the Autobuilder buildset for the nightly x86_64 build.

Listing 13-6 **Buildset nightly-x86-64 (`buildset-config/nightly-x86-64.conf`)**

```
[nightly-x86-64]
builders: 'example-worker'
repos: [{'poky':
          {'repourl':'git://git.yoctoproject.org/poky',
           'layerversion': {'core':'meta', 'yoctobsp':'meta-yocto-bsp'},
           'branch':'master'}}]
steps: [{'SetDest': {}},
       {'CheckOutLayers': {}},
       {'RunPreamble': {}},
       {'GetDistroVersion': {'distro': 'poky'}},
       {'CreateAutoConf': {'machine': 'qemux86-64', 'SDKMACHINE': 'i686',
                           'distro': 'poky', 'buildhistory': True}},
       {'CreateBBLayersConf': {'buildprovider': 'yocto'}},
       {'SyncPersistDB': {'distro': 'poky'}},
       {'GetBitbakeVersion': {}},
       {'BuildImages': {'images': 'core-image-sato core-image-sato-dev
                                   core-image-sato-sdk core-image-minimal
                                   core-image-minimal-dev'}},
       {'RunSanityTests': {'images': 'core-image-minimal core-image-sato
                                      core-image-sato-sdk'}},
       {'CreateAutoConf': {'machine': 'genericx86-64',
                           'SDKMACHINE': 'i686',
                           'buildhistory': False, 'distro': 'poky'}},
       {'BuildImages': {'images': 'core-image-sato core-image-sato-dev
                                   core-image-sato-sdk core-image-minimal
                                   core-image-minimal-dev'}},
       {'CreateAutoConf': {'machine': 'qemux86-64',
                           'SDKMACHINE': 'i686',
                           'distro': 'poky', 'buildhistory': False}},
       {'BuildToolchainImages': {}},
       {'RunSDKSanityTests': {'images': 'core-image-sato'}},
       {'CreateAutoConf': {'machine': 'qemux86-64',
                           'SDKMACHINE': 'x86_64',
                           'distro': 'poky', 'buildhistory': False}},
       {'BuildToolchainImages': {}},
       {'RunSDKSanityTests': {'images': 'core-image-sato'}},
```

```
{'SyncPersistDB': {'commit': True, 'distro':'poky'}},
{'PublishLayerTarballs': {}},
{'SendErrorReport': {}},
{'UploadToasterEventlog': {}},
{'PublishArtifacts': {'artifacts': ['qemux86-64', 'genericx86-64',
                       'ipk', 'toolchain', 'md5sums']}}]
```

A buildset typically contains at least these elements:

- **Buildset Name**: Name of the buildset in square brackets.
- **Repos**: A list of dictionaries containing the descriptions of the repositories to monitor. A repository description is itself a dictionary with the keys repourl, layerversion, and branch.
- **Steps**: A list of dictionaries with buildsteps. The build steps are Python classes located in lib/python2.7/site-packages/autobuilder/buildsteps of the Autobuilder root directory. Steps may take arguments, which are provided as dictionaries.

The Buildbot documentation contains general examples and explanations on how to create buildsets and buildsteps. The file README-NEW-AUTOBUILDER explains how Autobuilder buildsets and buildsteps are configured.

13.5 Summary

In this chapter, we described tools and techniques you can employ to scale the Yocto Project build system to development teams and production environment.

- Toaster extends the build system with a web user interface, allowing remote deployment and shared build resources.
- The build history provides tracking of build configuration and build output. It is an important tool to maintain build quality and repeatability. Starting from a baseline created by an initial build, changes to configuration and metadata artifacts are stored in a Git repository to create a seamless history of cause and effect.
- Through the use of source mirrors, development teams can share source downloads, and production environments can control from which software packages images for product deployment are created.
- Autobuilder provides an automated continuous build and integration system for Yocto Project builds. It is a complete out-of-the-box solution ready to be deployed within a short amount of time. Its default buildsets cover all standard Yocto Project build targets. They are a solid foundation that can easily be extended and adapted to your own requirements.

13.6 References

Buildbot Documentation, http://docs.buildbot.net

Yocto Project Autobuilder, https://www.yoctoproject.org/tools-resources/projects/autobuilder

Yocto Project Reference Manual, www.yoctoproject.org/docs/2.0/ref-manual/ref-manual.html

Yocto Project Toaster Manual, www.yoctoproject.org/docs/2.0/toaster-manual/toaster-manual.html

A

Open Source Licenses

In This Appendix

The list of open source licenses is rather long. The OpenEmbedded Build System provides the texts of 173 licenses used in its `meta/files/common-licenses` directory. The Open Source Initiative (OSI)[1] analyzes and reviews licenses and publishes a list of approved open source licenses with the goal to educate users, developers, businesses, and government agencies about open source licensing. For reference, the verbatim texts of four of the most common open source licenses are provided in this appendix.

A.1 MIT License (MIT)

The MIT License (MIT)
Copyright (c) <year> <copyright holders>
Permission is hereby granted, free of charge, to any person obtaining a copy of this software and associated documentation files (the "Software"), to deal in the Software without restriction, including without limitation the rights to use, copy, modify, merge, publish, distribute, sublicense, and/or sell copies of the Software, and to permit persons to whom the Software is furnished to do so, subject to the following conditions:

The above copyright notice and this permission notice shall be included in all copies or substantial portions of the Software.

THE SOFTWARE IS PROVIDED "AS IS", WITHOUT WARRANTY OF ANY KIND, EXPRESS OR IMPLIED, INCLUDING BUT NOT LIMITED TO THE WARRANTIES OF MERCHANTABILITY, FITNESS FOR A PARTICULAR PURPOSE AND NONINFRINGEMENT. IN NO EVENT SHALL THE AUTHORS OR COPYRIGHT HOLDERS BE LIABLE FOR ANY CLAIM, DAMAGES OR OTHER LIABILITY, WHETHER IN AN ACTION OF CONTRACT, TORT OR OTHERWISE, ARISING FROM, OUT OF OR IN CONNECTION WITH THE SOFTWARE OR THE USE OR OTHER DEALINGS IN THE SOFTWARE.

---

1. https://opensource.org

A.2 GNU General Public License (GPL) Version 2

GNU GENERAL PUBLIC LICENSE

Version 2, June 1991

Copyright (C) 1989, 1991 Free Software Foundation, Inc.

51 Franklin Street, Fifth Floor, Boston, MA 02110-1301 USA

Everyone is permitted to copy and distribute verbatim copies of this license document, but changing it is not allowed.

Preamble

The licenses for most software are designed to take away your freedom to share and change it. By contrast, the GNU General Public License is intended to guarantee your freedom to share and change free software—to make sure the software is free for all its users. This General Public License applies to most of the Free Software Foundation's software and to any other program whose authors commit to using it. (Some other Free Software Foundation software is covered by the GNU Library General Public License instead.) You can apply it to your programs, too.

When we speak of free software, we are referring to freedom, not price. Our General Public Licenses are designed to make sure that you have the freedom to distribute copies of free software (and charge for this service if you wish), that you receive source code or can get it if you want it, that you can change the software or use pieces of it in new free programs; and that you know you can do these things.

To protect your rights, we need to make restrictions that forbid anyone to deny you these rights or to ask you to surrender the rights. These restrictions translate to certain responsibilities for you if you distribute copies of the software, or if you modify it.

For example, if you distribute copies of such a program, whether gratis or for a fee, you must give the recipients all the rights that you have. You must make sure that they, too, receive or can get the source code. And you must show them these terms so they know their rights.

We protect your rights with two steps: (1) copyright the software, and (2) offer you this license which gives you legal permission to copy, distribute and/or modify the software.

Also, for each author's protection and ours, we want to make certain that everyone understands that there is no warranty for this free software. If the software is modified by someone else and passed on, we want its recipients to know that what they have is not the original, so that any problems introduced by others will not reflect on the original authors' reputations.

Finally, any free program is threatened constantly by software patents. We wish to avoid the danger that redistributors of a free program will individually obtain patent licenses, in effect making the program proprietary. To prevent this, we have made it clear that any patent must be licensed for everyone's free use or not licensed at all.

The precise terms and conditions for copying, distribution and modification follow.

Terms and Conditions for Copying, Distribution and Modification

0. This License applies to any program or other work which contains a notice placed by the copyright holder saying it may be distributed under the terms of this General Public License. The "Program", below, refers to any such program or work, and a "work based on the Program" means either the Program or any derivative work under copyright law: that is to say, a work containing the Program or a portion of it, either verbatim or with modifications and/or translated into another language. (Hereinafter, translation is included without limitation in the term "modification".) Each licensee is addressed as "you".

   Activities other than copying, distribution and modification are not covered by this License; they are outside its scope. The act of running the Program is not restricted, and the output from the Program is covered only if its contents constitute a work based on the Program (independent of having been made by running the Program). Whether that is true depends on what the Program does.

1. You may copy and distribute verbatim copies of the Program's source code as you receive it, in any medium, provided that you conspicuously and appropriately publish on each copy an appropriate copyright notice and disclaimer of warranty; keep intact all the notices that refer to this License and to the absence of any warranty; and give any other recipients of the Program a copy of this License along with the Program.

   You may charge a fee for the physical act of transferring a copy, and you may at your option offer warranty protection in exchange for a fee.

2. You may modify your copy or copies of the Program or any portion of it, thus forming a work based on the Program, and copy and distribute such modifications or work under the terms of Section 1 above, provided that you also meet all of these conditions:

   a. You must cause the modified files to carry prominent notices stating that you changed the files and the date of any change.

   b. You must cause any work that you distribute or publish, that in whole or in part contains or is derived from the Program or any part thereof, to be licensed as a whole at no charge to all third parties under the terms of this License.

   c. If the modified program normally reads commands interactively when run, you must cause it, when started running for such interactive use in the most ordinary way, to print or display an announcement including an appropriate copyright notice and a notice that there is no warranty (or else, saying that you provide a warranty) and that users may redistribute the program under these conditions, and telling the user how to view a copy of this License. (Exception: if the Program itself is interactive but does not normally print such an announcement, your work based on the Program is not required to print an announcement.)

These requirements apply to the modified work as a whole. If identifiable sections of that work are not derived from the Program, and can be reasonably considered independent and separate works in themselves, then this License, and its terms, do not apply to those sections when you distribute them as separate works. But when you distribute the same sections as part of a whole which is a work based on the Program, the distribution of the whole must be on the terms of this License, whose permissions for other licensees extend to the entire whole, and thus to each and every part regardless of who wrote it.

Thus, it is not the intent of this section to claim rights or contest your rights to work written entirely by you; rather, the intent is to exercise the right to control the distribution of derivative or collective works based on the Program.

In addition, mere aggregation of another work not based on the Program with the Program (or with a work based on the Program) on a volume of a storage or distribution medium does not bring the other work under the scope of this License.

3. You may copy and distribute the Program (or a work based on it, under Section 2) in object code or executable form under the terms of Sections 1 and 2 above provided that you also do one of the following:

   a. Accompany it with the complete corresponding machine-readable source code, which must be distributed under the terms of Sections 1 and 2 above on a medium customarily used for software interchange; or,

   b. Accompany it with a written offer, valid for at least three years, to give any third party, for a charge no more than your cost of physically performing source distribution, a complete machine-readable copy of the corresponding source code, to be distributed under the terms of Sections 1 and 2 above on a medium customarily used for software interchange; or,

   c. Accompany it with the information you received as to the offer to distribute corresponding source code. (This alternative is allowed only for noncommercial distribution and only if you received the program in object code or executable form with such an offer, in accord with Subsection b above.)

The source code for a work means the preferred form of the work for making modifications to it. For an executable work, complete source code means all the source code for all modules it contains, plus any associated interface definition files, plus the scripts used to control compilation and installation of the executable. However, as a special exception, the source code distributed need not include anything that is normally distributed (in either source or binary form) with the major components (compiler, kernel, and so on) of the operating system on which the executable runs, unless that component itself accompanies the executable.

If distribution of executable or object code is made by offering access to copy from a designated place, then offering equivalent access to copy the source code from the same place counts as distribution of the source code, even though third parties are not compelled to copy the source along with the object code.

4. You may not copy, modify, sublicense, or distribute the Program except as expressly provided under this License. Any attempt otherwise to copy, modify, sublicense or distribute the Program is void, and will automatically terminate your rights under this License. However, parties who have received copies, or rights, from you under this License will not have their licenses terminated so long as such parties remain in full compliance.

5. You are not required to accept this License, since you have not signed it. However, nothing else grants you permission to modify or distribute the Program or its derivative works. These actions are prohibited by law if you do not accept this License. Therefore, by modifying or distributing the Program (or any work based on the Program), you indicate your acceptance of this License to do so, and all its terms and conditions for copying, distributing or modifying the Program or works based on it.

6. Each time you redistribute the Program (or any work based on the Program), the recipient automatically receives a license from the original licensor to copy, distribute or modify the Program subject to these terms and conditions. You may not impose any further restrictions on the recipients' exercise of the rights granted herein. You are not responsible for enforcing compliance by third parties to this License.

7. If, as a consequence of a court judgment or allegation of patent infringement or for any other reason (not limited to patent issues), conditions are imposed on you (whether by court order, agreement or otherwise) that contradict the conditions of this License, they do not excuse you from the conditions of this License. If you cannot distribute so as to satisfy simultaneously your obligations under this License and any other pertinent obligations, then as a consequence you may not distribute the Program at all. For example, if a patent license would not permit royalty-free redistribution of the Program by all those who receive copies directly or indirectly through you, then the only way you could satisfy both it and this License would be to refrain entirely from distribution of the Program.

If any portion of this section is held invalid or unenforceable under any particular circumstance, the balance of the section is intended to apply and the section as a whole is intended to apply in other circumstances.

It is not the purpose of this section to induce you to infringe any patents or other property right claims or to contest validity of any such claims; this section has the sole purpose of protecting the integrity of the free software distribution system, which is implemented by public license practices. Many people have made generous contributions to the wide range of software distributed through that system in reliance on consistent application of that system; it is up to the author/donor to decide if he or she is willing to distribute software through any other system and a licensee cannot impose that choice.

This section is intended to make thoroughly clear what is believed to be a consequence of the rest of this License.

8. If the distribution and/or use of the Program is restricted in certain countries either by patents or by copyrighted interfaces, the original copyright holder who places the Program under this License may add an explicit geographical distribution limitation excluding those countries, so that distribution is permitted only in or among countries not thus excluded. In such case, this License incorporates the limitation as if written in the body of this License.

9. The Free Software Foundation may publish revised and/or new versions of the General Public License from time to time. Such new versions will be similar in spirit to the present version, but may differ in detail to address new problems or concerns.

Each version is given a distinguishing version number. If the Program specifies a version number of this License which applies to it and "any later version," you have the option of following the terms and conditions either of that version or of any later version published by the Free Software Foundation. If the Program does not specify a version number of this License, you may choose any version ever published by the Free Software Foundation.

10. If you wish to incorporate parts of the Program into other free programs whose distribution conditions are different, write to the author to ask for permission. For software which is copyrighted by the Free Software Foundation, write to the Free Software Foundation; we sometimes make exceptions for this. Our decision will be guided by the two goals of preserving the free status of all derivatives of our free software and of promoting the sharing and reuse of software generally.

No Warranty

11. BECAUSE THE PROGRAM IS LICENSED FREE OF CHARGE, THERE IS NO WARRANTY FOR THE PROGRAM, TO THE EXTENT PERMITTED BY APPLICABLE LAW. EXCEPT WHEN OTHERWISE STATED IN WRITING THE COPYRIGHT HOLDERS AND/OR OTHER PARTIES PROVIDE THE PROGRAM "AS IS" WITHOUT WARRANTY OF ANY KIND, EITHER EXPRESSED OR IMPLIED, INCLUDING, BUT NOT LIMITED TO, THE IMPLIED WARRANTIES OF MERCHANTABILITY AND FITNESS FOR A PARTICULAR PURPOSE. THE ENTIRE RISK AS TO THE QUALITY AND PERFORMANCE OF THE PROGRAM

IS WITH YOU. SHOULD THE PROGRAM PROVE DEFECTIVE, YOU ASSUME THE COST OF ALL NECESSARY SERVICING, REPAIR OR CORRECTION.

12. IN NO EVENT UNLESS REQUIRED BY APPLICABLE LAW OR AGREED TO IN WRITING WILL ANY COPYRIGHT HOLDER, OR ANY OTHER PARTY WHO MAY MODIFY AND/OR REDISTRIB-UTE THE PROGRAM AS PERMITTED ABOVE, BE LIABLE TO YOU FOR DAMAGES, INCLUDING ANY GENERAL, SPECIAL, INCIDEN-TAL OR CONSEQUENTIAL DAMAGES ARISING OUT OF THE USE OR INABILITY TO USE THE PROGRAM (INCLUDING BUT NOT LIMITED TO LOSS OF DATA OR DATA BEING RENDERED INAC-CURATE OR LOSSES SUSTAINED BY YOU OR THIRD PARTIES OR A FAILURE OF THE PROGRAM TO OPERATE WITH ANY OTHER PROGRAMS), EVEN IF SUCH HOLDER OR OTHER PARTY HAS BEEN ADVISED OF THE POSSIBILITY OF SUCH DAMAGES.

END OF TERMS AND CONDITIONS

How to Apply These Terms to Your New Programs

If you develop a new program, and you want it to be of the greatest possible use to the public, the best way to achieve this is to make it free software which everyone can redistribute and change under these terms.

To do so, attach the following notices to the program. It is safest to attach them to the start of each source file to most effectively convey the exclusion of warranty; and each file should have at least the "copyright" line and a pointer to where the full notice is found.

One line to give the program's name and a brief idea of what it does.

Copyright (C) <year> <name of author>

This program is free software; you can redistribute it and/or modify it under the terms of the GNU General Public License as published by the Free Software Foundation; either version 2 of the License, or (at your option) any later version.

This program is distributed in the hope that it will be useful, but WITHOUT ANY WARRANTY; without even the implied warranty of MERCHANT-ABILITY or FITNESS FOR A PARTICULAR PURPOSE. See the GNU General Public License for more details.

You should have received a copy of the GNU General Public License along with this program; if not, write to the Free Software Foundation, Inc., 59 Temple Place, Suite 330, Boston, MA 02111-1307 USA

Also add information on how to contact you by electronic and paper mail.

If the program is interactive, make it output a short notice like this when it starts in an interactive mode:

Gnomovision version 69, Copyright (C) year name of author Gnomovision comes with ABSOLUTELY NO WARRANTY; for details type `show w'. This is free software, and you are welcome to redistribute it under certain conditions; type `show c' for details.

The hypothetical commands `show w' and `show c' should show the appropriate parts of the General Public License. Of course, the commands you use may be called something other than `show w' and `show c'; they could even be mouse-clicks or menu items—whatever suits your program.

You should also get your employer (if you work as a programmer) or your school, if any, to sign a "copyright disclaimer" for the program, if necessary. Here is a sample; alter the names:

Yoyodyne, Inc., hereby disclaims all copyright interest in the program `Gnomovision' (which makes passes at compilers) written by James Hacker.

signature of Ty Coon, 1 April 1989

Ty Coon, President of Vice

This General Public License does not permit incorporating your program into proprietary programs. If your program is a subroutine library, you may consider it more useful to permit linking proprietary applications with the library. If this is what you want to do, use the GNU Library General Public License instead of this License.

A.3 GNU General Public License (GPL) Version 3

GNU GENERAL PUBLIC LICENSE
Version 3, 29 June 2007
Copyright (C) 2007 Free Software Foundation, Inc. <http://fsf.org/>
Everyone is permitted to copy and distribute verbatim copies of this license document, but changing it is not allowed.

Preamble

The GNU General Public License is a free, copyleft license for software and other kinds of works.

The licenses for most software and other practical works are designed to take away your freedom to share and change the works. By contrast, the GNU General Public License is intended to guarantee your freedom to share and change all versions of a program—to make sure it remains free software for all its users. We, the Free Software Foundation, use the GNU General Public License for most of our software; it applies also to any other work released this way by its authors. You can apply it to your programs, too.

When we speak of free software, we are referring to freedom, not price. Our General Public Licenses are designed to make sure that you have the freedom to distribute copies of free software (and charge for them if you wish), that you receive source code or can get it if you want it, that you can change the software or use pieces of it in new free programs, and that you know you can do these things.

To protect your rights, we need to prevent others from denying you these rights or asking you to surrender the rights. Therefore, you have certain responsibilities if you distribute copies of the software, or if you modify it: responsibilities to respect the freedom of others.

For example, if you distribute copies of such a program, whether gratis or for a fee, you must pass on to the recipients the same freedoms that you received. You must make sure that they, too, receive or can get the source code. And you must show them these terms so they know their rights.

Developers that use the GNU GPL protect your rights with two steps: (1) assert copyright on the software, and (2) offer you this License giving you legal permission to copy, distribute and/or modify it.

For the developers' and authors' protection, the GPL clearly explains that there is no warranty for this free software. For both users' and authors' sake, the GPL requires that modified versions be marked as changed, so that their problems will not be attributed erroneously to authors of previous versions.

Some devices are designed to deny users access to install or run modified versions of the software inside them, although the manufacturer can do so. This is fundamentally incompatible with the aim of protecting users' freedom to change the software. The systematic pattern of such abuse occurs in the area of products for individuals to use, which is precisely where it is most unacceptable. Therefore, we have designed this version of the GPL to prohibit the practice for those products. If such problems arise substantially in other domains, we stand ready to extend this provision to those domains in future versions of the GPL, as needed to protect the freedom of users.

Finally, every program is threatened constantly by software patents. States should not allow patents to restrict development and use of software on general-purpose computers, but in those that do, we wish to avoid the special danger that patents applied to a free program could make it effectively proprietary. To prevent this, the GPL assures that patents cannot be used to render the program non-free.

The precise terms and conditions for copying, distribution and modification follow.

Terms and Conditions

0. **Definitions.**

"This License" refers to version 3 of the GNU General Public License.

"Copyright" also means copyright-like laws that apply to other kinds of works, such as semiconductor masks.

"The Program" refers to any copyrightable work licensed under this License. Each licensee is addressed as "you". "Licensees" and "recipients" may be individuals or organizations.

To "modify" a work means to copy from or adapt all or part of the work in a fashion requiring copyright permission, other than the making of an exact copy. The resulting work is called a "modified version" of the earlier work or a work "based on" the earlier work.

A "covered work" means either the unmodified Program or a work based on the Program.

To "propagate" a work means to do anything with it that, without permission, would make you directly or secondarily liable for infringement under applicable copyright law, except executing it on a computer or modifying a private copy. Propagation includes copying, distribution (with or without modification), making available to the public, and in some countries other activities as well.

To "convey" a work means any kind of propagation that enables other parties to make or receive copies. Mere interaction with a user through a computer network, with no transfer of a copy, is not conveying.

An interactive user interface displays "Appropriate Legal Notices" to the extent that it includes a convenient and prominently visible feature that (1) displays an appropriate copyright notice, and (2) tells the user that there is no warranty for the work (except to the extent that warranties are provided), that licensees may convey the work under this License, and how to view a copy of this License. If the interface presents a list of user commands or options, such as a menu, a prominent item in the list meets this criterion.

1. **Source Code.**

The "source code" for a work means the preferred form of the work for making modifications to it. "Object code" means any non-source form of a work.

A "Standard Interface" means an interface that either is an official standard defined by a recognized standards body, or, in the case of interfaces specified for a particular programming language, one that is widely used among developers working in that language.

The "System Libraries" of an executable work include anything, other than the work as a whole, that (a) is included in the normal form of packaging a Major Component, but which is not part of that Major Component, and (b) serves only to enable use of the work with that Major Component, or to implement a Standard Interface for which an implementation is available to the public in source code form. A "Major Component", in this context, means a major essential component (kernel, window system, and so on) of the specific operating system (if any) on which the executable work runs, or a compiler used to produce the work, or an object code interpreter used to run it.

The "Corresponding Source" for a work in object code form means all the source code needed to generate, install, and (for an executable work) run the object code and to modify the work, including scripts to control those activities. However, it does not include the work's System Libraries, or general-purpose tools or generally available free programs which are used unmodified in performing those activities but which are not part of the work. For example, Corresponding Source includes interface definition files associated with source files for the work, and the source code for shared libraries and dynamically linked subprograms that the work is specifically designed to require, such as by intimate data communication or control flow between those subprograms and other parts of the work.

The Corresponding Source need not include anything that users can regenerate automatically from other parts of the Corresponding Source.

The Corresponding Source for a work in source code form is that same work.

2. **Basic Permissions.**

All rights granted under this License are granted for the term of copyright on the Program, and are irrevocable provided the stated conditions are met. This License explicitly affirms your unlimited permission to run the unmodified Program. The output from running a covered work is covered by this License only if the output, given its content, constitutes a covered work. This License acknowledges your rights of fair use or other equivalent, as provided by copyright law.

You may make, run and propagate covered works that you do not convey, without conditions so long as your license otherwise remains in force. You may convey covered works to others for the sole purpose of having them make modifications exclusively for you, or provide you with facilities for running those works, provided that you comply with the terms of this License in conveying all material for which you do not control copyright. Those thus making or running the covered works for you must do so exclusively on your behalf, under your direction and control, on terms that prohibit them from making any copies of your copyrighted material outside their relationship with you.

Conveying under any other circumstances is permitted solely under the conditions stated below. Sublicensing is not allowed; section 10 makes it unnecessary.

3. **Protecting Users' Legal Rights From Anti-Circumvention Law.**

No covered work shall be deemed part of an effective technological measure under any applicable law fulfilling obligations under article 11 of the WIPO copyright treaty adopted on 20 December 1996, or similar laws prohibiting or restricting circumvention of such measures.

When you convey a covered work, you waive any legal power to forbid circumvention of technological measures to the extent such circumvention is effected by exercising rights under this License with respect to the covered work, and you disclaim any intention to limit operation or modification of the work as a means of enforcing, against the work's users, your or third parties' legal rights to forbid circumvention of technological measures.

4. **Conveying Verbatim Copies.**

You may convey verbatim copies of the Program's source code as you receive it, in any medium, provided that you conspicuously and appropriately publish on each copy an appropriate copyright notice; keep intact all notices stating that this License and any non-permissive terms added in accord with section 7 apply to the code; keep intact all notices of the absence of any warranty; and give all recipients a copy of this License along with the Program.

You may charge any price or no price for each copy that you convey, and you may offer support or warranty protection for a fee.

5. **Conveying Modified Source Versions.**

You may convey a work based on the Program, or the modifications to produce it from the Program, in the form of source code under the terms of section 4, provided that you also meet all of these conditions:

a. The work must carry prominent notices stating that you modified it, and giving a relevant date.

b. The work must carry prominent notices stating that it is released under this License and any conditions added under section 7. This requirement modifies the requirement in section 4 to "keep intact all notices".

c. You must license the entire work, as a whole, under this License to anyone who comes into possession of a copy. This License will therefore apply, along with any applicable section 7 additional terms, to the whole of the work, and all its parts, regardless of how they are packaged. This License gives no permission to license the work in any other way, but it does not invalidate such permission if you have separately received it.

d. If the work has interactive user interfaces, each must display Appropriate Legal Notices; however, if the Program has interactive interfaces that do not display Appropriate Legal Notices, your work need not make them do so.

A compilation of a covered work with other separate and independent works, which are not by their nature extensions of the covered work, and which are not combined with it such as to form a larger program, in or on a volume of a storage or distribution medium, is called an "aggregate" if the compilation and its resulting copyright are not used to limit the access or legal rights of the compilation's users beyond what the individual works permit. Inclusion of a covered work in an aggregate does not cause this License to apply to the other parts of the aggregate.

6. **Conveying Non-Source Forms.**

You may convey a covered work in object code form under the terms of sections 4 and 5, provided that you also convey the machine-readable Corresponding Source under the terms of this License, in one of these ways:

a. Convey the object code in, or embodied in, a physical product (including a physical distribution medium), accompanied by the Corresponding Source fixed on a durable physical medium customarily used for software interchange.

b. Convey the object code in, or embodied in, a physical product (including a physical distribution medium), accompanied by a written offer, valid for at least three years and valid for as long as you offer spare parts or customer support for that product model, to give anyone who possesses the object code either (1) a copy of the Corresponding Source for all the software in the product that is covered by this License, on a durable physical medium customarily used for software interchange, for a price no more than your reasonable cost of physically performing this conveying of source, or (2) access to copy the Corresponding Source from a network server at no charge.

c. Convey individual copies of the object code with a copy of the written offer to provide the Corresponding Source. This alternative is allowed only occasionally and noncommercially, and only if you received the object code with such an offer, in accord with subsection 6b.

d. Convey the object code by offering access from a designated place (gratis or for a charge), and offer equivalent access to the Corresponding Source in the same way through the same place at no further charge. You need not require recipients to copy the Corresponding Source along with the object code. If the place to copy the object code is a network server, the Corresponding Source may be on a different server (operated by you or a third party) that supports equivalent copying facilities, provided you maintain clear directions next to the object code saying where to find the Corresponding Source. Regardless of what server hosts the Corresponding Source, you remain obligated to ensure that it is available for as long as needed to satisfy these requirements.

e. Convey the object code using peer-to-peer transmission, provided you inform other peers where the object code and Corresponding Source of the work are being offered to the general public at no charge under subsection 6d.

A separable portion of the object code, whose source code is excluded from the Corresponding Source as a System Library, need not be included in conveying the object code work.

A "User Product" is either (1) a "consumer product", which means any tangible personal property which is normally used for personal, family, or household purposes, or (2) anything designed or sold for incorporation into a dwelling. In determining whether a product is a consumer product, doubtful cases shall be resolved in favor of coverage. For a particular product received by a particular user, "normally used" refers to a typical or common use of that class of product, regardless of the status of the particular user or of the way in which the particular user actually uses, or expects or is expected to use, the product. A product is a consumer product regardless of whether the product has substantial commercial, industrial or non-consumer uses, unless such uses represent the only significant mode of use of the product.

"Installation Information" for a User Product means any methods, procedures, authorization keys, or other information required to install and execute modified versions of a covered work in that User Product from a modified version of its Corresponding Source. The information must suffice to ensure that the continued functioning of the modified object code is in no case prevented or interfered with solely because modification has been made.

If you convey an object code work under this section in, or with, or specifically for use in, a User Product, and the conveying occurs as part of a transaction in which the right of possession and use of the User Product is transferred to the recipient in perpetuity or for a fixed term (regardless of how the transaction is characterized), the Corresponding Source conveyed under this section must be accompanied by the Installation Information. But this requirement does not apply if neither you nor any third party retains the ability to install modified object code on the User Product (for example, the work has been installed in ROM).

The requirement to provide Installation Information does not include a requirement to continue to provide support service, warranty, or updates for a work that has been modified or installed by the recipient, or for the User Product in which it has been modified or installed. Access to a network may be denied when the modification itself materially and adversely affects the operation of the network or violates the rules and protocols for communication across the network.

Corresponding Source conveyed, and Installation Information provided, in accord with this section must be in a format that is publicly documented (and with an implementation available to the public in source code form), and must require no special password or key for unpacking, reading or copying.

7. **Additional Terms.**

"Additional permissions" are terms that supplement the terms of this License by making exceptions from one or more of its conditions. Additional permissions that are applicable to the entire Program shall be treated as though they were included in this License, to the extent that they are valid under applicable law. If additional permissions apply only to part of the Program, that part may be used separately under those permissions, but the entire Program remains governed by this License without regard to the additional permissions.

When you convey a copy of a covered work, you may at your option remove any additional permissions from that copy, or from any part of it. (Additional permissions may be written to require their own removal in certain cases when you modify the work.) You may place additional permissions on material, added by you to a covered work, for which you have or can give appropriate copyright permission.

Notwithstanding any other provision of this License, for material you add to a covered work, you may (if authorized by the copyright holders of that material) supplement the terms of this License with terms:

a. Disclaiming warranty or limiting liability differently from the terms of sections 15 and 16 of this License; or

b. Requiring preservation of specified reasonable legal notices or author attributions in that material or in the Appropriate Legal Notices displayed by works containing it; or

c. Prohibiting misrepresentation of the origin of that material, or requiring that modified versions of such material be marked in reasonable ways as different from the original version; or

d. Limiting the use for publicity purposes of names of licensors or authors of the material; or

e. Declining to grant rights under trademark law for use of some trade names, trademarks, or service marks; or

f. Requiring indemnification of licensors and authors of that material by anyone who conveys the material (or modified versions of it) with contractual assumptions of liability to the recipient, for any liability that these contractual assumptions directly impose on those licensors and authors.

All other non-permissive additional terms are considered "further restrictions" within the meaning of section 10. If the Program as you received it, or any part of it, contains a notice stating that it is governed by this License along with a term that is a further restriction, you may remove that term. If a license document contains a further restriction but permits relicensing or conveying under this License, you may add to a covered work material governed by the terms of that license document, provided that the further restriction does not survive such relicensing or conveying.

If you add terms to a covered work in accord with this section, you must place, in the relevant source files, a statement of the additional terms that apply to those files, or a notice indicating where to find the applicable terms.

Additional terms, permissive or non-permissive, may be stated in the form of a separately written license, or stated as exceptions; the above requirements apply either way.

8. **Termination.**

You may not propagate or modify a covered work except as expressly provided under this License. Any attempt otherwise to propagate or modify it is void, and will automatically terminate your rights under this License (including any patent licenses granted under the third paragraph of section 11).

However, if you cease all violation of this License, then your license from a particular copyright holder is reinstated (a) provisionally, unless and until the copyright holder explicitly and finally terminates your license, and (b) permanently, if the copyright holder fails to notify you of the violation by some reasonable means prior to 60 days after the cessation.

Moreover, your license from a particular copyright holder is reinstated permanently if the copyright holder notifies you of the violation by some reasonable means, this is the first time you have received notice of violation of this License (for any work) from that copyright holder, and you cure the violation prior to 30 days after your receipt of the notice.

Termination of your rights under this section does not terminate the licenses of parties who have received copies or rights from you under this License. If your rights have been terminated and not permanently reinstated, you do not qualify to receive new licenses for the same material under section 10.

9. **Acceptance Not Required for Having Copies.**

You are not required to accept this License in order to receive or run a copy of the Program. Ancillary propagation of a covered work occurring solely as a consequence of using peer-to-peer transmission to receive a copy likewise does not require acceptance. However, nothing other than this License grants you permission to propagate or modify any covered work. These actions infringe copyright if you do not accept this License. Therefore, by modifying or propagating a covered work, you indicate your acceptance of this License to do so.

10. **Automatic Licensing of Downstream Recipients.**

Each time you convey a covered work, the recipient automatically receives a license from the original licensors, to run, modify and propagate that work, subject to this License. You are not responsible for enforcing compliance by third parties with this License.

An "entity transaction" is a transaction transferring control of an organization, or substantially all assets of one, or subdividing an organization, or merging organizations. If propagation of a covered work results from an entity transaction, each party to that transaction who receives a copy of the work also receives whatever licenses to the work the party's predecessor in interest had or could give under the previous paragraph, plus a right to possession of the Corresponding Source of the work from the predecessor in interest, if the predecessor has it or can get it with reasonable efforts.

You may not impose any further restrictions on the exercise of the rights granted or affirmed under this License. For example, you may not impose a license fee, royalty, or other charge for exercise of rights granted under this License, and you may not initiate litigation (including a cross-claim or counterclaim in a lawsuit) alleging that any patent claim is infringed by making, using, selling, offering for sale, or importing the Program or any portion of it.

11. **Patents.**

A "contributor" is a copyright holder who authorizes use under this License of the Program or a work on which the Program is based. The work thus licensed is called the contributor's "contributor version".

A contributor's "essential patent claims" are all patent claims owned or controlled by the contributor, whether already acquired or hereafter acquired, that would be infringed by some manner, permitted by this License, of making, using, or selling its contributor version, but do not include claims that would be infringed only as a consequence of further modification of the contributor version. For purposes of this definition, "control" includes the right to grant patent sublicenses in a manner consistent with the requirements of this License.

Each contributor grants you a non-exclusive, worldwide, royalty-free patent license under the contributor's essential patent claims, to make, use, sell, offer for sale, import and otherwise run, modify and propagate the contents of its contributor version.

In the following three paragraphs, a "patent license" is any express agreement or commitment, however denominated, not to enforce a patent (such as an express permission to practice a patent or covenant not to sue for patent infringement). To "grant" such a patent license to a party means to make such an agreement or commitment not to enforce a patent against the party.

If you convey a covered work, knowingly relying on a patent license, and the Corresponding Source of the work is not available for anyone to copy, free of charge and under the terms of this License, through a publicly available network server or other readily accessible means, then you must either (1) cause the Corresponding Source to be so available, or (2) arrange to deprive yourself of the benefit of the patent license for this particular work, or (3) arrange, in a manner consistent with the requirements of this License, to extend the patent license to downstream recipients. "Knowingly relying" means you have actual knowledge that, but for the patent license, your conveying the covered work in a country, or your recipient's use of the covered work in a country, would infringe one or more identifiable patents in that country that you have reason to believe are valid.

If, pursuant to or in connection with a single transaction or arrangement, you convey, or propagate by procuring conveyance of, a covered work, and grant a patent license to some of the parties receiving the covered work authorizing them to use, propagate, modify or convey a specific copy of the covered work, then the patent license you grant is automatically extended to all recipients of the covered work and works based on it.

A patent license is "discriminatory" if it does not include within the scope of its coverage, prohibits the exercise of, or is conditioned on the non-exercise of one or more of the rights that are specifically granted under this License. You may not convey a covered work if you are a party to an arrangement with a third party that is in the business of distributing software, under which you make payment to the third party based on the extent of your activity of conveying the work, and under which the third party grants, to any of the parties who would receive the covered work from you, a discriminatory patent license (a) in connection with copies of the covered work conveyed by you (or copies made from those copies), or (b) primarily for and in connection with specific products or compilations that contain the covered work, unless you entered into that arrangement, or that patent license was granted, prior to 28 March 2007.

Nothing in this License shall be construed as excluding or limiting any implied license or other defenses to infringement that may otherwise be available to you under applicable patent law.

12. **No Surrender of Others' Freedom.**

If conditions are imposed on you (whether by court order, agreement or otherwise) that contradict the conditions of this License, they do not excuse you from the conditions of this License. If you cannot convey a covered work so as to satisfy simultaneously your obligations under this License and any other pertinent obligations, then as a consequence you may not convey it at all. For example, if you agree to terms that obligate you to collect a royalty for further conveying from those to whom you convey the Program, the only way you could satisfy both those terms and this License would be to refrain entirely from conveying the Program.

13. **Use with the GNU Affero General Public License.**

Notwithstanding any other provision of this License, you have permission to link or combine any covered work with a work licensed under version 3 of the GNU Affero General Public License into a single combined work, and to convey the resulting work. The terms of this License will continue to apply to the part which is the covered work, but the special requirements of the GNU Affero General Public License, section 13, concerning interaction through a network will apply to the combination as such.

14. **Revised Versions of this License.**

The Free Software Foundation may publish revised and/or new versions of the GNU General Public License from time to time. Such new versions will be similar in spirit to the present version, but may differ in detail to address new problems or concerns.

Each version is given a distinguishing version number. If the Program specifies that a certain numbered version of the GNU General Public License "or any later version" applies to it, you have the option of following the terms and conditions either of that numbered version or of any later version published by the Free Software Foundation. If the Program does not specify a version number of the GNU General Public License, you may choose any version ever published by the Free Software Foundation.

If the Program specifies that a proxy can decide which future versions of the GNU General Public License can be used, that proxy's public statement of acceptance of a version permanently authorizes you to choose that version for the Program.

Later license versions may give you additional or different permissions. However, no additional obligations are imposed on any author or copyright holder as a result of your choosing to follow a later version.

15. **Disclaimer of Warranty.**

   THERE IS NO WARRANTY FOR THE PROGRAM, TO THE EXTENT PERMITTED BY APPLICABLE LAW. EXCEPT WHEN OTHERWISE STATED IN WRITING THE COPYRIGHT HOLDERS AND/OR OTHER PARTIES PROVIDE THE PROGRAM "AS IS" WITHOUT WARRANTY OF ANY KIND, EITHER EXPRESSED OR IMPLIED, INCLUDING, BUT NOT LIMITED TO, THE IMPLIED WARRANTIES OF MERCHANTABILITY AND FITNESS FOR A PARTICULAR PURPOSE. THE ENTIRE RISK AS TO THE QUALITY AND PERFORMANCE OF THE PROGRAM IS WITH YOU. SHOULD THE PROGRAM PROVE DEFECTIVE, YOU ASSUME THE COST OF ALL NECESSARY SERVICING, REPAIR OR CORRECTION.

16. **Limitation of Liability.**

   IN NO EVENT UNLESS REQUIRED BY APPLICABLE LAW OR AGREED TO IN WRITING WILL ANY COPYRIGHT HOLDER, OR ANY OTHER PARTY WHO MODIFIES AND/OR CONVEYS THE PROGRAM AS PERMITTED ABOVE, BE LIABLE TO YOU FOR DAMAGES, INCLUDING ANY GENERAL, SPECIAL, INCIDENTAL OR CONSEQUENTIAL DAMAGES ARISING OUT OF THE USE OR INABILITY TO USE THE PROGRAM (INCLUDING BUT NOT LIMITED TO LOSS OF DATA OR DATA BEING RENDERED INACCURATE OR LOSSES SUSTAINED BY YOU OR THIRD PARTIES OR A FAILURE OF THE PROGRAM TO OPERATE WITH ANY OTHER PROGRAMS), EVEN IF SUCH HOLDER OR OTHER PARTY HAS BEEN ADVISED OF THE POSSIBILITY OF SUCH DAMAGES.

17. **Interpretation of Sections 15 and 16.**

> If the disclaimer of warranty and limitation of liability provided above cannot be given local legal effect according to their terms, reviewing courts shall apply local law that most closely approximates an absolute waiver of all civil liability in connection with the Program, unless a warranty or assumption of liability accompanies a copy of the Program in return for a fee.

END OF TERMS AND CONDITIONS

How to Apply These Terms to Your New Programs

If you develop a new program, and you want it to be of the greatest possible use to the public, the best way to achieve this is to make it free software which everyone can redistribute and change under these terms.

To do so, attach the following notices to the program. It is safest to attach them to the start of each source file to most effectively state the exclusion of warranty; and each file should have at least the "copyright" line and a pointer to where the full notice is found.

<one line to give the program's name and a brief idea of what it does.>

Copyright (C) <year> <name of author>

This program is free software: you can redistribute it and/or modify it under the terms of the GNU General Public License as published by the Free Software Foundation, either version 3 of the License, or (at your option) any later version.

This program is distributed in the hope that it will be useful, but WITHOUT ANY WARRANTY; without even the implied warranty of MERCHANT-ABILITY or FITNESS FOR A PARTICULAR PURPOSE. See the GNU General Public License for more details.

You should have received a copy of the GNU General Public License along with this program. If not, see <http://www.gnu.org/licenses/>.

Also add information on how to contact you by electronic and paper mail.

If the program does terminal interaction, make it output a short notice like this when it starts in an interactive mode:

<program> Copyright (C) <year> <name of author>

This program comes with ABSOLUTELY NO WARRANTY; for details type `show w'.

This is free software, and you are welcome to redistribute it under certain conditions; type `show c' for details.

The hypothetical commands `show w'` and `show c'` should show the appropriate parts of the General Public License. Of course, your program's commands might be different; for a GUI interface, you would use an "about box".

You should also get your employer (if you work as a programmer) or school, if any, to sign a "copyright disclaimer" for the program, if necessary. For more information on this, and how to apply and follow the GNU GPL, see <http://www.gnu.org/licenses/>.

The GNU General Public License does not permit incorporating your program into proprietary programs. If your program is a subroutine library, you may consider it more useful to permit linking proprietary applications with the library. If this is what you want to do, use the GNU Lesser General Public License instead of this License. But first, please read <http://www.gnu.org/philosophy/why-not-lgpl.html>.

A.4 Apache License Version 2.0

Apache License
Version 2.0, January 2004
http://www.apache.org/licenses/

TERMS AND CONDITIONS FOR USE, REPRODUCTION, AND DISTRIBUTION

1. **Definitions.**

   "License" shall mean the terms and conditions for use, reproduction, and distribution as defined by Sections 1 through 9 of this document.

   "Licensor" shall mean the copyright owner or entity authorized by the copyright owner that is granting the License.

   "Legal Entity" shall mean the union of the acting entity and all other entities that control, are controlled by, or are under common control with that entity. For the purposes of this definition, "control" means (i) the power, direct or indirect, to cause the direction or management of such entity, whether by contract or otherwise, or (ii) ownership of fifty percent (50%) or more of the outstanding shares, or (iii) beneficial ownership of such entity.

   "You" (or "Your") shall mean an individual or Legal Entity exercising permissions granted by this License.

   "Source" form shall mean the preferred form for making modifications, including but not limited to software source code, documentation source, and configuration files.

   "Object" form shall mean any form resulting from mechanical transformation or translation of a Source form, including but not limited to compiled object code, generated documentation, and conversions to other media types.

"Work" shall mean the work of authorship, whether in Source or Object form, made available under the License, as indicated by a copyright notice that is included in or attached to the work (an example is provided in the Appendix below).

"Derivative Works" shall mean any work, whether in Source or Object form, that is based on (or derived from) the Work and for which the editorial revisions, annotations, elaborations, or other modifications represent, as a whole, an original work of authorship. For the purposes of this License, Derivative Works shall not include works that remain separable from, or merely link (or bind by name) to the interfaces of, the Work and Derivative Works thereof.

"Contribution" shall mean any work of authorship, including the original version of the Work and any modifications or additions to that Work or Derivative Works thereof, that is intentionally submitted to Licensor for inclusion in the Work by the copyright owner or by an individual or Legal Entity authorized to submit on behalf of the copyright owner. For the purposes of this definition, "submitted" means any form of electronic, verbal, or written communication sent to the Licensor or its representatives, including but not limited to communication on electronic mailing lists, source code control systems, and issue tracking systems that are managed by, or on behalf of, the Licensor for the purpose of discussing and improving the Work, but excluding communication that is conspicuously marked or otherwise designated in writing by the copyright owner as "Not a Contribution."

"Contributor" shall mean Licensor and any individual or Legal Entity on behalf of whom a Contribution has been received by Licensor and subsequently incorporated within the Work.

2. **Grant of Copyright License.**

Subject to the terms and conditions of this License, each Contributor hereby grants to You a perpetual, worldwide, non-exclusive, no-charge, royalty-free, irrevocable copyright license to reproduce, prepare Derivative Works of, publicly display, publicly perform, sublicense, and distribute the Work and such Derivative Works in Source or Object form.

3. **Grant of Patent License.**

Subject to the terms and conditions of this License, each Contributor hereby grants to You a perpetual, worldwide, non-exclusive, no-charge, royalty-free, irrevocable (except as stated in this section) patent license to make, have made, use, offer to sell, sell, import, and otherwise transfer the Work, where such license applies only to those patent claims licensable by such Contributor that are necessarily infringed by their Contribution(s) alone or by combination of their Contribution(s) with the Work to which such Contribution(s) was submitted. If You institute patent litigation against any entity (including a cross-claim or counterclaim in a lawsuit) alleging that the Work or a Contribution incorporated within the Work constitutes direct or contributory patent infringement, then any patent licenses granted to You under this License for that Work shall terminate as of the date such litigation is filed.

4. **Redistribution.**

You may reproduce and distribute copies of the Work or Derivative Works thereof in any medium, with or without modifications, and in Source or Object form, provided that You meet the following conditions:

a. You must give any other recipients of the Work or Derivative Works a copy of this License; and

b. You must cause any modified files to carry prominent notices stating that You changed the files; and

c. You must retain, in the Source form of any Derivative Works that You distribute, all copyright, patent, trademark, and attribution notices from the Source form of the Work, excluding those notices that do not pertain to any part of the Derivative Works; and

d. If the Work includes a "NOTICE" text file as part of its distribution, then any Derivative Works that You distribute must include a readable copy of the attribution notices contained within such NOTICE file, excluding those notices that do not pertain to any part of the Derivative Works, in at least one of the following places: within a NOTICE text file distributed as part of the Derivative Works; within the Source form or documentation, if provided along with the Derivative Works; or, within a display generated by the Derivative Works, if and wherever such third-party notices normally appear. The contents of the NOTICE file are for informational purposes only and do not modify the License. You may add Your own attribution notices within Derivative Works that You distribute, alongside or as an addendum to the NOTICE text from the Work, provided that such additional attribution notices cannot be construed as modifying the License.

You may add Your own copyright statement to Your modifications and may provide additional or different license terms and conditions for use, reproduction, or distribution of Your modifications, or for any such Derivative Works as a whole, provided Your use, reproduction, and distribution of the Work otherwise complies with the conditions stated in this License.

5. **Submission of Contributions.**

Unless You explicitly state otherwise, any Contribution intentionally submitted for inclusion in the Work by You to the Licensor shall be under the terms and conditions of this License, without any additional terms or conditions. Notwithstanding the above, nothing herein shall supersede or modify the terms of any separate license agreement you may have executed with Licensor regarding such Contributions.

6. **Trademarks.**

This License does not grant permission to use the trade names, trademarks, service marks, or product names of the Licensor, except as required for reasonable and customary use in describing the origin of the Work and reproducing the content of the NOTICE file.

7. **Disclaimer of Warranty.**

Unless required by applicable law or agreed to in writing, Licensor provides the Work (and each Contributor provides its Contributions) on an "AS IS" BASIS, WITHOUT WARRANTIES OR CONDITIONS OF ANY KIND, either express or implied, including, without limitation, any warranties or conditions of TITLE, NON-INFRINGEMENT, MERCHANTABILITY, or FITNESS FOR A PARTICULAR PURPOSE. You are solely responsible for determining the appropriateness of using or redistributing the Work and assume any risks associated with Your exercise of permissions under this License.

8. **Limitation of Liability.**

In no event and under no legal theory, whether in tort (including negligence), contract, or otherwise, unless required by applicable law (such as deliberate and grossly negligent acts) or agreed to in writing, shall any Contributor be liable to You for damages, including any direct, indirect, special, incidental, or consequential damages of any character arising as a result of this License or out of the use or inability to use the Work (including but not limited to damages for loss of goodwill, work stoppage, computer failure or malfunction, or any and all other commercial damages or losses), even if such Contributor has been advised of the possibility of such damages.

9. **Accepting Warranty or Additional Liability.**

While redistributing the Work or Derivative Works thereof, You may choose to offer, and charge a fee for, acceptance of support, warranty, indemnity, or other liability obligations and/or rights consistent with this License. However, in accepting such obligations, You may act only on Your own behalf and on Your sole responsibility, not on behalf of any other Contributor, and only if You agree to indemnify, defend, and hold each Contributor harmless for any liability incurred by, or claims asserted against, such Contributor by reason of your accepting any such warranty or additional liability.

END OF TERMS AND CONDITIONS

APPENDIX: How to Apply the Apache License to Your Work

To apply the Apache License to your work, attach the following boilerplate notice, with the fields enclosed by brackets "[]" replaced with your own identifying information.

(Don't include the brackets!) The text should be enclosed in the appropriate comment syntax for the file format. We also recommend that a file or class name and description of purpose be included on the same "printed page" as the copyright notice for easier identification within third-party archives.

Copyright [yyyy] [name of copyright owner]

Licensed under the Apache License, Version 2.0 (the "License"); you may not use this file except in compliance with the License. You may obtain a copy of the License at

http://www.apache.org/licenses/LICENSE-2.0

Unless required by applicable law or agreed to in writing, software distributed under the License is distributed on an "AS IS" BASIS, WITHOUT WARRANTIES OR CONDITIONS OF ANY KIND, either express or implied. See the License for the specific language governing permissions and limitations under the License.

B

Metadata Reference

Tables B-1 and B-2, listing layers and machines, respectively, appear on the following pages. For a searchable reference, go to http://layers.openembedded.org/layerindex/branch/master/layers/.

Table B-1 Layers

Layer name	Description	Type	Repository
meta-oe	Additional shared OpenEmbedded (OE) metadata	Base	git://git.openembedded.org/meta-openembedded
openembedded-core	Core metadata	Base	git://git.openembedded.org/openembedded-core
e100-bsp	Ettus E1XX series board support package (BSP)	Machine (BSP)	git://github.com/EttusResearch/meta-ettus.git
e300-bsp	Ettus E3XX Series BSP	Machine (BSP)	https://github.com/EttusResearch/meta-ettus.git
meta-aarch64	Aarch64 (64-bit ARM) architecture support	Machine (BSP)	git://git.linaro.org/openembedded/meta-linaro.git
meta-acer	Acer machines support	Machine (BSP)	git://github.com/shr-distribution/meta-smartphone.git
meta-altera	Altera SoC BSP layer	Machine (BSP)	https://github.com/kraj/meta-altera
meta-amd	AMD board support common layer (official)	Machine (BSP)	git://git.yoctoproject.org/meta-amd
meta-asus	Asus machines support	Machine (BSP)	git://github.com/shr-distribution/meta-smartphone.git
meta-atmel	Official Yocto Project layer for Atmel SoCs	Machine (BSP)	git://github.com/linux4sam/meta-atmel.git
meta-baldeagle	AMD Bald Eagle platform BSP	Machine (BSP)	http://git.yoctoproject.org/cgit/cgit.cgi/meta-amd/
meta-beagleboard	Support for beagleboard.org devices	Machine (BSP)	git://github.com/beagleboard/meta-beagleboard.git
meta-bug	BugLabs bug20 machine support	Machine (BSP)	git://github.com/buglabs/meta-bug.git
meta-bytesatwork	Official BSP layer for Bytesatwork-based platform	Machine (BSP)	https://github.com/bytesatwork/meta-bytesatwork.git
meta-chip	Yocto BSP layer for CHIP boards	Machine (BSP)	https://github.com/agherzan/meta-chip.git
meta-ci20	Meta layer to support Creator CI20 MIPS boards	Machine (BSP)	https://github.com/akuster/meta-ci20
meta-crownbay	Intel Crown Bay platform BSP	Machine (BSP)	git://git.yoctoproject.org/meta-intel
meta-crystalforest	Intel Crystal Forest platform BSP	Machine (BSP)	git://git.yoctoproject.org/meta-intel
meta-cubox	SolidRun CuBox platform BSP	Machine (BSP)	git://github.com/dv1/meta-cubox.git
meta-digi-arm	Support for Digi ConnectCore/ConnectCard modules	Machine (BSP)	https://github.com/dgii/meta-digi.git
meta-dra7xx-evm	Tizen BSP layer for DRA7XX-EVM	Machine (BSP)	https://github.com/vitalyvch/meta-dra7xx-evm.git
meta-efikamx	Genesi Efika MX machine support	Machine (BSP)	git://github.com/kraj/meta-efikamx.git

Layer name	Description	Type	Repository
meta-emenlow	Intel eMenlow platform BSP	Machine (BSP)	git://git.yoctoproject.org/meta-intel
meta-exynos	BSP layer for Exynos-based machines	Machine (BSP)	https://github.com/slimlogic/meta-exynos.git
meta-fri2	Kontron Fish River Island 2 BSP	Machine (BSP)	git://git.yoctoproject.org/meta-intel
meta-fsl-arm	Freescale ARM hardware support	Machine (BSP)	git://git.yoctoproject.org/meta-fsl-arm
meta-fsl-arm-extra	Freescale ARM hardware support (extra boards)	Machine (BSP)	git://github.com/Freescale/meta-fsl-arm-extra.git
meta-fsl-ppc	Freescale PowerPC hardware support	Machine (BSP)	git://git.yoctoproject.org/meta-fsl-ppc
meta-geeksphone	Geeksphone device support	Machine (BSP)	git://github.com/shr-distribution/meta-smartphone.git
meta-gumstix	Gumstix board support (official)	Machine (BSP)	git://github.com/gumstix/meta-gumstix.git
meta-gumstix-community	Gumstix board support (unofficial community BSP)	Machine (BSP)	https://github.com/schnitzeltony/meta-gumstix-community
meta-gumstix-extras	Gumstix board support extras (official)	Machine (BSP)	https://github.com/gumstix/meta-gumstix-extras.git
meta-handheld	Older handheld device support (Zaurus, iPAQ, etc.)	Machine (BSP)	git://git.openembedded.org/meta-handheld
meta-hipos	BSP and related Distro for embedded devices from the DResearch Fahrzeugelektronik GmbH	Machine (BSP)	git://github.com/DFE/meta-hipos.git
meta-htc	HTC smartphone support	Machine (BSP)	git://github.com/shr-distribution/meta-smartphone.git
meta-igep	IGEP board support	Machine (BSP)	git://github.com/ebutera/meta-igep.git
meta-intel	Intel board support common layer (official)	Machine (BSP)	git://git.yoctoproject.org/meta-intel
meta-intel-edison-bsp	Intel Edison module support	Machine (BSP)	git://git.yoctoproject.org/meta-intel-edison
meta-intel-quark	Intel Quark platform support	Machine (BSP)	git://git.yoctoproject.org/meta-intel-quark
meta-ivi-bsp	BSP layer for IVI reference hardware	Machine (BSP)	git://git.yoctoproject.org/meta-ivi
meta-jasperforest	Intel Jasper Forest platform BSP	Machine (BSP)	git://git.yoctoproject.org/meta-intel
meta-jz-mips	BSP for devices with Ingenic MIPS SoC	Machine (BSP)	https://github.com/leon-anavi/meta-jz-mips.git

Continues

Table B-1 Layers (*Continued*)

Layer name	Description	Type	Repository
meta-kirkwood	Marvell Kirkwood-based device support	Machine (BSP)	git://github.com/kelvinlawson/meta-kirkwood.git
meta-lsi	LS Axxia Communication Processors Platform BSP	Machine (BSP)	git://git.yoctoproject.org/meta-lsi
meta-minnow	MinnowBoard BSP layer	Machine (BSP)	git://git.yoctoproject.org/meta-minnow
meta-nanopi	FriendlyARM NanoPi board support	Machine (BSP)	git://git.kernelconcepts.de/meta-nanopi.git
meta-netbookpro	Ps on NetBook Pro device support	Machine (BSP)	git://github.com/tworaz/meta-netbookpro
meta-netmodule	BSP Layer from NetModule for various boards	Machine (BSP)	https://github.com/netmodule/meta-netmodule.git
meta-nokia	Nokia N900 support	Machine (BSP)	git://github.com/shr-distribution/meta-smartphone.git
meta-nslu2	Linksys NSLU2 device support	Machine (BSP)	git://github.com/kraj/meta-nslu2
meta-nuc	Intel Next Unit of Computing BSP	Machine (BSP)	git://git.yoctoproject.org/meta-intel
meta-odroid	Supports the series of Odroid boards made by Hardkernel	Machine (BSP)	https://github.com/akuster/meta-odroid
meta-openmoko	OpenMoko device support	Machine (BSP)	git://github.com/shr-distribution/meta-smartphone.git
meta-openpandora	OpenPandora machine support	Machine (BSP)	git://github.com/openpandora/meta-openpandora.git
meta-ouya	Support Ouya game console	Machine (BSP)	https://github.com/pwgen/meta-ouya
meta-palm	Palm Pre machine support	Machine (BSP)	git://github.com/shr-distribution/meta-smartphone.git
meta-parallella	Support for the Parallella board from Adapteva	Machine (BSP)	https://github.com/nathanrossi/meta-parallella.git
meta-phytec	Phytec board support (official)	Machine (BSP)	git://git.phytec.de/meta-phytec
meta-picosam9	Picosam9 board support	Machine (BSP)	https://gitorious.org/picopc-tools/meta-picosam9.git
meta-qemu-bsps	Layer for other QEMU machines	Machine (BSP)	https://github.com/akuster/meta-qemu-bsps
meta-raspberrypi	Raspberry Pi board support	Machine (BSP)	git://git.yoctoproject.org/meta-raspberrypi
meta-renesas-rza1	Official BSP layer for Renesas RZ/A1 platforms	Machine (BSP)	git://github.com/renesas-rz/meta-renesas-rza1
meta-rockchip	Layer supporting public Rockchip-based development boards and products	Machine (BSP)	git://git.yoctoproject.org/meta-rockchip

Layer name	Description	Type	Repository
meta-romley	Intel Romley platform BSP	Machine (BSP)	git://git.yoctoproject.org/meta-intel
meta-samsung	Samsung smartphone support	Machine (BSP)	git://github.com/shr-distribution/meta-smartphone.git
meta-sugarbay	Intel Sugar Bay platform BSP	Machine (BSP)	git://git.yoctoproject.org/meta-intel
meta-sunxi	Allwinner sunxi board support	Machine (BSP)	https://github.com/linux-sunxi/meta-sunxi
meta-ti	Texas Instruments board support (official)	Machine (BSP)	git://git.yoctoproject.org/meta-ti
meta-via-vab820-bsp	VIA VAB-820/AMOS-820 BSP layer	Machine (BSP)	git://github.com/viaembedded/meta-via-vab820-bsp.git
meta-xilinx	Xilinx hardware support	Machine (BSP)	git://git.yoctoproject.org/meta-xilinx
meta-xilinx-community	Additional Xilinx hardware support	Machine (BSP)	git://git.yoctoproject.org/meta-xilinx-community
meta-yocto-bsp	BSP layer for Yocto Project reference hardware	Machine (BSP)	git://git.yoctoproject.org/meta-yocto
meta-yocto-bsp-old	Former Yocto Project reference BSPs	Machine (BSP)	git://git.yoctoproject.org/meta-yocto-bsp-old
meta-angstrom	Ångström distribution	Distribution	git://github.com/Angstrom-distribution/meta-angstrom.git
meta-arago-distro	Arago/TI-SDK distribution	Distribution	git://arago-project.org/git/meta-arago.git
meta-debian	Using Debian source code to BitBake images	Distribution	git://github.com/meta-debian/meta-debian.git
meta-digi-dey	Provides the Digi Embedded Linux distribution images	Distribution	https://github.com/dgii/meta-digi
meta-eca	Mobile access point	Distribution	git://git.yoctoproject.org/meta-eca
meta-eldk	Denx ELDK distribution	Distribution	git://git.denx.de/eldk.git
meta-guacamayo	Guacamayo distribution	Distribution	git://github.com/Guacamayo/meta-guacamayo.git
meta-intel-edison-distro	Distro layer for official Intel Edison images	Distribution	git://git.yoctoproject.org/meta-intel-edison
meta-intel-iot-devkit	Distro layer for the Intel IoT Developer Kit	Distribution	git://git.yoctoproject.org/meta-intel-iot-devkit

Continues

Table B-1 Layers (*Continued*)

Layer name	Description	Type	Repository
meta-ivi	Collection of software related to in-vehicle infotainment systems	Distribution	git://git.yoctoproject.org/meta-ivi
meta-luneos	Distro layer for LuneOS	Distribution	https://github.com/webOS-ports/meta-webos-ports
meta-luv	luvOS distribution	Distribution	git://git.yoctoproject.org/meta-luv
meta-mel	Mentor Embedded Linux distribution (from Mentor Graphics Corporation)	Distribution	https://github.com/MentorEmbedded/meta-mentor
meta-micro	Micro distribution	Distribution	git://git.openembedded.org/meta-micro
meta-mmmpi	An example distro layer customized for the Raspberry Pi	Distribution	https://bitbucket.org/mmmpi/meta-mmmpi.git
meta-overc	Full-featured, container-based distribution	Distribution	git://github.com/WindRiver-OpenSourceLabs/meta-overc.git
meta-shr-distro	SHR distribution	Distribution	git://github.com/shr-distribution/meta-smartphone.git
meta-slugos	SlugOS distribution	Distribution	git://github.com/kraj/meta-slugos
meta-tizen	Tizen reference for the Yocto Project	Distribution	git://review.tizen.org/scm/bb/meta-tizen
meta-webos	WebOS distribution (official)	Distribution	git://github.com/openwebos/meta-webos
meta-webos-ports	Distro layer for LuneOS	Distribution	https://github.com/webOS-ports/meta-webos-ports
meta-woce	WebOS Community Edition distribution	Distribution	git://github.com/kraj/meta-woce
meta-yocto	Poky reference distribution for the Yocto Project	Distribution	git://git.yoctoproject.org/meta-yocto
meta-alt-desktop-extras	Lightweight (legacy) X desktop, tools, and recipe extensions	Miscellaneous	https://github.com/sarnold/meta-alt-desktop-extras
meta-axon	Using Erlang on YP	Miscellaneous	https://github.com/joaohf/meta-axon
meta-baryon	Baryon example NAS distribution	Miscellaneous	git://git.yoctoproject.org/meta-baryon
meta-cgl	Carrier Grade Linux compliance packages	Miscellaneous	git://git.yoctoproject.org/meta-cgl
meta-darwin	OE meta layer for darwin-based SDKs	Miscellaneous	git://git.yoctoproject.org/meta-darwin
meta-gir	GObject Introspection Support	Miscellaneous	git://github.com/meta-gir/meta-gir.git

Layer name	Description	Type	Repository
meta-intel-galileo	Intel Galileo platform support	Miscellaneous	git://git.yoctoproject.org/meta-intel-galileo
meta-kernel-dev	Kernel development extras	Miscellaneous	git://git.yoctoproject.org/meta-yocto-kernel-extras
meta-linaro	Linaro layer for OE	Miscellaneous	git://git.linaro.org/openembedded/meta-linaro.git
meta-mentor-staging	Mentor Graphics Staging Layer for Yocto/OE	Miscellaneous	https://github.com/MentorEmbedded/meta-mentor
meta-mingw	OE meta layer for mingw-based SDKs	Miscellaneous	git://git.yoctoproject.org/meta-mingw
meta-pareon	This layer automates using Pareon Verify with OE	Miscellaneous	https://github.com/vectorfabrics/meta-pareon
meta-ro-rootfs	Staging area for improvements to read-only-rootfs handling	Miscellaneous	https://github.com/MentorEmbedded/meta-ro-rootfs
meta-security-isafw	Image Security Analyser FW layer	Miscellaneous	https://github.com/01org/meta-security-isafw
meta-security-rockwell	OE layer that assists developers in hardening their Yocto-built systems, focusing on the Daisy release	Miscellaneous	https://github.com/IrdetoServices/meta-security-rockwell.git
meta-tlk	Time-limited kernel layer	Miscellaneous	git://git.yoctoproject.org/meta-intel
meta-ada	Ada support	Software	git://github.com/Lucretia/meta-ada.git
meta-android	Android-specific tools	Software	git://github.com/shr-distribution/meta-smartphone.git
meta-arago-extras	Arago/TI extra apps	Software	git://arago-project.org/git/meta-arago.git
meta-aspnet	ASP.NET 5	Software	git://github.com/Tragetaschen/meta-aspnet.git
meta-audio	Contains recipes for various audio DSP tools	Software	https://github.com/errordeveloper/oe-meta-audio
meta-aurora	Aurora UI	Software	git://github.com/shr-distribution/meta-smartphone.git
meta-beagleboard-extras	BeagleBoard extras	Software	git://github.com/beagleboard/meta-beagleboard
meta-browser	Web browsers (Chromium, Firefox, etc.)	Software	git://github.com/OSSystems/meta-browser.git
meta-buglabs	BugLabs middleware and specific OSGi components	Software	git://github.com/buglabs/meta-buglabs.git

Continues

Table B-1 Layers (*Continued*)

Layer name	Description	Type	Repository
meta-chicken	Chicken toolchain support	Software	git://github.com/OSSystems/meta-chicken
meta-ci	The OE/Yocto BSP layer for CI-related things	Software	https://github.com/koenkooi/meta-ci.git
meta-clang	Clang/LLVM alternative to gcc for C/C++ cross compiler	Software	https://github.com/kraj/meta-clang
meta-cloud-services	General package support for cloud and clustering development	Software	git://git.yoctoproject.org/meta-cloud-services
meta-clutter	Recipes for Cogl, Clutter, and friends	Software	git://github.com/Guacamayo/meta-clutter.git
meta-cpan	CPAN distributions as meant by CPAN authors	Software	https://github.com/rehsack/meta-cpan.git
meta-crosswalk	Web runtime for ambitious HTML5 applications	Software	git://github.com/crosswalk-project/meta-crosswalk
meta-efl	Enlightenment UI support	Software	git://git.openembedded.org/meta-openembedded
meta-erlang	Erlang support	Software	https://github.com/joaohf/meta-erlang
meta-filesystems	Support for additional filesystems	Software	git://git.openembedded.org/meta-openembedded
meta-fsl-demos	OE/Yocto layer for Freescale's demonstration images	Software	https://github.com/Freescale/meta-fsl-demos.git
meta-fso	Freesmartphone.org framework support	Software	git://github.com/shr-distribution/meta-smartphone.git
meta-game-emulators	Software layer for video game system emulators	Software	https://github.com/sergioprado/meta-game-emulators
meta-games	Open source games	Software	git://github.com/cazfi/meta-games.git
meta-gnome	GNOME UI support	Software	git://git.openembedded.org/meta-openembedded
meta-go	Provides support for cross-compiling programs written in Go language	Software	https://github.com/errordeveloper/oe-meta-go
meta-gpe	GPE UI support (very minimal currently)	Software	git://git.openembedded.org/meta-openembedded
meta-gstreamer10	OE layer for GStreamer 1.0	Software	git://github.com/dv1/meta-gstreamer1.0.git
meta-hamradio	Ham radio-related software	Software	https://github.com/hambedded-linux/meta-hamradio.git

Layer name	Description	Type	Repository
meta-initramfs	initramfs tools	Software	git://git.openembedded.org/meta-openembedded
meta-intel-iot-middleware	Shared middleware recipes for Intel IoT platforms	Software	git://git.yoctoproject.org/meta-intel-iot-middleware
meta-iot	Provides support for building an Internet of Things device manager and translator	Software	https://github.com/cablelabs/meta-iot
meta-ivi-demo	GENIVI Yocto Demo Platform	Software	git://git.yoctoproject.org/meta-ivi
meta-java	Java support	Software	git://git.yoctoproject.org/meta-java
meta-kali	Kali penetration test tools	Software	https://github.com/akuster/meta-kali
meta-kde4	KDE 4/Plasma Active	Software	https://bitbucket.org/gen_dev_sst/meta-kde4.git
meta-kf5	KDE Frameworks 5	Software	https://github.com/e8johan/meta-kf5.git
meta-linaro-toolchain	Linaro toolchain support	Software	git://git.linaro.org/openembedded/meta-linaro.git
meta-luneui	Recipes for LuneOS UI	Software	https://github.com/webOS-ports/meta-webos-ports
meta-lxcbench	Yocto layer for the LXCBENCH project	Software	git://git.projects.genivi.org/lxcbench.git
meta-maker	OE recipes for makers	Software	http://git.yoctoproject.org/git/meta-maker
meta-measured	Tools and utilities related to measuring software and trusted computing	Software	https://github.com/flihp/meta-measured.git
meta-mel-support	Mentor Embedded Linux Support Layer for Yocto/OE	Software	https://github.com/MentorEmbedded/meta-mentor
meta-mono	Mono	Software	git://git.yoctoproject.org/meta-mono
meta-multimedia	Multimedia-related software	Software	git://git.openembedded.org/meta-openembedded
meta-musl	Support for the musl C library	Software	https://github.com/kraj/meta-musl.git
meta-netmodule-extras	Additional packets used by NetModule	Software	https://github.com/netmodule/meta-netmodule-extras.git

Continues

Table B-1 Layers (Continued)

Layer name	Description	Type	Repository
meta-networking	Network-related software	Software	git://git.openembedded.org/meta-openembedded
meta-office	Office applications and libs	Software	git://github.com/schnitzeltony/meta-office.git
meta-oic	Support for building the Open Interconnect Consortium Iotivity framework	Software	git://git.yoctoproject.org/meta-oic
meta-openclovis	Layer to support SAFplus middleware components	Software	https://github.com/joaohf/meta-openclovis
meta-openhab	Yocto layer providing openHAB (home automation software)	Software	https://github.com/ulfwin/meta-openhab
meta-openstack	OpenStack support	Software	git://git.yoctoproject.org/meta-cloud-services
meta-openstack-compute-deploy	OpenStack compute node support	Software	git://git.yoctoproject.org/meta-cloud-services
meta-openstack-controller-deploy	OpenStack controller node support	Software	git://git.yoctoproject.org/meta-cloud-services
meta-openstack-qemu	OpenStack QEMU image support	Software	git://git.yoctoproject.org/meta-cloud-services
meta-openwrt	OE metadata for OpenWRT packages	Software	https://github.com/kraj/meta-openwrt
meta-opie	Opie UI support	Software	git://git.openembedded.org/meta-opie
meta-oracle-java	Oracle Java support	Software	git://git.yoctoproject.org/meta-oracle-java
meta-osmocombb	OsmocomBB support	Software	git://github.com/shr-distribution/meta-smartphone.git
meta-perl	Additional Perl recipes	Software	git://git.openembedded.org/meta-openembedded
meta-pypy	Cross/Embedded PyPy (https://bitbucket.org/pypy/pypy) support	Software	https://github.com/mzakharo/meta-pypy.git
meta-python	Python support	Software	git://git.openembedded.org/meta-openembedded
meta-qt3	Qt 3.x support	Software	git://git.yoctoproject.org/meta-qt3
meta-qt4	Qt 4.x support	Software	git://git.yoctoproject.org/meta-qt4

Layer name	Description	Type	Repository
meta-qt5	Qt5 modules	Software	git://github.com/meta-qt5/meta-qt5.git
meta-qt5-extra	Desktop environments and applications based on qt5	Software	git://github.com/schnitzeltony/meta-qt5-extra.git
meta-realtime	Additional real-time support	Software	git://git.yoctoproject.org/meta-realtime
meta-ros	Robot Operating System (ROS) support layer	Software	git://github.com/bmwcarit/meta-ros.git
meta-ruby	Ruby support	Software	git://git.openembedded.org/meta-openembedded
meta-rust	Rust compiler and package manager	Software	https://github.com/starlab-io/meta-rust.git
meta-sdr	Software-defined radio (SDR)–related recipes	Software	https://github.com/balister/meta-sdr.git
meta-security	Security tools for Internet connected devices	Software	git://git.yoctoproject.org/meta-security
meta-security-framework	Adds higher-level security middleware and tools	Software	https://github.com/01org/meta-intel-iot-security.git
meta-security-smack	Adds the Smack LSM to OE distros	Software	https://github.com/01org/meta-intel-iot-security.git
meta-selinux	SELinux support	Software	git://git.yoctoproject.org/meta-selinux
meta-shr	SHR applications	Software	git://github.com/shr-distribution/meta-smartphone.git
meta-smalltalk	GNU Smalltalk and ports	Software	git://github.com/sysmocom/meta-smalltalk.git
meta-sourcery	CodeSourcery toolchain support layer by Mentor Graphics Corporation	Software	git://github.com/MentorEmbedded/meta-sourcery.git
meta-spec	Support for the Simple PCIe FMC Carrier (SPEC)	Software	git://ohwr.org/fmc-projects/spec/spec-getting-started/meta-spec.git
meta-swupdate	Layer supporting Software Update via swupdate	Software	https://github.com/sbabic/meta-swupdate
meta-systemd	systemd support	Software	git://git.openembedded.org/meta-openembedded
meta-telephony	Telephony-related software	Software	https://github.com/sysmocom/meta-telephony
meta-telldus	TellStick support layer	Software	https://github.com/maxinbjohn/meta-telldus

Continues

Table B-1 Layers (Continued)

Layer name	Description	Type	Repository
meta-tracing	Layer to add necessary agent support for Sourcery Analyzer (lttng+systemtap bits)	Software	git://github.com/MentorEmbedded/meta-tracing.git
meta-uav	Software for drones	Software	https://github.com/koenkooi/meta-uav.git
meta-virtualization	Hypervisor, virtualization tool stack, and cloud support	Software	git://git.yoctoproject.org/meta-virtualization
meta-web-kiosk	Layer enabling browser-based kiosk devices with virtual keyboard support	Software	git://git.yoctoproject.org/meta-web-kiosk
meta-webkit	WebKit engines and browsers: WebKitForWayland, WebKitGTK+	Software	https://github.com/Igalia/meta-webkit
meta-webserver	Web server–related software	Software	git://git.openembedded.org/meta-openembedded
meta-wolfssl	Lightweight, portable, C-language-based SSL/TLS library	Software	https://github.com/wolfSSL/meta-wolfssl
meta-x10	x10 protocol related software	Software	git://github.com/baillaw/meta-x10.git
meta-xfce	XFCE UI support	Software	git://git.openembedded.org/meta-openembedded
toolchain-layer	Older/newer toolchains	Software	git://git.openembedded.org/meta-openembedded

Table B-2 Machines

Machine name	Description	Layer
a500	Acer IconiaTab A500	meta-acer
akita	Sharp Zaurus SL-C1000 device	meta-handheld
am180x-evm	TI AM180x EVM board	meta-ti
am335x-evm	TI AM335x EVM	meta-ti
am3517-evm	TI Sitara AM3517 EVM	meta-ti
am37x-evm	TI AM37x EVM	meta-ti
am437x-evm	TI AM437x EVM	meta-ti
am57xx-evm	TI DRA7xx EVM	meta-ti
apalis-imx6	Toradex Apalis iMX6 SOM	meta-fsl-arm-extra
arago	Unified/fake Arago machine configuration for TI/Arago ARMv5 platforms	meta-arago-distro
arago-armv5	Unified/fake Arago machine configuration for TI/Arago ARMv5 platforms	meta-arago-distro
arago-armv7	Unified/fake Arago machine configuration for TI/Arago ARMv7 platforms	meta-arago-distro
arndale	Arndale board	meta-exynos
arndale-octa	Arndale Octa board	meta-exynos
arria10	Arria 10 SoC	meta-altera
arria5	Arria V SoC	meta-altera
at91sam9m10g45ek	Atmel evaluation board	meta-atmel
at91sam9rlek	Atmel evaluation board	meta-atmel
at91sam9x5ek	Atmel evaluation board	meta-atmel
axxiaarm	LSI Axxia ARM systems	meta-lsi
axxiapowerpc	LSI Axxia PowerPC systems	meta-lsi

Continues

Table B-2 Machines (Continued)

Machine name	Description	Layer
b4420qds	Freescale QorIQ Qonverge B4420	`meta-fsl-ppc`
b4420qds-64b	Freescale QorIQ Qonverge B4420	`meta-fsl-ppc`
b4860qds	Freescale QorIQ Qonverge B4860	`meta-fsl-ppc`
b4860qds-64b	Freescale QorIQ Qonverge B4860	`meta-fsl-ppc`
baldeagle	Bald Eagle systems	`meta-baldeagle`
balto	Balto Board RZ/A1H	`meta-renesas-rza1`
balto-xip	Balto Board RZ/A1H	`meta-renesas-rza1`
bananapi	Banana Pi, based on Allwinner A20 CPU (http://bananapi.org)	`meta-sunxi`
beagleboard	BeagleBoard board (http://beagleboard.org)	`meta-ti`
beagleboard	BeagleBoard board	`meta-yocto-bsp-old`
beaglebone	BeagleBone board (http://beagleboard.org/bone)	`meta-ti`
beaglebone	BeagleBone and BeagleBone Black boards (http://beagleboard.org/black)	`meta-yocto-bsp`
beaglebone	BeagleBone board	`meta-beagleboard`
ben-nanonote	Qi-Hardware Ben Nanonote	`meta-handheld`
bsc9131rdb	Freescale QorIQ Qonverge BSC9131	`meta-fsl-ppc`
bsc9132qds	Freescale QorIQ Qonverge BSC9132	`meta-fsl-ppc`
bug	BUG 1.x board (imx31 based)	`meta-bug`
bug20	BUG 2.0 board (OMAP3530 based)	`meta-bug`
bytepanel	bytePANEL by bytes at work AG	`meta-bytesatwork`
c293pcie	Freescale C29x Crypto Coprocessor	`meta-fsl-ppc`
c7x0	Sharp Zaurus SL-C700, Sharp Zaurus SL-C750, Sharp Zaurus SL-C760, Sharp Zaurus SL-C860 devices	`meta-handheld`
ccardimx28js	Digi ConnectCore for MX28 JSK	`meta-digi-arm`

Machine name	Description	Layer
ccimx51js	Digi ConnectCore for MX51 JSK	meta-digi-arm
ccimx53js	Digi ConnectCore for MX53 JSK	meta-digi-arm
cfa10036	CFA-10036	meta-fsl-arm-extra
cfa10037	CFA-10037	meta-fsl-arm-extra
cfa10049	CFA-10049	meta-fsl-arm-extra
cfa10055	CFA-10055	meta-fsl-arm-extra
cfa10056	CFA-10056	meta-fsl-arm-extra
cfa10057	CFA-10057, also called CFA-920	meta-fsl-arm-extra
cfa10058	CFA-10058, also called CFA-921	meta-fsl-arm-extra
cgtqmx6	Congatec QMX6 evaluation board	meta-fsl-arm-extra
chip	CHIP board	meta-chip
chromebook-snow	Arndale board	meta-exynos
ci20	ci20 systems	meta-ci20
cm-fx6	CompuLab CM-FX6 machines	meta-fsl-arm-extra
colibri-imx6	Toradex Colibri iMX6 SOM	meta-fsl-arm-extra
colibri-vf	Toradex Colibri VF50/VF61 powered by Freescale Vybrid SoC	meta-fsl-arm-extra
collie	SA1100 based Sharp Zaurus SL-5000 and SL-5500 devices	meta-handheld
creator-ci20	MIPS Creator CI20	meta-jz-mips
crespo	Samsung Crespo	meta-samsung
crownbay-noemgd	Crown Bay systems, without Intel-proprietary graphics bits	meta-crownbay
crystalforest	Crystal Forest Gladden systems	meta-crystalforest
cubieboard	Cubieboard, based on Allwinner a10 CPU (http://cubieboard.org)	meta-sunxi

Continues

Table B-2 **Machines** (*Continued*)

Machine name	Description	Layer
cubieboard2	Cubieboard2, based on Allwinner A20 CPU	`meta-sunxi`
cubietruck	Cubietruck, based on Allwinner A20 CPU (www.cubietruck.com)	`meta-sunxi`
cubox	www.solid-run.com/products/cubox	`meta-cubox`
cubox-i	SolidRun CuBox-i and HummingBoard machines	`meta-fsl-arm-extra`
cyclone5	Cyclone V SoC	`meta-altera`
dra7xx-evm	TI DRA7xx EVM	`meta-ti`
dra7xx-evm	TI DRA7xx EVM	`meta-dra7xx-evm`
duovero	Gumstix DuoVero	`meta-gumstix`
edgerouter	Edgerouter	`meta-yocto-bsp`
edison	Edison systems	`meta-intel-edison-bsp`
efikamx	EFIKA MX development platform (www.powerdeveloper.org/platforms/efikamx)	`meta-efikamx`
emenlow-noemgd	eMenlow-based systems, such as the Webs-2120 box, without the Intel-proprietary graphics bits	`meta-emenlow`
ep108-zynqmp	Xilinx EP108 ZynqMP emulation platform	`meta-xilinx`
ettus-e1xx	USRP E1XX	`e100-bsp`
ettus-e300	Ettus Research E3XX SDR	`e300-bsp`
example		`meta-kernel-dev`
forfun-q88db	Forfun Q88DB tablet with A13 CPU	`meta-sunxi`
fri2-noemgd	Fish River Island 2 systems, without Intel-proprietary graphics bits	`meta-fri2`
gcw0	Game Consoles Worldwide (GCW) Zero	`meta-handheld`
geeksphone-one	Geeksphone One	`meta-geeksphone`
generic-armv4t	ARMv4T-based boards	`meta-eldk`
generic-armv5te	ARMv5TE-based boards	`meta-eldk`

Machine name	Description	Layer
generic-armv6	ARMv6-based boards	meta-eldk
generic-armv7a	ARMv7a-based boards	meta-eldk
generic-armv7a-hf	ARMv7a-based boards	meta-eldk
generic-mips	MIPS-based boards	meta-eldk
generic-nios2	Nios II machines	meta-altera
generic-powerpc	Generic PowerPC machine with FPU	meta-eldk
generic-powerpc-4xx	APM PPC4xx-based boards (with FPU)	meta-eldk
generic-powerpc-4xx-softfloat	APM PPC4xx-based boards (without FPU)	meta-eldk
generic-powerpc-e500v2		meta-eldk
generic-powerpc-softfloat	Generic PowerPC machine without FPU	meta-eldk
genericarmv7a	Generic machine to be used by linaro-media-create	meta-linaro
genericarmv7ab	Generic machine to be used by linaro-media-create	meta-linaro
genericarmv8	Generic machine to be used by linaro-media-create	meta-aarch64
genericarmv8b	Generic machine to be used by linaro-media-create	meta-aarch64
genericx86	Generic X86 (32-bit) PCs; supports moderately wide range of drivers that should boot and be usable on typical hardware	meta-yocto-bsp
genericx86-64	generic X86_64 (64-bit) PCs and servers; supports moderately wide range of drivers that should boot and be usable on typical hardware	meta-yocto-bsp
grouper	Asus Grouper	meta-asus
guruplug	ARM-based Marvell SheevaPlug	meta-kirkwood
h1940	HP iPAQ h1930 and h1940	meta-handheld
h3600	Compaq iPAQ 36xx, Compaq iPAQ 37xx, and Compaq iPAQ 38xx devices	meta-handheld

Continues

Table B-2 Machines (*Continued*)

Machine name	Description	Layer
hpveer	HP Veer handset	meta-palm
htccream	HTC Dream phone (aka T-Mobile G1 and Google ADP-1)	meta-htc
htcleo	HTC Leo smartphone (aka HTC HD2)	meta-htc
hx4700	hx4700 iPAQ with a PXA27x CPU	meta-handheld
i9300	Samsung Galaxy SIII	meta-samsung
igep0020	IGEPv2 AM/DM37x processor board	meta-igep
igep0030	IGEP COM module AM/DM37x processor board	meta-igep
igep0033	IGEP COM AQUILA AM335x processor board	meta-igep
imx233-olinuxino-maxi	OLIMEX iMX233-OLinuXino-Maxi	meta-fsl-arm-extra
imx233-olinuxino-micro	OLIMEX iMX233-OLinuXino-Micro	meta-fsl-arm-extra
imx233-olinuxino-mini	OLIMEX iMX233-OLinuXino-Mini	meta-fsl-arm-extra
imx233-olinuxino-nano	OLIMEX iMX233-OLinuXino-Nano	meta-fsl-arm-extra
imx23evk	Freescale i.MX23 Evaluation Kit (EVK)	meta-fsl-arm
imx28evk	Freescale i.MX28 EVK	meta-fsl-arm
imx51evk	Freescale i.MX51 EVK	meta-fsl-arm
imx53ard	Freescale i.MX53 SABRE Automotive Board	meta-fsl-arm
imx53qsb	Freescale i.MX53 Quick Start Board	meta-fsl-arm
imx6dl-riotboard	i.MX6S RIoTboard	meta-fsl-arm-extra
imx6dlsabreauto	Freescale i.MX6DL SABRE Automotive	meta-fsl-arm
imx6dlsabresd	Freescale i.MX6DL SABRE Smart Device	meta-fsl-arm
imx6qpsabreauto	Freescale i.MX6QP SABRE Automotive	meta-fsl-arm
imx6qsabreauto	Freescale i.MX6Q SABRE Automotive	meta-fsl-arm

Machine name	Description	Layer
imx6qsabrelite	Boundary Devices i.MX6Q SABRE Lite	meta-fsl-arm-extra
imx6qsabresd	Freescale i.MX6Q SABRE Smart Device	meta-fsl-arm
imx6qvab820	VAB-820	meta-via-vab820-bsp
imx6sl-warp	i.MX6SL WaRP board	meta-fsl-arm-extra
imx6slevk	Freescale i.MX6SL EVK	meta-fsl-arm
imx6solosabreauto	Freescale i.MX6Solo SABRE Automotive	meta-fsl-arm
imx6solosabresd	Freescale i.MX6Solo SABRE Smart Device	meta-fsl-arm
imx6sxsabreauto	Freescale i.MX6SoloX Sabre Automotive	meta-fsl-arm
imx6sxsabresd	Freescale i.MX6SoloX Sabre Smart Device	meta-fsl-arm
imx6ulevk	Freescale i.MX6UL EVK	meta-fsl-arm
imx7dsabresd	Freescale i.MX7D SABRE Smart Device	meta-fsl-arm
intel-core2-32	32-bit Intel Core 2 CPU (and later) with MMX, SSE, SSE2, SSE3, and SSSE3 instruction set support; supports moderately wide range of drivers that should boot and be usable on typical hardware	meta-intel
intel-corei7-64	64-bit Intel Core i7 CPU (and later) with MMX, SSE, SSE2, SSE3, and SSSE3 instruction set support; supports moderately wide range of drivers that should boot and be usable on typical hardware	meta-intel
intel-quark	Quark systems	meta-intel
jasperforest	Jasper Forest Picket Post	meta-jasperforest
k2e-evm	TI Keystone 2 K2E Evaluation Module (EVM)	meta-ti
k2g-evm	TI Keystone 2 K2G EVM	meta-ti
k2hk-evm	TI Keystone 2 K2HK EVM	meta-ti
k2l-evm	TI Keystone 2 K2L EVM	meta-ti
kc705-trd-microblazeel	Machine support for Xilinx KC705 Embedded Kit targeted reference design (TRD)	meta-xilinx

Continues

Table B-2 Machines (*Continued*)

Machine name	Description	Layer
lng-rt-x86-64		meta-linaro
lng-x86-64		meta-linaro
ls1021atwr	LS1021ATWR in 32-bit mode	meta-fsl-arm
m28evk	DENX M28 SoM EVK	meta-eldk
m28evk	DENX M28 SoM EVK	meta-fsl-arm-extra
m53evk	DENX M53 SoM EVK	meta-eldk
m53evk	DENX M53 SoM EVK	meta-fsl-arm-extra
maguro	Samsung Tuna	meta-samsung
mele	Mele a1000 and a2000, based on Allwinner a10 CPU	meta-sunxi
meleg	Mele a1000g and a2000g, based on Allwinner a10 CPU	meta-sunxi
microzed-zynq7	Machine support for microZed (www.microzed.org)	meta-xilinx-community
microzed-zynq7	Machine support for microZed (www.microzed.org)	meta-xilinx
minnow	MinnowBoard v1 (Intel Atom E640T); for the MinnowBoard MAX (Intel Atom E38xx), use the meta-intel intel-corei7-64 BSP (www.elinux.org/Minnowboard:MinnowMaxYoctoProject)	meta-minnow
minnow-emgd	MinnowBoard v1 (Intel Atom E640T); for the MinnowBoard MAX (Intel Atom E38xx), use the meta-intel intel-corei7-64 BSP (www.elinux.org/Minnowboard:MinnowMaxYoctoProject)	meta-minnow
ml405-virtex4-ppc405	Xilinx ML405 FPGA development platform with a Virtex-4 PowerPC 405 processor (with APU FPU)	meta-xilinx-community
ml507-virtex5-ppc440	Xilinx ML507 FPGA development platform with a Virtex-5 PowerPC 440 processor (with APU FPU)	meta-xilinx-community
mpc5200		meta-eldk
mpc5200xenomai		meta-eldk
mpc8315e-rdb		meta-yocto-bsp
nanopi	FriendlyARM NanoPi board	meta-nanopi
netbookpro	Psion Teklogix NetBook Pro	meta-netbookpro

Machine name	Description	Layer
netstora	ARM-based Netgear Stora	meta-kirkwood
nexusone	Nexus One smartphone	meta-htc
nitrogen6sx	Boundary Devices Nitrogen6SX	meta-fsl-arm-extra
nitrogen6x	Boundary Devices Nitrogen6X	meta-fsl-arm-extra
nitrogen6x-lite	Boundary Devices Nitrogen6X Lite	meta-fsl-arm-extra
nokia900	Nokia 900	meta-nokia
nslu2be	NSLU2 in big-endian mode	meta-nslu2
nslu2le	NSLU2 in little-endian mode	meta-nslu2
nuc	Intel NUC model DC3217IYE	meta-nuc
odroid-c1	ODROID-C1 by Hardkernel	meta-odroid
odroid-u2	ODROID-U2 by Hardkernel	meta-odroid
odroid-ux3	ODROID-UX3 systems	meta-odroid
odroid-xu	ODROID-XU by Hardkernel	meta-odroid
olinuxino-a10lime	Olimex A10-OLinuXino Lime Board, based on Allwinner A10 CPU	meta-sunxi
olinuxino-a10s	Olimex A10S-OLinuXino-MICRO Board, based on Allwinner A10s CPU	meta-sunxi
olinuxino-a13	Olime A13-OLinuXino Board, based on Allwinner a13 CPU	meta-sunxi
olinuxino-a13som	Olimex A13-SOM Evaluation Board, based on Allwinner A13 CPU	meta-sunxi
olinuxino-a20	Olimex A20-OLinuXino Board, based on Allwinner A20 CPU	meta-sunxi
olinuxino-a20lime	Olimex A20-OLinuXino Lime Board, based on Allwinner A20 CPU	meta-sunxi
olinuxino-a20lime2	Olimex A20-OLinuXino Lime2 Board, based on Allwinner A20 CPU	meta-sunxi
olinuxino-a20som	Olimex A20-SOM Evaluation Board, based on Allwinner A20 CPU	meta-sunxi
om-gta01	OM Neo1973 GSM phone	meta-openmoko

Continues

Table B-2 Machines (*Continued*)

Machine name	Description	Layer
om-gta02	Openmoko NeoFreerunner GSM phone	meta-openmoko
om-gta04	Godelico GTA04 GSM phone	meta-openmoko
omap3evm	Texas Instruments OMAP3 EVM	meta-ti
omap5-evm	Texas Instruments OMAP5 uEVM	meta-ti
openpandora	Pandora handheld console (www.openpandora.org)	meta-openpandora
ouya	ASUS tf201	meta-ouya
overo	Gumstix Overo	meta-gumstix
overo	Gumstix Overo	meta-gumstix-community
p1010rdb	Freescale QorIQ P1010 Reference	meta-fsl-ppc
p1020rdb	Freescale QorIQ P1020 Reference	meta-fsl-ppc
p1021rdb	Freescale QorIQ P1021 Reference	meta-fsl-ppc
p1022ds	Freescale QorIQ P1022 Development	meta-fsl-ppc
p1023rdb	Freescale QorIQ P1023 Reference	meta-fsl-ppc
p1025twr	Freescale QorIQ P1025 MPU Tower	meta-fsl-ppc
p2020rdb	Freescale QorIQ P2020 Reference	meta-fsl-ppc
p2041rdb	Freescale QorIQ P2041 Reference	meta-fsl-ppc
p3041ds	Freescale QorIQ P3041 Development	meta-fsl-ppc
p4080ds	Freescale QorIQ P4080 Development	meta-fsl-ppc
p5020ds	Freescale QorIQ P5020 Development	meta-fsl-ppc
p5020ds-64b	Freescale QorIQ P5020 Development	meta-fsl-ppc
p5040ds	Freescale QorIQ P5040 Development	meta-fsl-ppc
p5040ds-64b	Freescale QorIQ P5040 Development	meta-fsl-ppc

Machine name	Description	Layer
palmpre	Palm Pre handset	meta-palm
palmpre2	Palm Pre 2 handset	meta-palm
pandaboard	OMAP4430 Panda	meta-ti
parallella	Adapteva Parallella Board, headless	meta-parallella
parallella-hdmi	Adapteva Parallella Board with HDMI support	meta-parallella
pcm052	Phytec phyCORE Vybrid Development Kit	meta-fsl-arm-extra
pepper	Gumstix Pepper	meta-gumstix
picosam9	Picosam9 board (http://arm.mini-box.com)	meta-picosam9
picozed-zynq7	Machine support for picoZed (http://zedboard.org/product/picozed)	meta-xilinx
poodle	PXA250 based Sharp Zaurus SL-B500 and SHarp Zaurus SL-5600 devices	meta-handheld
qemuarm	arm_versatile_926ejs	openembedded-core
qemuarm64	Generic ARMv8	openembedded-core
qemumicroblaze	MicroBlaze QEMU machine support (Petalogix-ml605 model)	meta-xilinx
qemumicroblaze-s3adsp1800	MicroBlaze QEMU machine support (Petalogix-s3adsp1800 model)	meta-xilinx
qemumips	mti_malta32_be	openembedded-core
qemumips64	mti-malta64-be	openembedded-core
qemuppc	PPC system under QEMU emulation	openembedded-core
qemuppc64	PPC system under QEMU emulation	meta-qemu-bsps
qemux86	Common x86	openembedded-core
qemux86-64	Common x86	openembedded-core
qemuzynq	Zynq QEMU machine support (xilinx-zynq-a9 model)	meta-xilinx
quark	Quark systems	meta-intel-quark

Continues

425

Table B-2 Machines (*Continued*)

Machine name	Description	Layer
raspberrypi	RaspberryPi board (www.raspberrypi.org)	meta-raspberrypi
raspberrypi0	RaspberryPi Zero board (https://www.raspberrypi.org/blog/raspberry-pi-zero)	meta-raspberrypi
raspberrypi2	RaspberryPi 2	meta-raspberrypi
rk3066a-marsboard	The Marsboard-RK3066 is powered by the popular Rockchip dual-core SoC combining a power dual-core ARM Cortex-A9 CPU and quad-core Mali-400 MP4 GPU	meta-rockchip
rk3188-radxarock	Radxa Rock is a single-board computer with quad-core ARM Cortex-A9 processor, 80 pin headers, which makes it easy to connect other I/O or GPIO	meta-rockchip
rk3288-firefly	Firefly-RK3288 is a high-performance platform with strong computing power, graphic processing, and video decoding ability	meta-rockchip
romley	Romley systems	meta-romley
romley-ivb	Romley systems	meta-romley
routerstationpro	mt_malta32_be	meta-yocto-bsp-old
rskrza1	RSKRZA1 board	meta-renesas-rza1
rskrza1-xip	RSKRZA1 board	meta-renesas-rza1
sama5d2-xplained	Atmel evaluation board	meta-atmel
sama5d3-xplained	Atmel evaluation board	meta-atmel
sama5d3xek	Atmel evaluation board	meta-atmel
sama5d4-xplained	Atmel evaluation board	meta-atmel
sama5d4ek	Atmel evaluation board	meta-atmel
sheevaplug	ARM-based Marvell SheevaPlug	meta-kirkwood
spitz	Sharp Zaurus SL-C3000 device	meta-handheld
sugarbay	Sugar Bay systems	meta-sugarbay
t1023rdb	Freescale QorIQ T1023 Reference	meta-fsl-ppc
t1023rdb-64b	Freescale QorIQ T1023 Reference	meta-fsl-ppc

Machine name	Description	Layer
t1024rdb	Freescale QorIQ T1024 Reference	meta-fsl-ppc
t1024rdb-64b	Freescale QorIQ T1024 Reference	meta-fsl-ppc
t1040d4rdb	Freescale QorIQ T1040D4 Reference	meta-fsl-ppc
t1040d4rdb-64b	Freescale QorIQ T1040D4 Reference	meta-fsl-ppc
t1042d4rdb	Freescale QorIQ T1042D4 Reference	meta-fsl-ppc
t1042d4rdb-64b	Freescale QorIQ T1042D4 Reference	meta-fsl-ppc
t2080qds	Freescale QorIQ T2080 Development	meta-fsl-ppc
t2080qds-64b	Freescale QorIQ T2080 Development	meta-fsl-ppc
t2080rdb	Freescale QorIQ T2080 Reference	meta-fsl-ppc
t2080rdb-64b	Freescale QorIQ T2080 Reference	meta-fsl-ppc
t4160qds	Freescale QorIQ T4160 Development	meta-fsl-ppc
t4160qds-64b	Freescale QorIQ T4160 Development	meta-fsl-ppc
t4240qds	Freescale QorIQ T4240 Development	meta-fsl-ppc
t4240qds-64b	Freescale QorIQ T4240 Development	meta-fsl-ppc
t4240rdb	Freescale QorIQ T4240 Reference	meta-fsl-ppc
t4240rdb-64b	Freescale QorIQ T4240 Reference	meta-fsl-ppc
tilapia	Asus Tilapia	meta-asus
toro	Samsung Toro	meta-samsung
toroplus	Samsung Toro Plus	meta-samsung
tosa	PXA255-based Sharp Zaurus SL-6000 device	meta-handheld
twr-vf65gs10	Freescale Vybrid TWR-VF65GS10	meta-fsl-arm
tx6q-10x0	Ka-Ro electronics TX6Q Computer-On-Module	meta-fsl-arm-extra

Continues

Table B-2 Machines (*Continued*)

Machine name	Description	Layer
tx6q-11x0	Ka-Ro electronics TX6Q Computer-On-Module	meta-fsl-arm-extra
tx6s-8034	Ka-Ro electronics TX6S Computer-On-Module	meta-fsl-arm-extra
tx6s-8035	Ka-Ro electronics TX6S Computer-On-Module	meta-fsl-arm-extra
tx6dl-8033	Ka-Ro electronics TX6DL Computer-On-Module	meta-fsl-arm-extra
tx6u-80x0	Ka-Ro electronics TX6DL Computer-On-Module	meta-fsl-arm-extra
tx6u-81x0	Ka-Ro electronics TX6DL Computer-On-Module	meta-fsl-arm-extra
ventana	Gateworks Ventana boards	meta-fsl-arm-extra
vexpressa9	VExpress A9 board	meta-ivi-bsp
veyron-speedy	Google Veyron Speedy Rev 1+ board (formally known as Chromebook Asus C201)	meta-rockchip
wandboard	i.MX6 Wandboard Quad	meta-fsl-arm-extra
zc702-base-trd-zynq7	Machine support for ZC702 Base TRD	meta-xilinx-community
zc702-zynq7	Machine support for ZC702 Evaluation Board	meta-xilinx
zc706-pcie-trd-zynq7	Machine support for ZC706 PCIe TRD	meta-xilinx-community
zc706-zynq7	Machine support for ZC706 Evaluation Board	meta-xilinx
ze7000-zynq7	Machine configuration for the ze7000 from NetModule device	meta-xilinx-community
zedboard-zynq7	Machine support for ZedBoard (www.zedboard.org)	meta-xilinx
zx3-pm3-zynq7	Enclustra PM3 evaluation board with ZX3 module	meta-xilinx-community
zybo-zynq7	Machine support for ZYBO	meta-xilinx
zynq-ze7000	Poky image generated by NetModule AG (www.netmodule.com) for the ZE7000 (Z4E) Platform	meta-netmodule
zynq-zx3-pm3	Poky image generated by NetModule AG (www.netmodule.com) for the Mars ZX3 Module + Mars PM3 development kit from Enclustra AG (www.enclustra.com)	meta-netmodule
zynq-zx3-starter	Poky image generated by NetModule AG (www.netmodule.com) for the Mars ZX3 Module + Mars Starter development kit from Enclustra AG (www.enclustra.com)	meta-netmodule

Index

REGISTER YOUR PRODUCT at informit.com/register
Access Additional Benefits and SAVE 35% on Your Next Purchase

- Download available product updates.

- Access bonus material when applicable.

- Receive exclusive offers on new editions and related products.
  (Just check the box to hear from us when setting up your account.)

- Get a coupon for 35% for your next purchase, valid for 30 days. Your code will
  be available in your InformIT cart. (You will also find it in the Manage Codes
  section of your account page.)

Registration benefits vary by product. Benefits will be listed on your account page
under Registered Products.

InformIT.com–The Trusted Technology Learning Source

InformIT is the online home of information technology brands at Pearson, the world's foremost
education company. At InformIT.com you can

- Shop our books, eBooks, software, and video training.
- Take advantage of our special offers and promotions (informit.com/promotions).
- Sign up for special offers and content newsletters (informit.com/newsletters).
- Read free articles and blogs by information technology experts.
- Access thousands of free chapters and video lessons.

Connect with InformIT–Visit informit.com/community
Learn about InformIT community events and programs.

informIT.com
the trusted technology learning source

Addison-Wesley · Cisco Press · IBM Press · Microsoft Press · Pearson IT Certification · Prentice Hall · Que · Sams · VMware Press

ALWAYS LEARNING   PEARSON